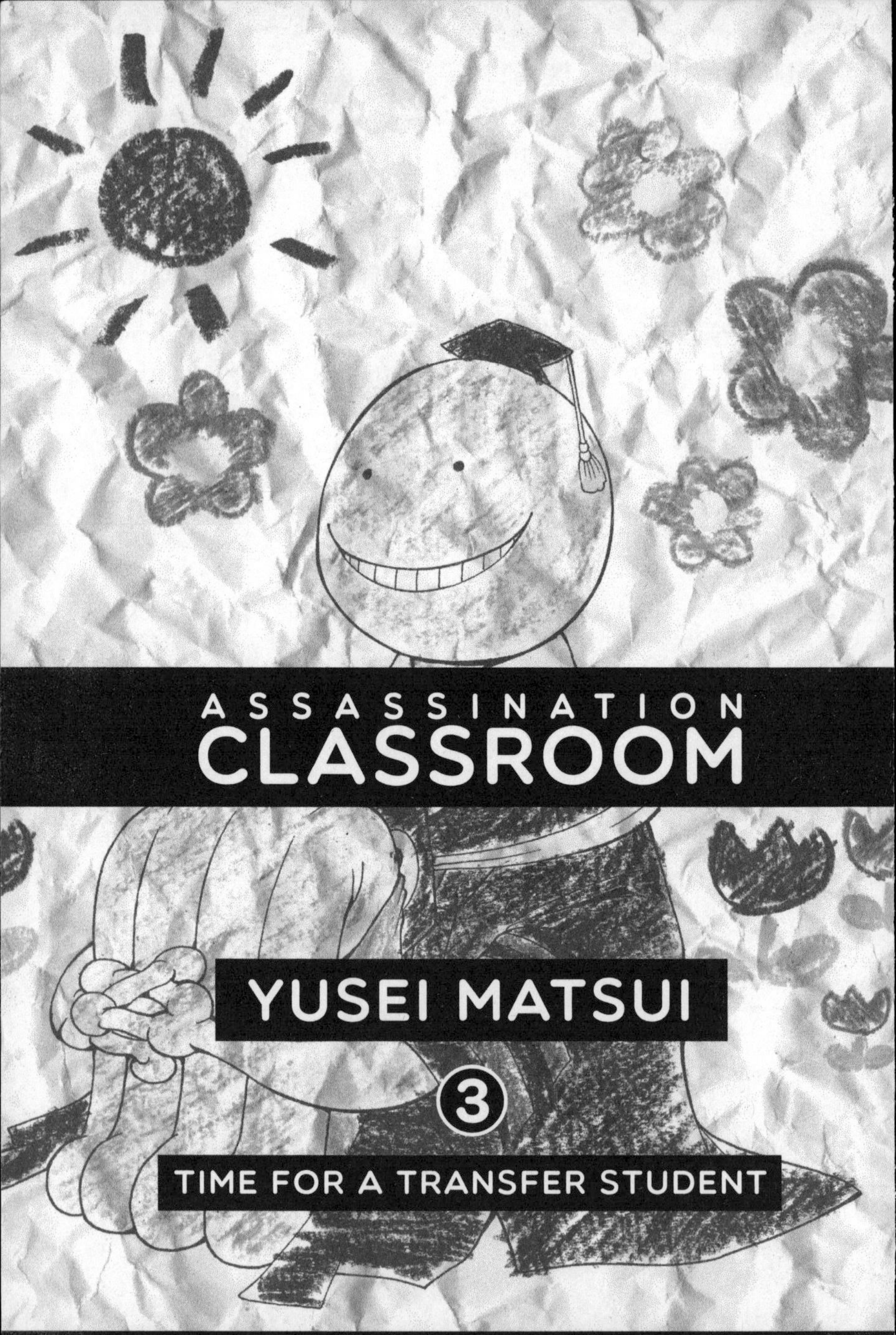

ASSASSINATION CLASSROOM

YUSEI MATSUI

3

TIME FOR A TRANSFER STUDENT

SHONEN JUMP ADVANCED

Koro Tribune

May Issue

Published by:
Class 3-E Newspaper Staff

Our new teacher is a creature who plans to destroy the world...?!

Story Thus Far

One day, something destroyed most of the moon.

I'M THE ONE WHO DISINTEGRATED PART OF THE MOON.
AND NEXT YEAR AT THIS TIME I'M GOING TO DO THE SAME THING TO YOUR PLANET EARTH.
ALSO, I'M YOUR NEW TEACHER. I HOPE WE

A mysterious creature showed up in our junior high classroom claiming that he had attacked the moon and promising to destroy the earth next March. And then... he took over as our teacher. What the—?! Faced with a creature beyond human understanding that no army could kill, the leaders of the world had no choice but to rely on the students of Kunugigaoka Junior High, Class 3-E, to do the job. For a reward of ten billion yen (100 million dollars)... SIGN ME UP!! Will the students of the so-called End Class, filled with losers and rejects, be able to kill their target Koro Sensei by graduation...?!

Koro Sensei

A mysterious octopus-like creature whose nick-name is a play on the words "koro senai," which means "can't be killed." He is capable of flying at Mach 20 and his versatile tentacles protect him from attacks and aid him in everyday activities.

He's a sucker for the ladies...

Nobody knows why he wants to teach Class 3-E, but he has proven to be an extremely capable teacher.

Kaede Kayano

Smart AND pretty.
My brain is up here!

Class E student. She's the one who named Koro Sensei. Sits at the desk next to Nagisa, and they seem to get along well.

Nagisa Shiota

Class E student. Skilled at information gathering, he has been taking notes on Koro Sensei's weaknesses.

Taiga Okajima

Pick up artist!

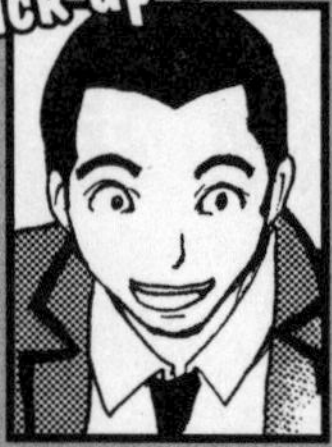

He has girls on the brain... If you want the scoop on any of the girls in Class 3-E, he's your go-to guy.

Karma Akabane

Class E student. A quick thinker skilled at surprise attacks. Succeeded in injuring Koro Sensei a few times.

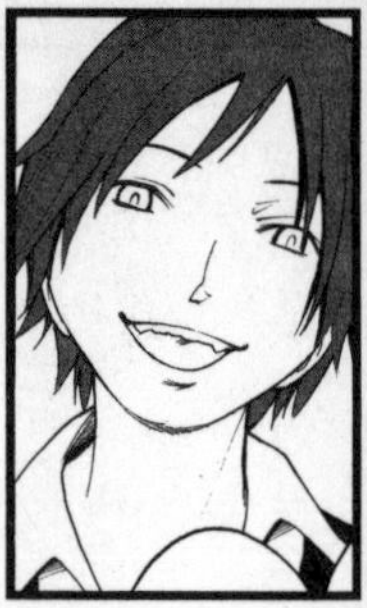

Our grades are getting better!!

Even though our midterms sucked (thanks to the principal) we still did great. Let's show Koro Sensei what we can do on the final!!

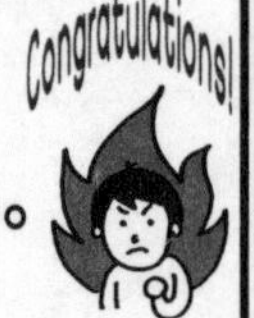
Congratulations!

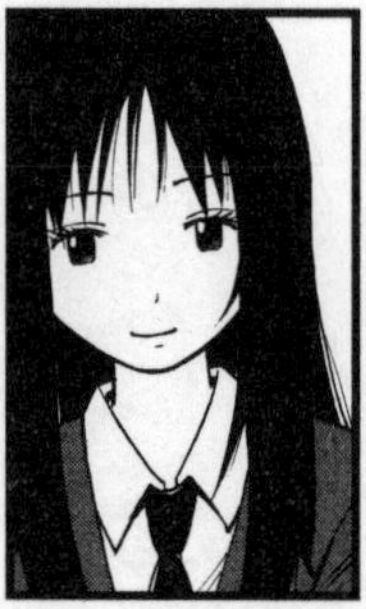

Yukiko Kanzaki

The most popular girl in Class E. She and Kayano were kidnapped during the School Trip.

Irina Jelavich

A sexy assassin hired as an English teacher. She's known for using her "womanly charms" to get close to a target, but has failed to kill Koro Sensei—yet.

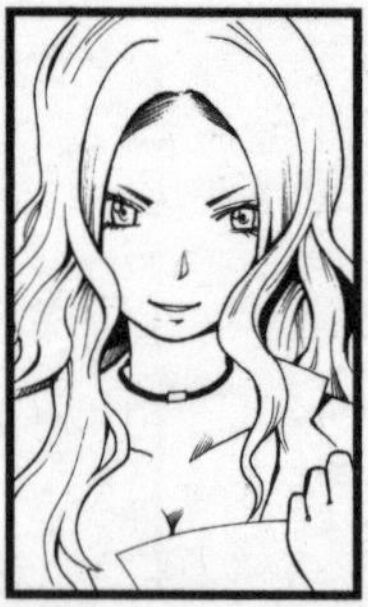

Tadaomi Karasuma

Member of the Ministry of Defense and the Class E students' P.E. teacher. Also in charge of managing visiting assassins.

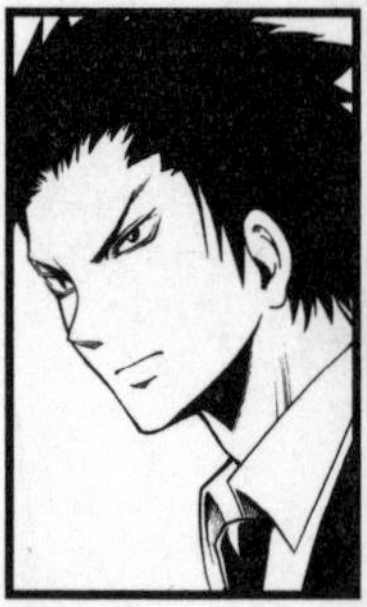

Kill them with cuteness! ♡
Koro Kawaii Knife Kovers

It's to die for! ♪

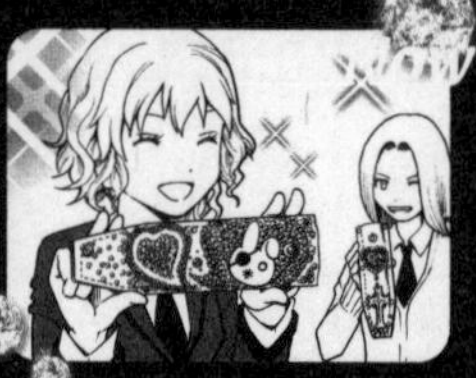

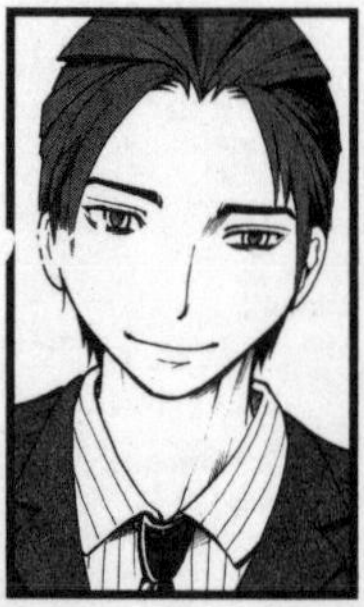

Gakuho Asano

The principal of Kunugigaoka Academy, who built this academically competitive school based on his faith in rationality and hierarchy.

ASSASSINATION
CLASSROOM 3 CONTENTS

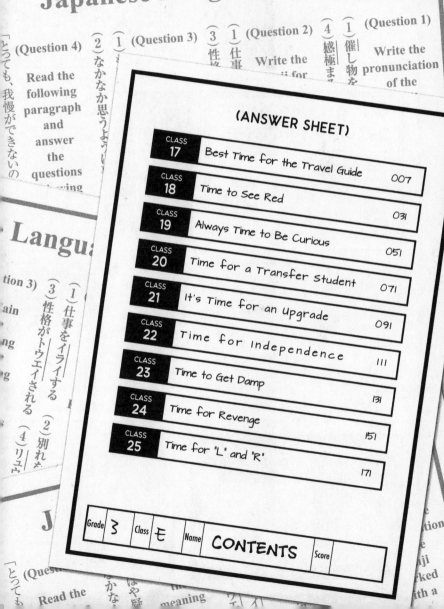

Japanese Language Test

(Question 1)
Write the pronunciation of the

(1)催し物を
(4)感極ま

(Question 2)
Write the

(1)仕事
(3)性格

(Question 3)
(1)
(2)なかなか思うよう

(Question 4)
Read the following paragraph and answer the questions

「とっても、我慢ができないの

Langu

tion 3)

(1)仕事をイライする
(3)性格がトウエイされる
(2)別れ
(4)リュウ

(ANSWER SHEET)

Grade	3	Class	E	Name	CONTENTS	Score	

「とって
(Ques
Read the
meaning

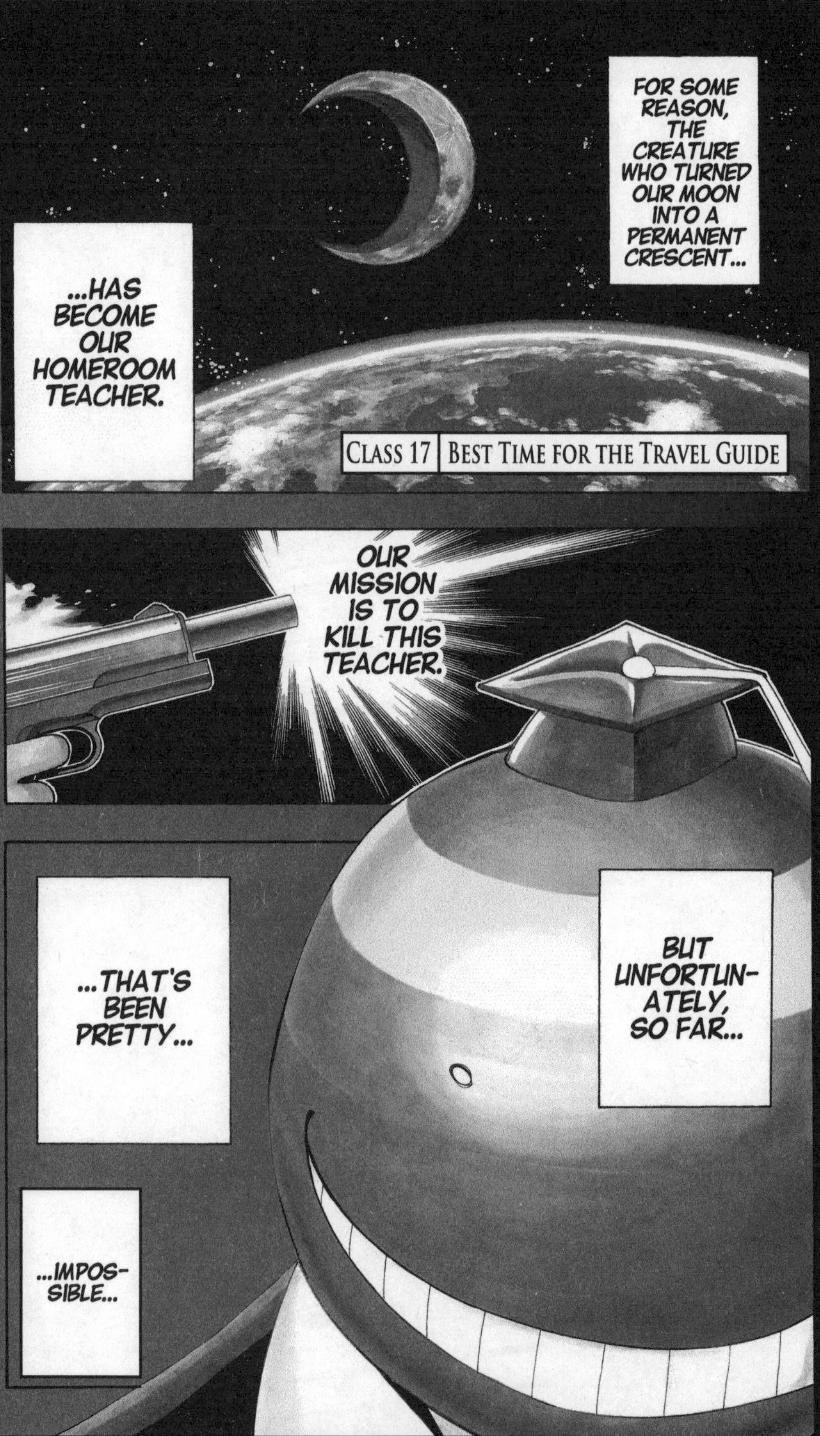
FOR SOME REASON, THE CREATURE WHO TURNED OUR MOON INTO A PERMANENT CRESCENT...
...HAS BECOME OUR HOMEROOM TEACHER.
CLASS 17 BEST TIME FOR THE TRAVEL GUIDE
OUR MISSION IS TO KILL THIS TEACHER.
BUT UNFORTUN-ATELY, SO FAR...
...THAT'S BEEN PRETTY...
...IMPOS-SIBLE...

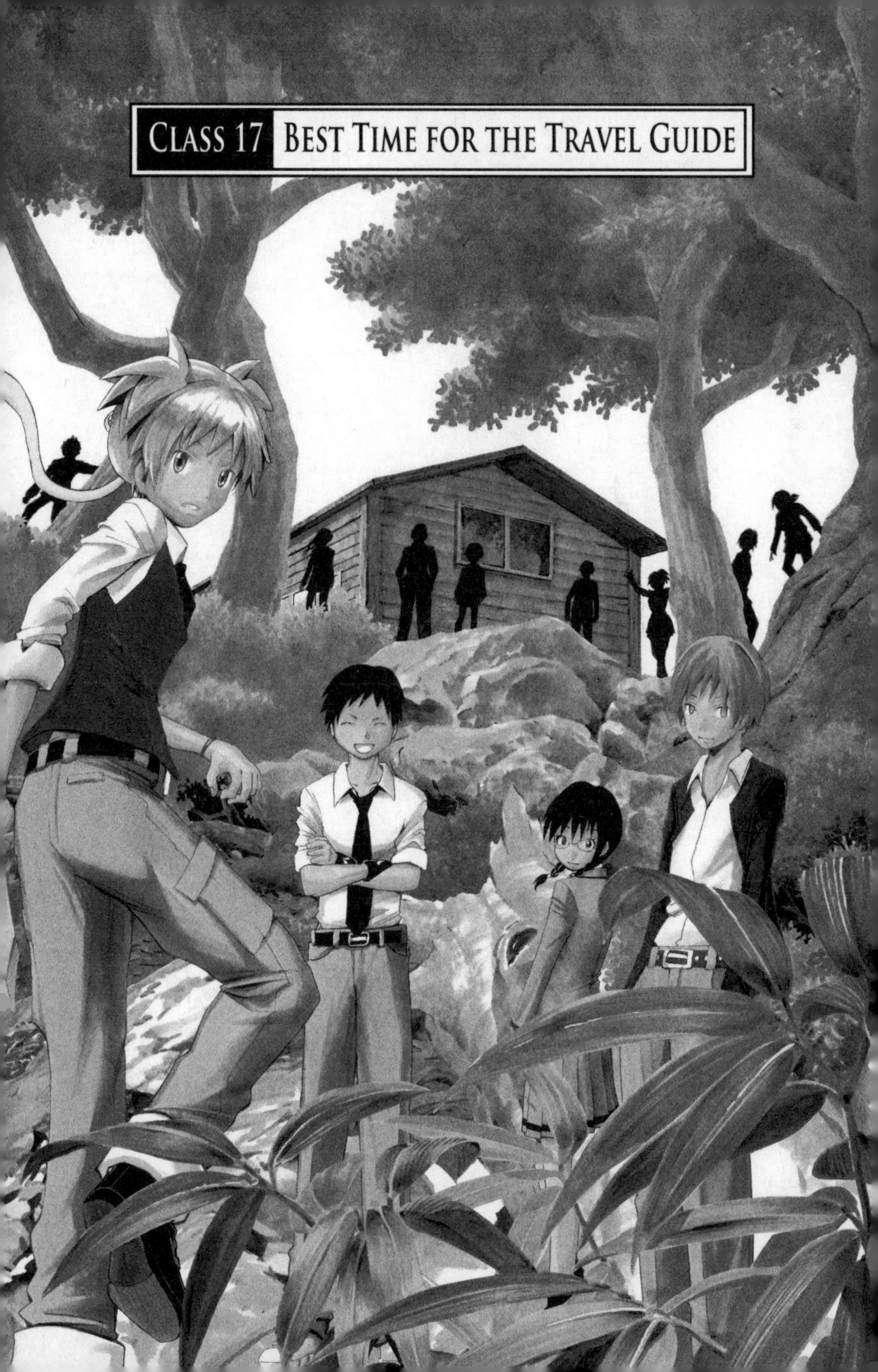
CLASS 17 BEST TIME FOR THE TRAVEL GUIDE

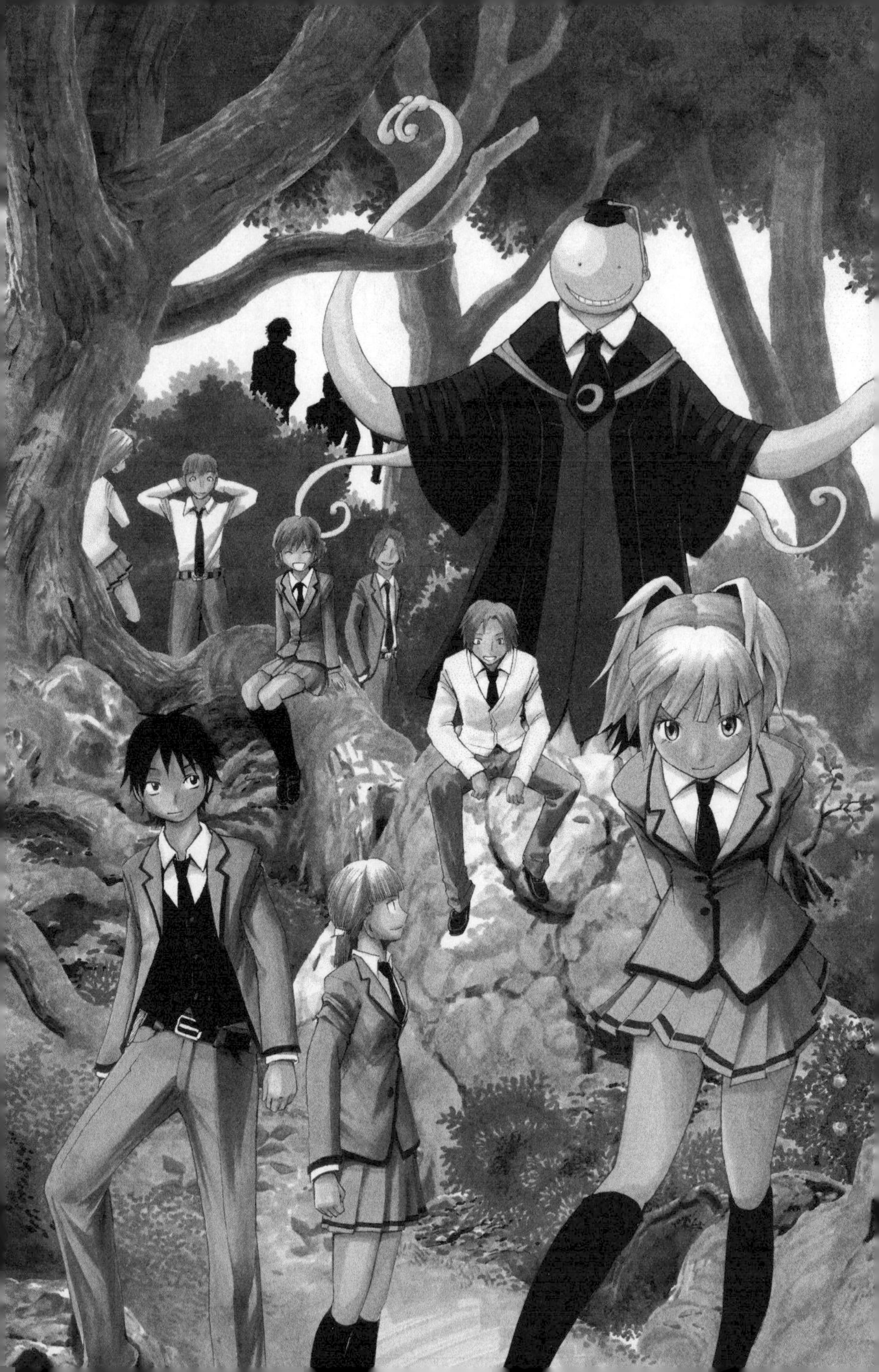

☞ THE MEANING OF THE NAME

"KORO SENSEI"

☞ IT'S A PLAY ON WORDS.

① "KOROSENAI" MEANS
"CAN'T BE KILLED."

殺せ|

② "SENSEI" MEANS
"TEACHER."

殺せんせー|

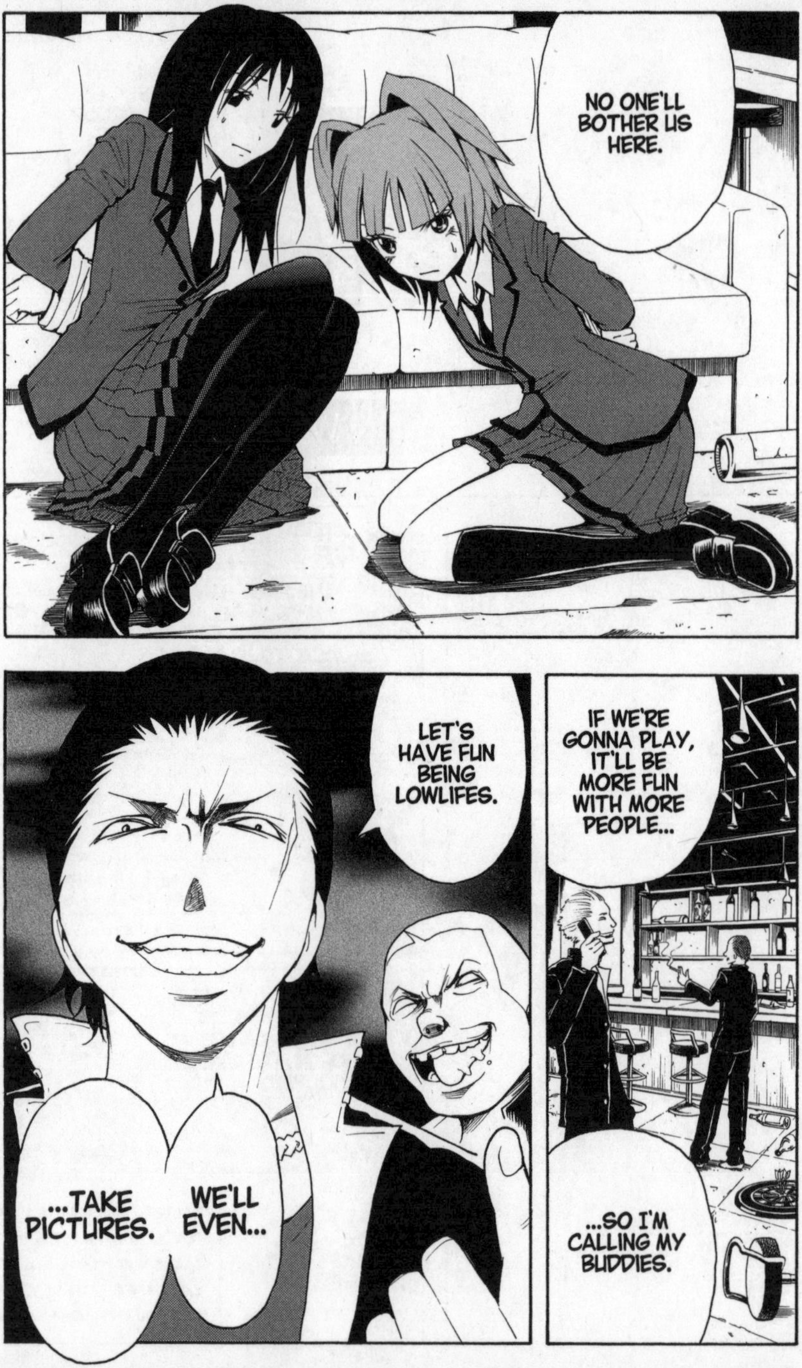
NO ONE'LL BOTHER US HERE.
IF WE'RE GONNA PLAY, IT'LL BE MORE FUN WITH MORE PEOPLE...
...SO I'M CALLING MY BUDDIES.
LET'S HAVE FUN BEING LOWLIFES.
WE'LL EVEN...
...TAKE PICTURES.

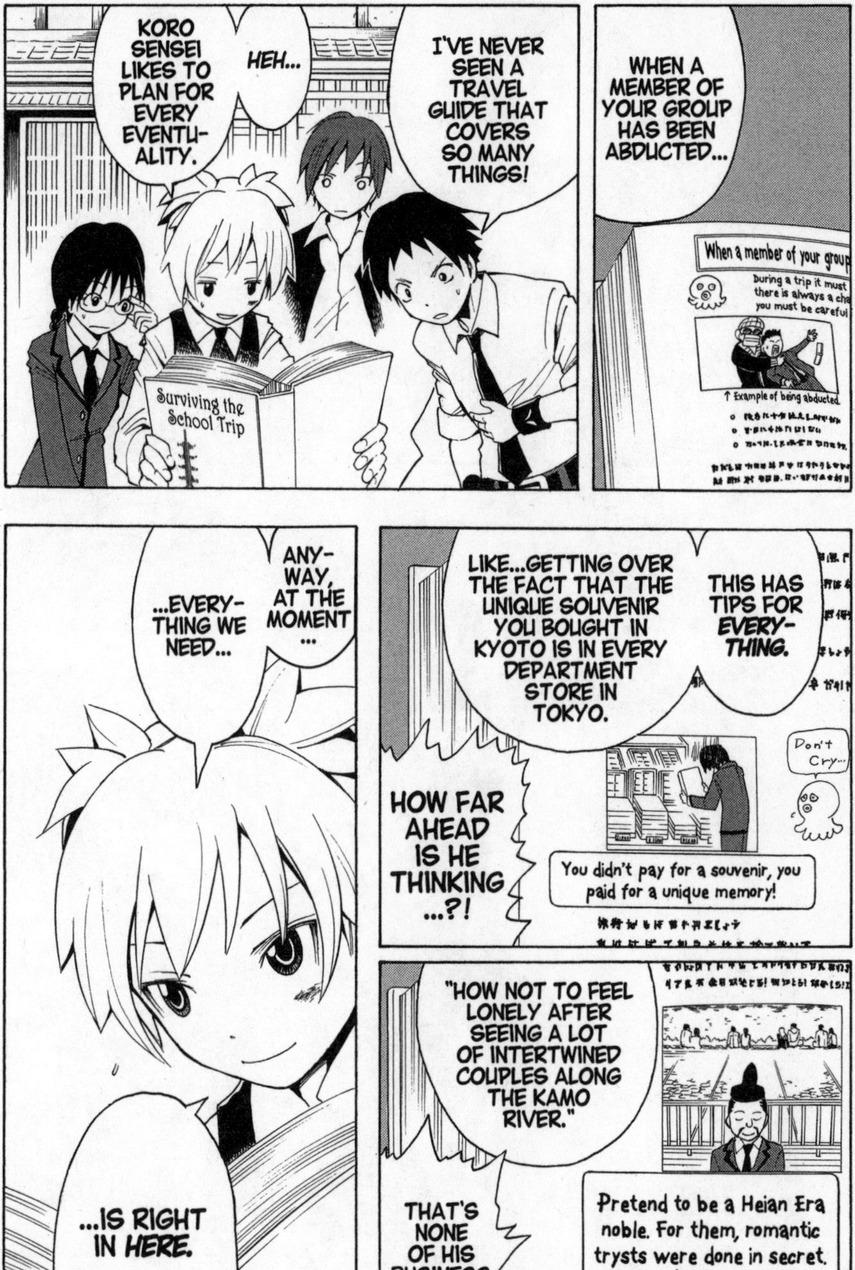
WHEN A MEMBER OF YOUR GROUP HAS BEEN ABDUCTED...
When a member of your group
During a trip it must
there is always a cha
you must be careful
↑ Example of being abducted.
I'VE NEVER SEEN A TRAVEL GUIDE THAT COVERS SO MANY THINGS!
HEH...
KORO SENSEI LIKES TO PLAN FOR EVERY EVENTU-ALITY.
Surviving the School Trip
THIS HAS TIPS FOR *EVERY-THING.*
LIKE...GETTING OVER THE FACT THAT THE UNIQUE SOUVENIR YOU BOUGHT IN KYOTO IS IN EVERY DEPARTMENT STORE IN TOKYO.
Don't Cry...
HOW FAR AHEAD IS HE THINKING ...?!
You didn't pay for a souvenir, you paid for a unique memory!
"HOW NOT TO FEEL LONELY AFTER SEEING A LOT OF INTERTWINED COUPLES ALONG THE KAMO RIVER."
Pretend to be a Heian Era noble. For them, romantic trysts were done in secret. So there's nothing wrong with you not having a date.
THAT'S NONE OF HIS BUSINESS !!
ANY-WAY, AT THE MOMENT ...
...EVERY-THING WE NEED...
...IS RIGHT IN *HERE.*

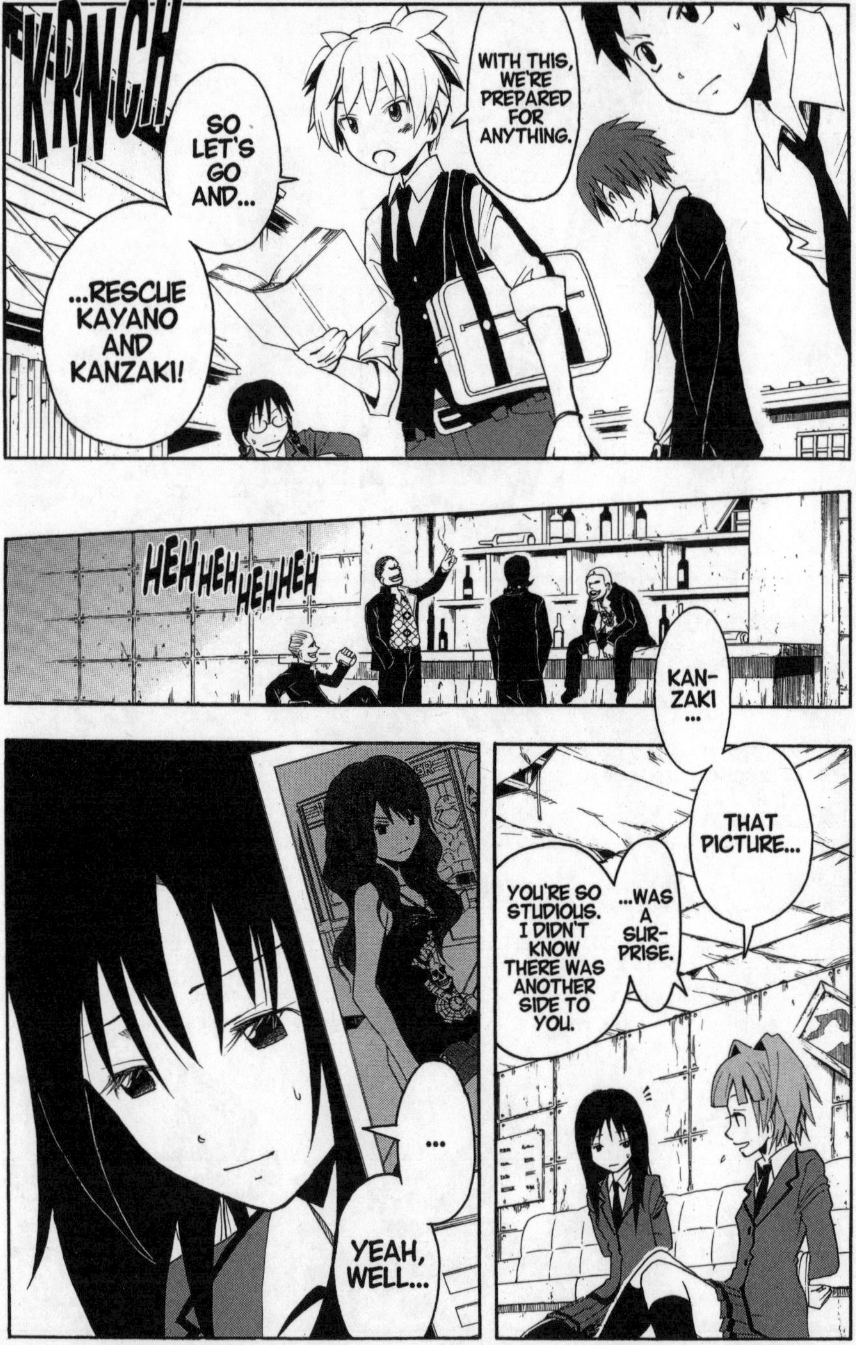
WITH THIS, WE'RE PREPARED FOR ANYTHING.
K-RNCH
SO LET'S GO AND...
...RESCUE KAYANO AND KANZAKI!
HEH HEH HEH HEH
KAN-ZAKI...
THAT PICTURE...
...WAS A SUR-PRISE.
YOU'RE SO STUDIOUS. I DIDN'T KNOW THERE WAS ANOTHER SIDE TO YOU.
...
YEAH, WELL...

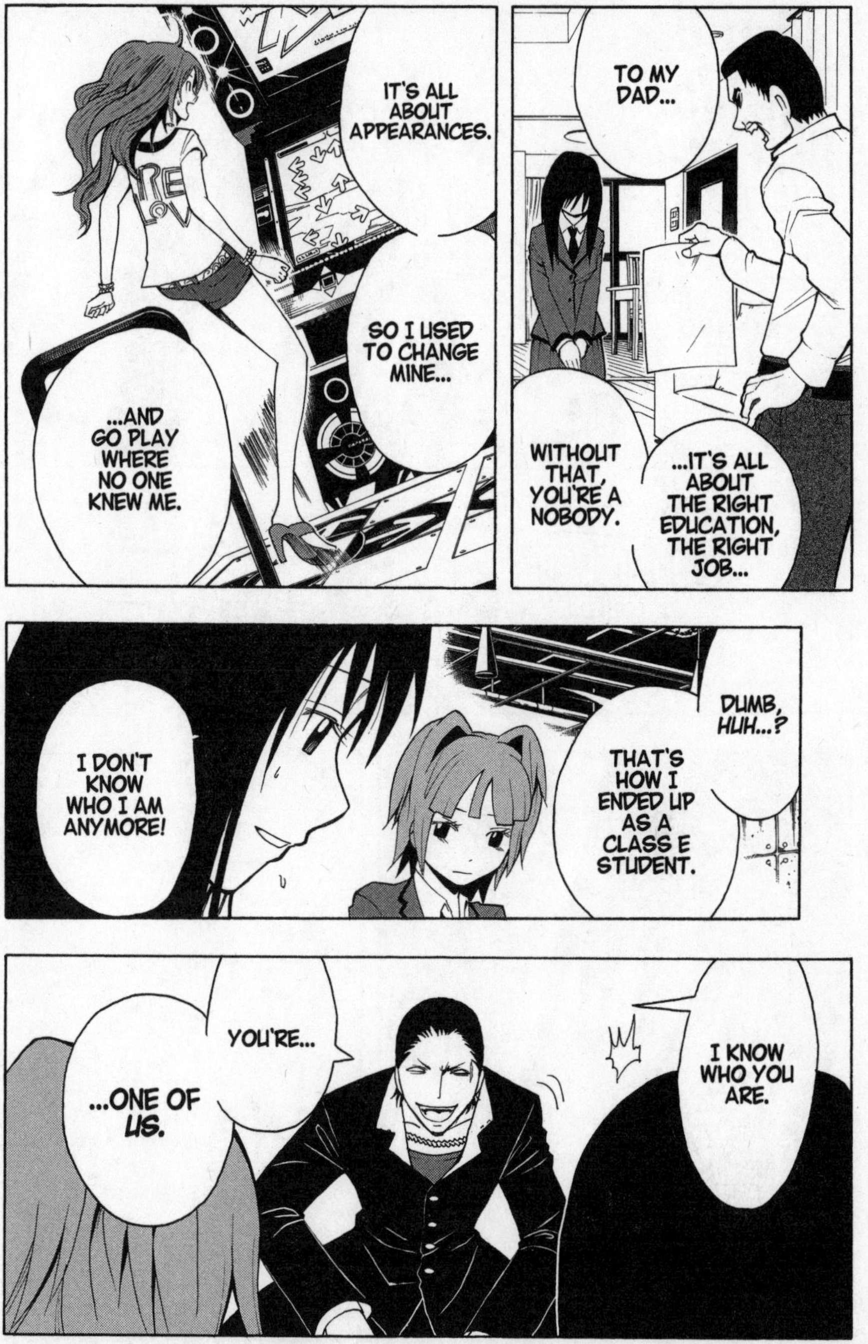
TO MY DAD...
...IT'S ALL ABOUT THE RIGHT EDUCATION, THE RIGHT JOB...
WITHOUT THAT, YOU'RE A NOBODY.
IT'S ALL ABOUT APPEARANCES.
SO I USED TO CHANGE MINE...
...AND GO PLAY WHERE NO ONE KNEW ME.
DUMB, HUH...?
THAT'S HOW I ENDED UP AS A CLASS E STUDENT.
I DON'T KNOW WHO I AM ANYMORE!
I KNOW WHO YOU ARE.
YOU'RE...
...ONE OF US.

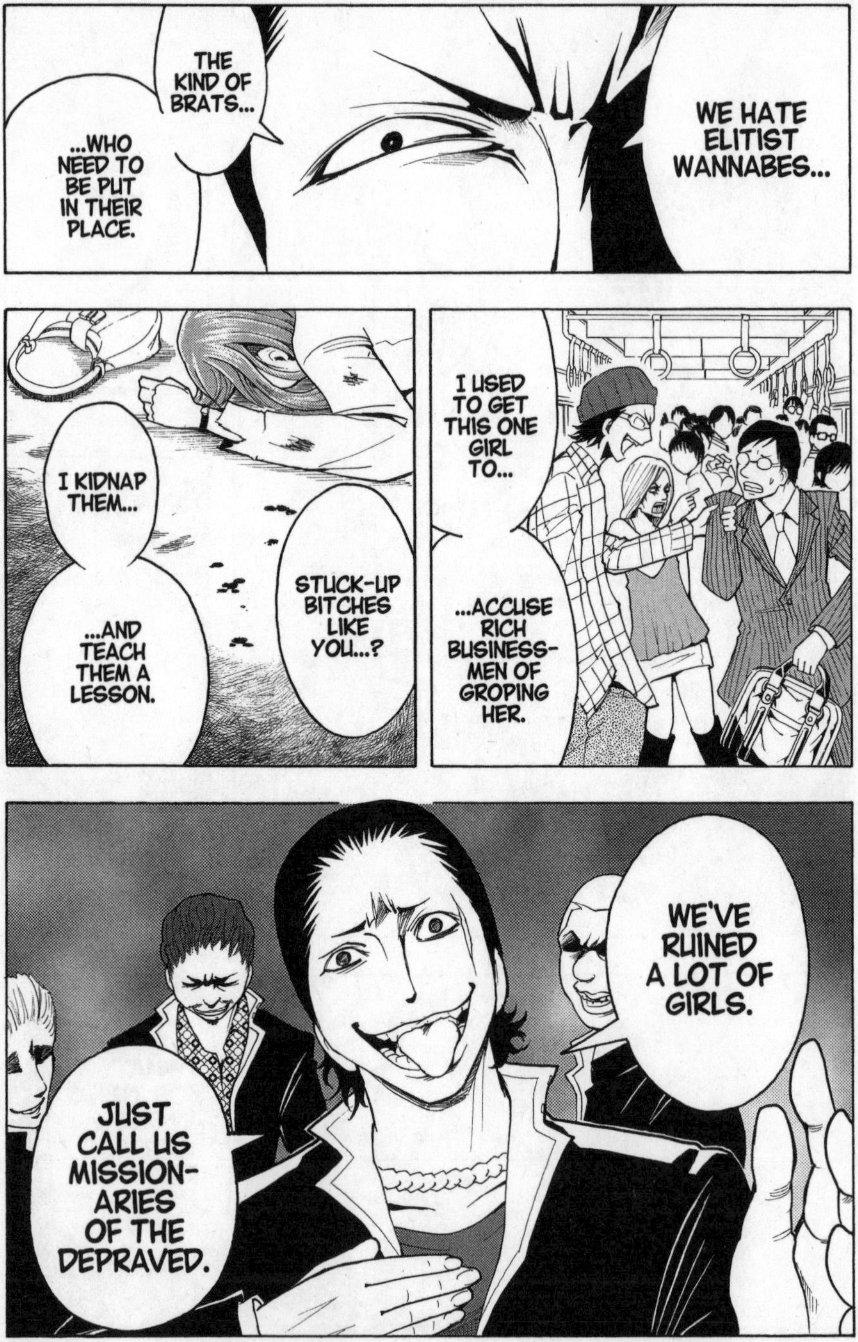
WE HATE ELITIST WANNABES...
THE KIND OF BRATS...
...WHO NEED TO BE PUT IN THEIR PLACE.
I USED TO GET THIS ONE GIRL TO...
...ACCUSE RICH BUSINESS-MEN OF GROPING HER.
STUCK-UP BITCHES LIKE YOU...?
I KIDNAP THEM...
...AND TEACH THEM A LESSON.
WE'VE RUINED A LOT OF GIRLS.
JUST CALL US MISSION-ARIES OF THE DEPRAVED.

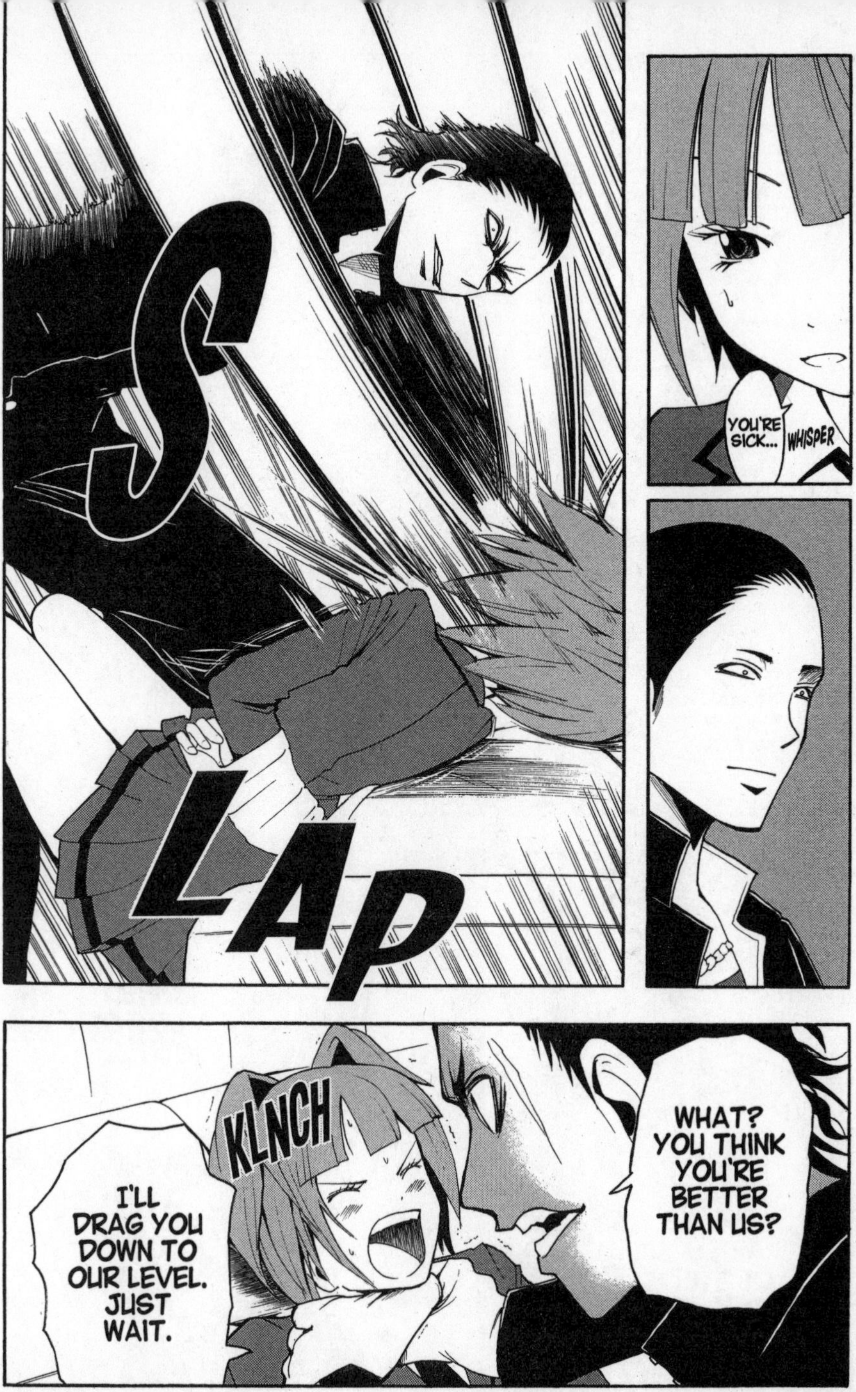
YOU'RE SICK...
WHISPER
SLAP
WHAT? YOU THINK YOU'RE BETTER THAN US?
KLNCH
I'LL DRAG YOU DOWN TO OUR LEVEL. JUST WAIT.

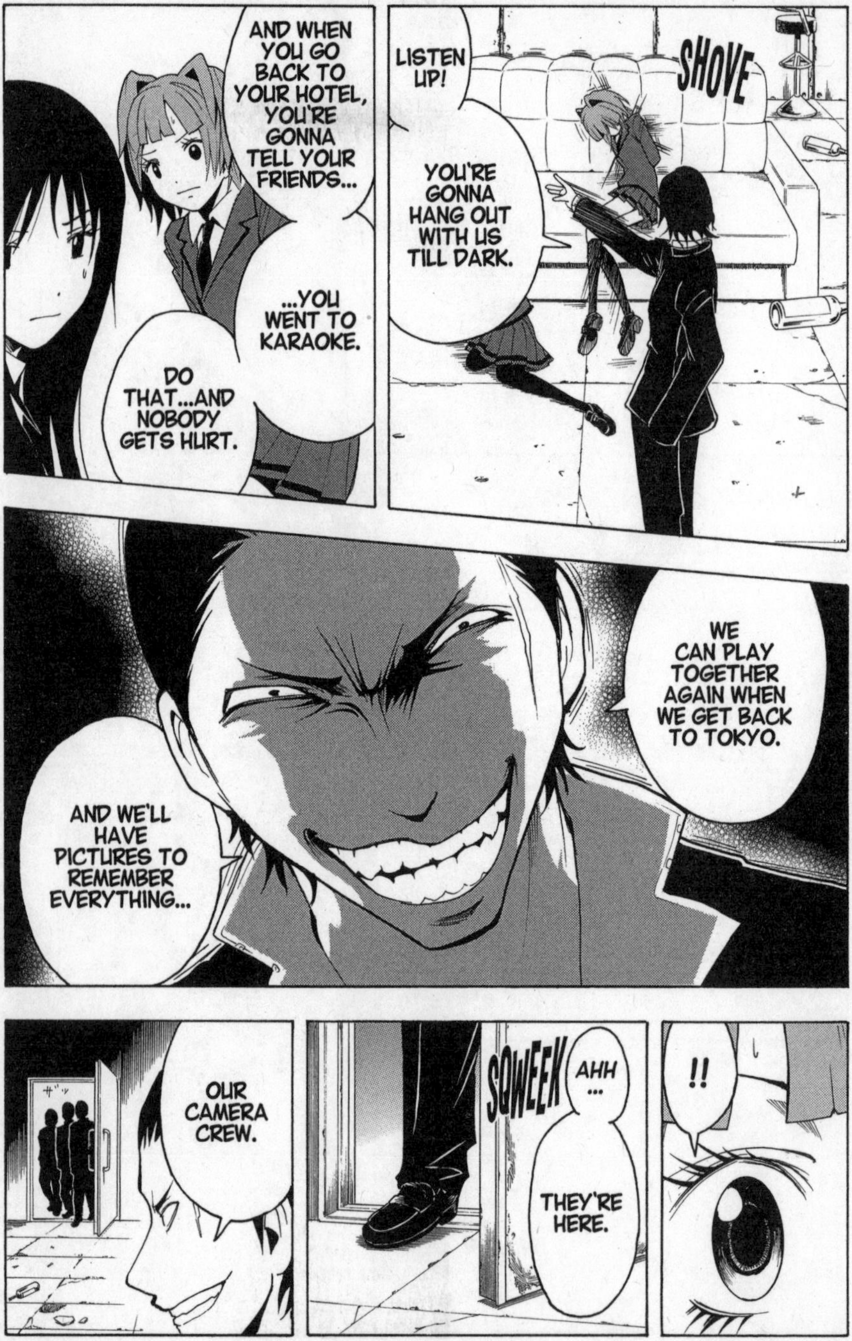
LISTEN UP!
SHOVE
YOU'RE GONNA HANG OUT WITH US TILL DARK.
AND WHEN YOU GO BACK TO YOUR HOTEL, YOU'RE GONNA TELL YOUR FRIENDS...
...YOU WENT TO KARAOKE.
DO THAT...AND NOBODY GETS HURT.
WE CAN PLAY TOGETHER AGAIN WHEN WE GET BACK TO TOKYO.
AND WE'LL HAVE PICTURES TO REMEMBER EVERYTHING...
!!
SQWEEK
AHH ...
THEY'RE HERE.
OUR CAMERA CREW.

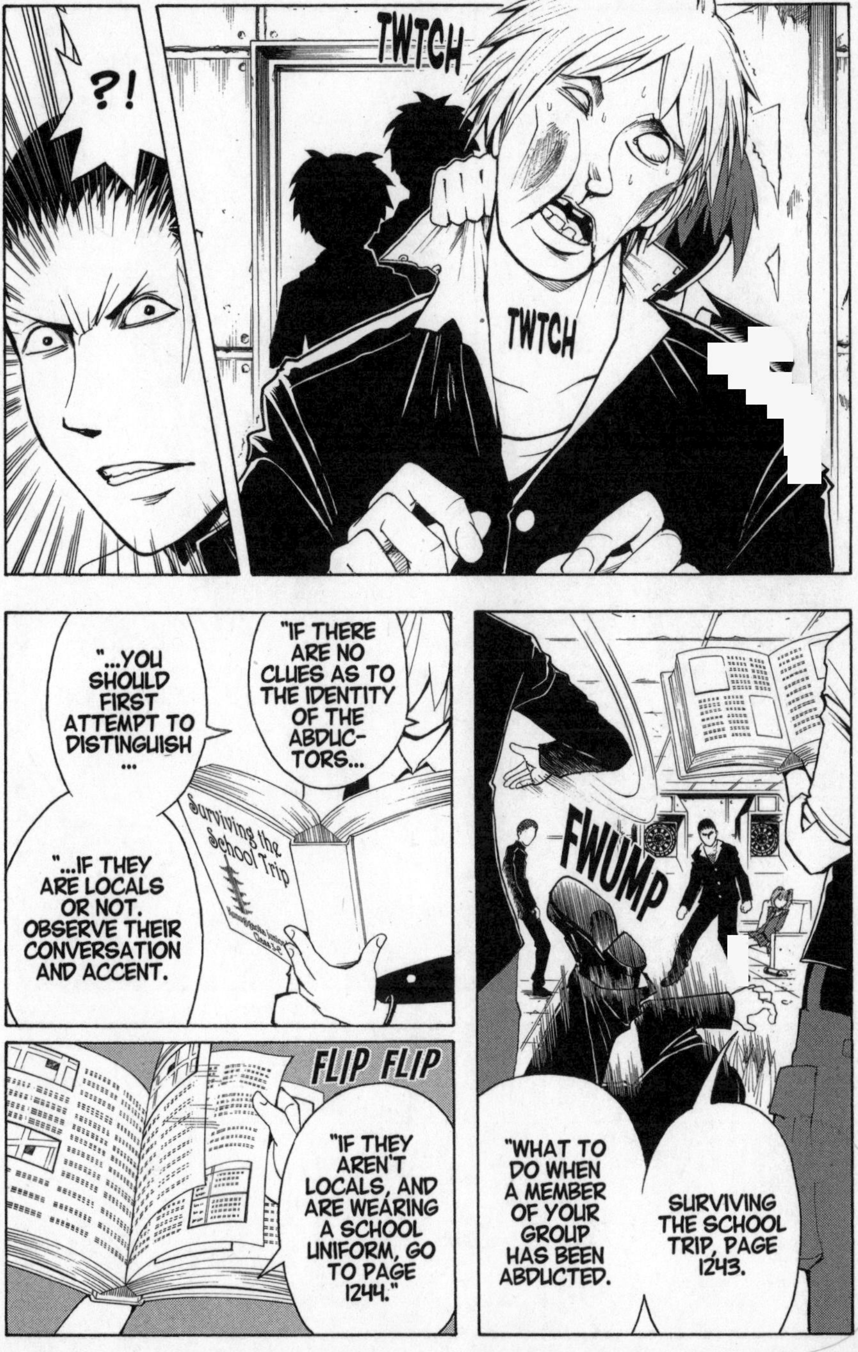
TWTCH
TWTCH
?!
FWUMP
SURVIVING THE SCHOOL TRIP, PAGE 1243.
"WHAT TO DO WHEN A MEMBER OF YOUR GROUP HAS BEEN ABDUCTED.
"IF THERE ARE NO CLUES AS TO THE IDENTITY OF THE ABDUC-TORS...
"...YOU SHOULD FIRST ATTEMPT TO DISTINGUISH ...
"...IF THEY ARE LOCALS OR NOT. OBSERVE THEIR CONVERSATION AND ACCENT.
Surviving the School Trip
FLIP FLIP
"IF THEY AREN'T LOCALS, AND ARE WEARING A SCHOOL UNIFORM, GO TO PAGE 1244."

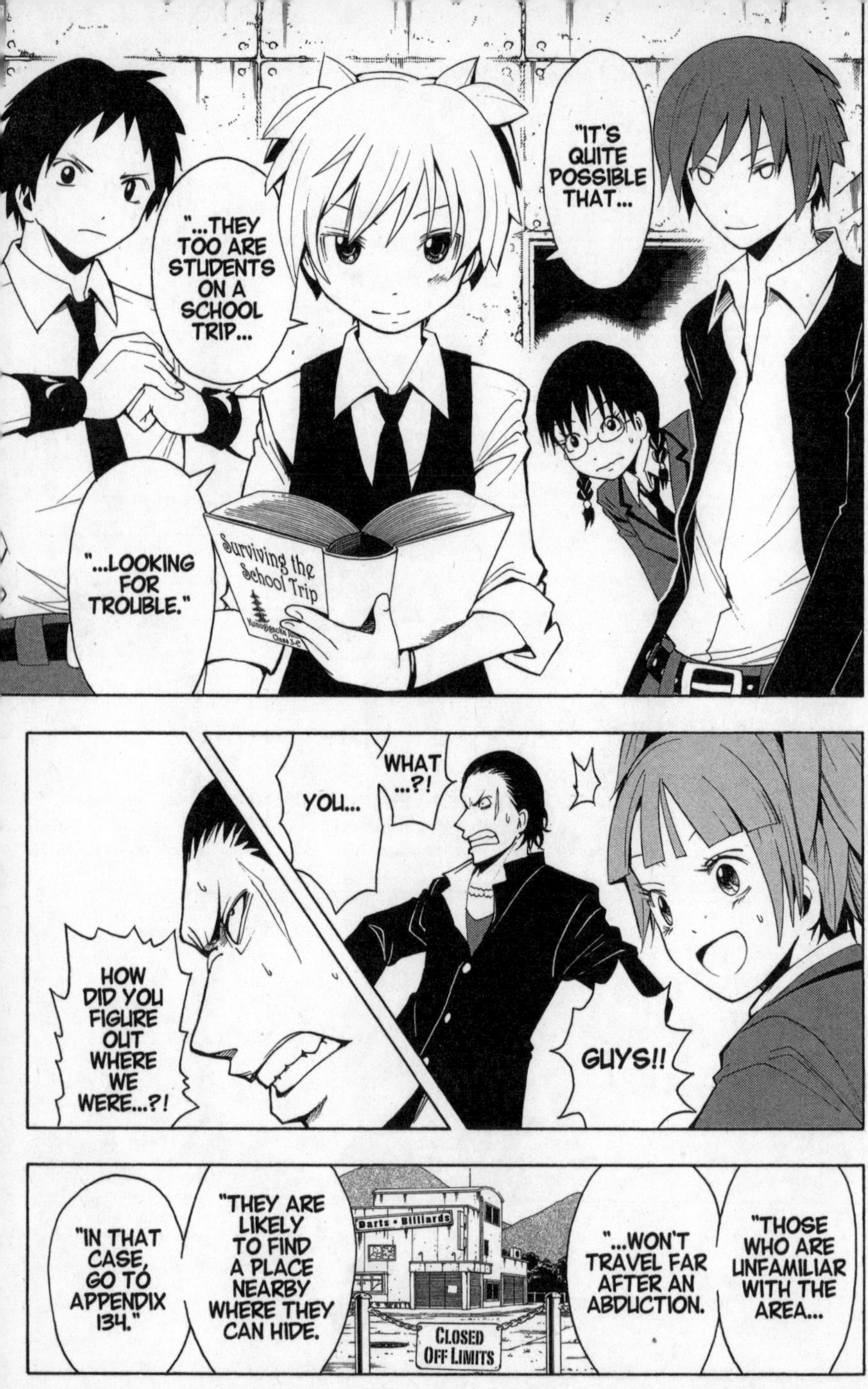
"IT'S QUITE POSSIBLE THAT...
"...THEY TOO ARE STUDENTS ON A SCHOOL TRIP...
"...LOOKING FOR TROUBLE."
Surviving the School Trip
GUYS!!
WHAT ...?!
YOU...
HOW DID YOU FIGURE OUT WHERE WE WERE...?!
"THOSE WHO ARE UNFAMILIAR WITH THE AREA...
"...WON'T TRAVEL FAR AFTER AN ABDUCTION.
"THEY ARE LIKELY TO FIND A PLACE NEARBY WHERE THEY CAN HIDE.
"IN THAT CASE, GO TO APPENDIX 134."
Darts • Billiards
CLOSED
OFF LIMITS

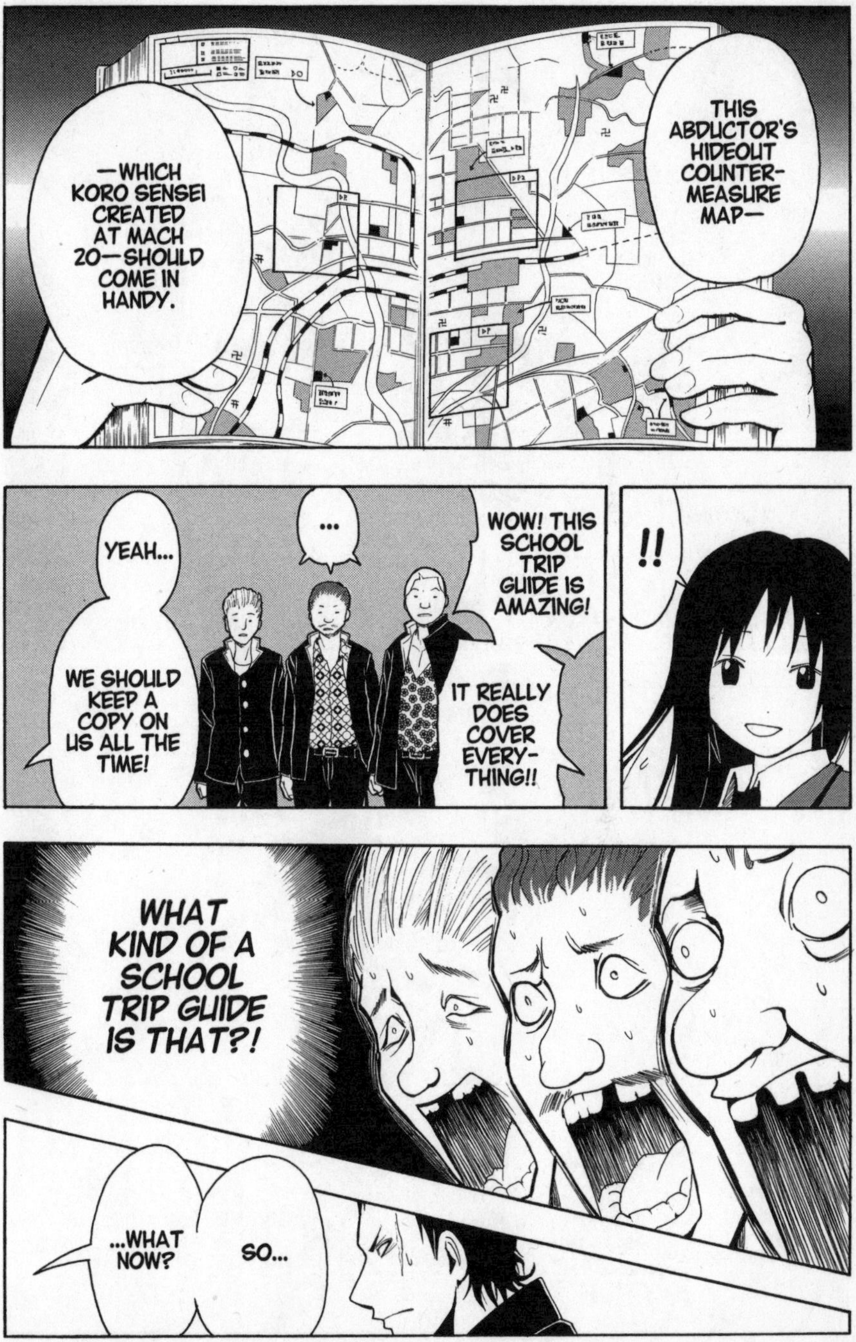
THIS ABDUCTOR'S HIDEOUT COUNTER-MEASURE MAP—
—WHICH KORO SENSEI CREATED AT MACH 20—SHOULD COME IN HANDY.
!!
WOW! THIS SCHOOL TRIP GUIDE IS AMAZING!
IT REALLY DOES COVER EVERY-THING!!
...
YEAH...
WE SHOULD KEEP A COPY ON US ALL THE TIME!
WHAT KIND OF A SCHOOL TRIP GUIDE IS THAT?!
SO...
...WHAT NOW?

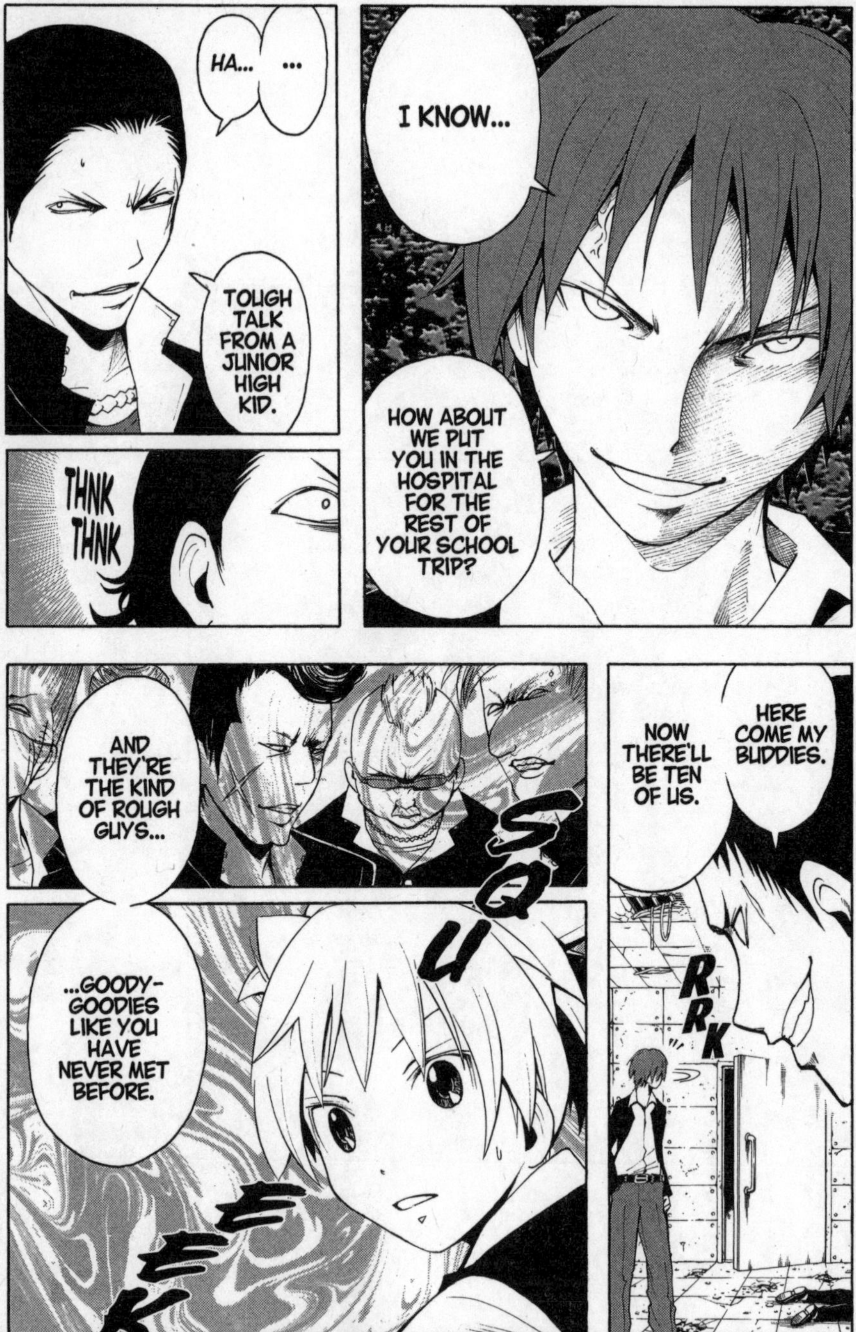
I KNOW...
HOW ABOUT WE PUT YOU IN THE HOSPITAL FOR THE REST OF YOUR SCHOOL TRIP?
...
HA...
TOUGH TALK FROM A JUNIOR HIGH KID.
THNK THNK
HERE COME MY BUDDIES.
NOW THERE'LL BE TEN OF US.
RRK
AND THEY'RE THE KIND OF ROUGH GUYS...
SQU
...GOODY-GOODIES LIKE YOU HAVE NEVER MET BEFORE.
EEEK

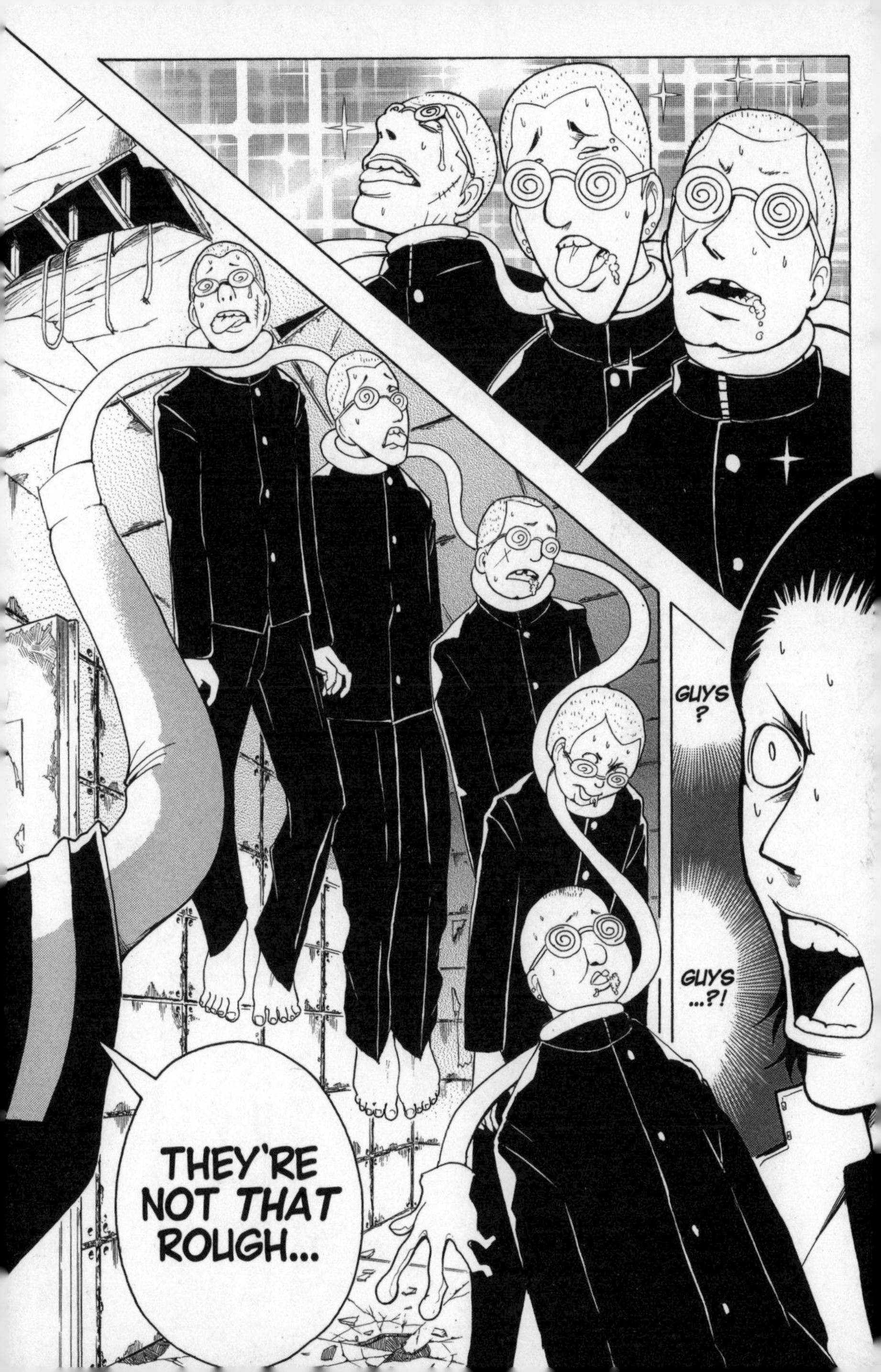
GUYS ?
GUYS ...?!
THEY'RE NOT THAT ROUGH...

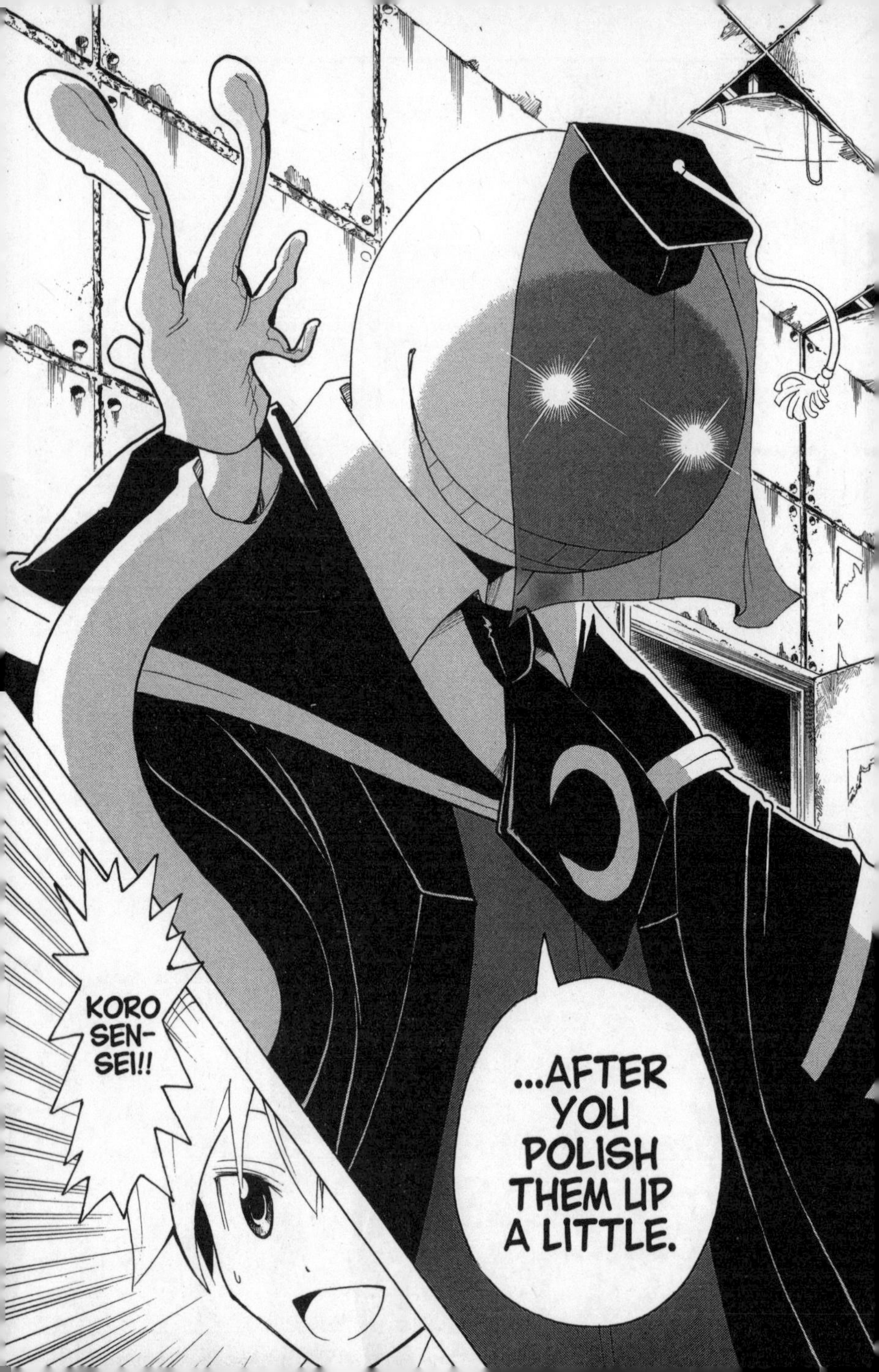
...AFTER YOU POLISH THEM UP A LITTLE.
KORO SEN-SEI!!

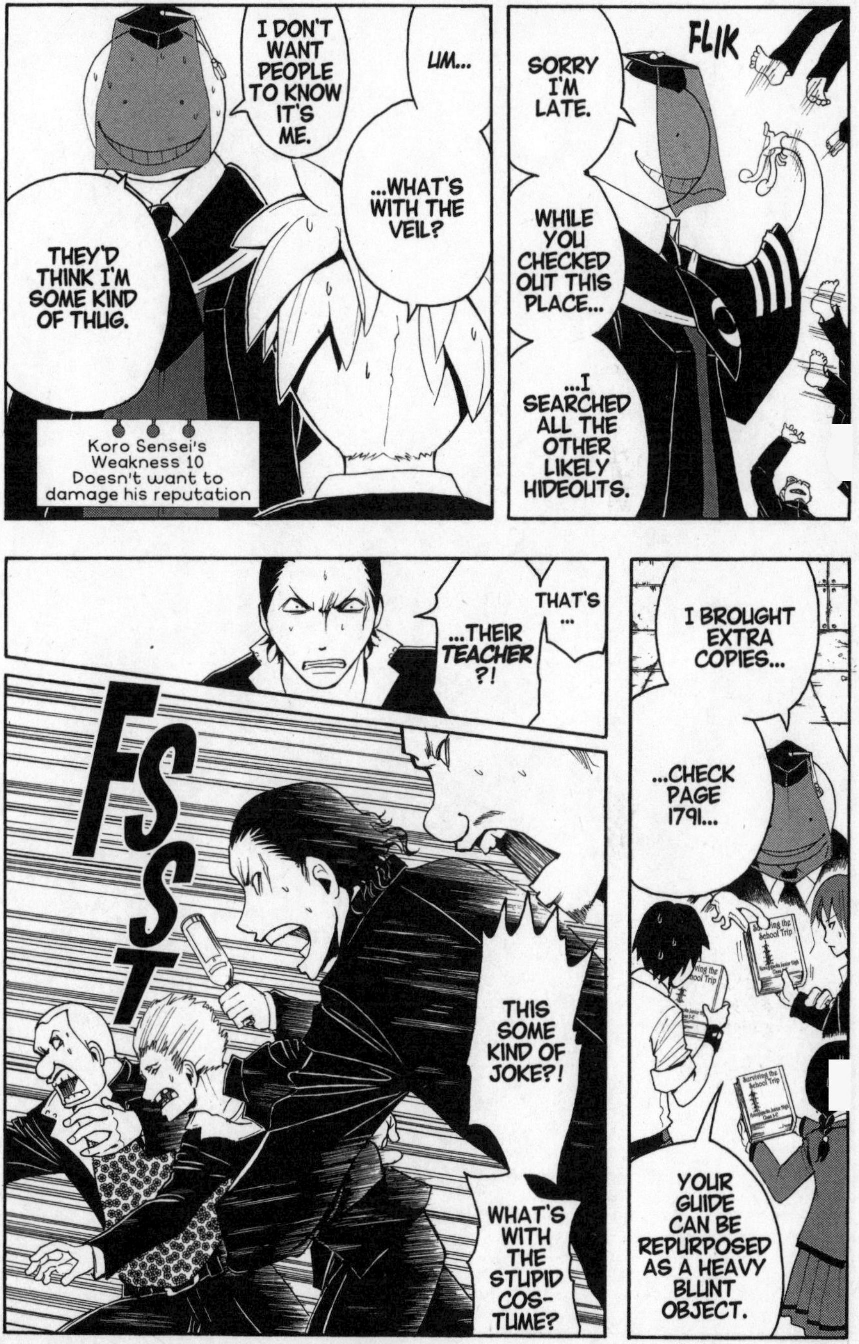
FLIK
SORRY I'M LATE.
WHILE YOU CHECKED OUT THIS PLACE...
...I SEARCHED ALL THE OTHER LIKELY HIDEOUTS.
UM...
...WHAT'S WITH THE VEIL?
I DON'T WANT PEOPLE TO KNOW IT'S ME.
THEY'D THINK I'M SOME KIND OF THUG.
Koro Sensei's Weakness 10
Doesn't want to damage his reputation
I BROUGHT EXTRA COPIES...
...CHECK PAGE 1791...
Surviving the School Trip
YOUR GUIDE CAN BE REPURPOSED AS A HEAVY BLUNT OBJECT.
THAT'S ...
...THEIR TEACHER?!
FSST
THIS SOME KIND OF JOKE?!
WHAT'S WITH THE STUPID COS-TUME?

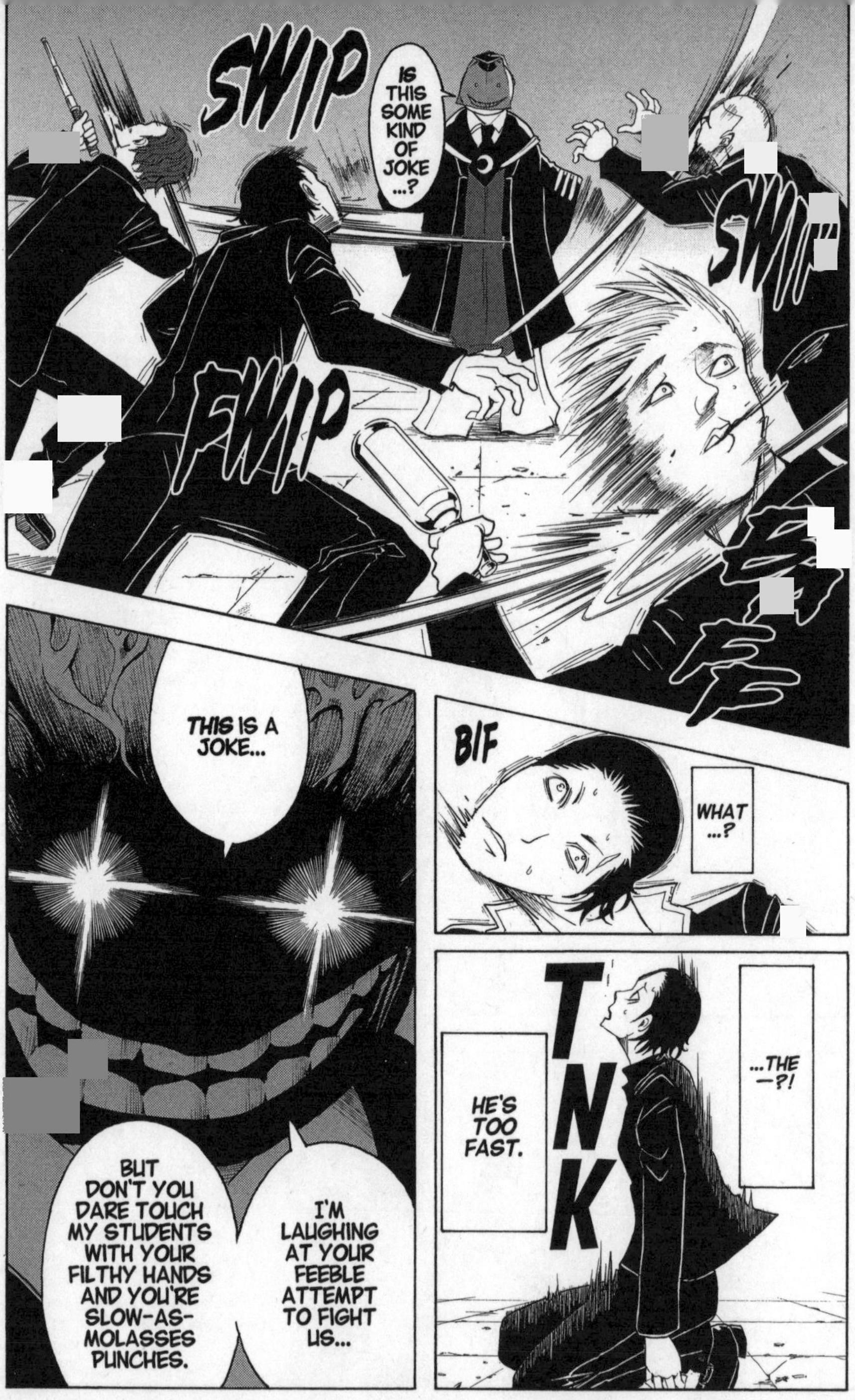
IS THIS SOME KIND OF JOKE ...?
SWIP
FWIP
BIF
WHAT ...?
TNK
...THE —?!
HE'S TOO FAST.
THIS IS A JOKE...
I'M LAUGHING AT YOUR FEEBLE ATTEMPT TO FIGHT US...
BUT DON'T YOU DARE TOUCH MY STUDENTS WITH YOUR FILTHY HANDS AND YOU'RE SLOW-AS-MOLASSES PUNCHES.

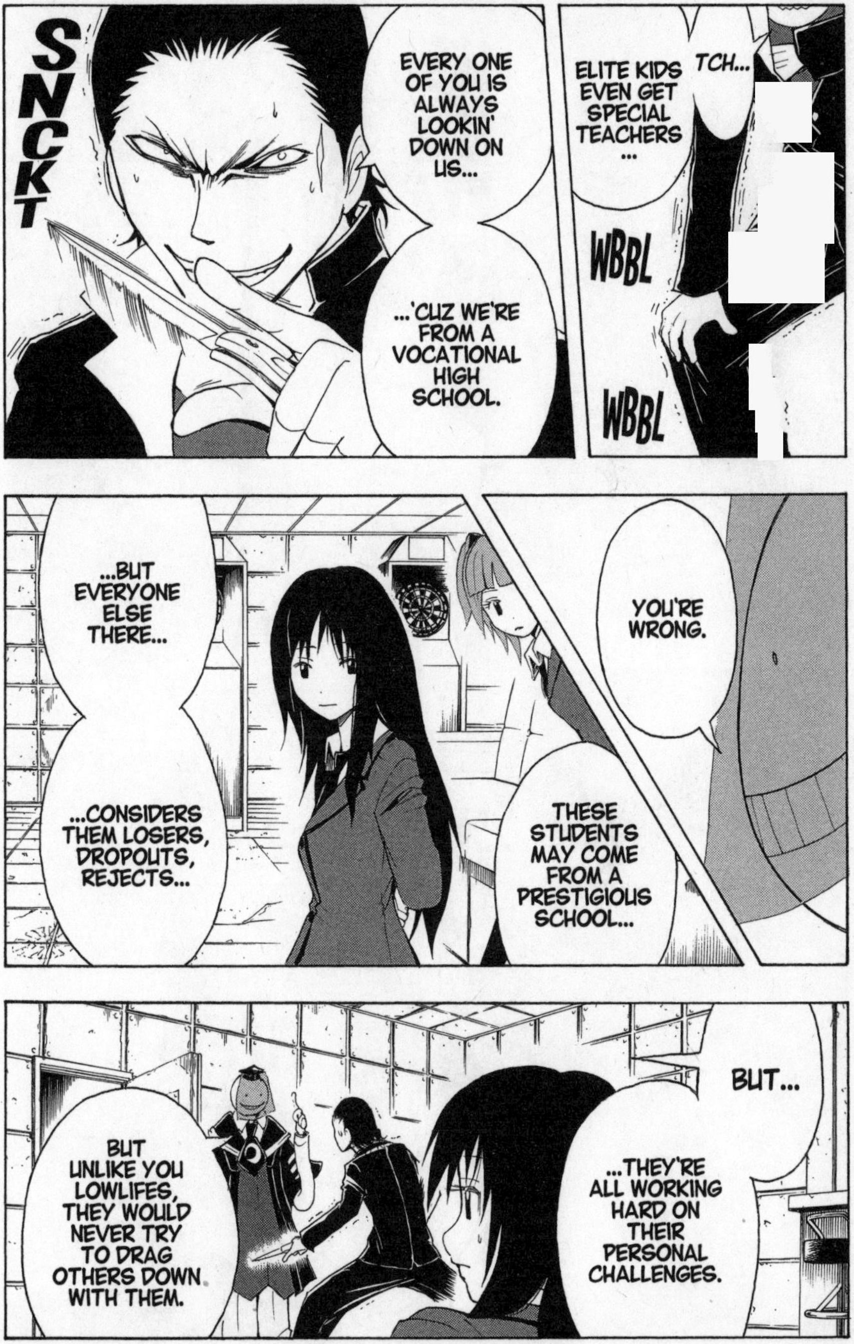
TCH...
ELITE KIDS EVEN GET SPECIAL TEACHERS...
WBBL
WBBL
SNCKT
EVERY ONE OF YOU IS ALWAYS LOOKIN' DOWN ON US...
...'CUZ WE'RE FROM A VOCATIONAL HIGH SCHOOL.
YOU'RE WRONG.
THESE STUDENTS MAY COME FROM A PRESTIGIOUS SCHOOL...
...BUT EVERYONE ELSE THERE...
...CONSIDERS THEM LOSERS, DROPOUTS, REJECTS...
BUT...
...THEY'RE ALL WORKING HARD ON THEIR PERSONAL CHALLENGES.
BUT UNLIKE YOU LOWLIFES, THEY WOULD NEVER TRY TO DRAG OTHERS DOWN WITH THEM.

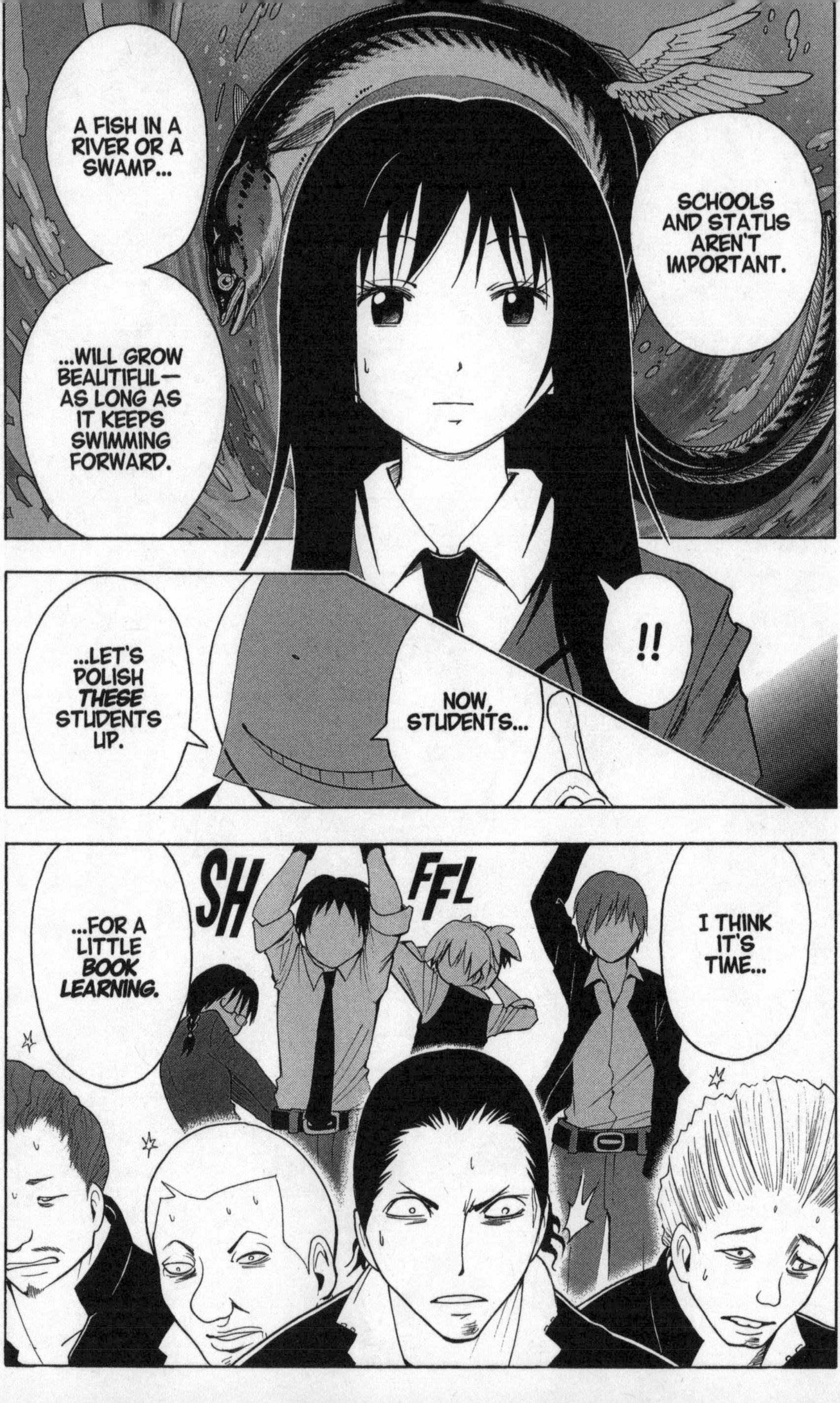
SCHOOLS AND STATUS AREN'T IMPORTANT.
A FISH IN A RIVER OR A SWAMP...
...WILL GROW BEAUTIFUL— AS LONG AS IT KEEPS SWIMMING FORWARD.
!!
NOW, STUDENTS...
...LET'S POLISH *THESE* STUDENTS UP.
I THINK IT'S TIME...
SHFFL
...FOR A LITTLE *BOOK LEARNING.*

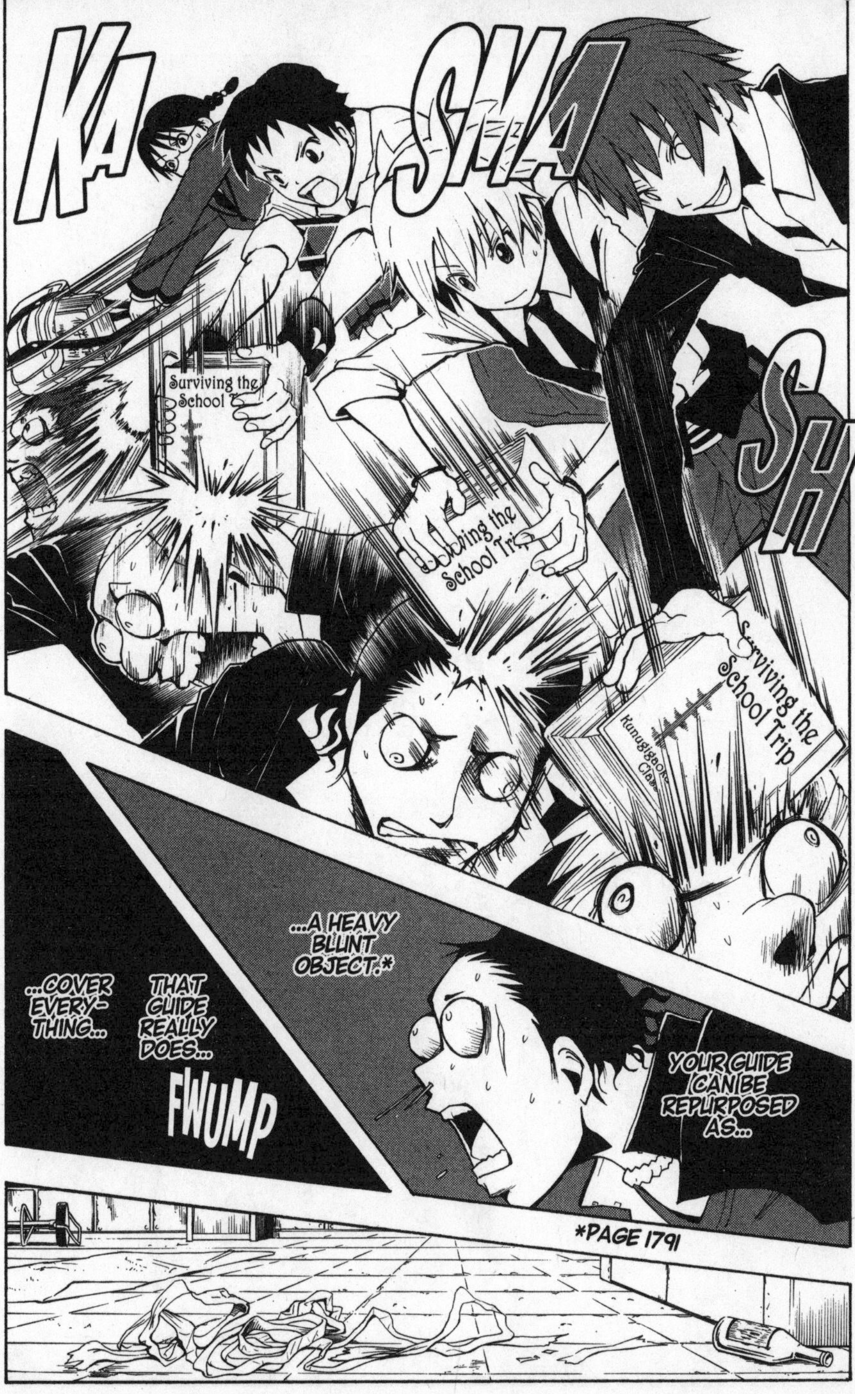
KA SHA SH
Surviving the School Trip
Surviving the School Trip
Surviving the School Trip
YOUR GUIDE CAN BE REPURPOSED AS...
...A HEAVY BLUNT OBJECT.*
THAT GUIDE REALLY DOES...
...COVER EVERY-THING...
FWUMP
*PAGE 1791

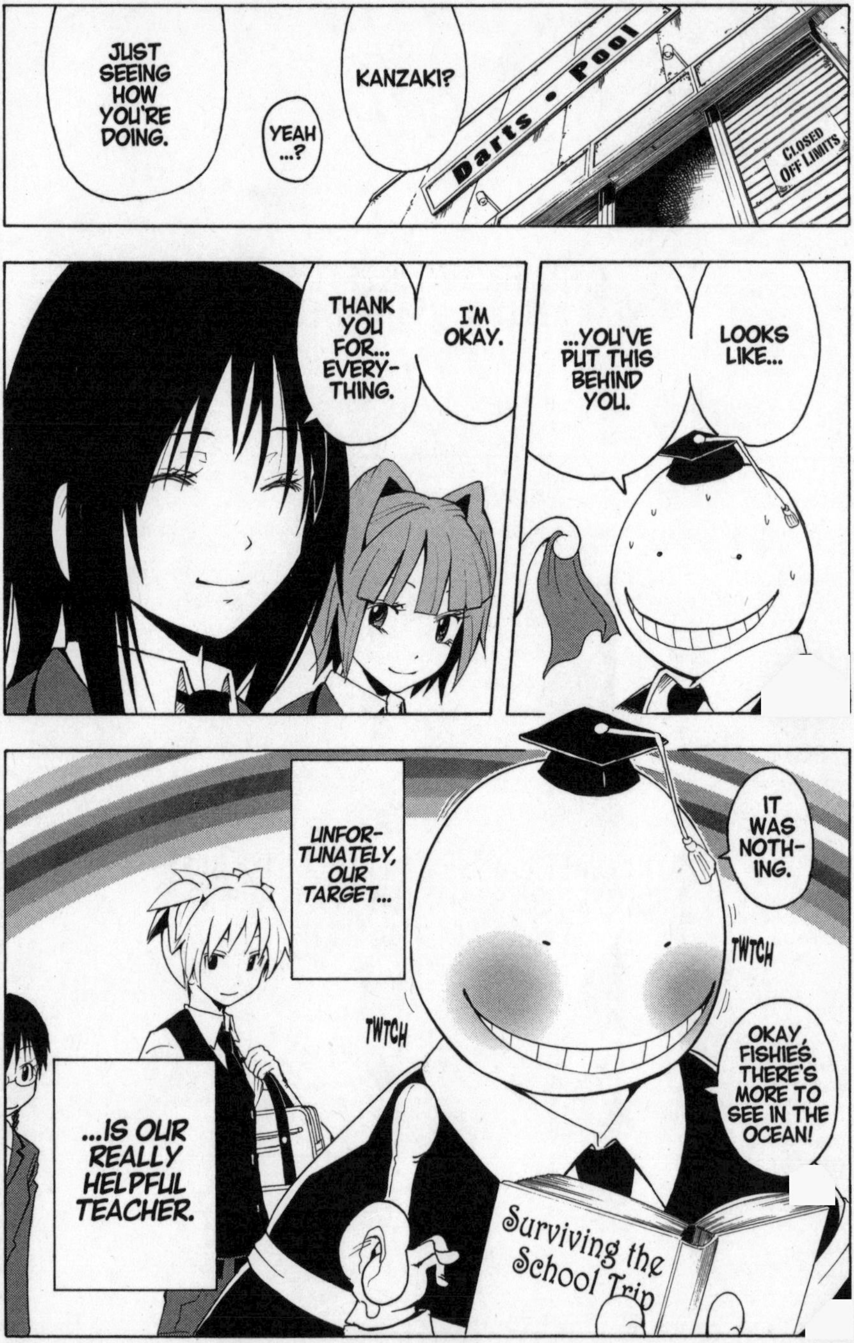
Darts • Pool
CLOSED OFF LIMITS
KANZAKI?
YEAH ...?
JUST SEEING HOW YOU'RE DOING.
LOOKS LIKE...
...YOU'VE PUT THIS BEHIND YOU.
I'M OKAY.
THANK YOU FOR... EVERYTHING.
IT WAS NOTHING.
UNFORTUNATELY, OUR TARGET...
TWTCH
TWTCH
OKAY, FISHIES. THERE'S MORE TO SEE IN THE OCEAN!
...IS OUR REALLY HELPFUL TEACHER.
Surviving the School Trip

RYUKI HAD TO REPEAT A
YEAR AFTER THIS INCIDENT.

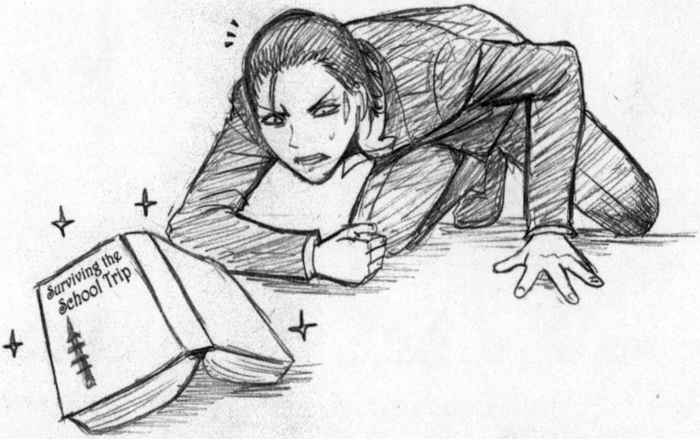
Surviving the School Trip

BUT SOMEHOW HE KNEW ALL THE BEST
PLACES TO SEE ON THE FOLLOWING
YEAR'S SCHOOL TRIP.

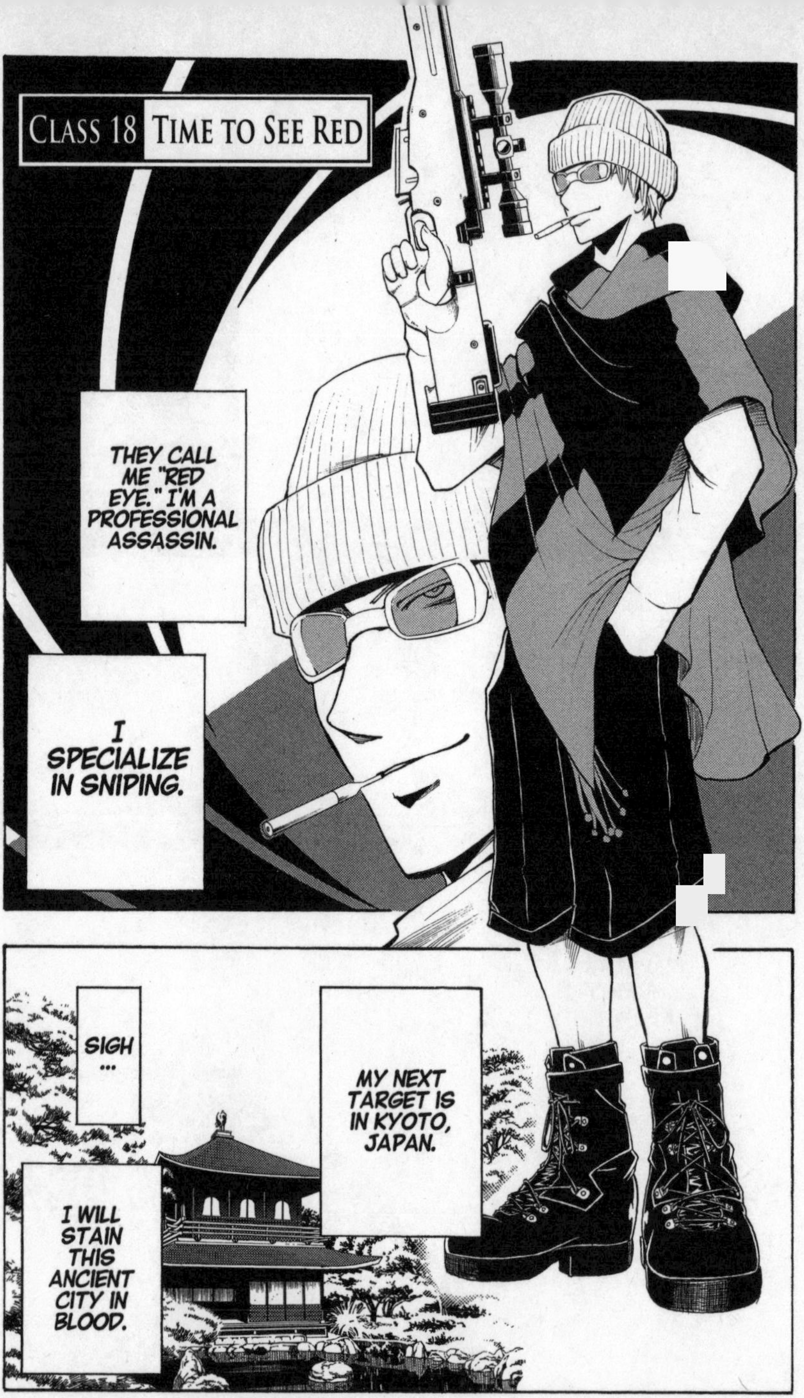
CLASS 18 TIME TO SEE RED
THEY CALL ME "RED EYE." I'M A PROFESSIONAL ASSASSIN.
I SPECIALIZE IN SNIPING.
MY NEXT TARGET IS IN KYOTO, JAPAN.
SIGH...
I WILL STAIN THIS ANCIENT CITY IN BLOOD.

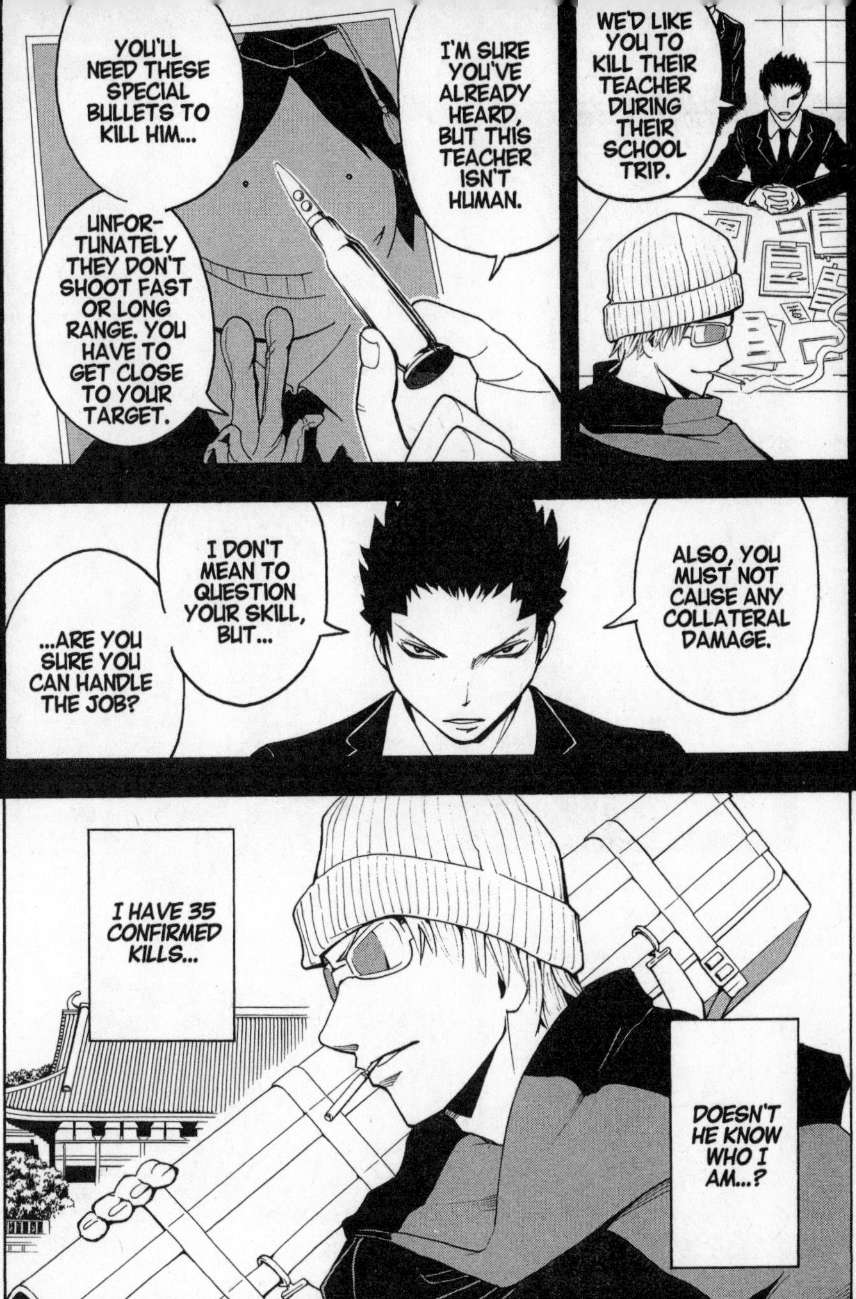
WE'D LIKE YOU TO KILL THEIR TEACHER DURING THEIR SCHOOL TRIP.
I'M SURE YOU'VE ALREADY HEARD, BUT THIS TEACHER ISN'T HUMAN.
YOU'LL NEED THESE SPECIAL BULLETS TO KILL HIM...
UNFOR-TUNATELY THEY DON'T SHOOT FAST OR LONG RANGE. YOU HAVE TO GET CLOSE TO YOUR TARGET.
ALSO, YOU MUST NOT CAUSE ANY COLLATERAL DAMAGE.
I DON'T MEAN TO QUESTION YOUR SKILL, BUT...
...ARE YOU SURE YOU CAN HANDLE THE JOB?
I HAVE 35 CONFIRMED KILLS...
DOESN'T HE KNOW WHO I AM...?

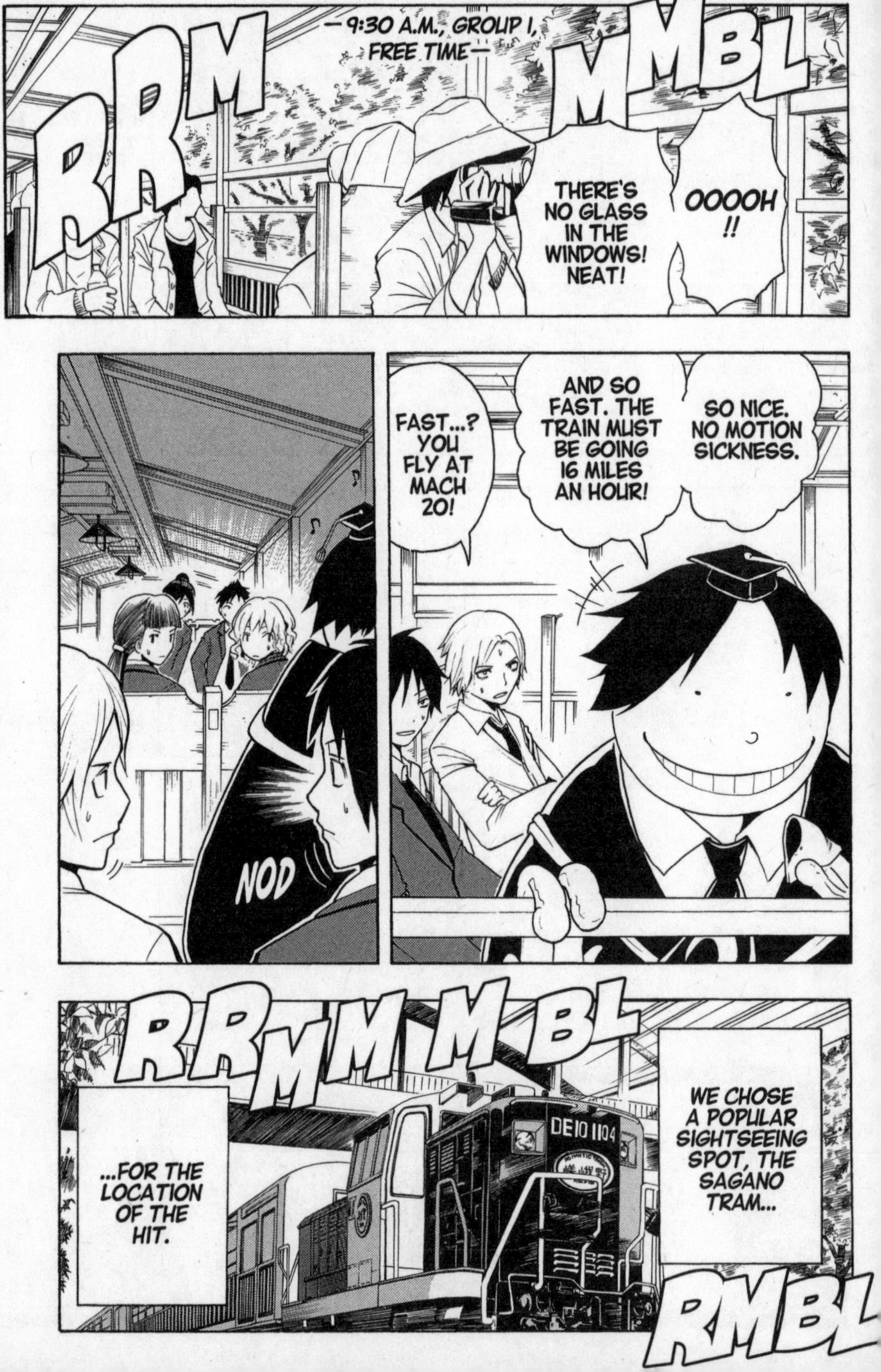
—9:30 A.M., GROUP 1, FREE TIME—
RRM
MMBL
OOOOH !!
THERE'S NO GLASS IN THE WINDOWS! NEAT!
SO NICE. NO MOTION SICKNESS.
AND SO FAST. THE TRAIN MUST BE GOING 16 MILES AN HOUR!
FAST...? YOU FLY AT MACH 20!
NOD
RRMMM M MBL
WE CHOSE A POPULAR SIGHTSEEING SPOT, THE SAGANO TRAM...
DE10 1104
...FOR THE LOCATION OF THE HIT.
RMBL

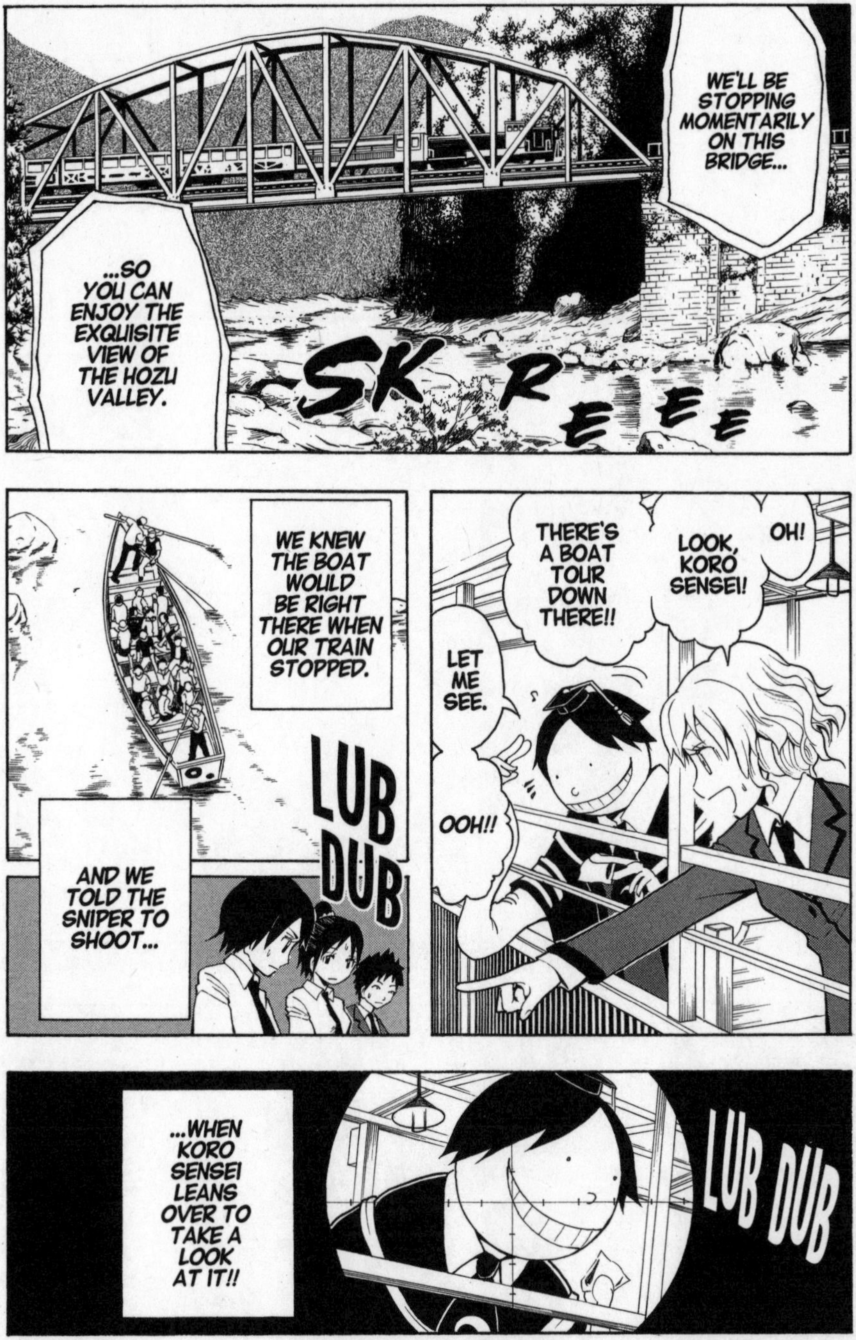
WE'LL BE STOPPING MOMENTARILY ON THIS BRIDGE...
...SO YOU CAN ENJOY THE EXQUISITE VIEW OF THE HOZU VALLEY.
SKREEE
OH!
LOOK, KORO SENSEI!
THERE'S A BOAT TOUR DOWN THERE!!
LET ME SEE.
OOH!!
WE KNEW THE BOAT WOULD BE RIGHT THERE WHEN OUR TRAIN STOPPED.
LUB DUB
AND WE TOLD THE SNIPER TO SHOOT...
...WHEN KORO SENSEI LEANS OVER TO TAKE A LOOK AT IT!!
LUB DUB

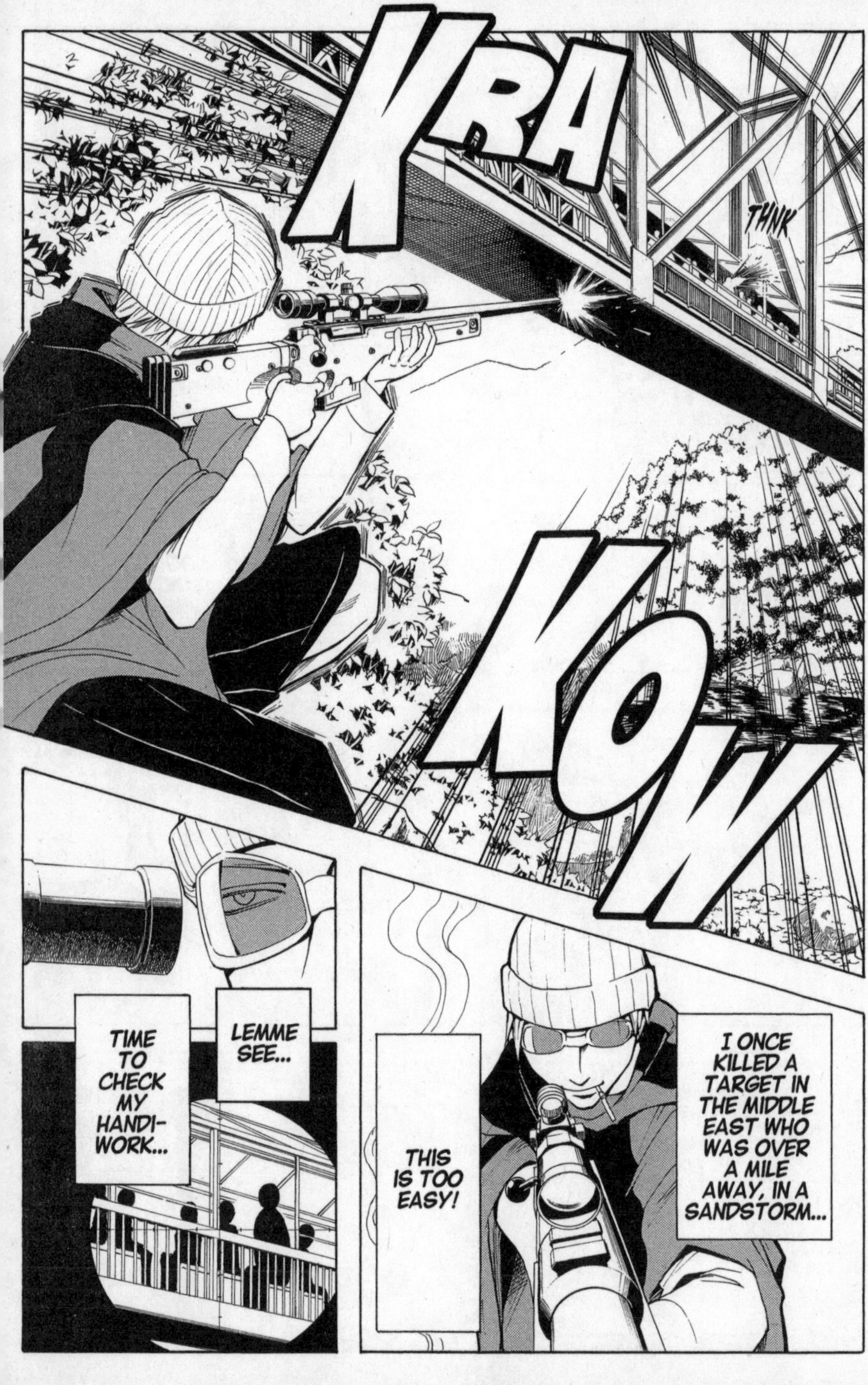
KRA
THNK
KOW
I ONCE KILLED A TARGET IN THE MIDDLE EAST WHO WAS OVER A MILE AWAY, IN A SANDSTORM...
THIS IS TOO EASY!
LEMME SEE...
TIME TO CHECK MY HANDIWORK...

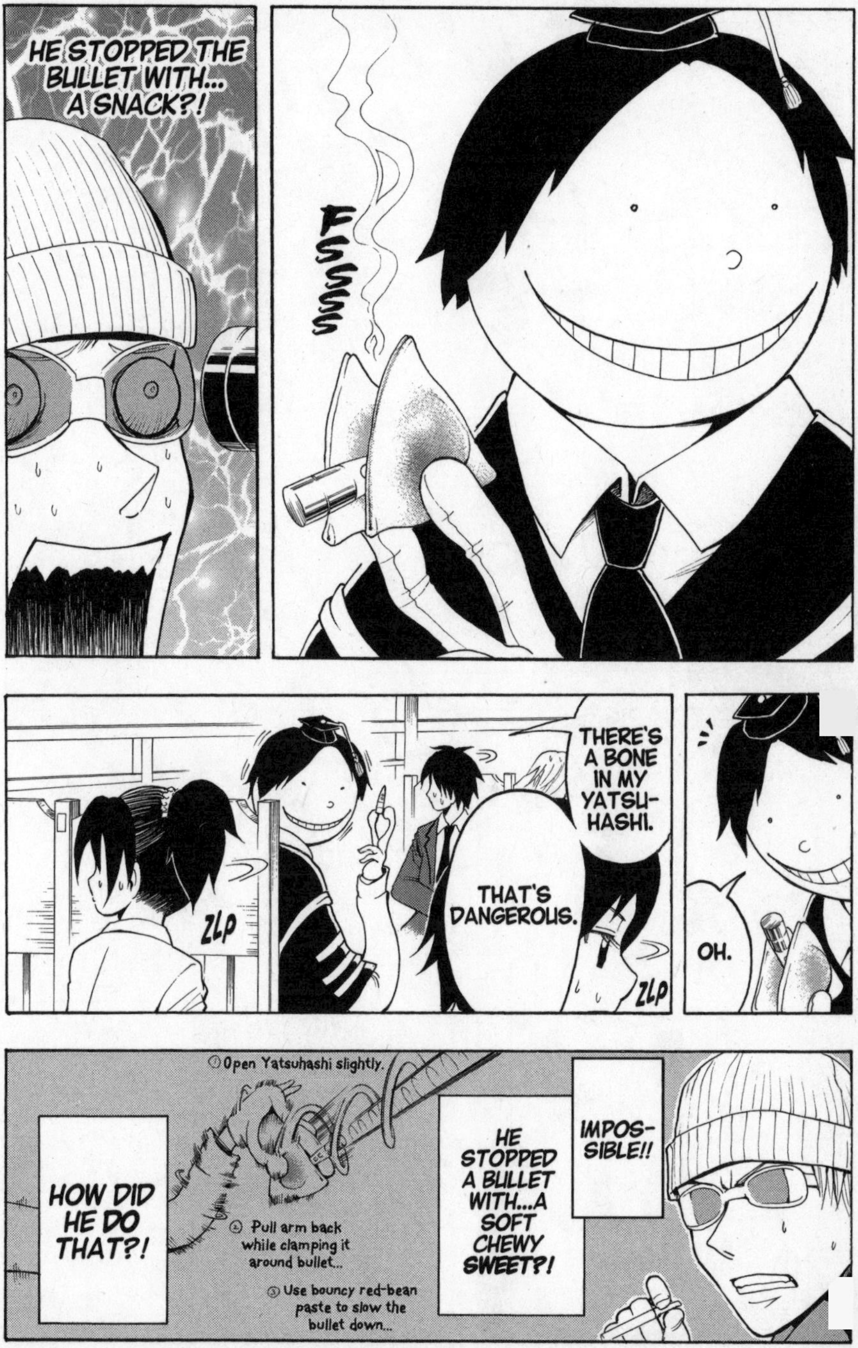
FSSSS
HE STOPPED THE BULLET WITH... A SNACK?!
OH.
THERE'S A BONE IN MY YATSU-HASHI.
THAT'S DANGEROUS.
ZLP
ZLP
IMPOS-SIBLE!!
HE STOPPED A BULLET WITH...A SOFT CHEWY SWEET?!
HOW DID HE DO THAT?!
① Open Yatsuhashi slightly.
② Pull arm back while clamping it around bullet...
③ Use bouncy red-bean paste to slow the bullet down...

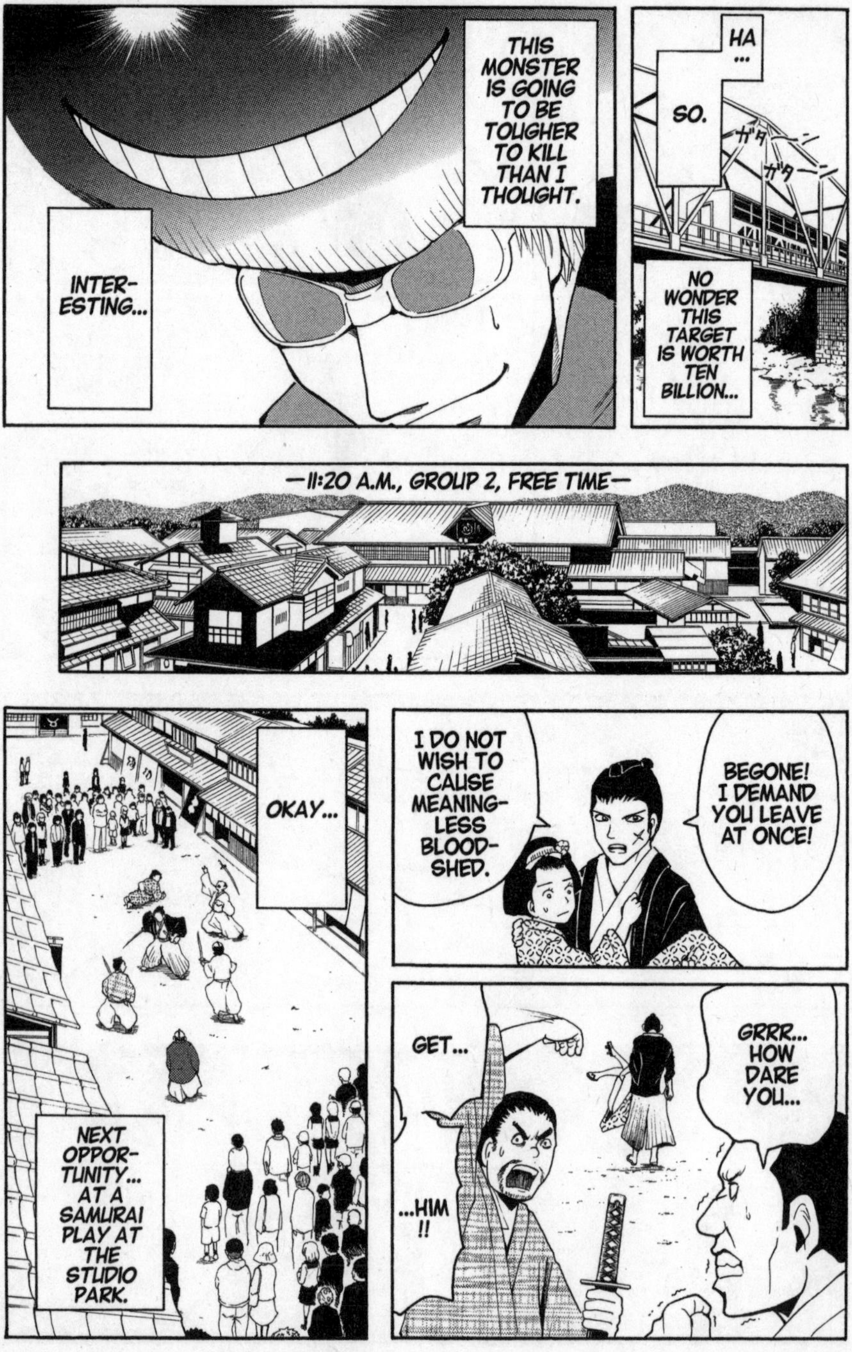
HA... SO.
ガタ―ン
ガタ―ン
NO WONDER THIS TARGET IS WORTH TEN BILLION...
THIS MONSTER IS GOING TO BE TOUGHER TO KILL THAN I THOUGHT.
INTER-ESTING...
—11:20 A.M., GROUP 2, FREE TIME—
BEGONE! I DEMAND YOU LEAVE AT ONCE!
I DO NOT WISH TO CAUSE MEANING-LESS BLOOD-SHED.
GRRR... HOW DARE YOU...
GET...
...HIM!!
OKAY...
NEXT OPPOR-TUNITY... AT A SAMURAI PLAY AT THE STUDIO PARK.

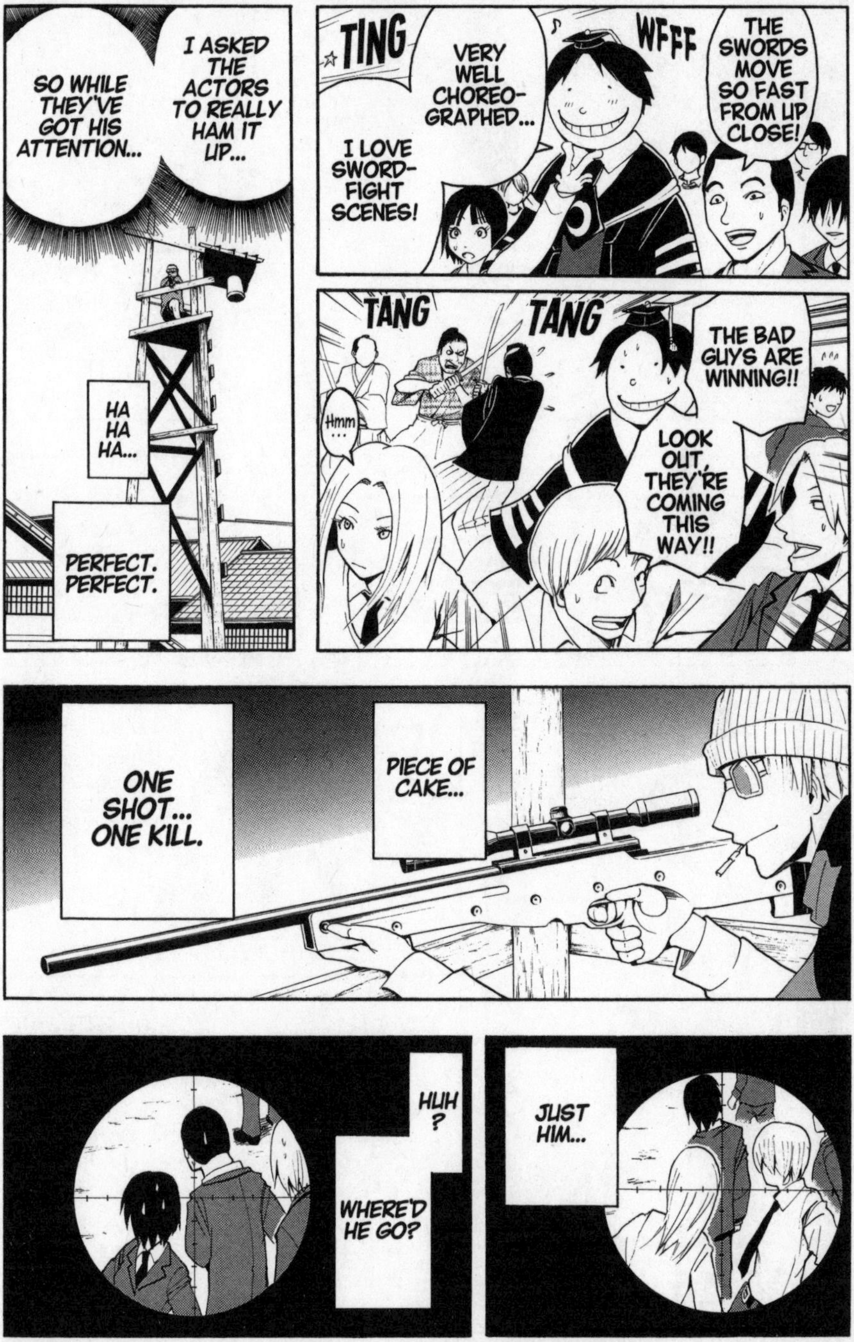
THE SWORDS MOVE SO FAST FROM UP CLOSE!
WFFF
VERY WELL CHOREOGRAPHED...
TING
I LOVE SWORD-FIGHT SCENES!
THE BAD GUYS ARE WINNING!!
TANG
TANG
LOOK OUT, THEY'RE COMING THIS WAY!!
Hmm...
I ASKED THE ACTORS TO REALLY HAM IT UP...
SO WHILE THEY'VE GOT HIS ATTENTION...
HA HA HA...
PERFECT. PERFECT.
PIECE OF CAKE...
ONE SHOT... ONE KILL.
JUST HIM...
HUH?
WHERE'D HE GO?

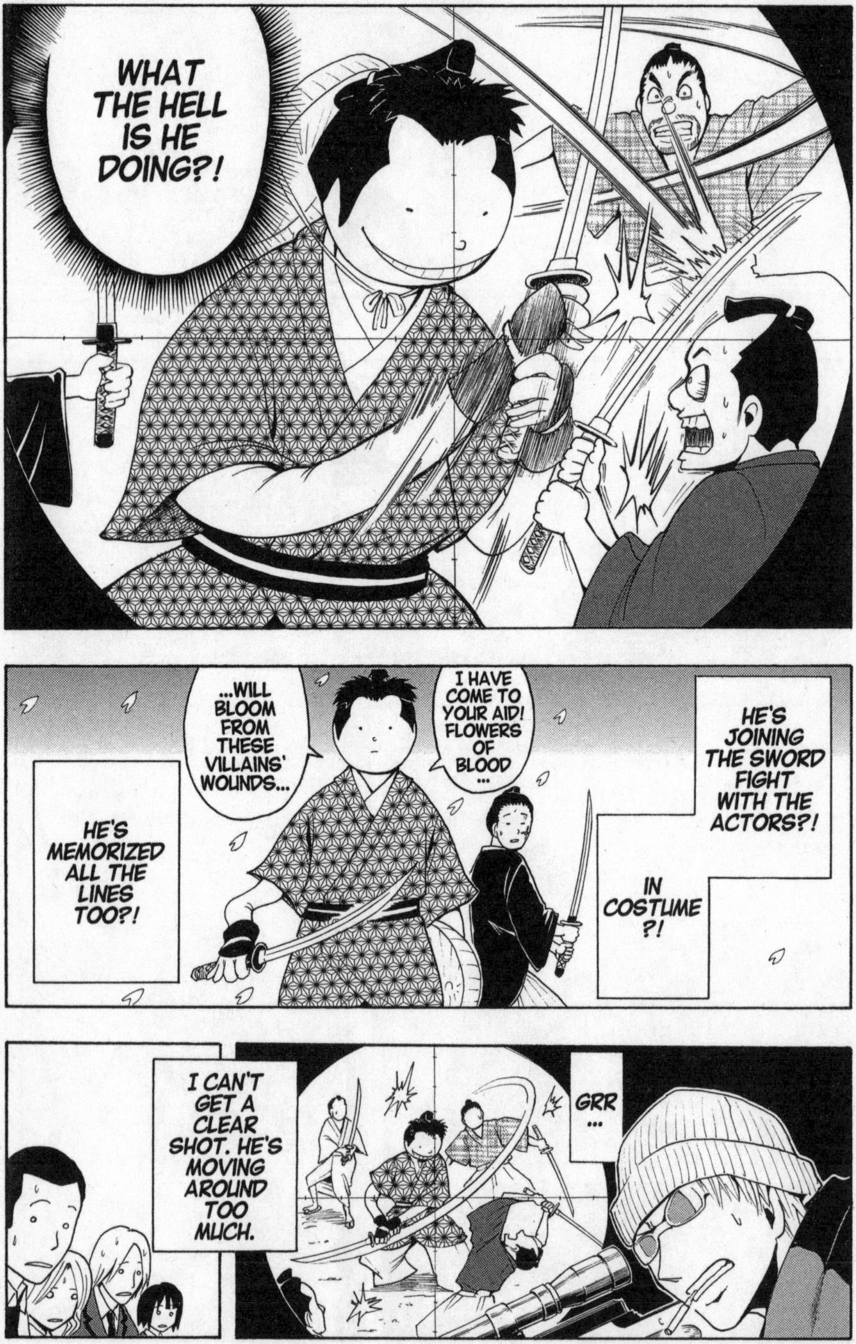
WHAT THE HELL IS HE DOING?!
HE'S JOINING THE SWORD FIGHT WITH THE ACTORS?!
IN COSTUME ?!
I HAVE COME TO YOUR AID! FLOWERS OF BLOOD ...
...WILL BLOOM FROM THESE VILLAINS' WOUNDS...
HE'S MEMORIZED ALL THE LINES TOO?!
GRR ...
I CAN'T GET A CLEAR SHOT. HE'S MOVING AROUND TOO MUCH.

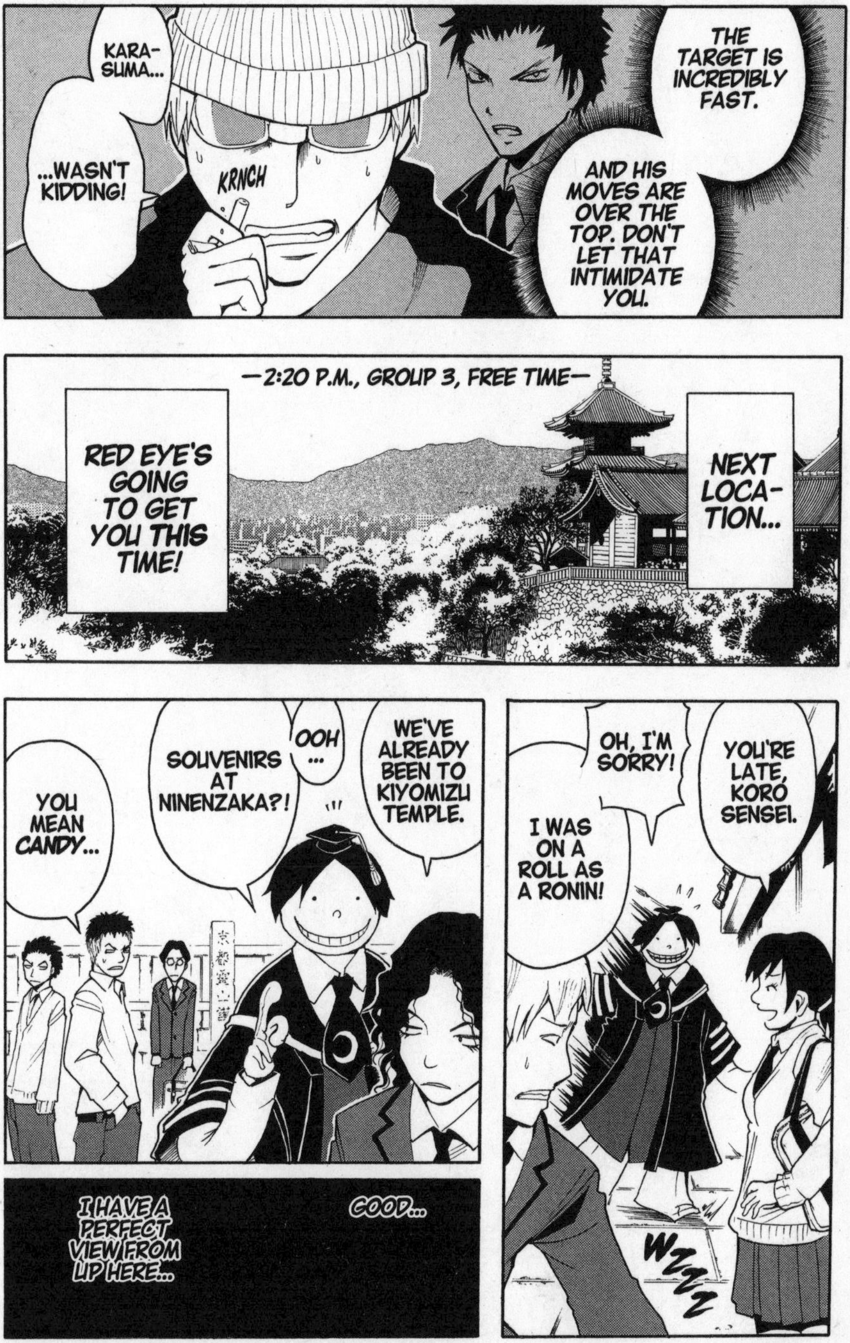
THE TARGET IS INCREDIBLY FAST.
AND HIS MOVES ARE OVER THE TOP. DON'T LET THAT INTIMIDATE YOU.
KARA-SUMA...
...WASN'T KIDDING!
KRNCH
—2:20 P.M., GROUP 3, FREE TIME—
NEXT LOCA-TION...
RED EYE'S GOING TO GET YOU THIS TIME!
YOU'RE LATE, KORO SENSEI.
OH, I'M SORRY!
I WAS ON A ROLL AS A RONIN!
WZZZ
WE'VE ALREADY BEEN TO KIYOMIZU TEMPLE.
OOH...
SOUVENIRS AT NINENZAKA?!
YOU MEAN CANDY...
GOOD...
I HAVE A PERFECT VIEW FROM UP HERE...

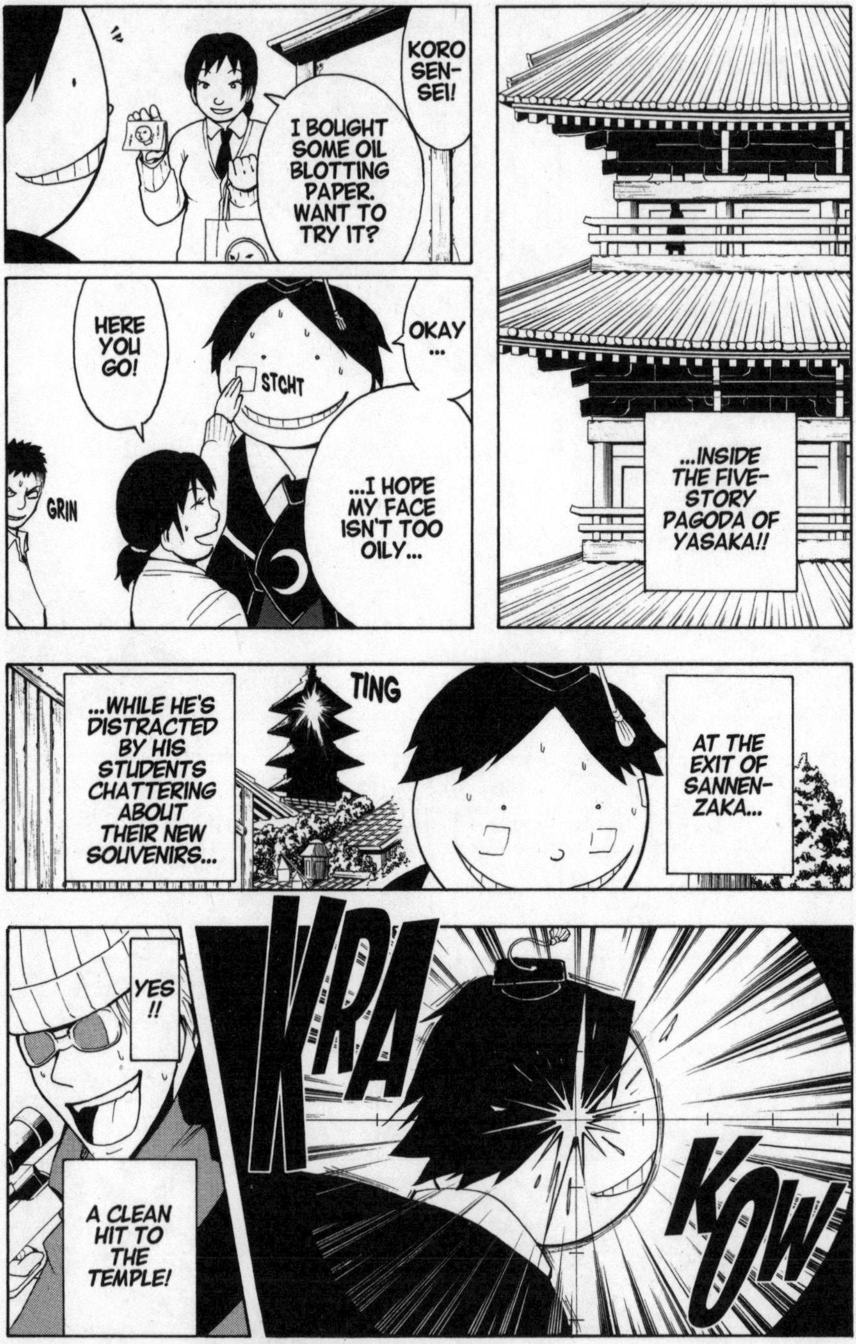
...INSIDE THE FIVE-STORY PAGODA OF YASAKA!!
KORO SENSEI!
I BOUGHT SOME OIL BLOTTING PAPER. WANT TO TRY IT?
OKAY ...
HERE YOU GO!
STCHT
...I HOPE MY FACE ISN'T TOO OILY...
GRIN
AT THE EXIT OF SANNEN-ZAKA...
TING
...WHILE HE'S DISTRACTED BY HIS STUDENTS CHATTERING ABOUT THEIR NEW SOUVENIRS...
KRA
KOW
YES !!
A CLEAN HIT TO THE TEMPLE!

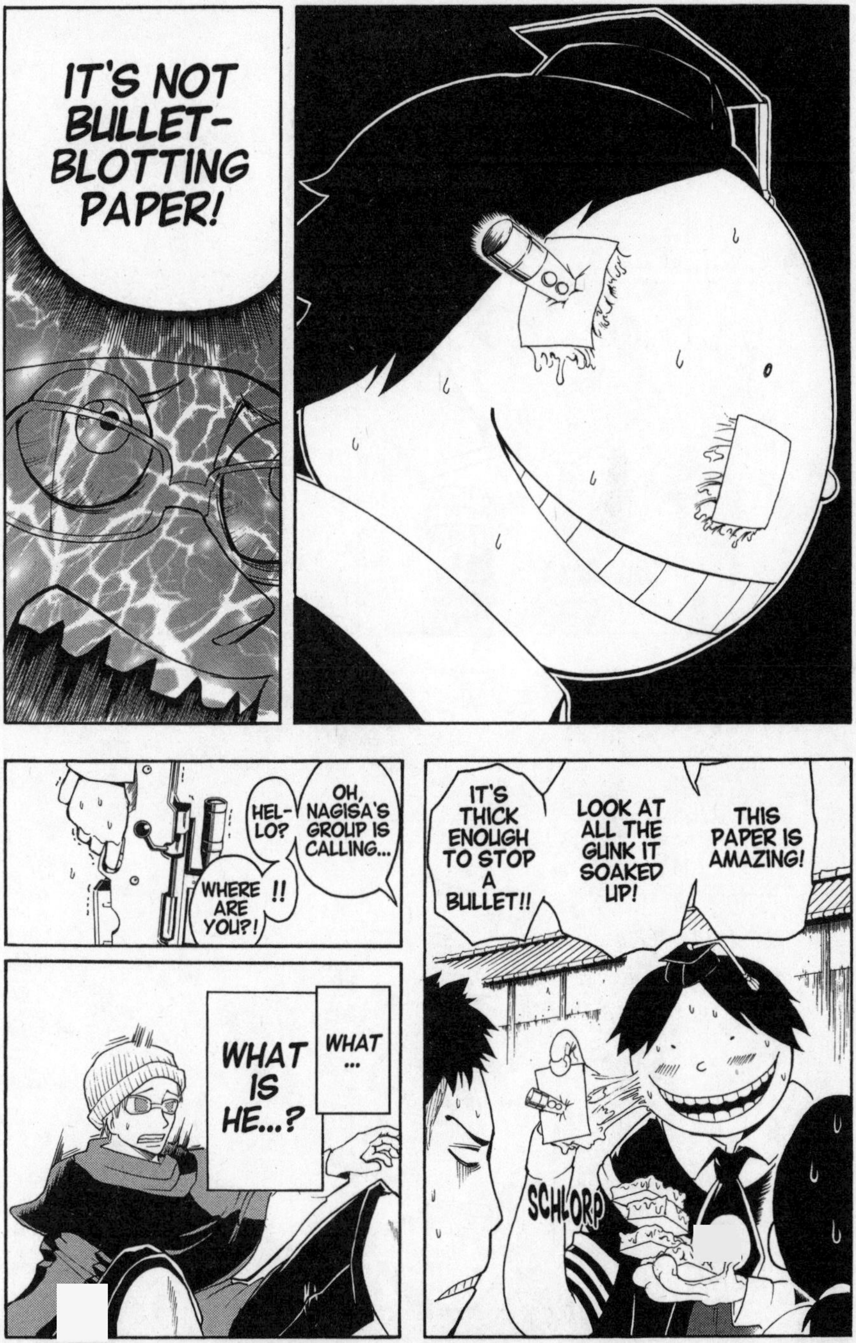
IT'S NOT BULLET-BLOTTING PAPER!
THIS PAPER IS AMAZING!
LOOK AT ALL THE GUNK IT SOAKED UP!
IT'S THICK ENOUGH TO STOP A BULLET!!
SCHLORP
OH, NAGISA'S GROUP IS CALLING...
HEL-LO?
!!
WHERE ARE YOU?!
WHAT...
WHAT IS HE...?

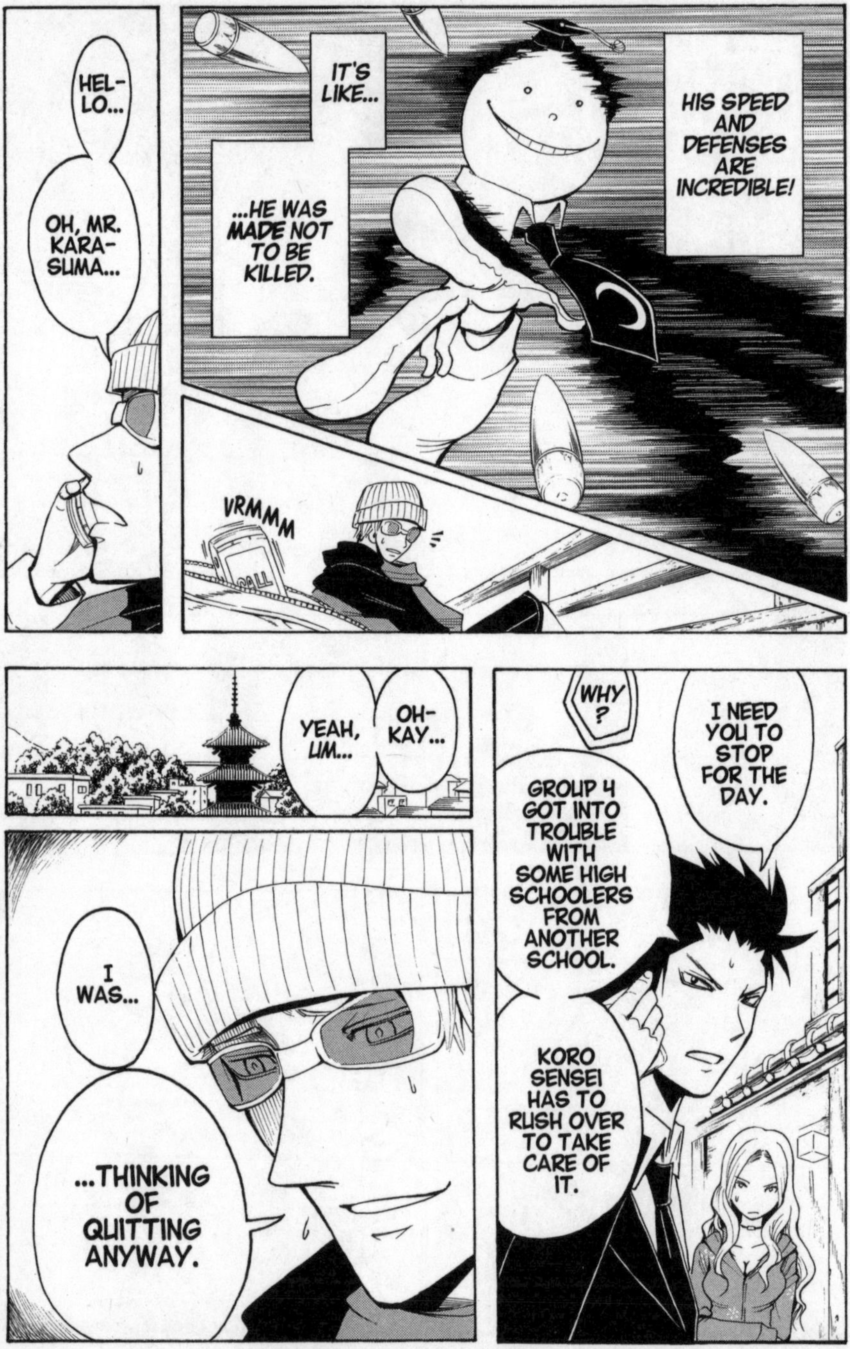
HIS SPEED AND DEFENSES ARE INCREDIBLE!
IT'S LIKE...
...HE WAS MADE NOT TO BE KILLED.
VRMMM
HEL-LO...
OH, MR. KARA-SUMA...
I NEED YOU TO STOP FOR THE DAY.
WHY?
GROUP 4 GOT INTO TROUBLE WITH SOME HIGH SCHOOLERS FROM ANOTHER SCHOOL.
KORO SENSEI HAS TO RUSH OVER TO TAKE CARE OF IT.
OH-KAY...
YEAH, UM...
I WAS...
...THINKING OF QUITTING ANYWAY.

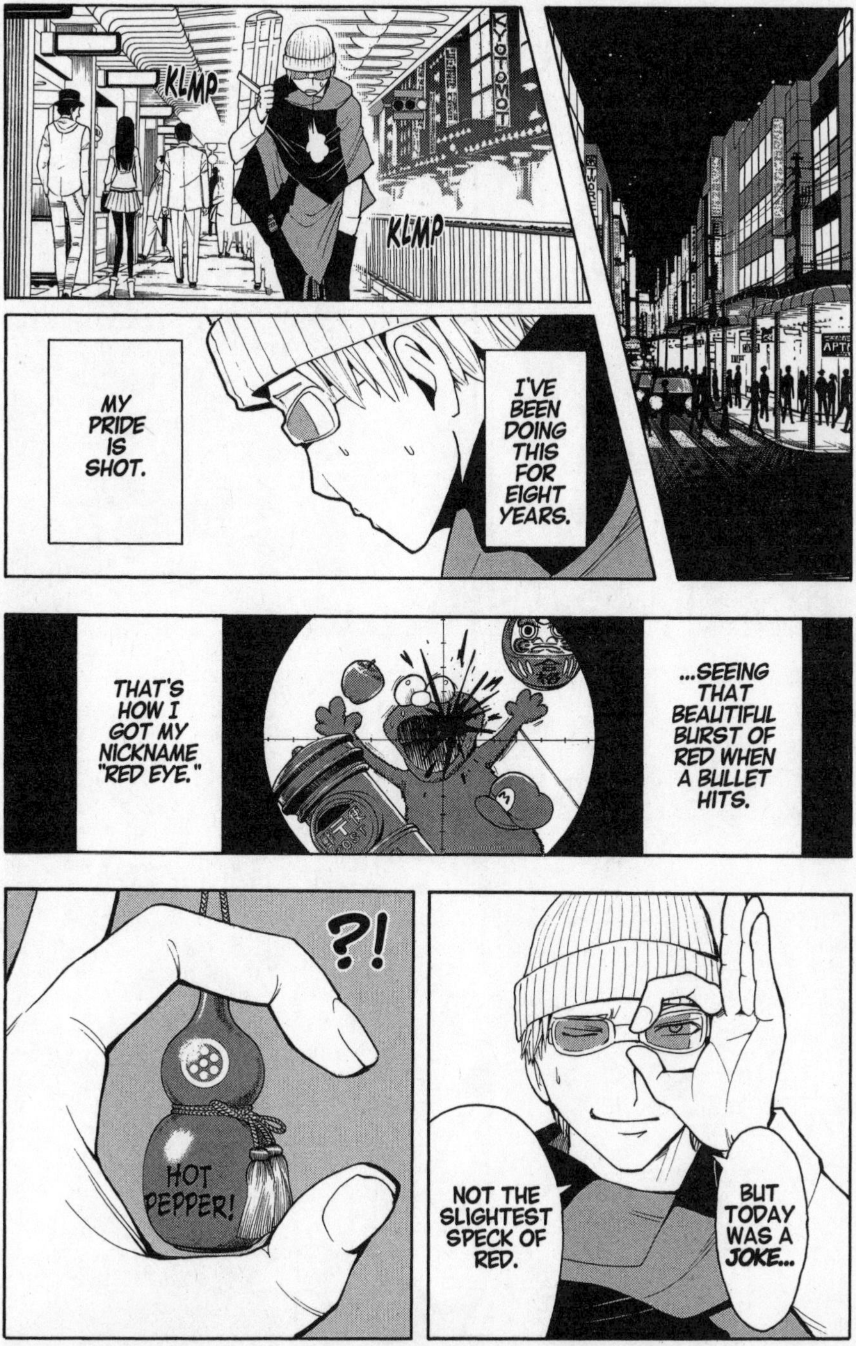
KLMP
KLMP
I'VE BEEN DOING THIS FOR EIGHT YEARS.
MY PRIDE IS SHOT.
...SEEING THAT BEAUTIFUL BURST OF RED WHEN A BULLET HITS.
THAT'S HOW I GOT MY NICKNAME "RED EYE."
BUT TODAY WAS A JOKE...
NOT THE SLIGHTEST SPECK OF RED.
?!
HOT PEPPER!

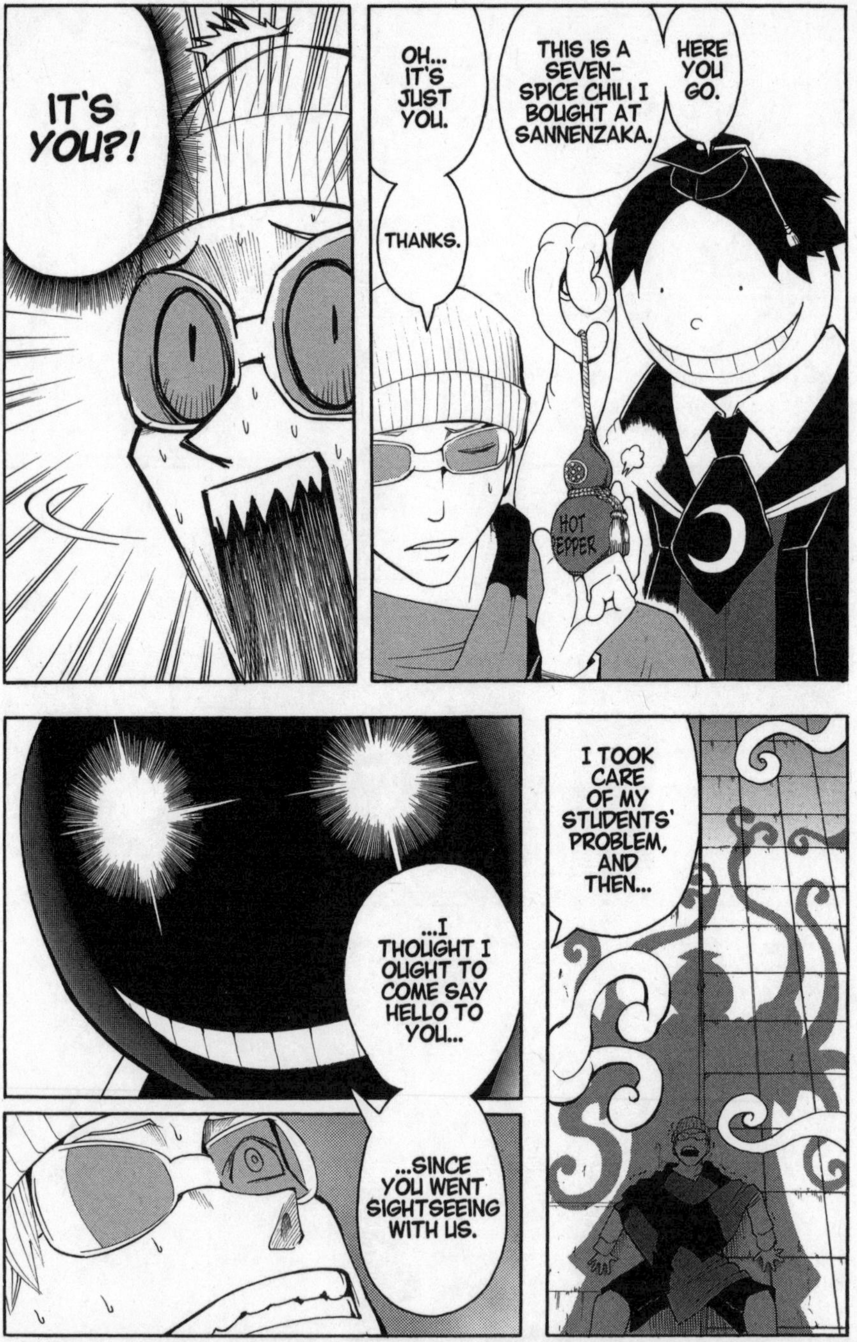
HERE YOU GO.
THIS IS A SEVEN-SPICE CHILI I BOUGHT AT SANNENZAKA.
OH... IT'S JUST YOU.
THANKS.
HOT PEPPER
IT'S YOU?!
I TOOK CARE OF MY STUDENTS' PROBLEM, AND THEN...
...I THOUGHT I OUGHT TO COME SAY HELLO TO YOU...
...SINCE YOU WENT SIGHTSEEING WITH US.

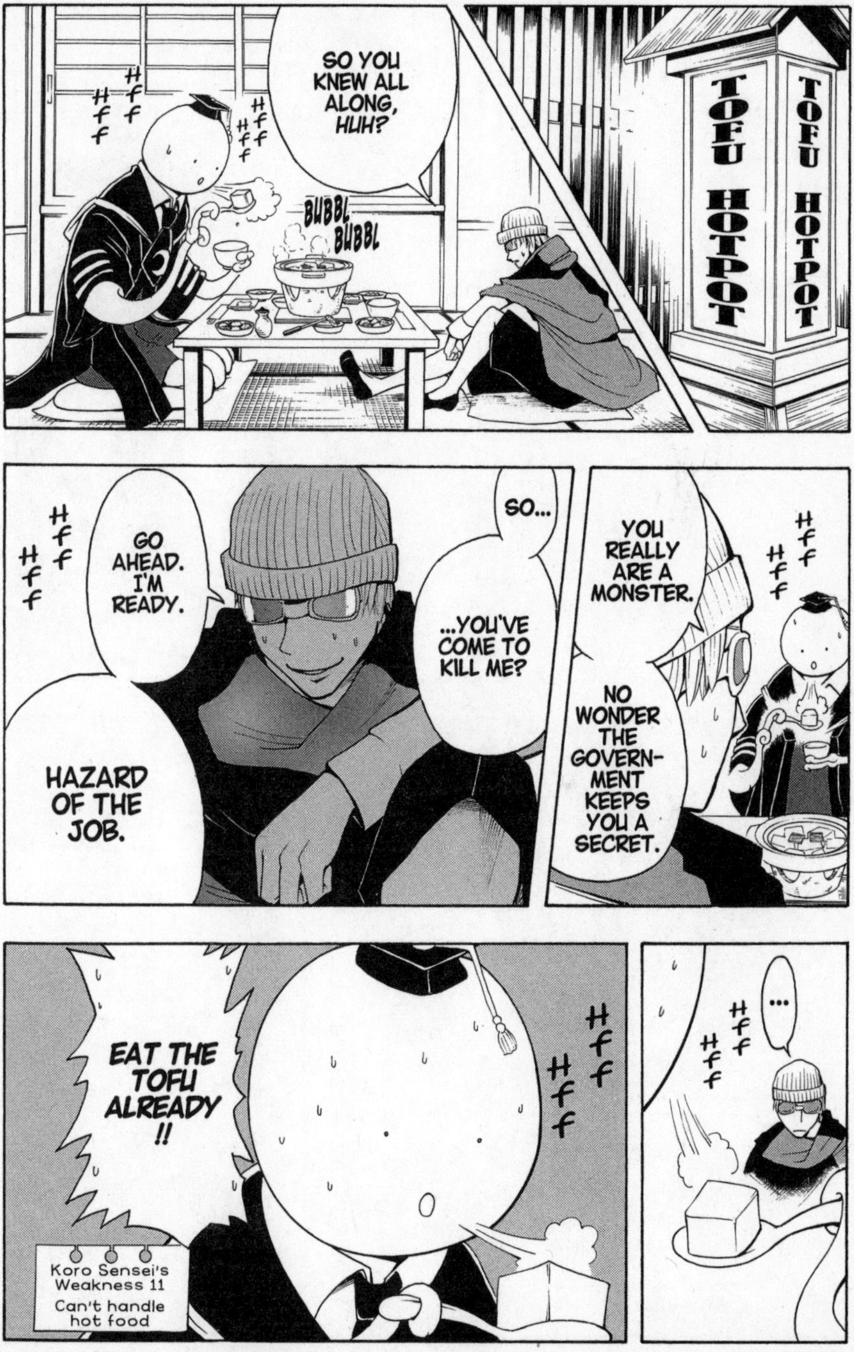
TOFU HOTPOT
TOFU HOTPOT
SO YOU KNEW ALL ALONG, HUH?
HFF HFF
HFF HFF
BUBBL BUBBL
YOU REALLY ARE A MONSTER.
NO WONDER THE GOVERN-MENT KEEPS YOU A SECRET.
HFF HFF
SO...
...YOU'VE COME TO KILL ME?
GO AHEAD. I'M READY.
HFF HFF
HAZARD OF THE JOB.
...
HFF HFF
HFF HFF
EAT THE TOFU ALREADY!!
Koro Sensei's Weakness 11
Can't handle hot food

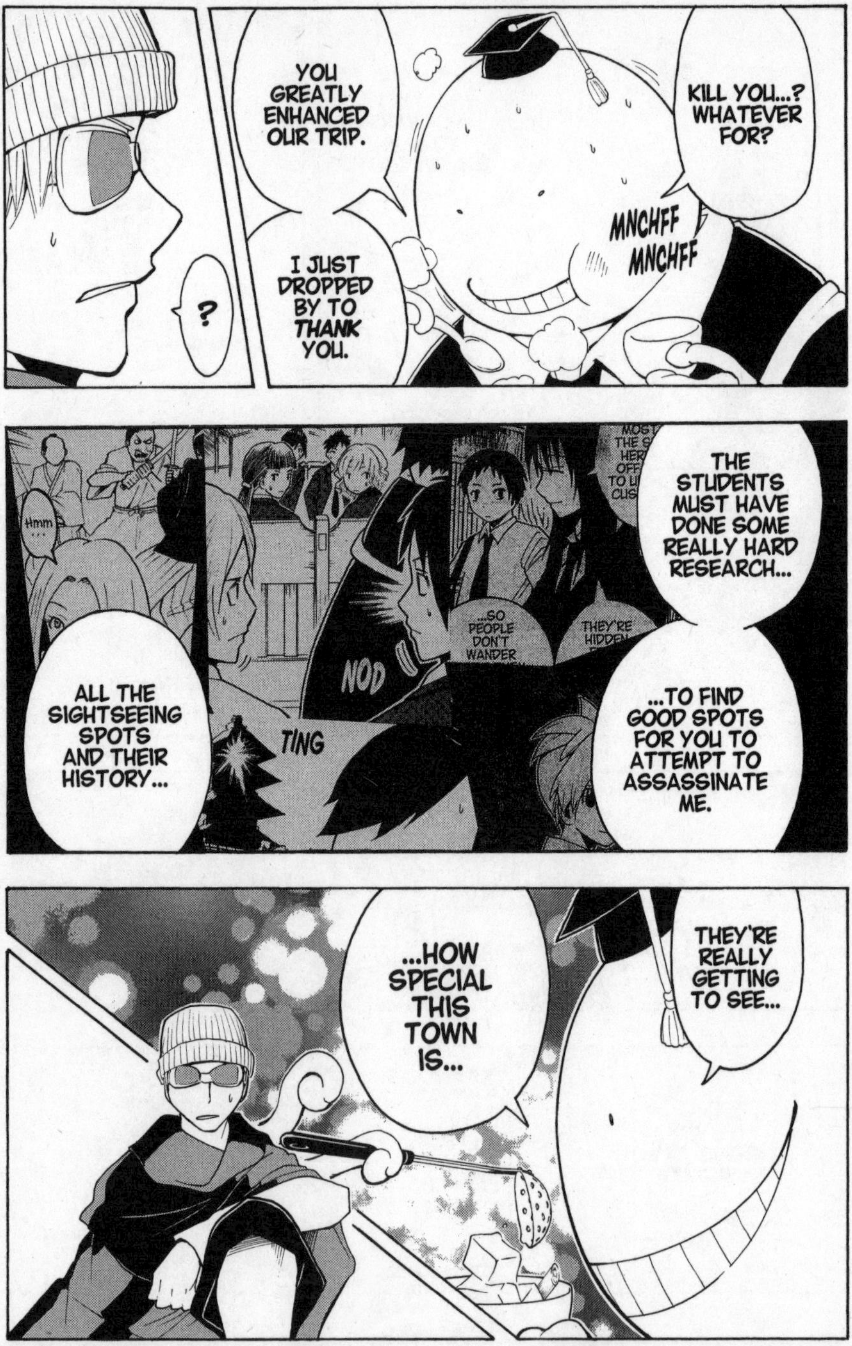
KILL YOU...? WHATEVER FOR?
MNCHFF MNCHFF
YOU GREATLY ENHANCED OUR TRIP.
I JUST DROPPED BY TO THANK YOU.
?
THE STUDENTS MUST HAVE DONE SOME REALLY HARD RESEARCH...
...TO FIND GOOD SPOTS FOR YOU TO ATTEMPT TO ASSASSINATE ME.
THEY'RE HIDDEN
...SO PEOPLE DON'T WANDER
NOD
TING
ALL THE SIGHTSEEING SPOTS AND THEIR HISTORY...
Hmm...
THEY'RE REALLY GETTING TO SEE...
...HOW SPECIAL THIS TOWN IS...

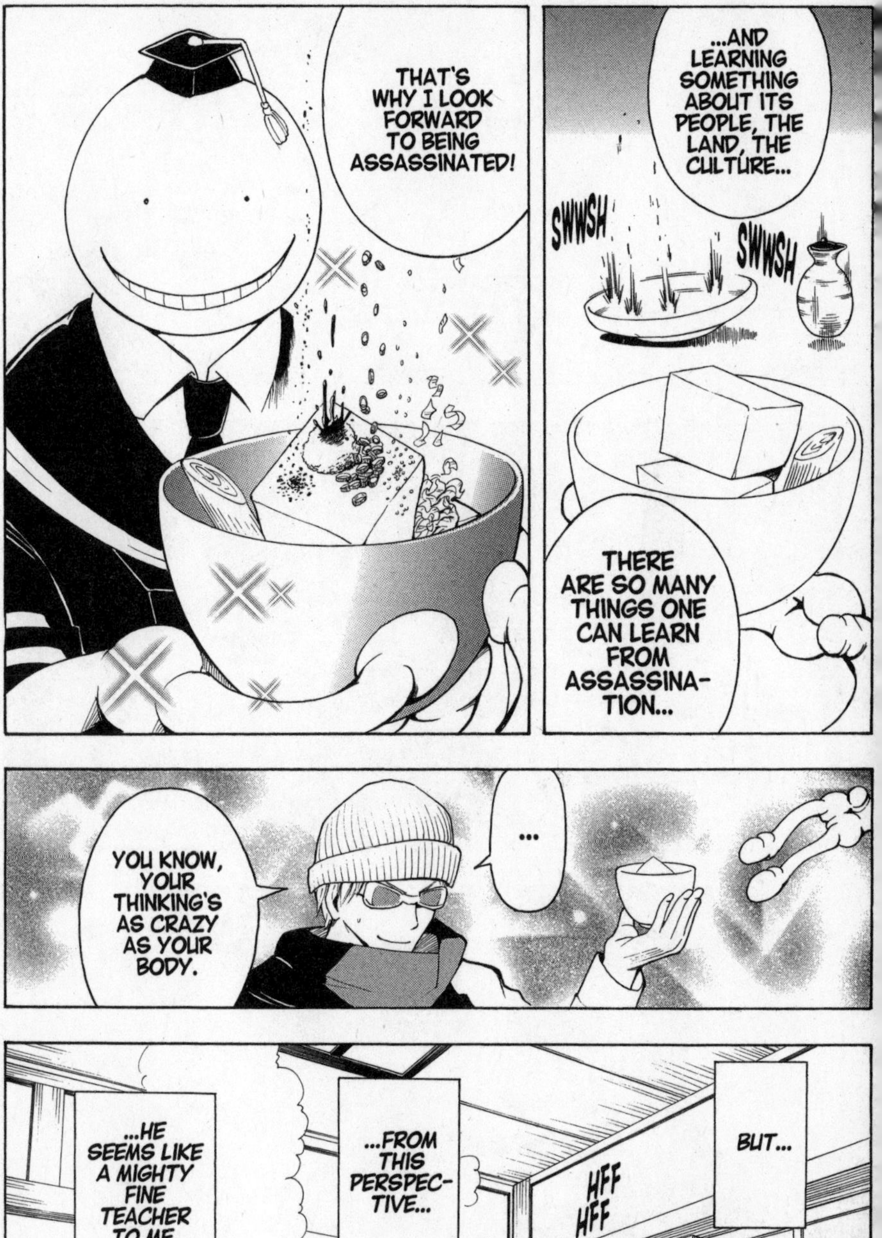
...AND LEARNING SOMETHING ABOUT ITS PEOPLE, THE LAND, THE CULTURE...
SWWSH
SWWSH
THERE ARE SO MANY THINGS ONE CAN LEARN FROM ASSASSINATION...
THAT'S WHY I LOOK FORWARD TO BEING ASSASSINATED!
...
YOU KNOW, YOUR THINKING'S AS CRAZY AS YOUR BODY.
BUT...
HFF HFF
...FROM THIS PERSPECTIVE...
...HE SEEMS LIKE A MIGHTY FINE TEACHER TO ME.

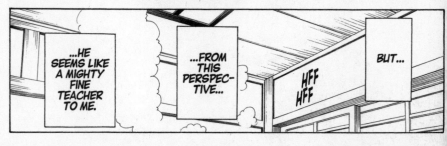

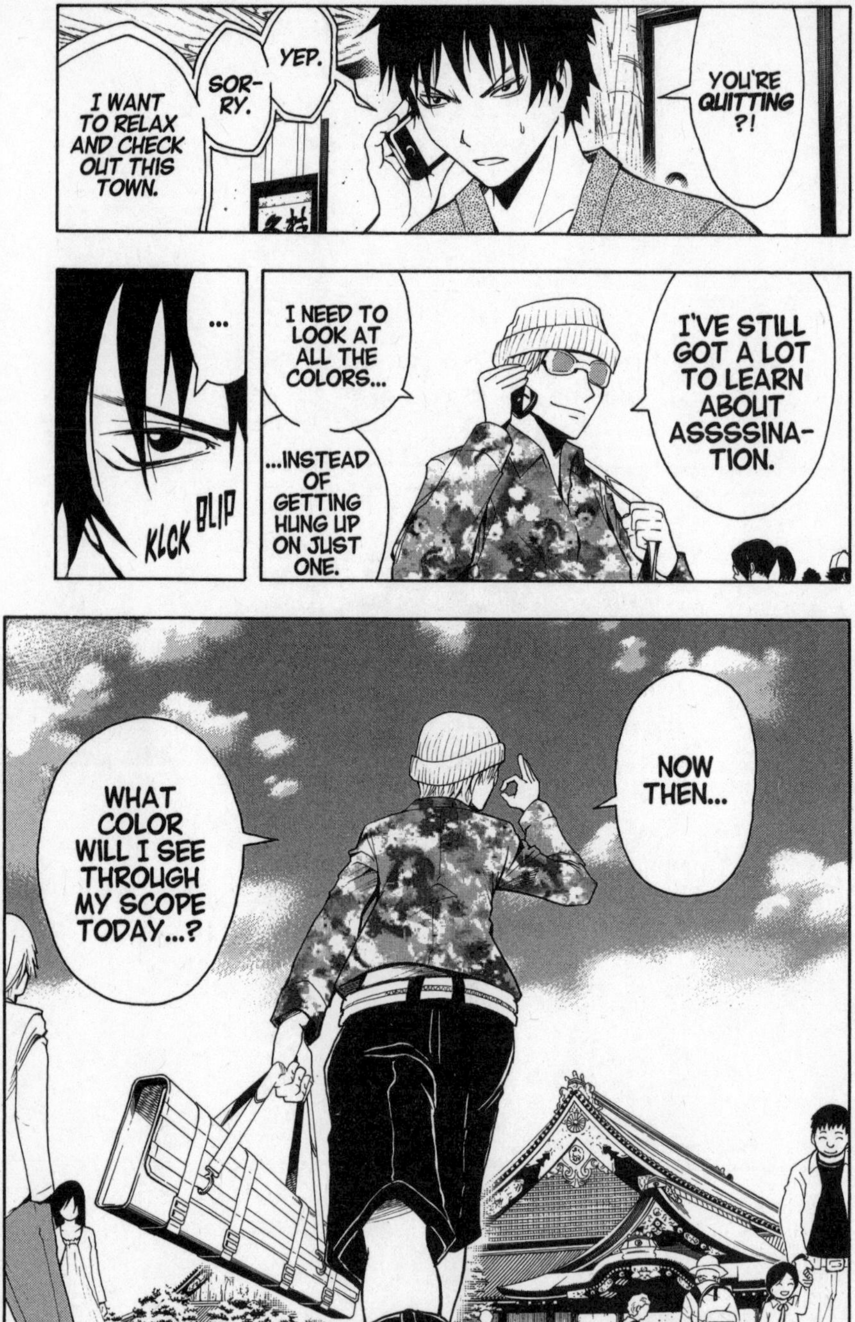
YOU'RE QUITTING?!
YEP.
SOR-RY.
I WANT TO RELAX AND CHECK OUT THIS TOWN.
I'VE STILL GOT A LOT TO LEARN ABOUT ASSSSINA-TION.
I NEED TO LOOK AT ALL THE COLORS...
...INSTEAD OF GETTING HUNG UP ON JUST ONE.
...
BLIP
KLCK
NOW THEN...
WHAT COLOR WILL I SEE THROUGH MY SCOPE TODAY...?

I only realized how cool the Silver
Pavilion was after I grew up.

When I was a kid, I just thought, "They must not
have enough money to buy gold-leaf for it."

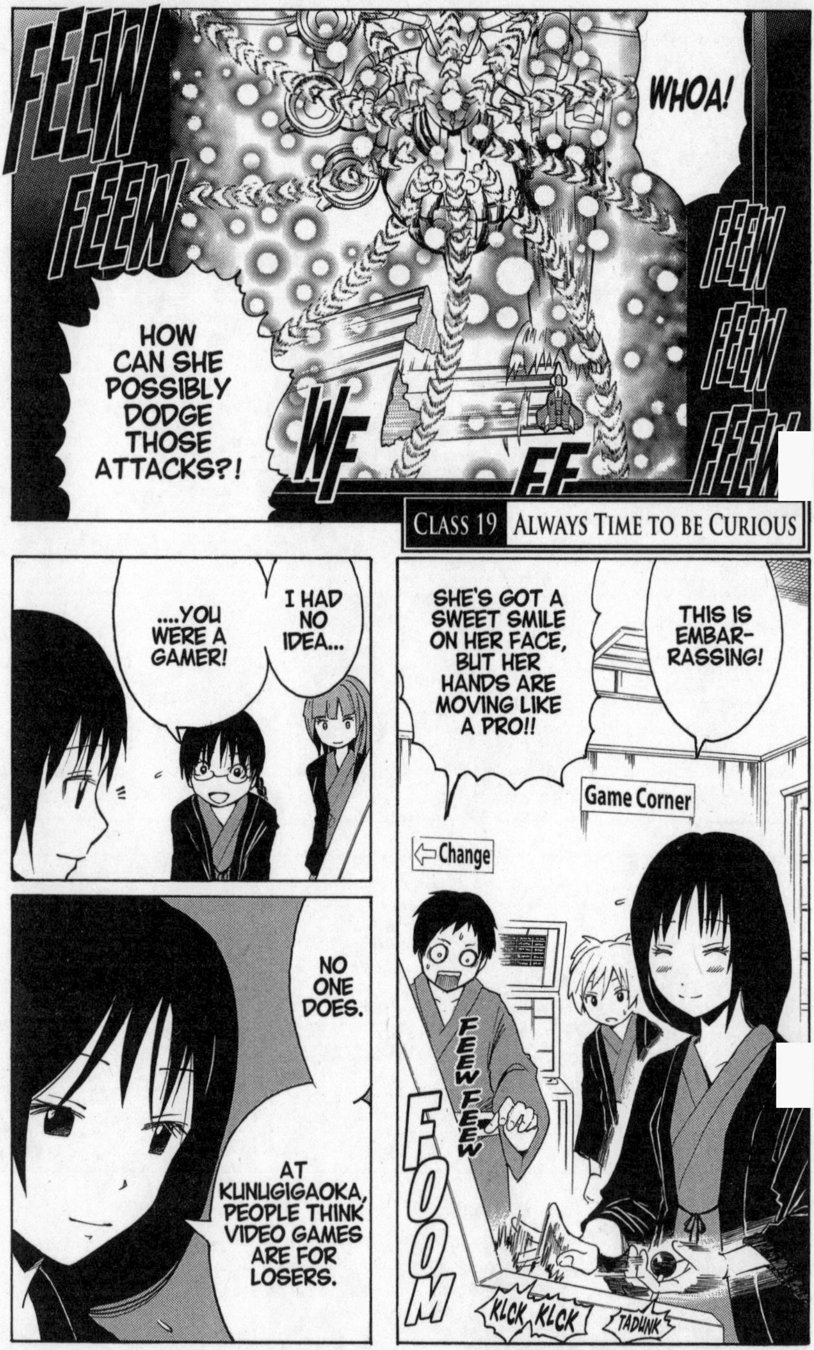
WHOA!
FEEW FEEW FEEW
FEEW FEEW
HOW CAN SHE POSSIBLY DODGE THOSE ATTACKS?!
FF
WF
CLASS 19 ALWAYS TIME TO BE CURIOUS
THIS IS EMBAR-RASSING!
SHE'S GOT A SWEET SMILE ON HER FACE, BUT HER HANDS ARE MOVING LIKE A PRO!!
Game Corner
Change
FEEW FEEW
FOOM
TADUNK
KLCK, KLCK
I HAD NO IDEA...
....YOU WERE A GAMER!
NO ONE DOES.
AT KUNUGIGAOKA, PEOPLE THINK VIDEO GAMES ARE FOR LOSERS.

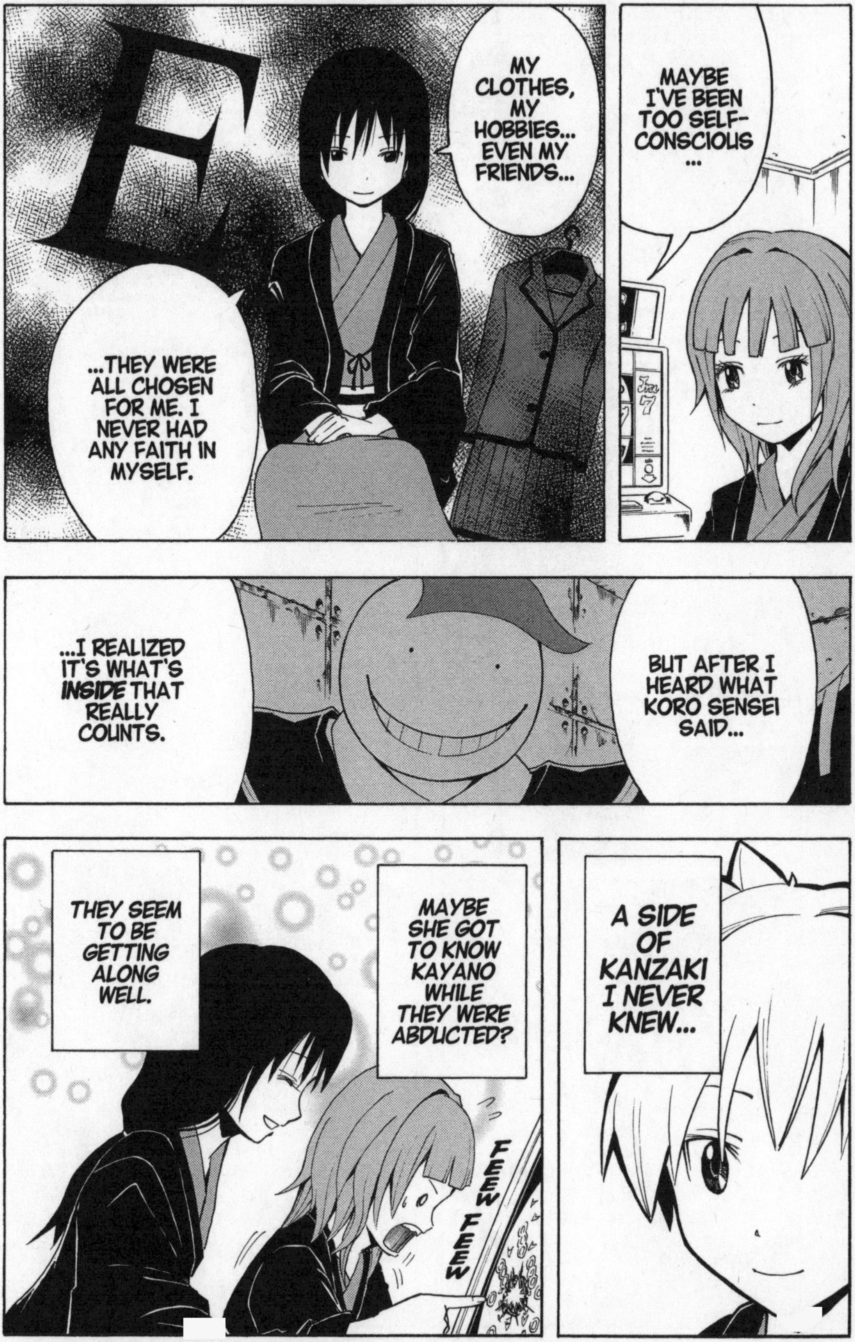
MAYBE I'VE BEEN TOO SELF-CONSCIOUS...
MY CLOTHES, MY HOBBIES... EVEN MY FRIENDS...
...THEY WERE ALL CHOSEN FOR ME. I NEVER HAD ANY FAITH IN MYSELF.
BUT AFTER I HEARD WHAT KORO SENSEI SAID...
...I REALIZED IT'S WHAT'S **INSIDE** THAT REALLY COUNTS.
A SIDE OF KANZAKI I NEVER KNEW...
MAYBE SHE GOT TO KNOW KAYANO WHILE THEY WERE ABDUCTED?
THEY SEEM TO BE GETTING ALONG WELL.
FEEEW FEEEW

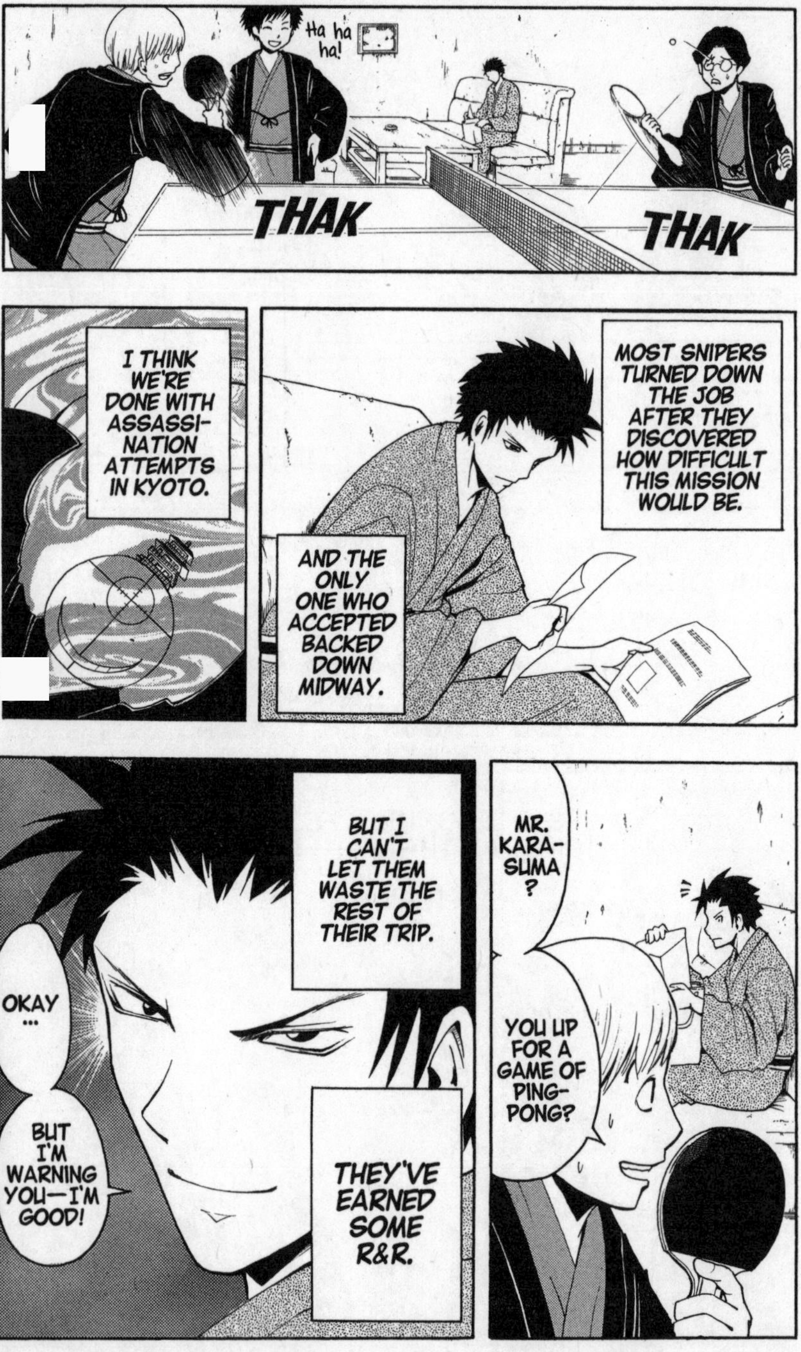
Ha ha ha!
THAK
THAK
MOST SNIPERS TURNED DOWN THE JOB AFTER THEY DISCOVERED HOW DIFFICULT THIS MISSION WOULD BE.
AND THE ONLY ONE WHO ACCEPTED BACKED DOWN MIDWAY.
I THINK WE'RE DONE WITH ASSASSI-NATION ATTEMPTS IN KYOTO.
MR. KARA-SUMA?
YOU UP FOR A GAME OF PING-PONG?
BUT I CAN'T LET THEM WASTE THE REST OF THEIR TRIP.
THEY'VE EARNED SOME R&R.
OKAY...
BUT I'M WARNING YOU—I'M GOOD!

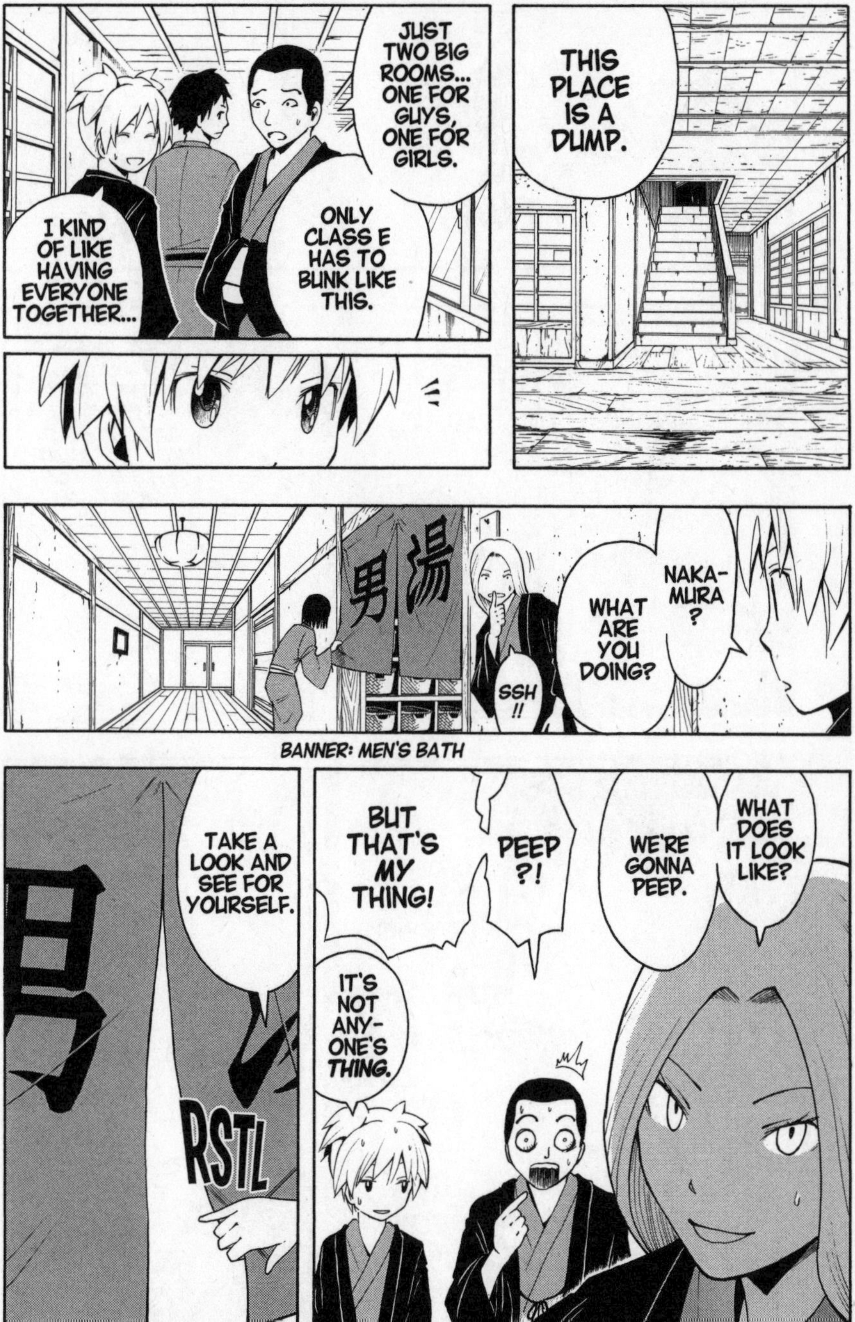
THIS PLACE IS A DUMP.
JUST TWO BIG ROOMS... ONE FOR GUYS, ONE FOR GIRLS.
ONLY CLASS E HAS TO BUNK LIKE THIS.
I KIND OF LIKE HAVING EVERYONE TOGETHER...
NAKA-MURA?
WHAT ARE YOU DOING?
SSH!!
男湯
WHAT DOES IT LOOK LIKE?
WE'RE GONNA PEEP.
PEEP?!
BUT THAT'S *MY* THING!
IT'S NOT ANYONE'S *THING.*
TAKE A LOOK AND SEE FOR YOURSELF.
RSTL

BANNER: MEN'S BATH

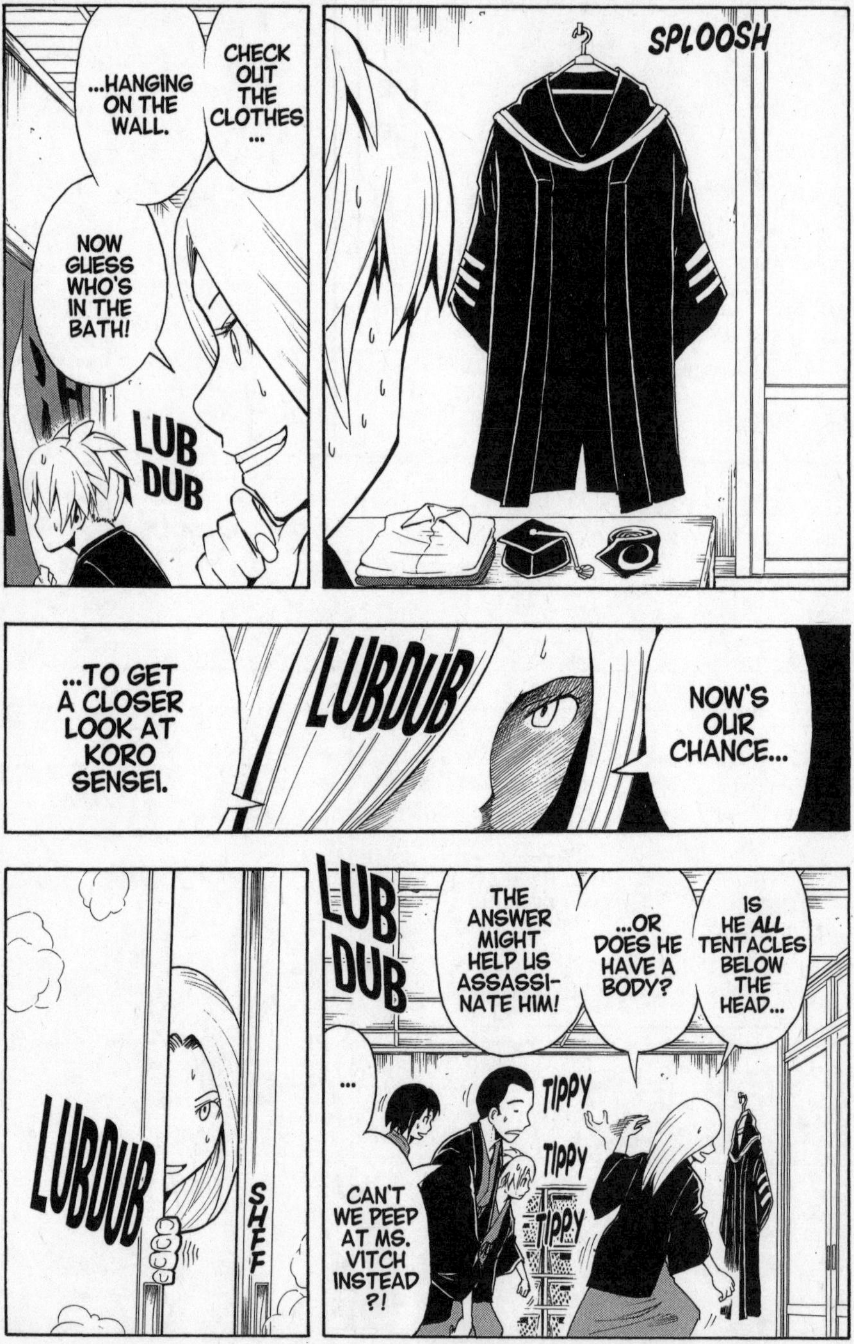
SPLOOSH
CHECK OUT THE CLOTHES...
...HANGING ON THE WALL.
NOW GUESS WHO'S IN THE BATH!
LUB DUB
NOW'S OUR CHANCE...
LUBDUB
...TO GET A CLOSER LOOK AT KORO SENSEI.
IS HE ALL TENTACLES BELOW THE HEAD...
...OR DOES HE HAVE A BODY?
THE ANSWER MIGHT HELP US ASSASSINATE HIM!
LUB DUB
TIPPY
TIPPY
TIPPY
...
CAN'T WE PEEP AT MS. VITCH INSTEAD?!
LUBDUB
SHFF

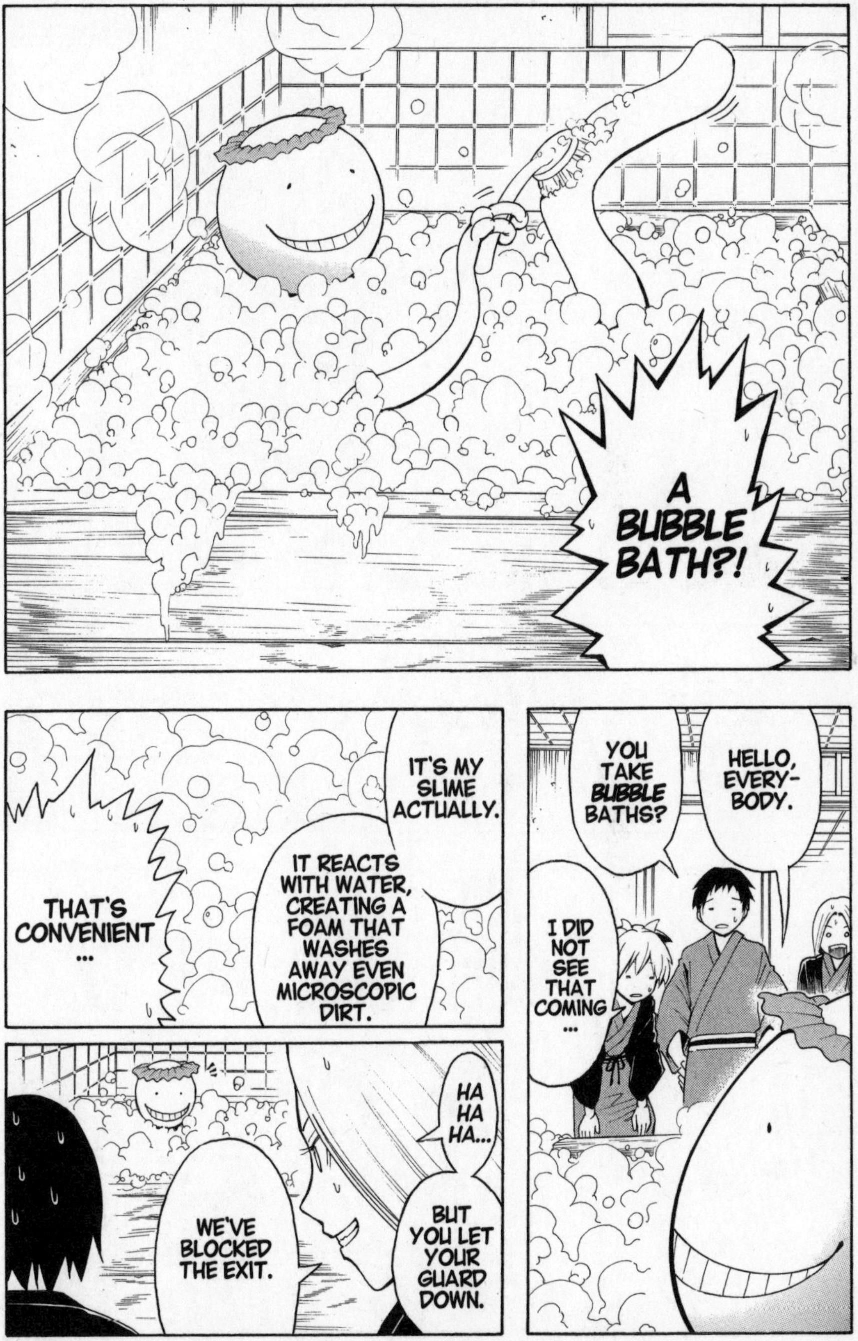
A BUBBLE BATH?!
HELLO, EVERYBODY.
YOU TAKE BUBBLE BATHS?
I DID NOT SEE THAT COMING...
IT'S MY SLIME ACTUALLY.
IT REACTS WITH WATER, CREATING A FOAM THAT WASHES AWAY EVEN MICROSCOPIC DIRT.
THAT'S CONVENIENT...
HA HA HA...
BUT YOU LET YOUR GUARD DOWN.
WE'VE BLOCKED THE EXIT.

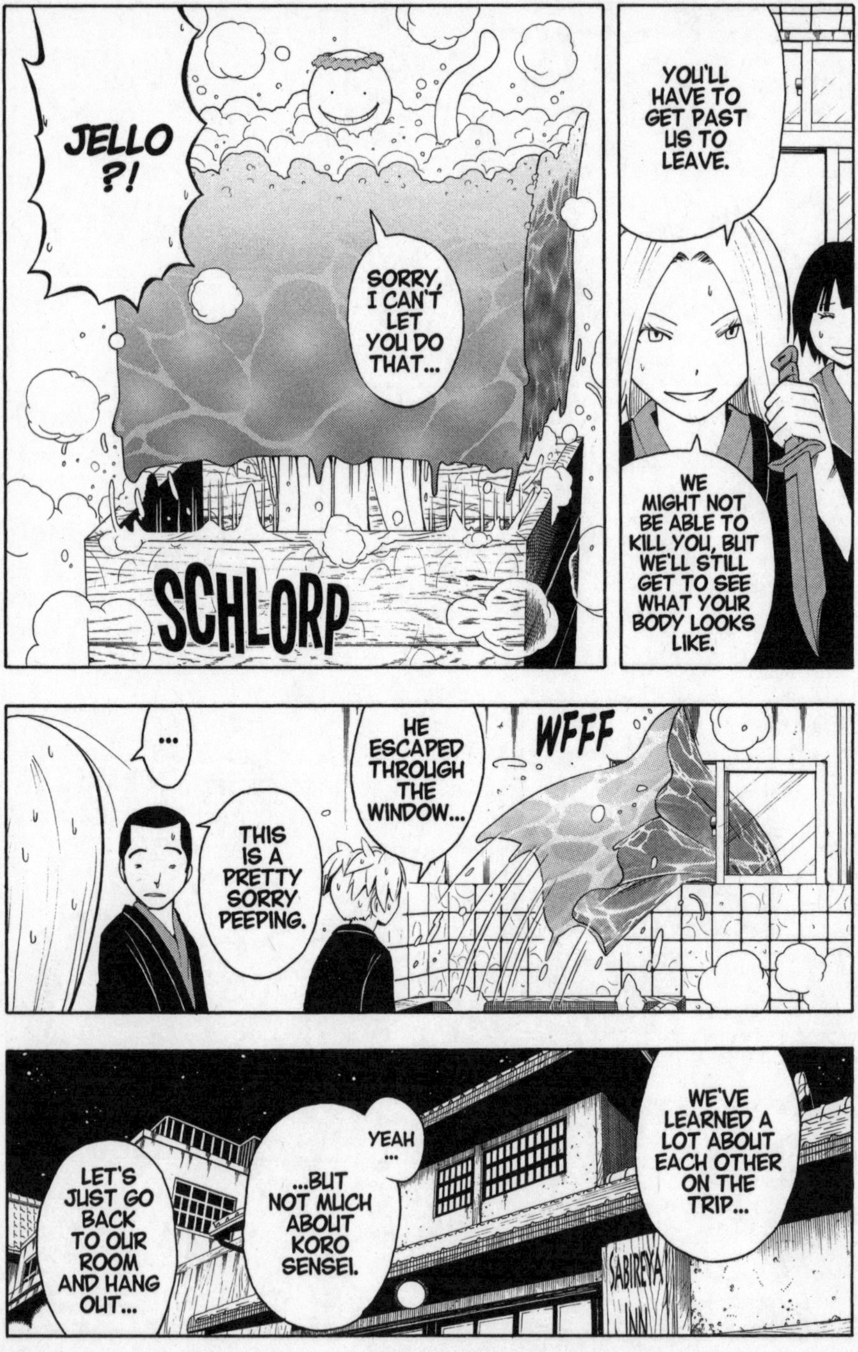
YOU'LL HAVE TO GET PAST US TO LEAVE.
WE MIGHT NOT BE ABLE TO KILL YOU, BUT WE'LL STILL GET TO SEE WHAT YOUR BODY LOOKS LIKE.
JELLO ?!
SORRY, I CAN'T LET YOU DO THAT...
SCHLORP
WFFF
HE ESCAPED THROUGH THE WINDOW...
THIS IS A PRETTY SORRY PEEPING.
...
WE'VE LEARNED A LOT ABOUT EACH OTHER ON THE TRIP...
YEAH ...
...BUT NOT MUCH ABOUT KORO SENSEI.
SABIREYA INN
LET'S JUST GO BACK TO OUR ROOM AND HANG OUT...

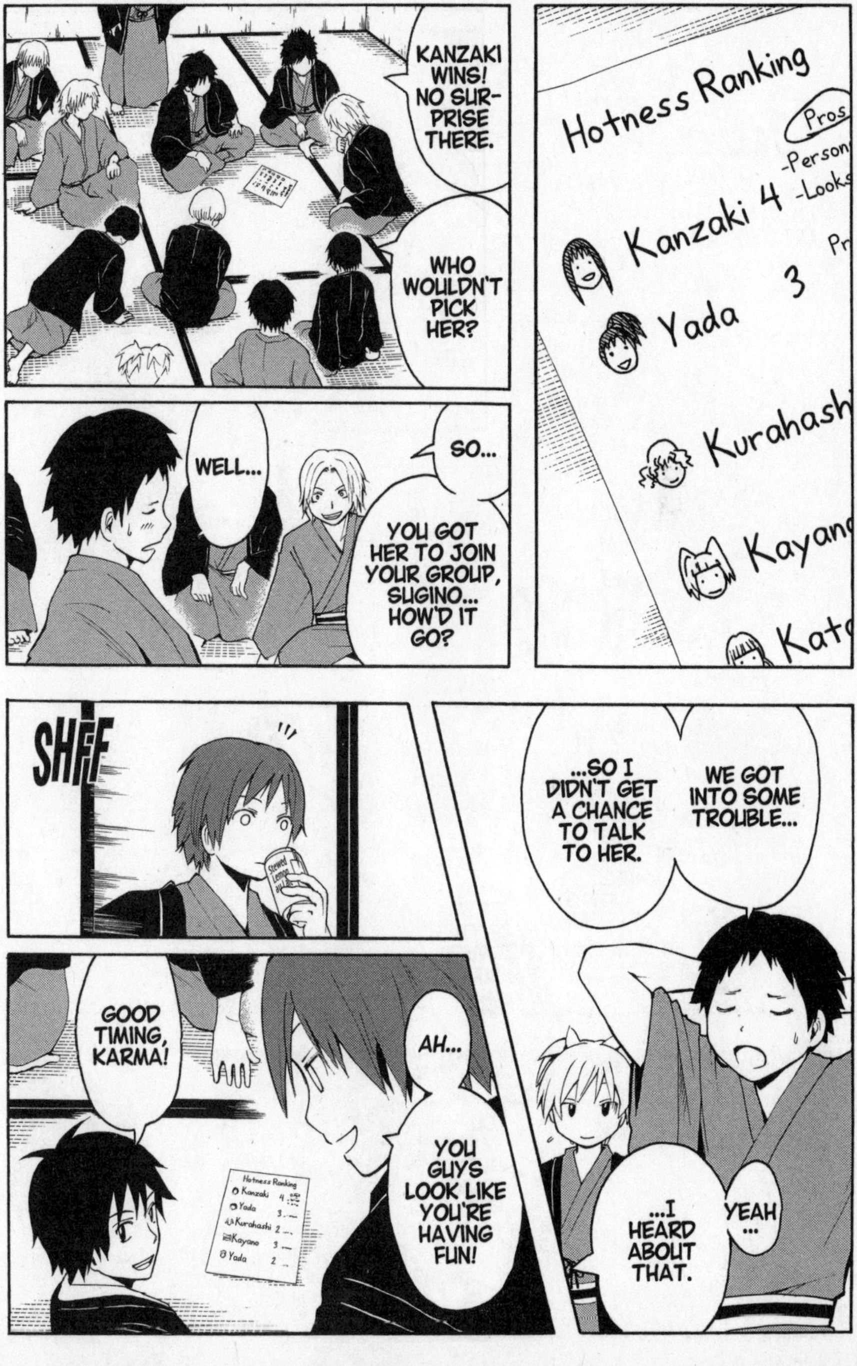
Hotness Ranking
Pros
-Person
-Looks
Kanzaki 4
Yada 3
Kurahashi
Kayano
KANZAKI WINS! NO SURPRISE THERE.
WHO WOULDN'T PICK HER?
SO...
YOU GOT HER TO JOIN YOUR GROUP, SUGINO... HOW'D IT GO?
WELL...
WE GOT INTO SOME TROUBLE...
...SO I DIDN'T GET A CHANCE TO TALK TO HER.
YEAH...
...I HEARD ABOUT THAT.
SHFF
Stewed Lemon
AH...
YOU GUYS LOOK LIKE YOU'RE HAVING FUN!
GOOD TIMING, KARMA!
Hotness Ranking
Kanzaki 4
Yada 3
Kurahashi 2
Kayano 3
Yada 2

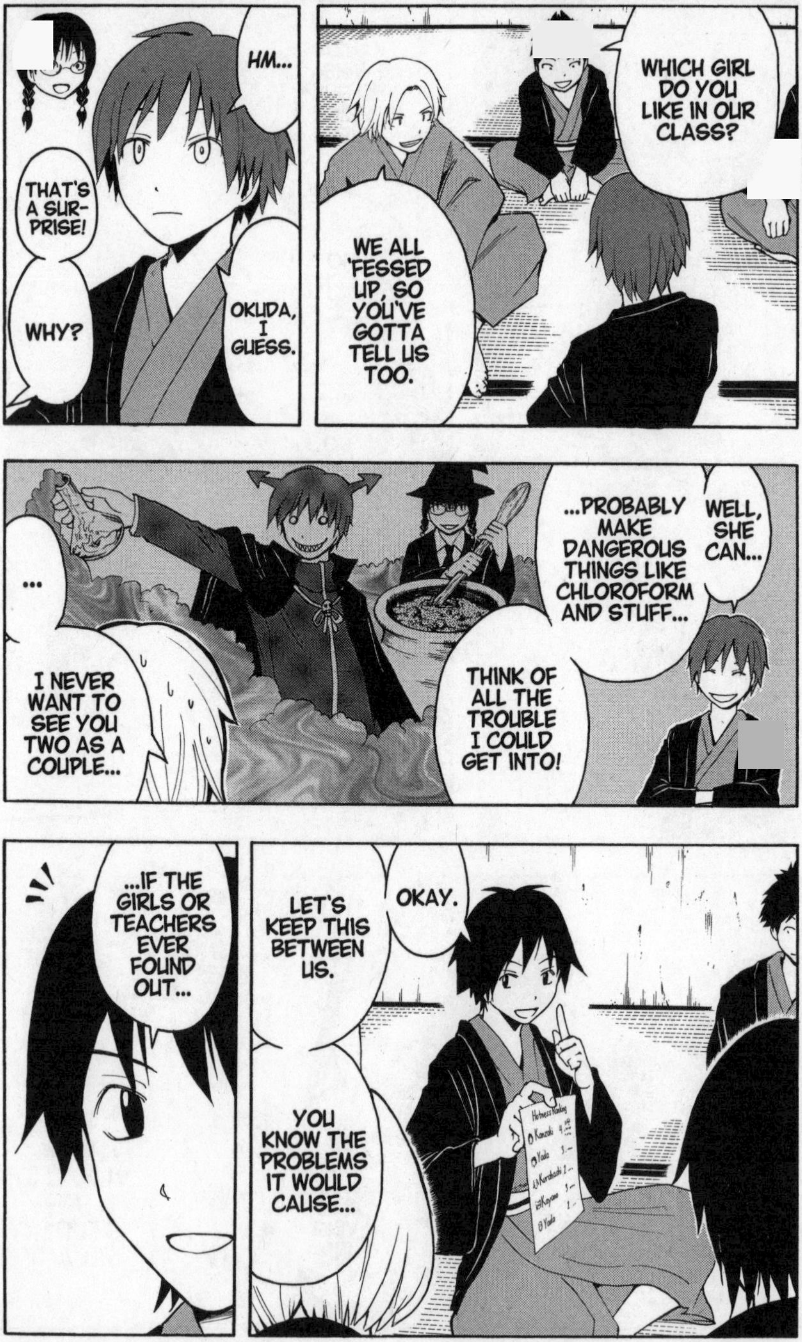
WHICH GIRL DO YOU LIKE IN OUR CLASS?
WE ALL 'FESSED UP, SO YOU'VE GOTTA TELL US TOO.
HM...
OKUDA, I GUESS.
THAT'S A SUR-PRISE!
WHY?
WELL, SHE CAN...
...PROBABLY MAKE DANGEROUS THINGS LIKE CHLOROFORM AND STUFF...
THINK OF ALL THE TROUBLE I COULD GET INTO!
...
I NEVER WANT TO SEE YOU TWO AS A COUPLE...
OKAY.
LET'S KEEP THIS BETWEEN US.
YOU KNOW THE PROBLEMS IT WOULD CAUSE...
...IF THE GIRLS OR TEACHERS EVER FOUND OUT...

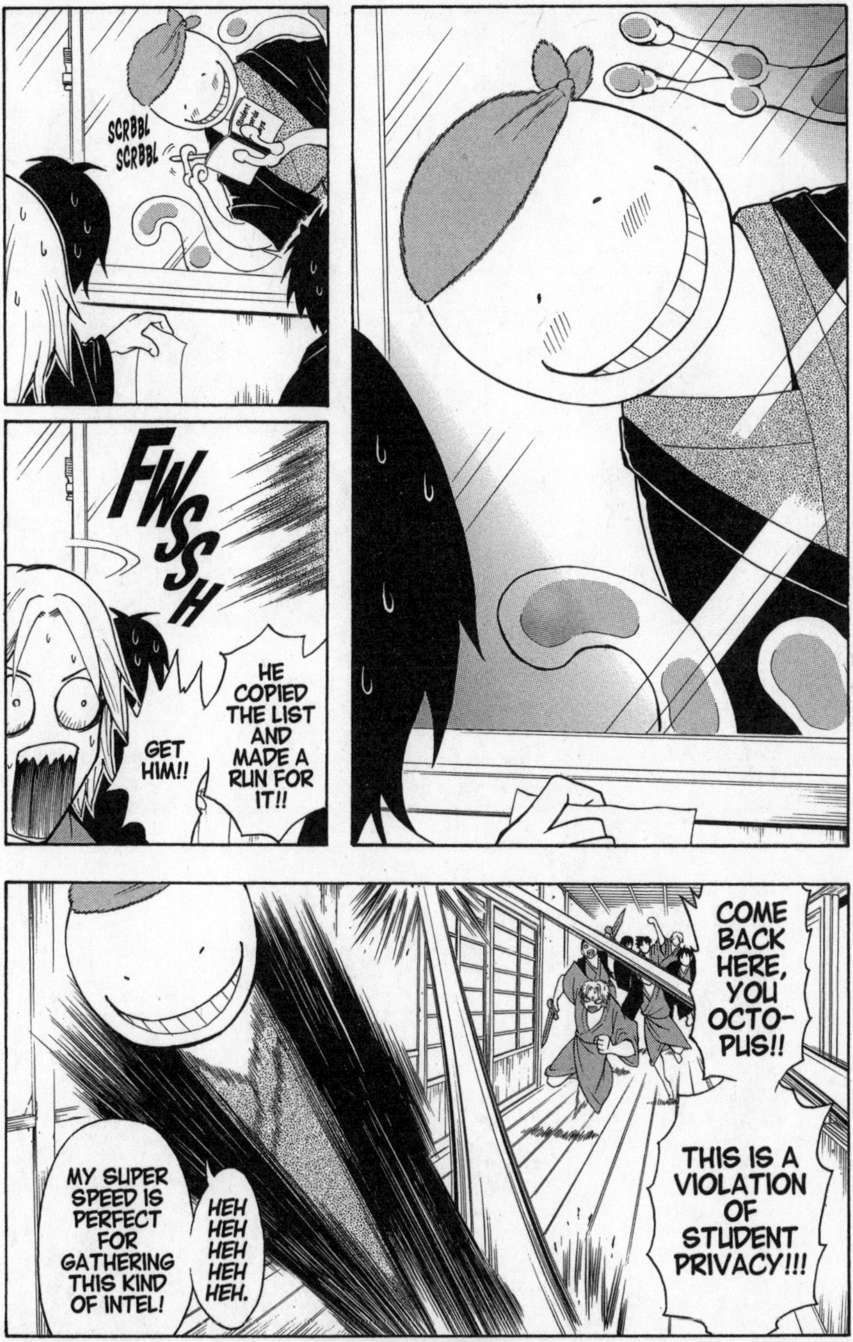
SCRBBL
SCRBBL
FWSSH
HE COPIED THE LIST AND MADE A RUN FOR IT!!
GET HIM!!
COME BACK HERE, YOU OCTO-PUS!!
THIS IS A VIOLATION OF STUDENT PRIVACY!!!
HEH HEH HEH HEH HEH.
MY SUPER SPEED IS PERFECT FOR GATHERING THIS KIND OF INTEL!

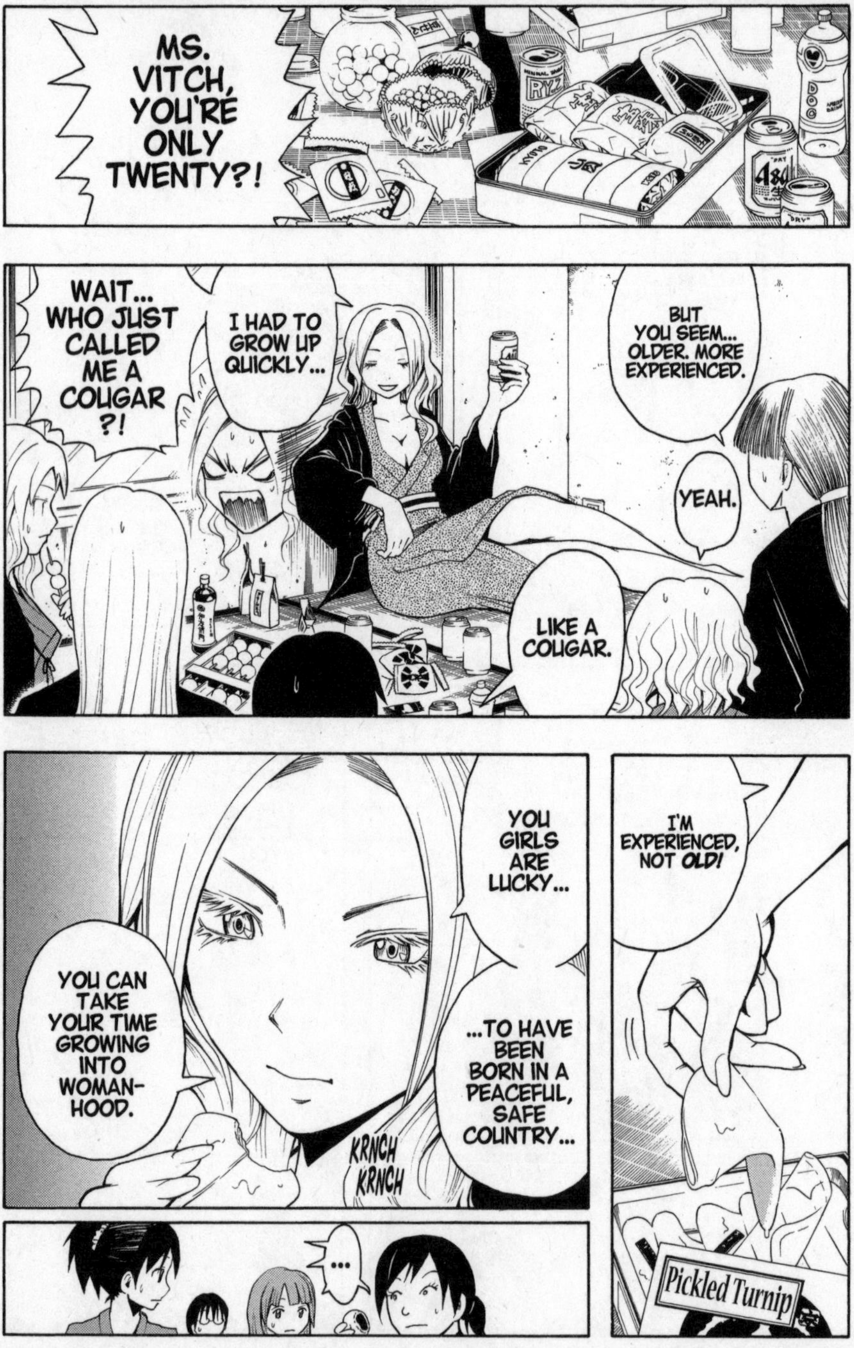
MS. VITCH, YOU'RE ONLY TWENTY?!
I HAD TO GROW UP QUICKLY...
BUT YOU SEEM... OLDER. MORE EXPERIENCED.
YEAH.
LIKE A COUGAR.
WAIT... WHO JUST CALLED ME A COUGAR?!
I'M EXPERIENCED, NOT OLD!
Pickled Turnip
YOU GIRLS ARE LUCKY...
...TO HAVE BEEN BORN IN A PEACEFUL, SAFE COUNTRY...
YOU CAN TAKE YOUR TIME GROWING INTO WOMAN-HOOD.
KRNCH KRNCH
...

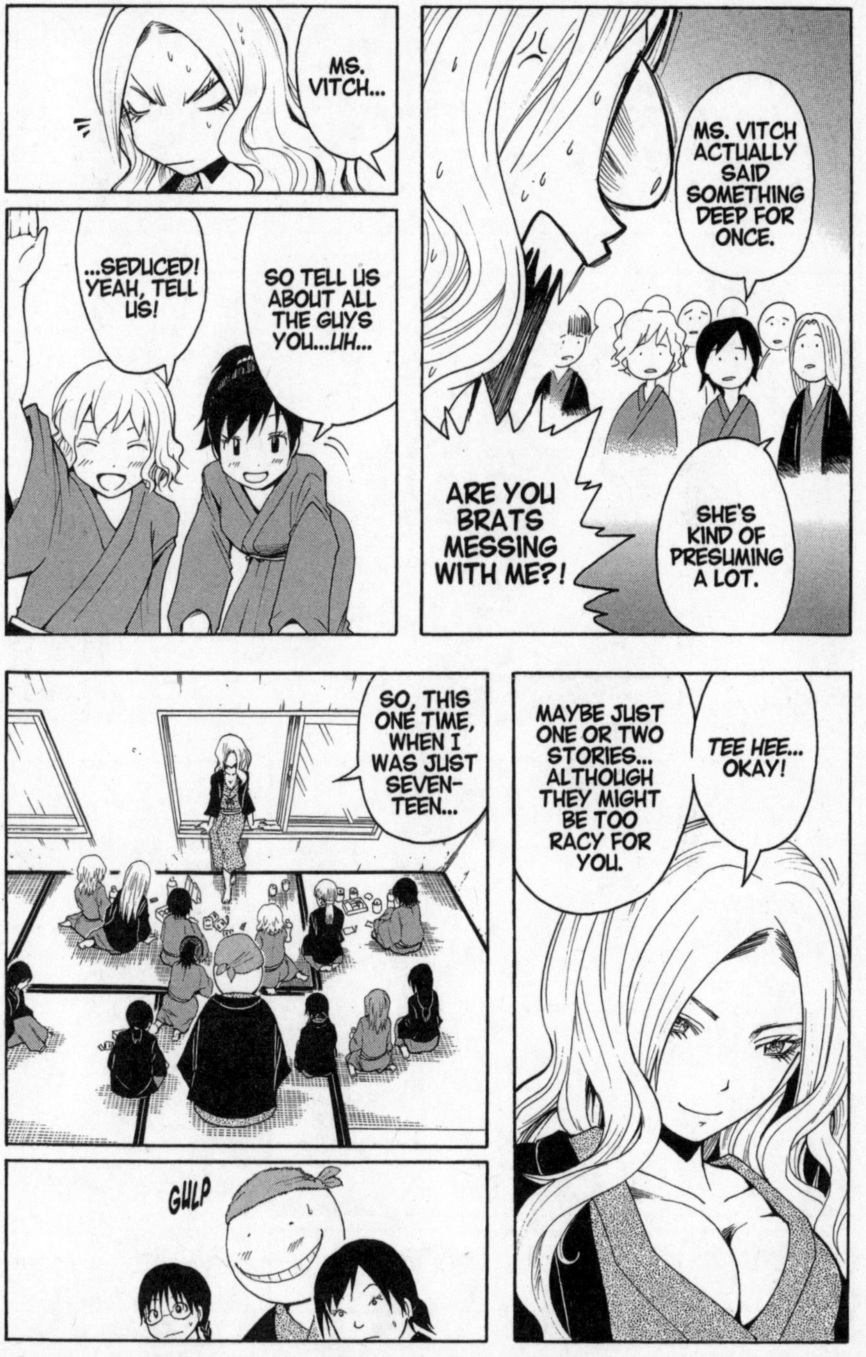
MS. VITCH ACTUALLY SAID SOMETHING DEEP FOR ONCE.
SHE'S KIND OF PRESUMING A LOT.
ARE YOU BRATS MESSING WITH ME?!
MS. VITCH...
SO TELL US ABOUT ALL THE GUYS YOU...UH...
...SEDUCED! YEAH, TELL US!
TEE HEE... OKAY!
MAYBE JUST ONE OR TWO STORIES... ALTHOUGH THEY MIGHT BE TOO RACY FOR YOU.
SO, THIS ONE TIME, WHEN I WAS JUST SEVENTEEN...
GULP

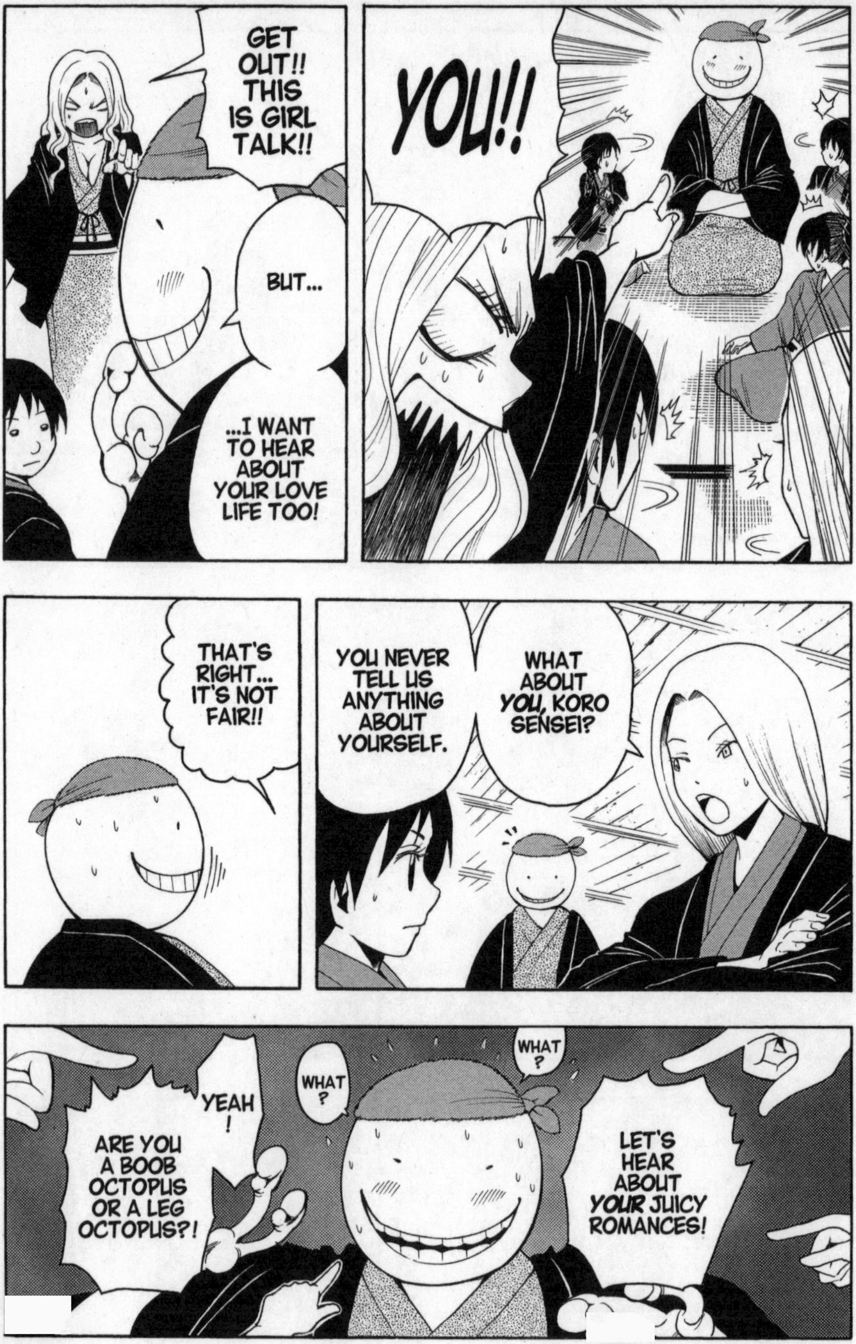
YOU!!
GET OUT!! THIS IS GIRL TALK!!
BUT...
...I WANT TO HEAR ABOUT YOUR LOVE LIFE TOO!
WHAT ABOUT YOU, KORO SENSEI?
YOU NEVER TELL US ANYTHING ABOUT YOURSELF.
THAT'S RIGHT... IT'S NOT FAIR!!
LET'S HEAR ABOUT YOUR JUICY ROMANCES!
WHAT?
WHAT?
YEAH!
ARE YOU A BOOB OCTOPUS OR A LEG OCTOPUS?!

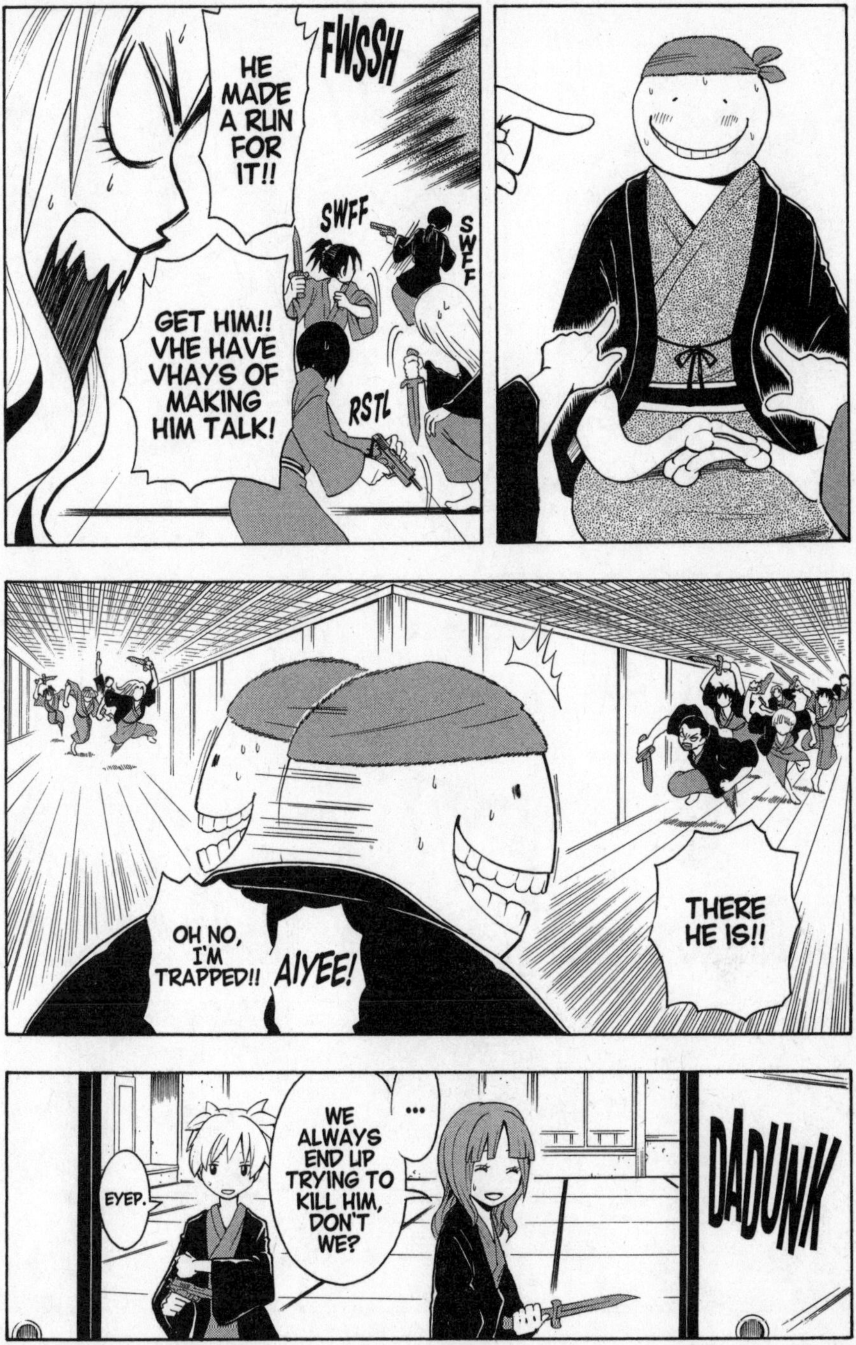
FWSSH
HE MADE A RUN FOR IT!!
SWFF
SWFF
GET HIM!! VHE HAVE VHAYS OF MAKING HIM TALK!
RSTL
THERE HE IS!!
AIYEE!
OH NO, I'M TRAPPED!!
DADUNK
...
WE ALWAYS END UP TRYING TO KILL HIM, DON'T WE?
EYEP.

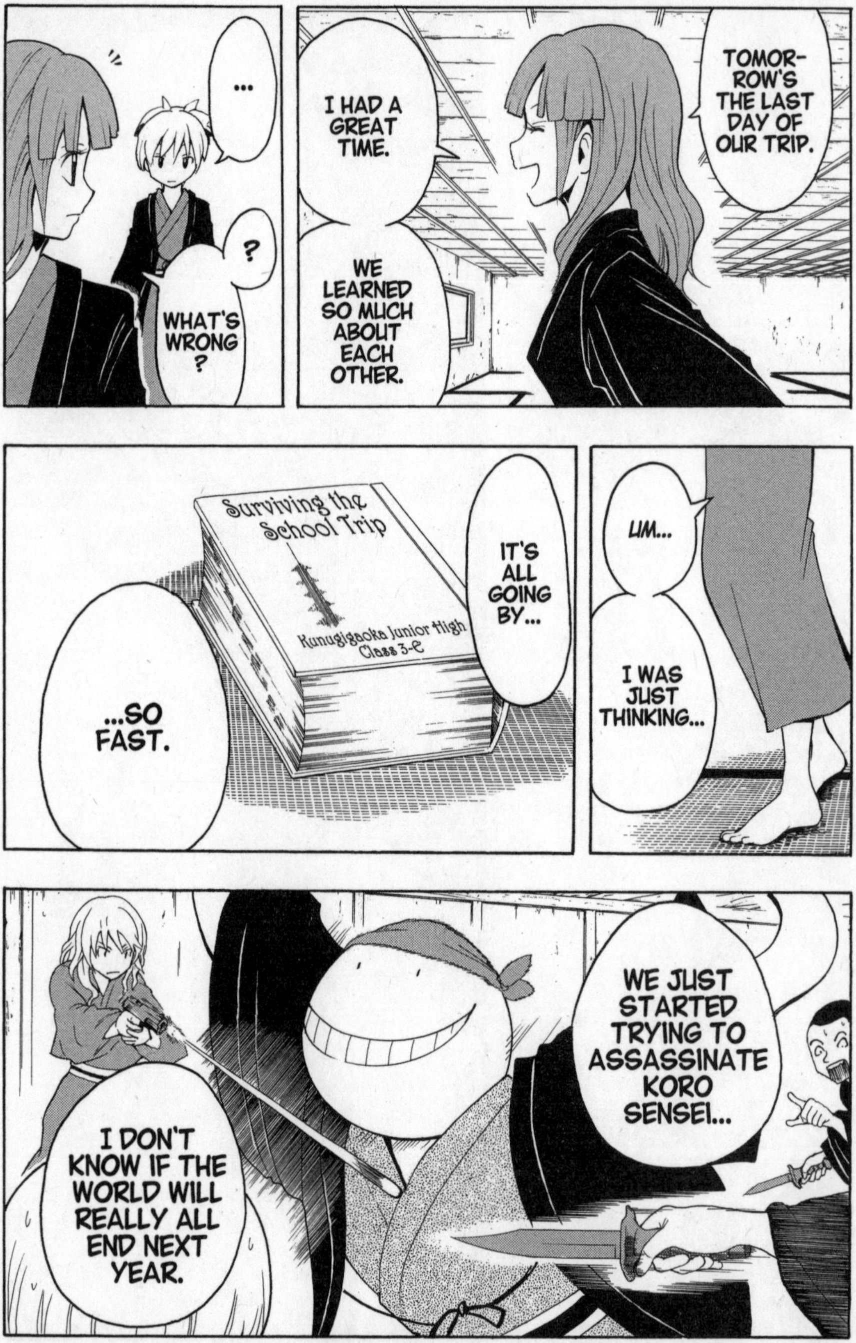
TOMOR-ROW'S THE LAST DAY OF OUR TRIP.
I HAD A GREAT TIME.
WE LEARNED SO MUCH ABOUT EACH OTHER.
...
?
WHAT'S WRONG?
UM...
I WAS JUST THINKING...
IT'S ALL GOING BY...
Surviving the School Trip
Kunugigaoka Junior High Class 3-E
...SO FAST.
WE JUST STARTED TRYING TO ASSASSINATE KORO SENSEI...
I DON'T KNOW IF THE WORLD WILL REALLY ALL END NEXT YEAR.

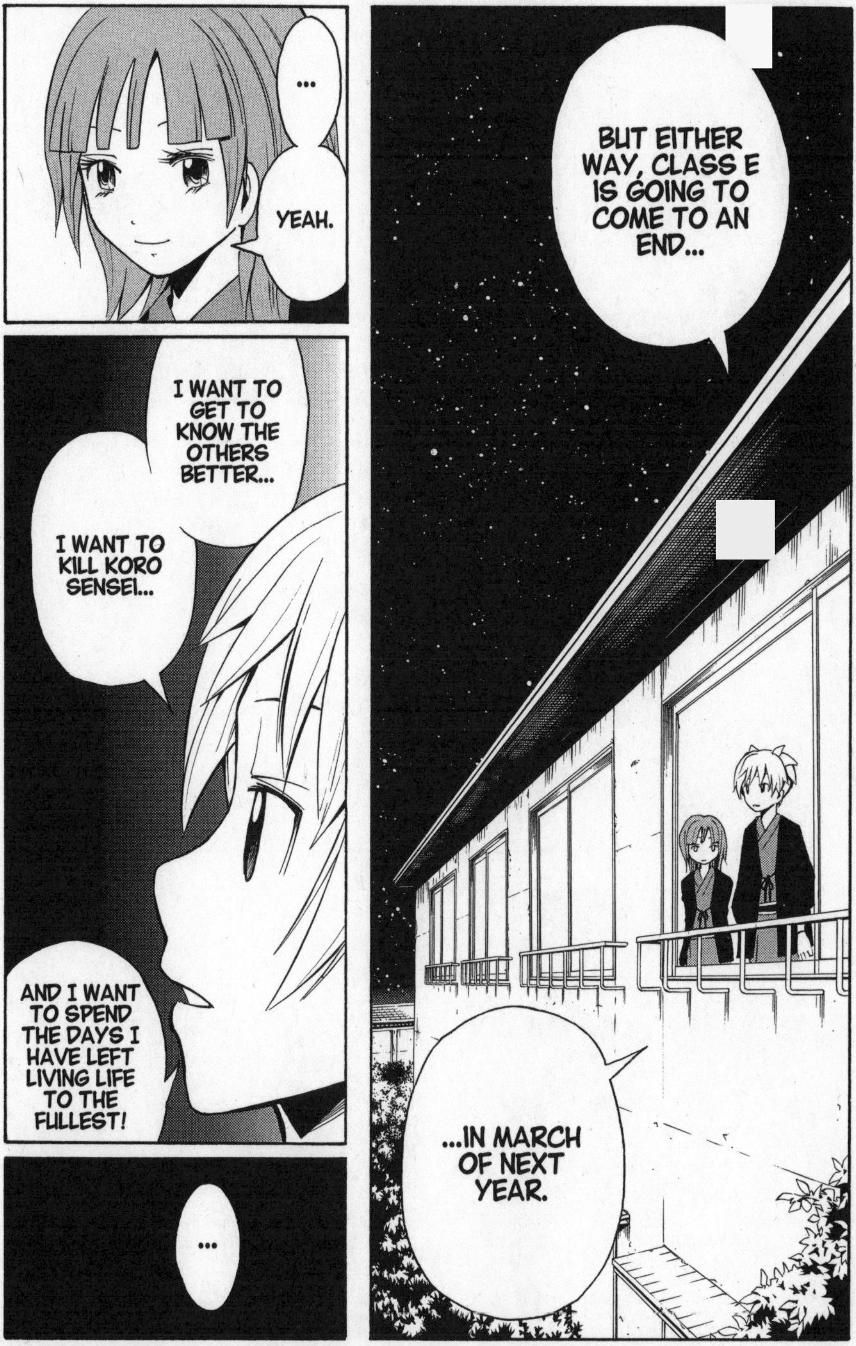
BUT EITHER WAY, CLASS E IS GOING TO COME TO AN END...
...IN MARCH OF NEXT YEAR.
...
YEAH.
I WANT TO GET TO KNOW THE OTHERS BETTER...
I WANT TO KILL KORO SENSEI...
AND I WANT TO SPEND THE DAYS I HAVE LEFT LIVING LIFE TO THE FULLEST!
...

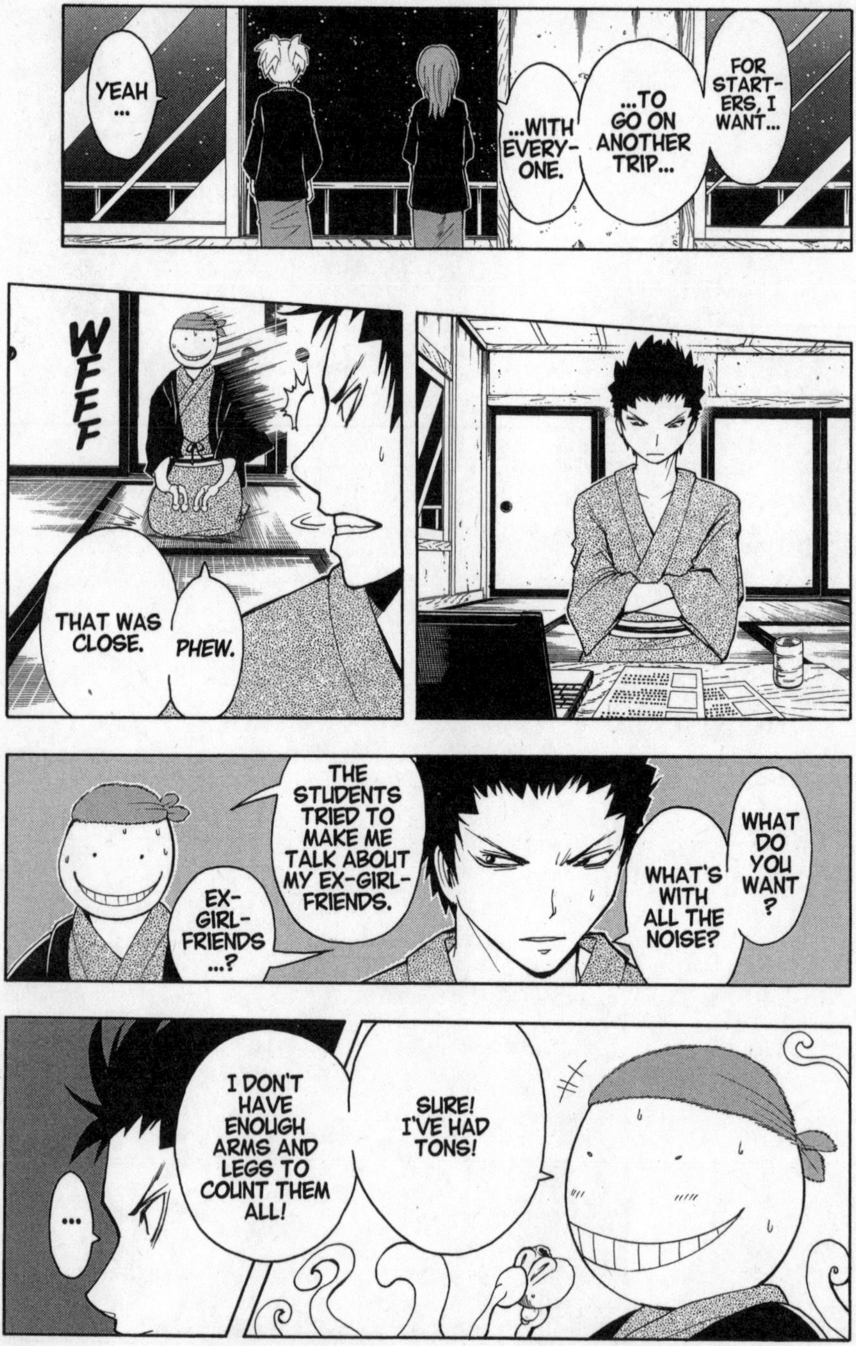
FOR START-ERS, I WANT...
...TO GO ON ANOTHER TRIP...
...WITH EVERY-ONE.
YEAH...
WFFF
PHEW.
THAT WAS CLOSE.
WHAT DO YOU WANT?
WHAT'S WITH ALL THE NOISE?
THE STUDENTS TRIED TO MAKE ME TALK ABOUT MY EX-GIRL-FRIENDS.
EX-GIRL-FRIENDS...?
SURE! I'VE HAD TONS!
I DON'T HAVE ENOUGH ARMS AND LEGS TO COUNT THEM ALL!
...

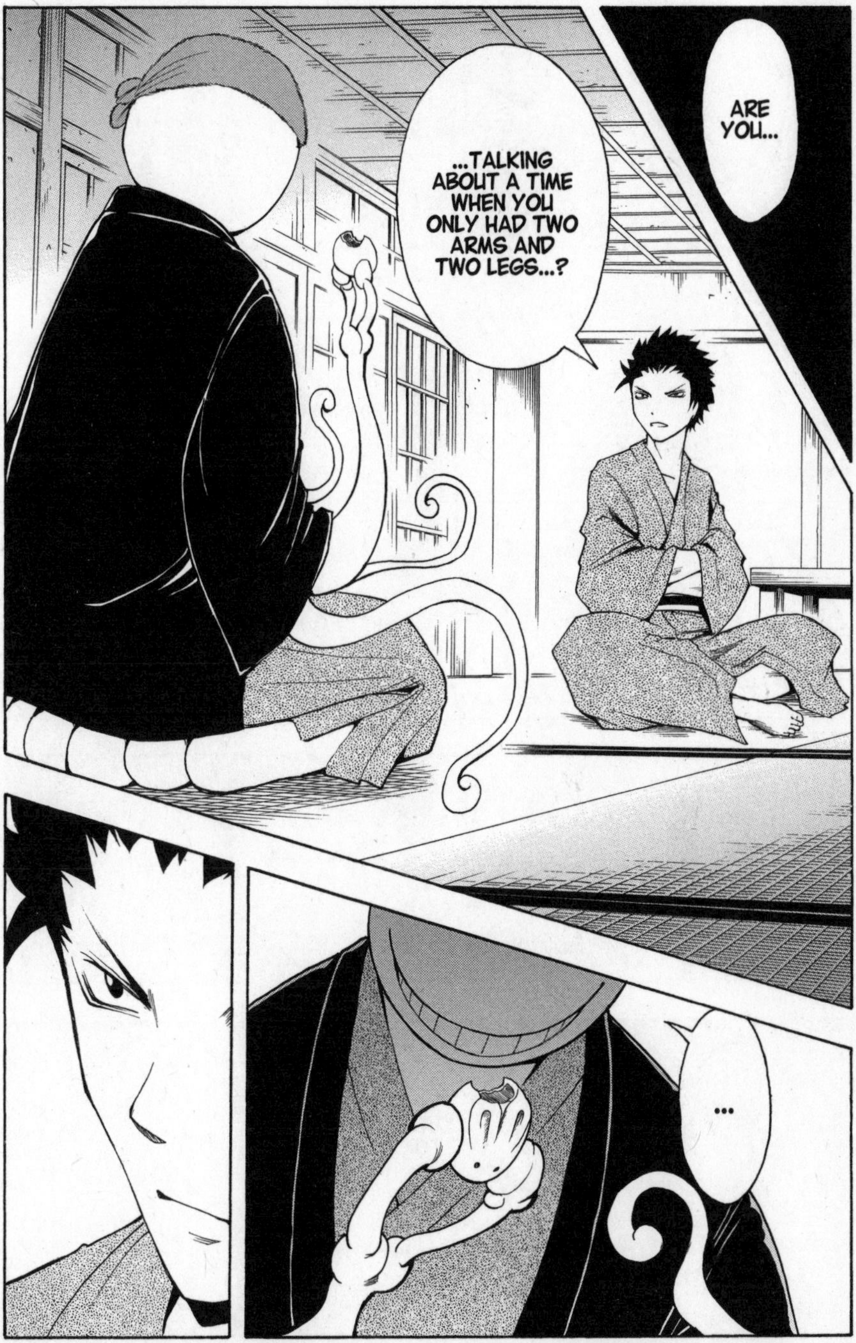
ARE YOU...
...TALKING ABOUT A TIME WHEN YOU ONLY HAD TWO ARMS AND TWO LEGS...?
...

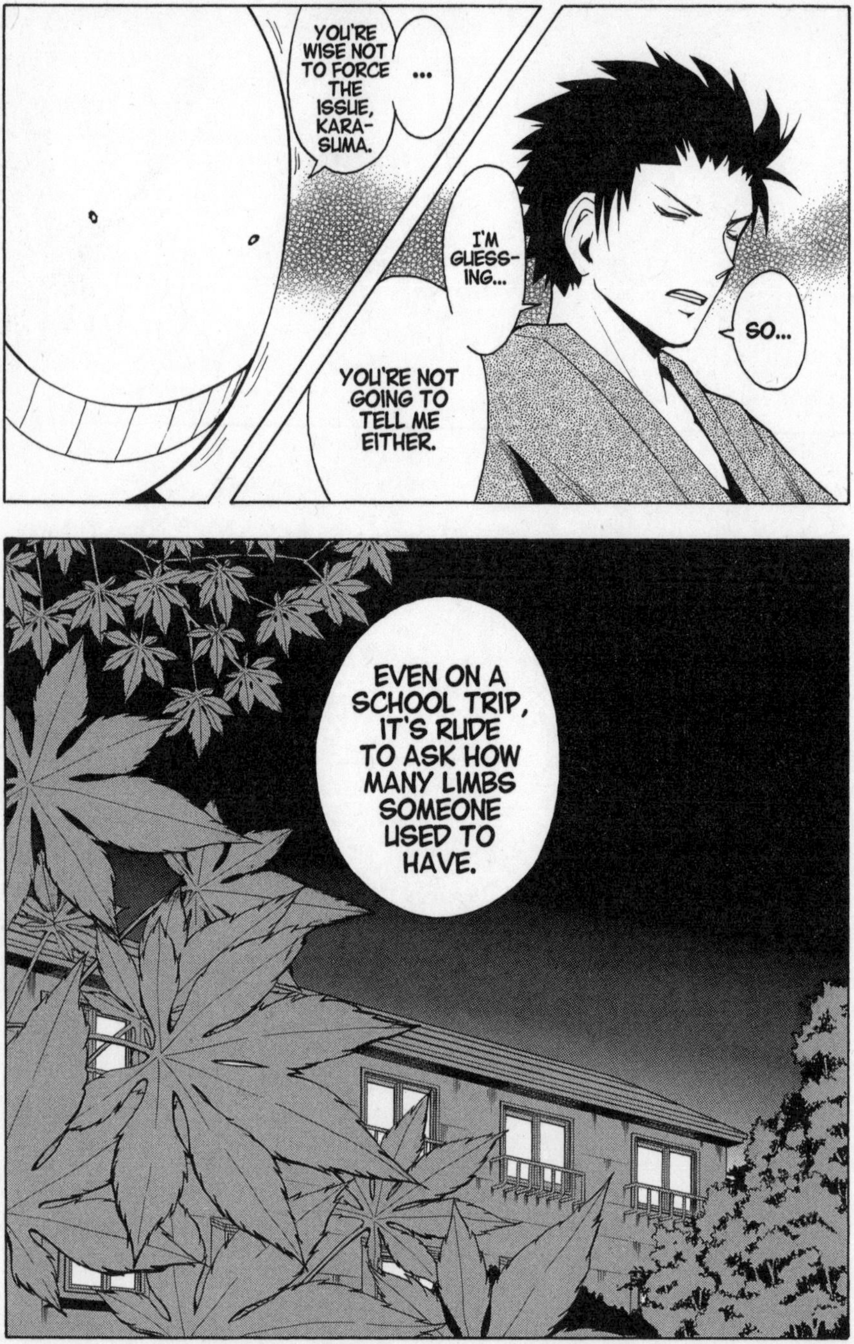
SO...
I'M GUESSING...
YOU'RE NOT GOING TO TELL ME EITHER.
YOU'RE WISE NOT TO FORCE THE ISSUE, KARASUMA.
...
EVEN ON A SCHOOL TRIP, IT'S RUDE TO ASK HOW MANY LIMBS SOMEONE USED TO HAVE.

When he had two arms and legs.

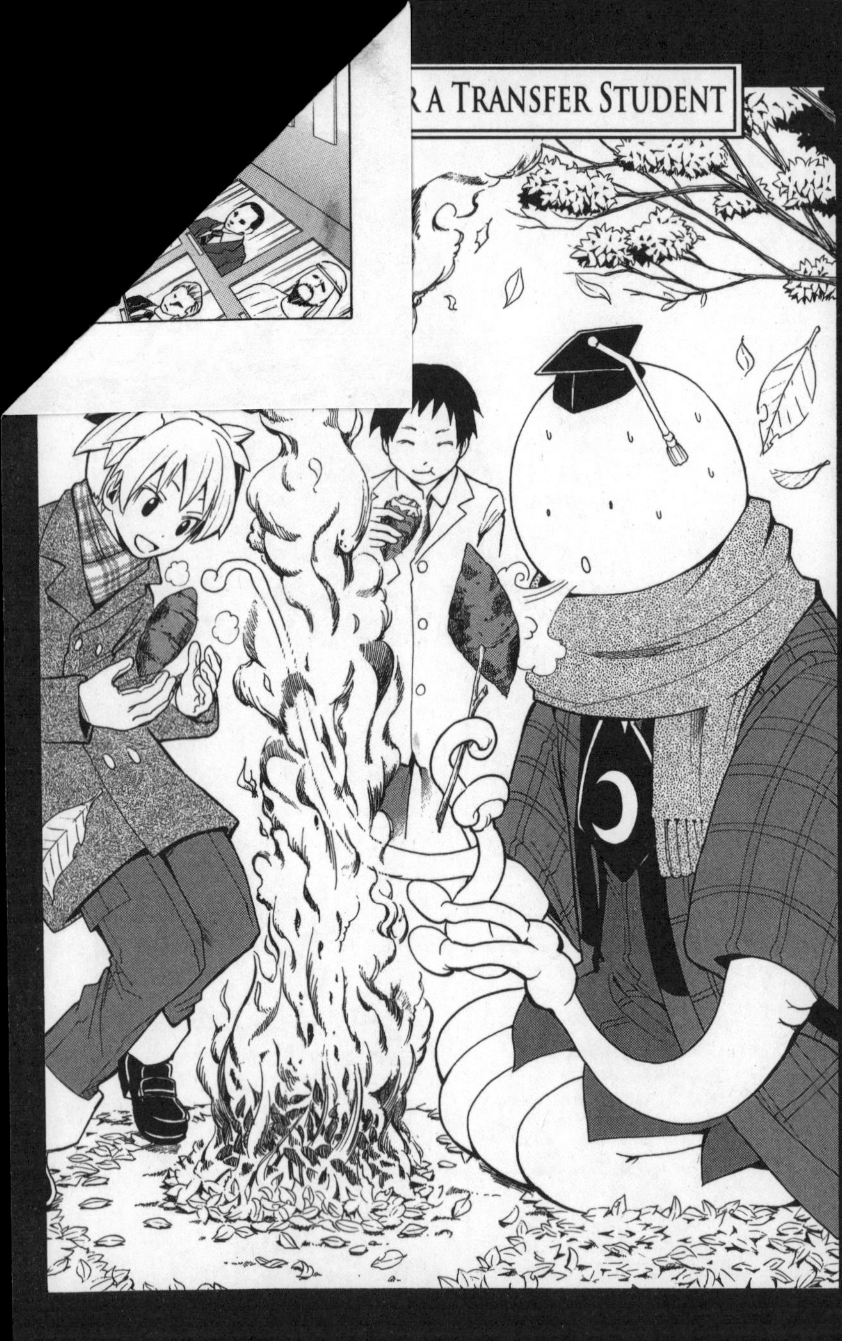
R A TRANSFER STUDENT

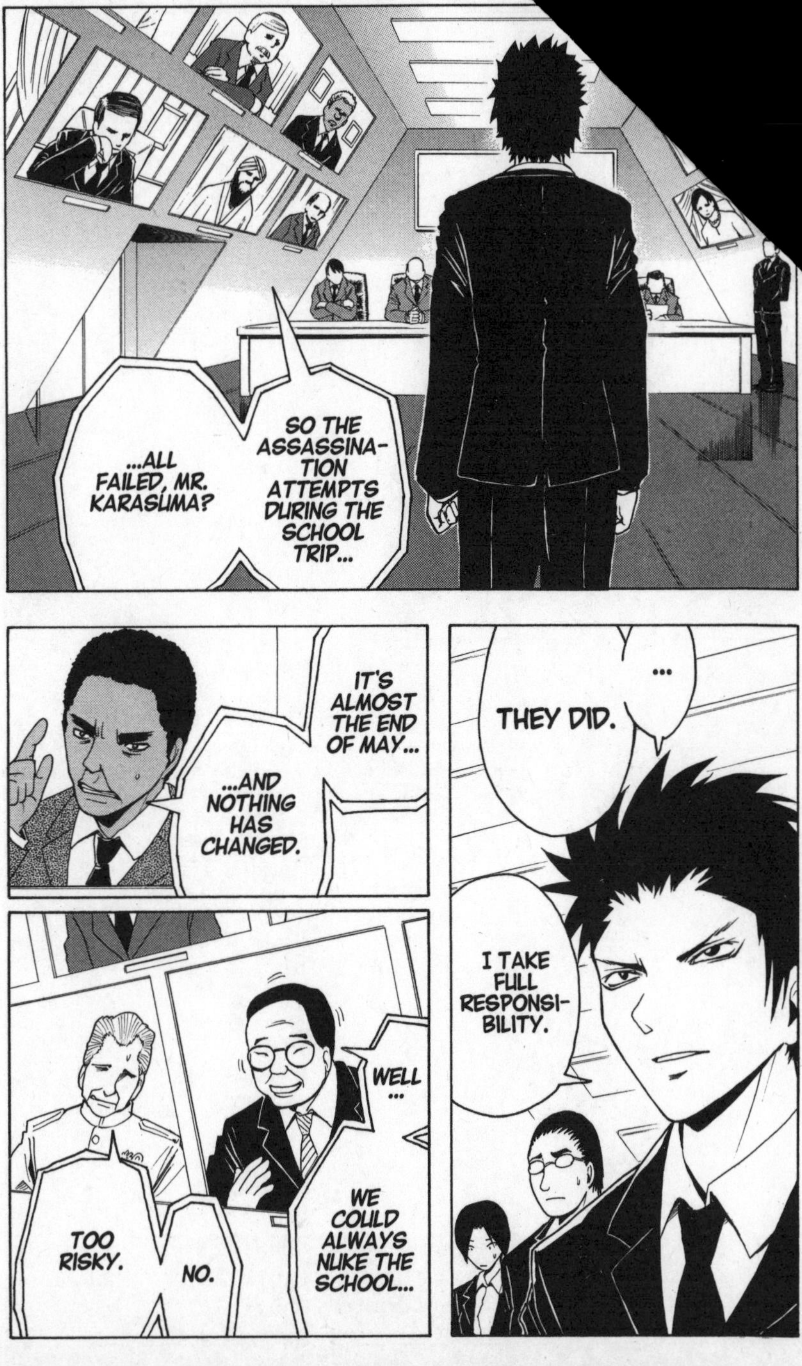
SO THE ASSASSINATION ATTEMPTS DURING THE SCHOOL TRIP...
...ALL FAILED, MR. KARASUMA?
...
THEY DID.
I TAKE FULL RESPONSIBILITY.
IT'S ALMOST THE END OF MAY...
...AND NOTHING HAS CHANGED.
WELL...
WE COULD ALWAYS NUKE THE SCHOOL...
NO.
TOO RISKY.

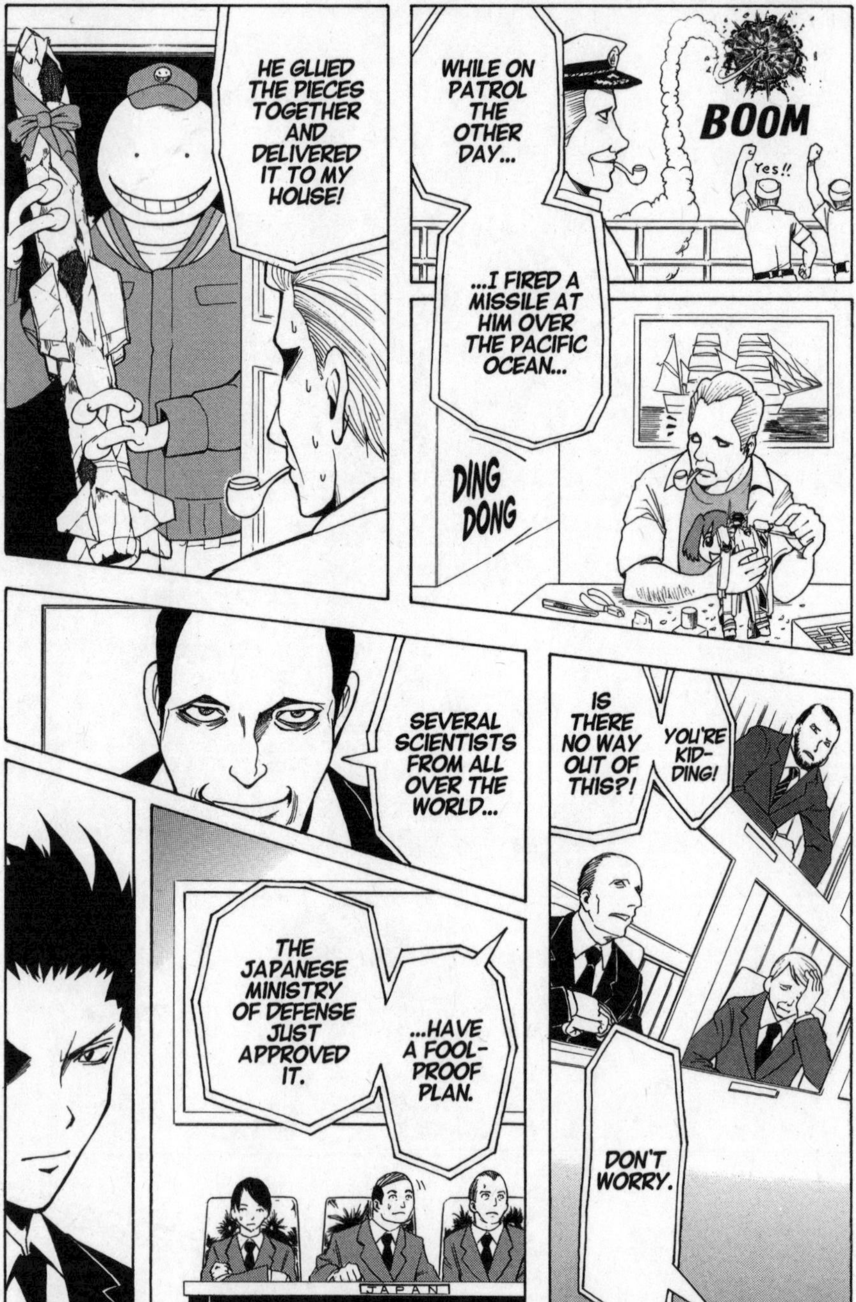
WHILE ON PATROL THE OTHER DAY...
BOOM
Yes!!
...I FIRED A MISSILE AT HIM OVER THE PACIFIC OCEAN...
DING DONG
HE GLUED THE PIECES TOGETHER AND DELIVERED IT TO MY HOUSE!
YOU'RE KID-DING!
IS THERE NO WAY OUT OF THIS?!
DON'T WORRY.
SEVERAL SCIENTISTS FROM ALL OVER THE WORLD...
...HAVE A FOOL-PROOF PLAN.
THE JAPANESE MINISTRY OF DEFENSE JUST APPROVED IT.
JAPAN

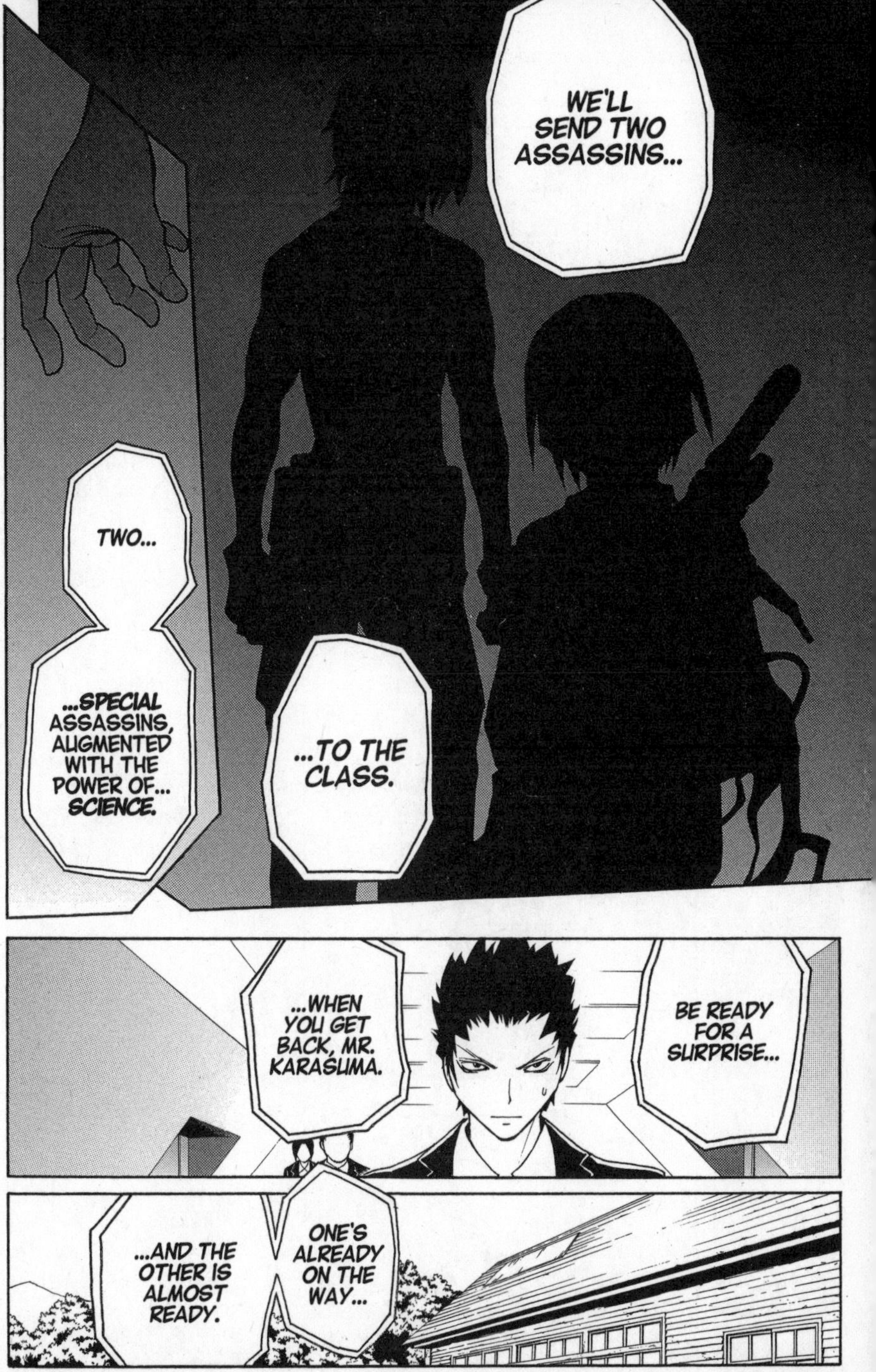
WE'LL SEND TWO ASSASSINS...
...TO THE CLASS.
TWO...
...SPECIAL ASSASSINS, AUGMENTED WITH THE POWER OF... SCIENCE.
BE READY FOR A SURPRISE...
...WHEN YOU GET BACK, MR. KARASUMA.
ONE'S ALREADY ON THE WAY...
...AND THE OTHER IS ALMOST READY.

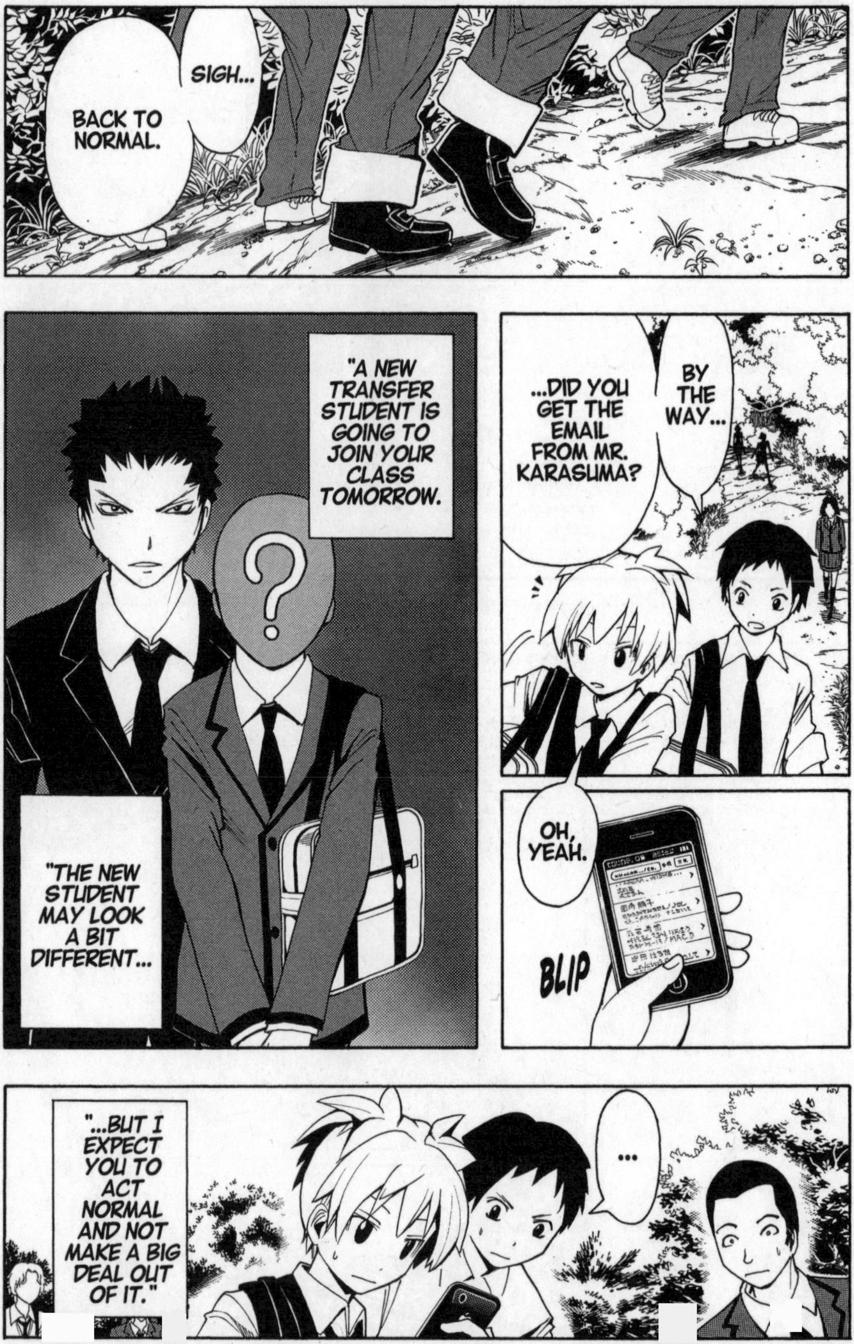
SIGH...
BACK TO NORMAL.
BY THE WAY...
...DID YOU GET THE EMAIL FROM MR. KARASUMA?
OH, YEAH.
BLIP
"A NEW TRANSFER STUDENT IS GOING TO JOIN YOUR CLASS TOMORROW.
"THE NEW STUDENT MAY LOOK A BIT DIFFERENT...
...
"...BUT I EXPECT YOU TO ACT NORMAL AND NOT MAKE A BIG DEAL OUT OF IT."

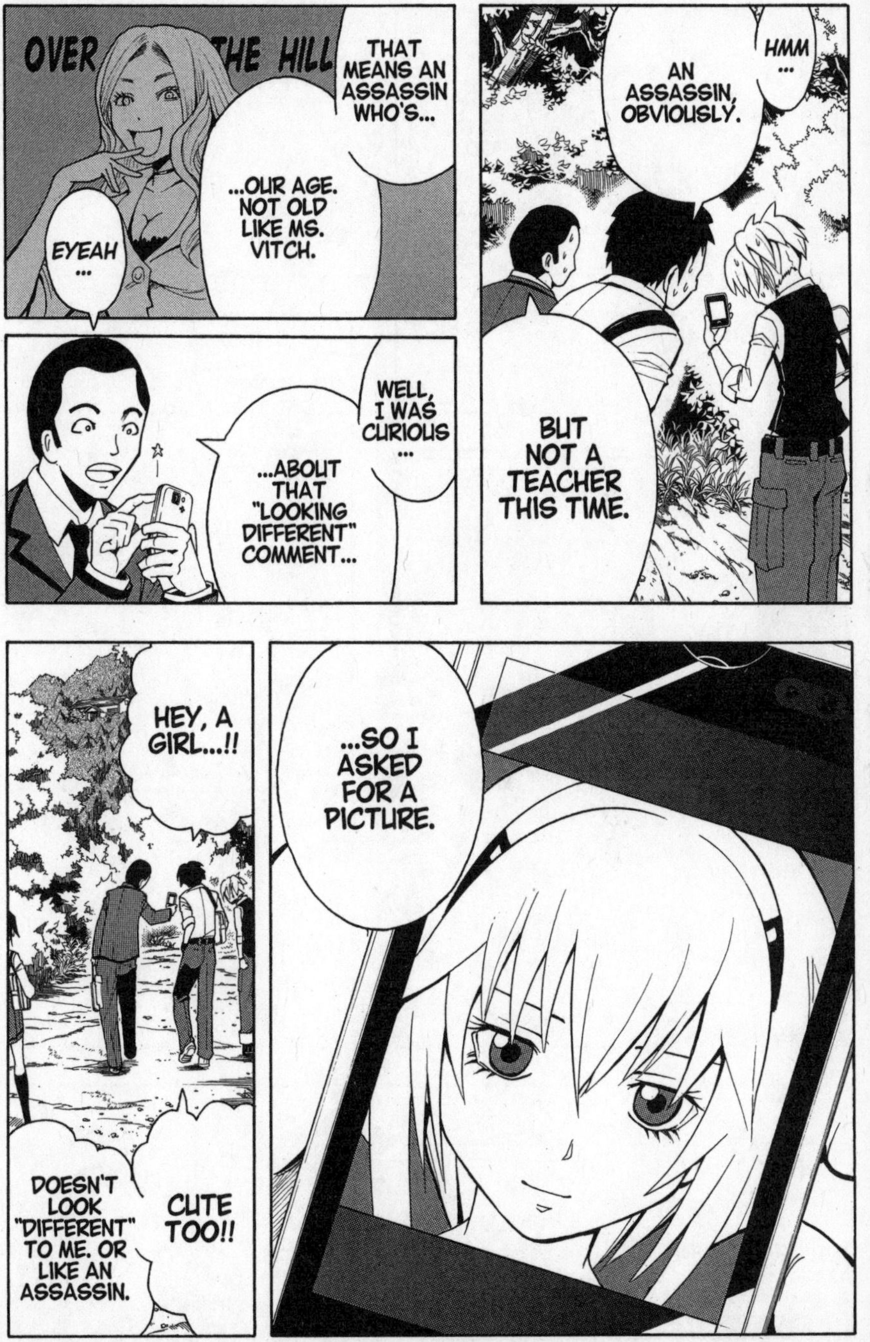
HMM ...
AN ASSASSIN, OBVIOUSLY.
BUT NOT A TEACHER THIS TIME.
THAT MEANS AN ASSASSIN WHO'S...
...OUR AGE. NOT OLD LIKE MS. VITCH.
OVER THE HILL
EYEAH ...
WELL, I WAS CURIOUS ...
...ABOUT THAT "LOOKING DIFFERENT" COMMENT...
...SO I ASKED FOR A PICTURE.
HEY, A GIRL...!!
CUTE TOO!!
DOESN'T LOOK "DIFFERENT" TO ME. OR LIKE AN ASSASSIN.

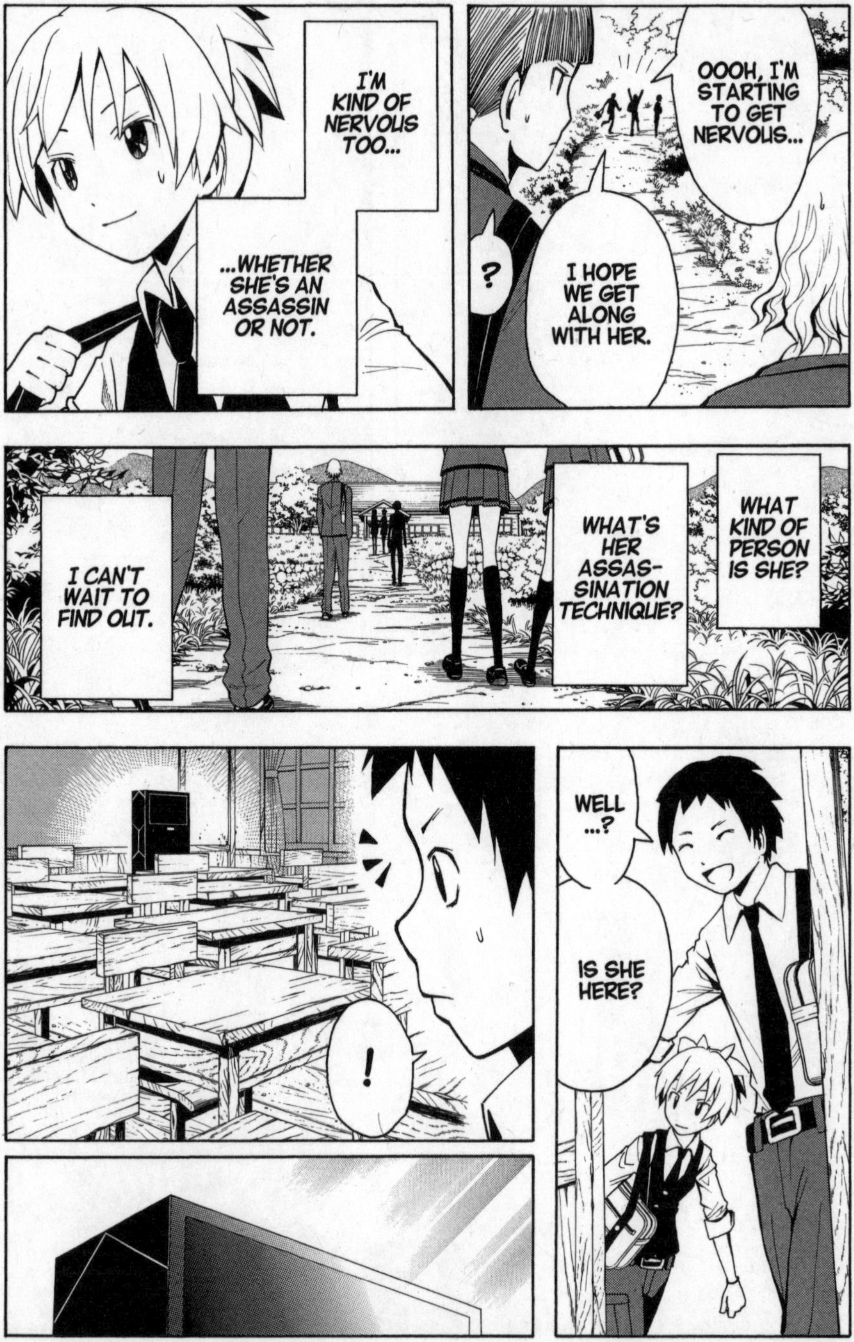
OOOH, I'M STARTING TO GET NERVOUS...
I HOPE WE GET ALONG WITH HER.
?
I'M KIND OF NERVOUS TOO...
...WHETHER SHE'S AN ASSASSIN OR NOT.
WHAT KIND OF PERSON IS SHE?
WHAT'S HER ASSAS-SINATION TECHNIQUE?
I CAN'T WAIT TO FIND OUT.
WELL ...?
IS SHE HERE?
!

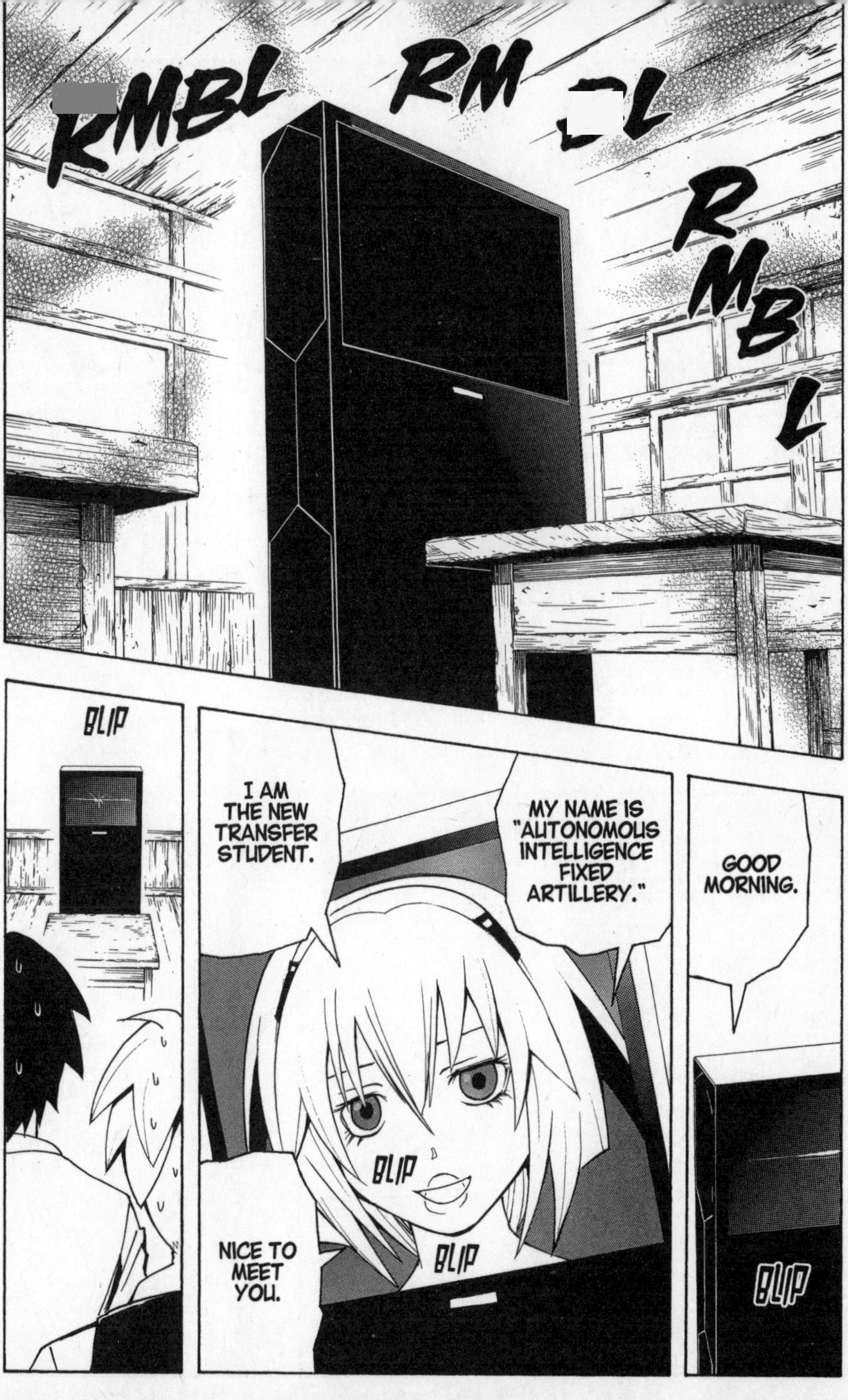
RMBL
RM
RMBL
BLIP
GOOD MORNING.
MY NAME IS "AUTONOMOUS INTELLIGENCE FIXED ARTILLERY."
I AM THE NEW TRANSFER STUDENT.
BLIP
NICE TO MEET YOU.
BLIP
BLIP

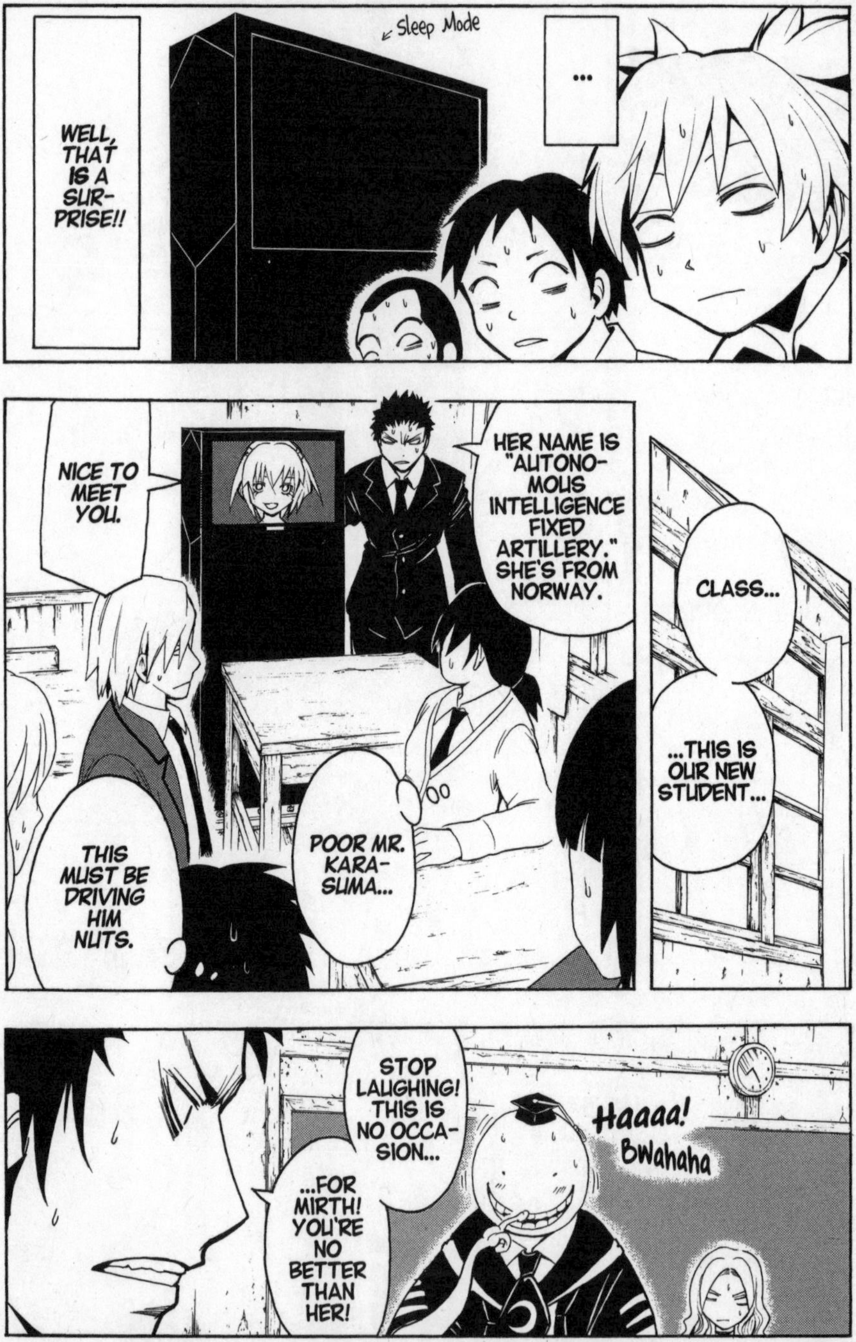
...
Sleep Mode
WELL, THAT IS A SURPRISE!!
CLASS...
...THIS IS OUR NEW STUDENT...
HER NAME IS "AUTONOMOUS INTELLIGENCE FIXED ARTILLERY." SHE'S FROM NORWAY.
NICE TO MEET YOU.
POOR MR. KARASUMA...
THIS MUST BE DRIVING HIM NUTS.
Haaaa!
Bwahaha
STOP LAUGHING! THIS IS NO OCCASION...
...FOR MIRTH! YOU'RE NO BETTER THAN HER!

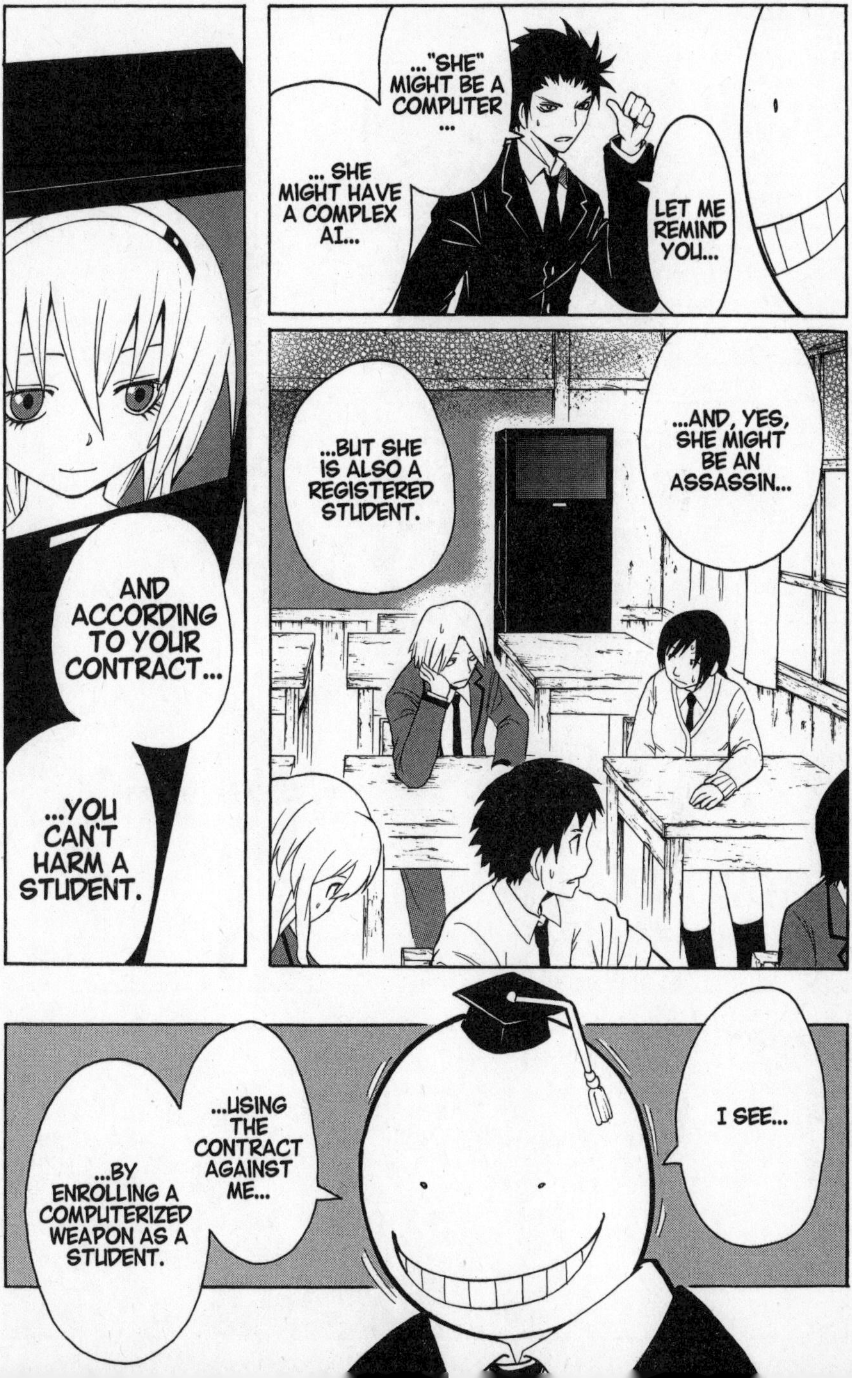
LET ME REMIND YOU...
..."SHE" MIGHT BE A COMPUTER ...
... SHE MIGHT HAVE A COMPLEX AI...
...AND, YES, SHE MIGHT BE AN ASSASSIN...
...BUT SHE IS ALSO A REGISTERED STUDENT.
AND ACCORDING TO YOUR CONTRACT...
...YOU CAN'T HARM A STUDENT.
I SEE...
...USING THE CONTRACT AGAINST ME...
...BY ENROLLING A COMPUTERIZED WEAPON AS A STUDENT.

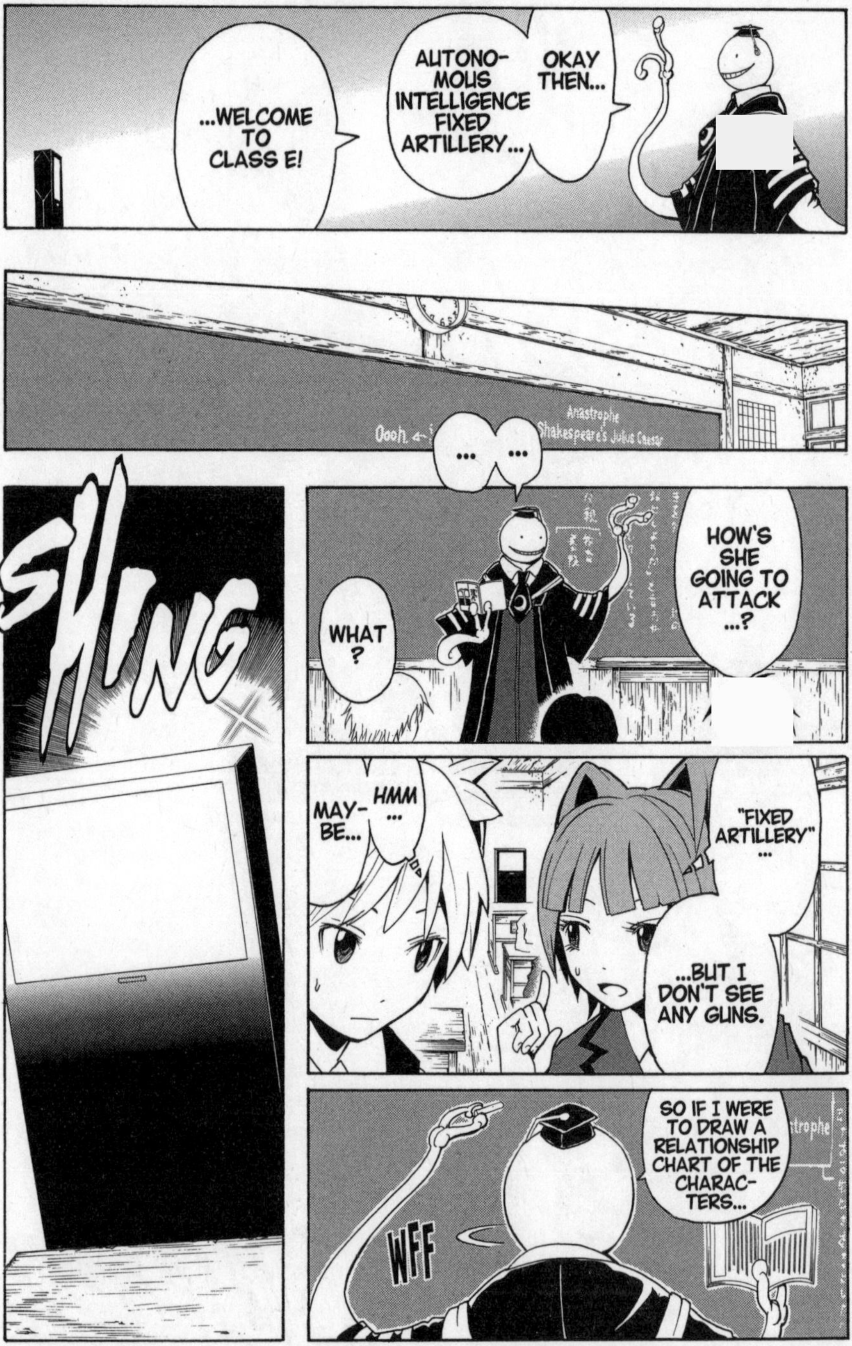
OKAY THEN...
AUTONO-MOUS INTELLIGENCE FIXED ARTILLERY...
...WELCOME TO CLASS E!
Anastrophe
Shakespeare's Julius Caesar
Oooh
... ...
HOW'S SHE GOING TO ATTACK ...?
WHAT ?
"FIXED ARTILLERY" ...
...BUT I DON'T SEE ANY GUNS.
HMM ...
MAY-BE...
SO IF I WERE TO DRAW A RELATIONSHIP CHART OF THE CHARAC-TERS...
WFF
SHING

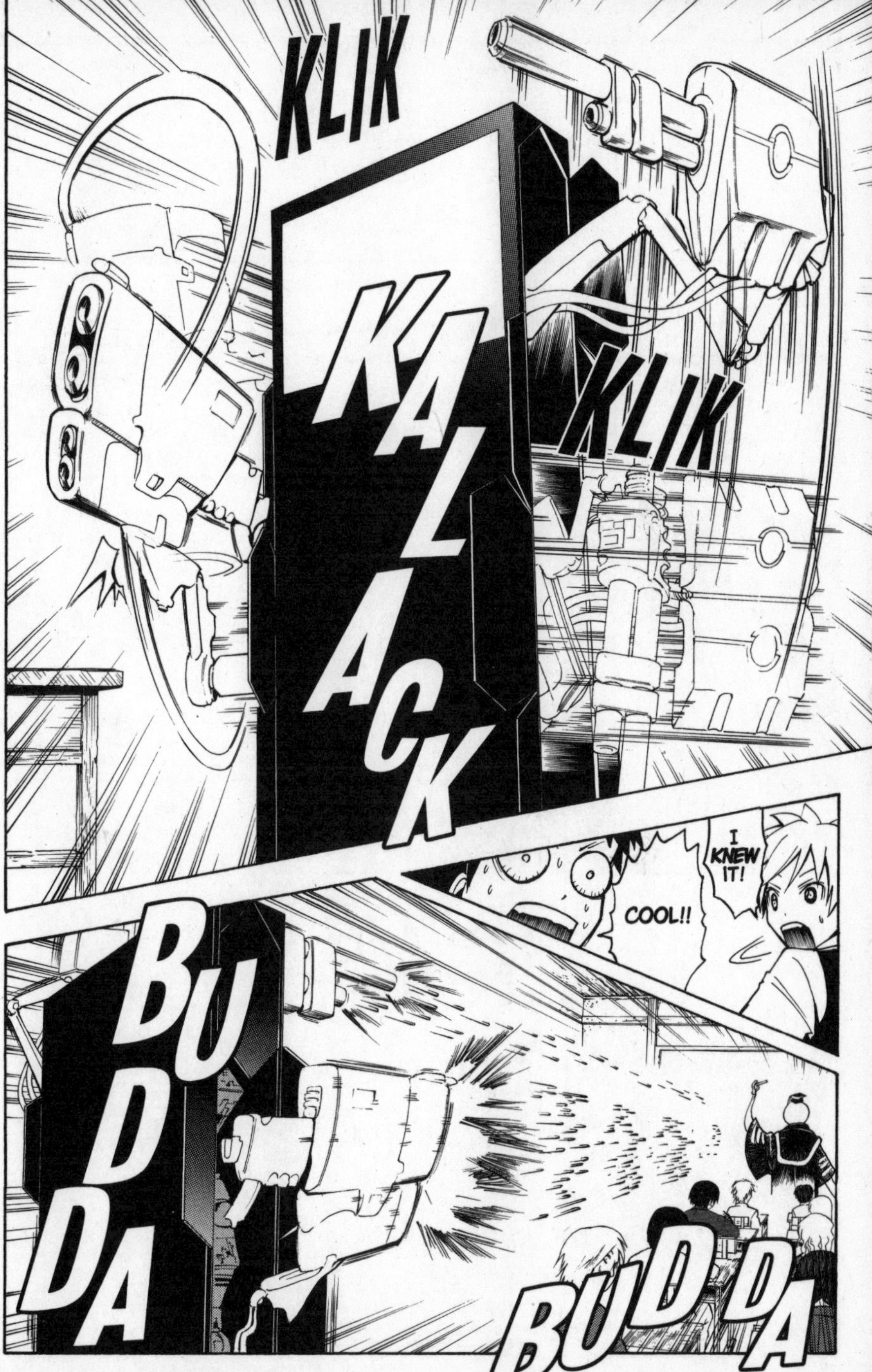
KLIK
KLIK
KALACK
I KNEW IT!
COOL!!
BUDDA
BUDDA

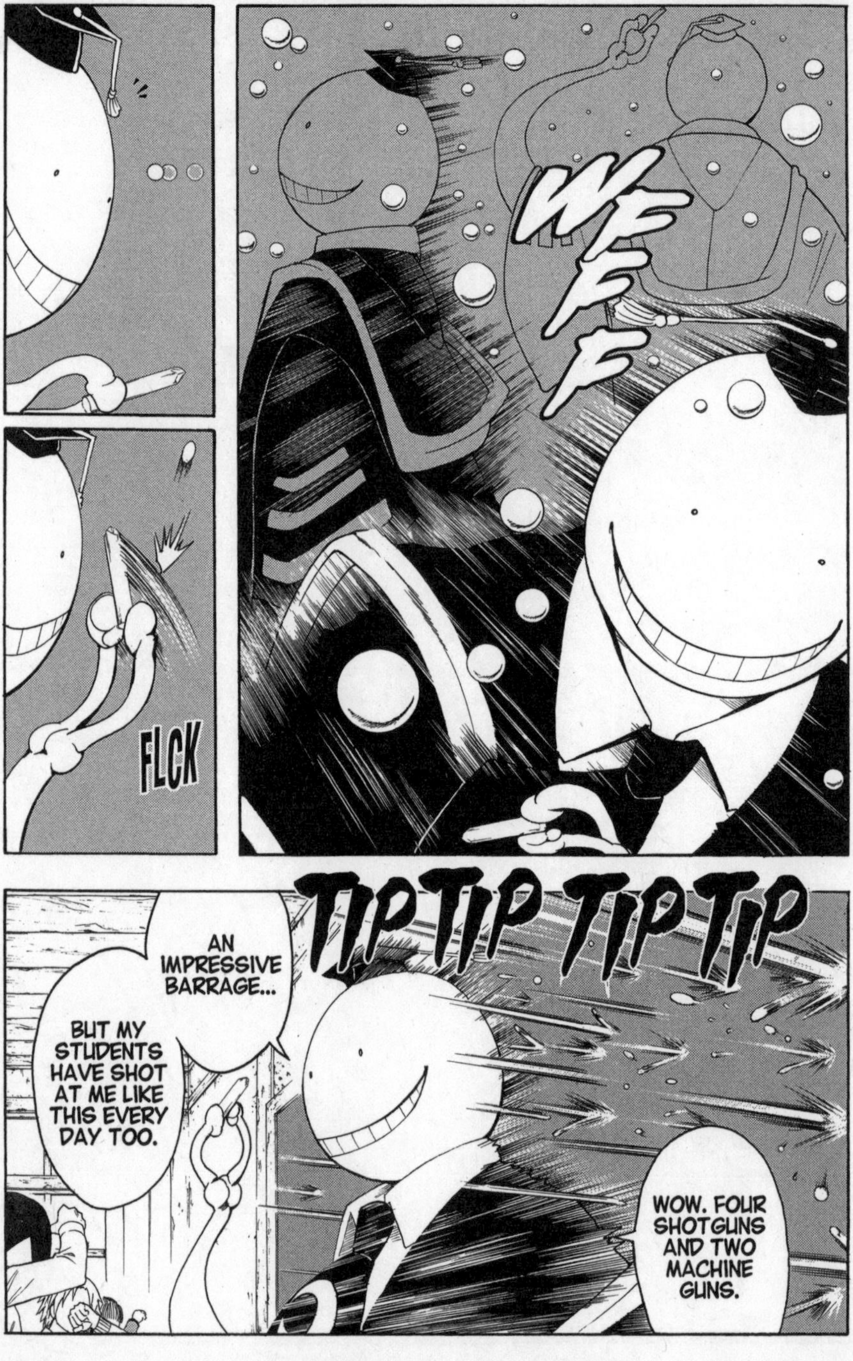
WEEE
FLCK
TIP TIP TIP TIP
WOW. FOUR SHOTGUNS AND TWO MACHINE GUNS.
AN IMPRESSIVE BARRAGE...
BUT MY STUDENTS HAVE SHOT AT ME LIKE THIS EVERY DAY TOO.

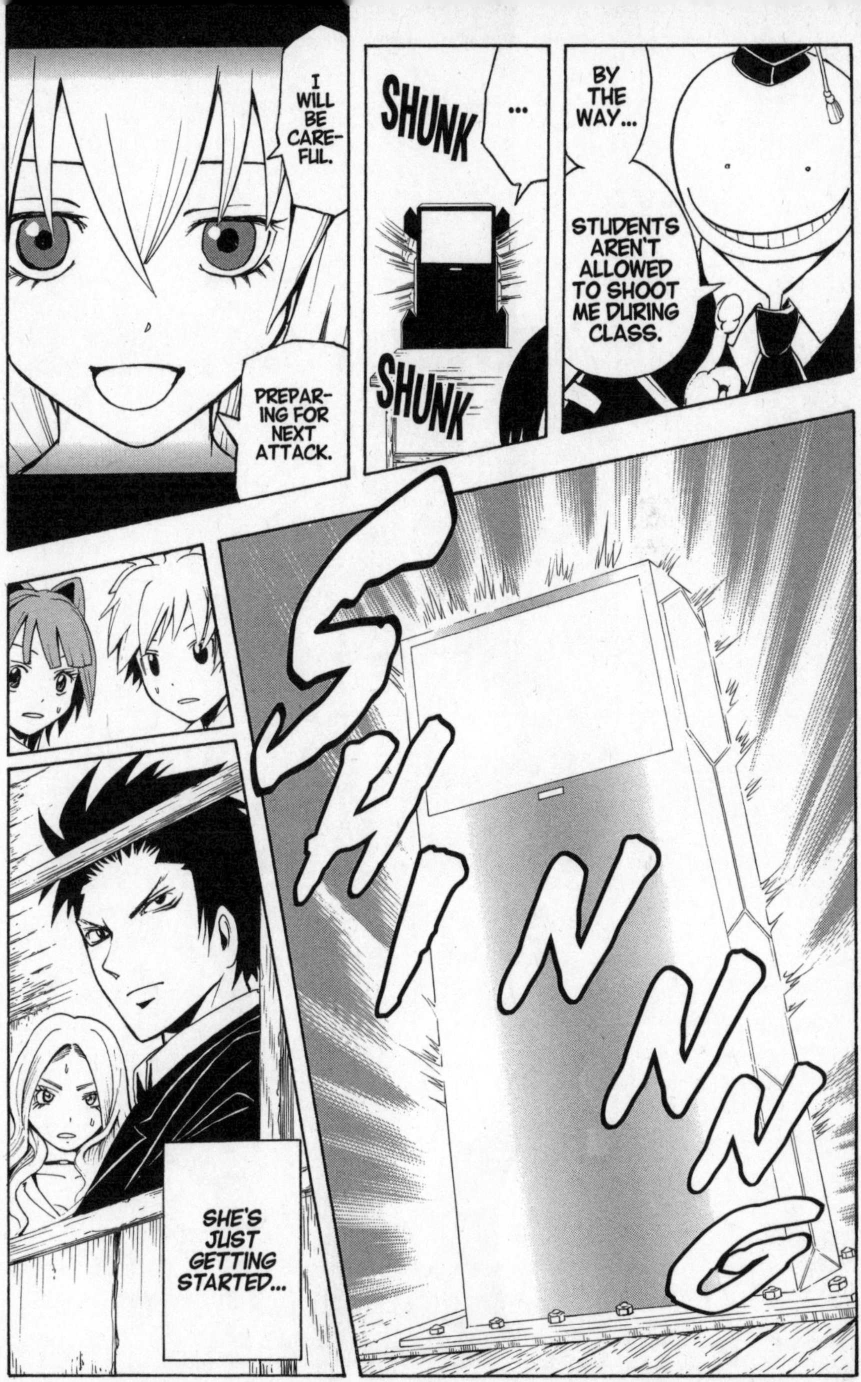
BY THE WAY...
STUDENTS AREN'T ALLOWED TO SHOOT ME DURING CLASS.
...
SHUNK
SHUNK
I WILL BE CAREFUL.
PREPARING FOR NEXT ATTACK.
SHINNNNG
SHE'S JUST GETTING STARTED...

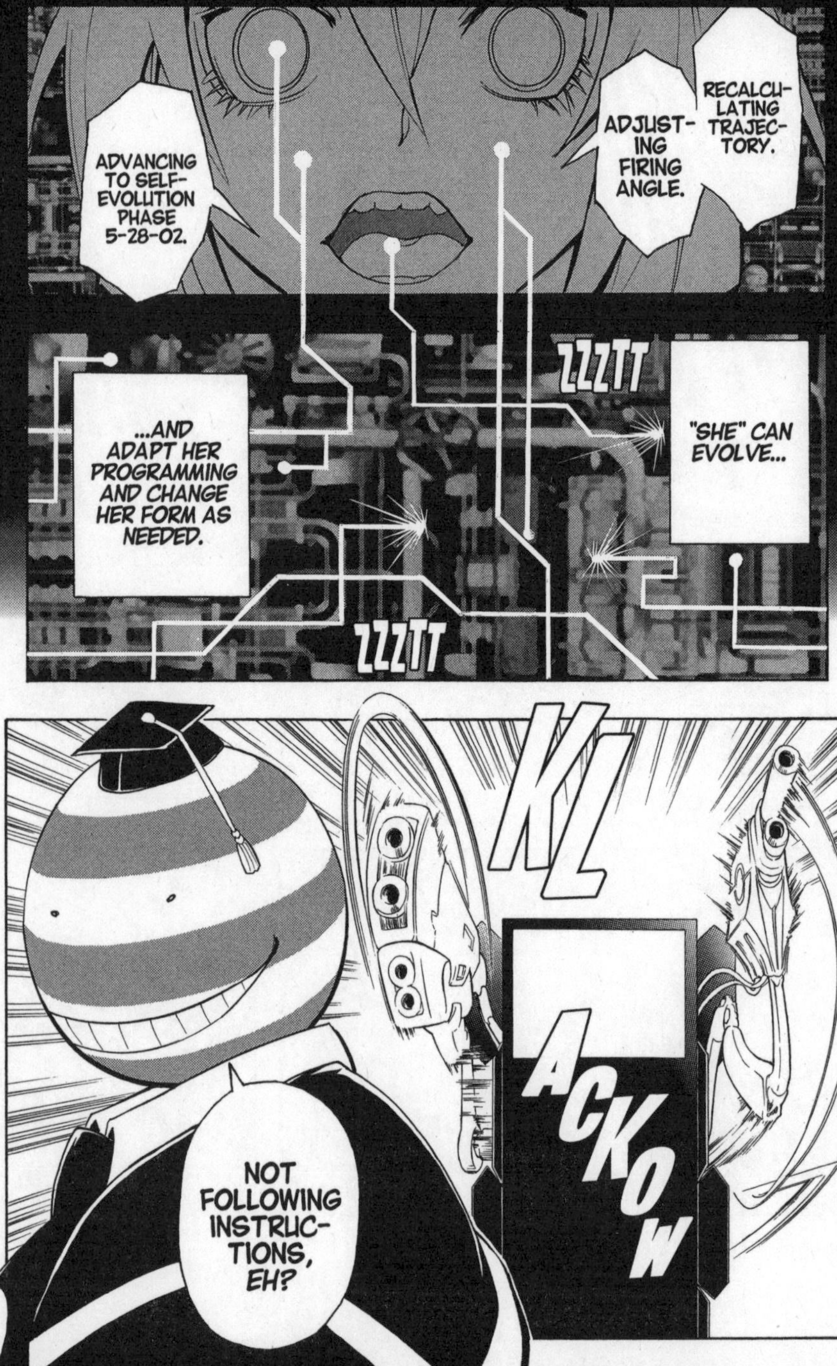
RECALCULATING TRAJECTORY.
ADJUSTING FIRING ANGLE.
ADVANCING TO SELF-EVOLUTION PHASE 5-28-02.
ZZZTT
"SHE" CAN EVOLVE...
...AND ADAPT HER PROGRAMMING AND CHANGE HER FORM AS NEEDED.
ZZZTT
KLACKOW
NOT FOLLOWING INSTRUCTIONS, EH?

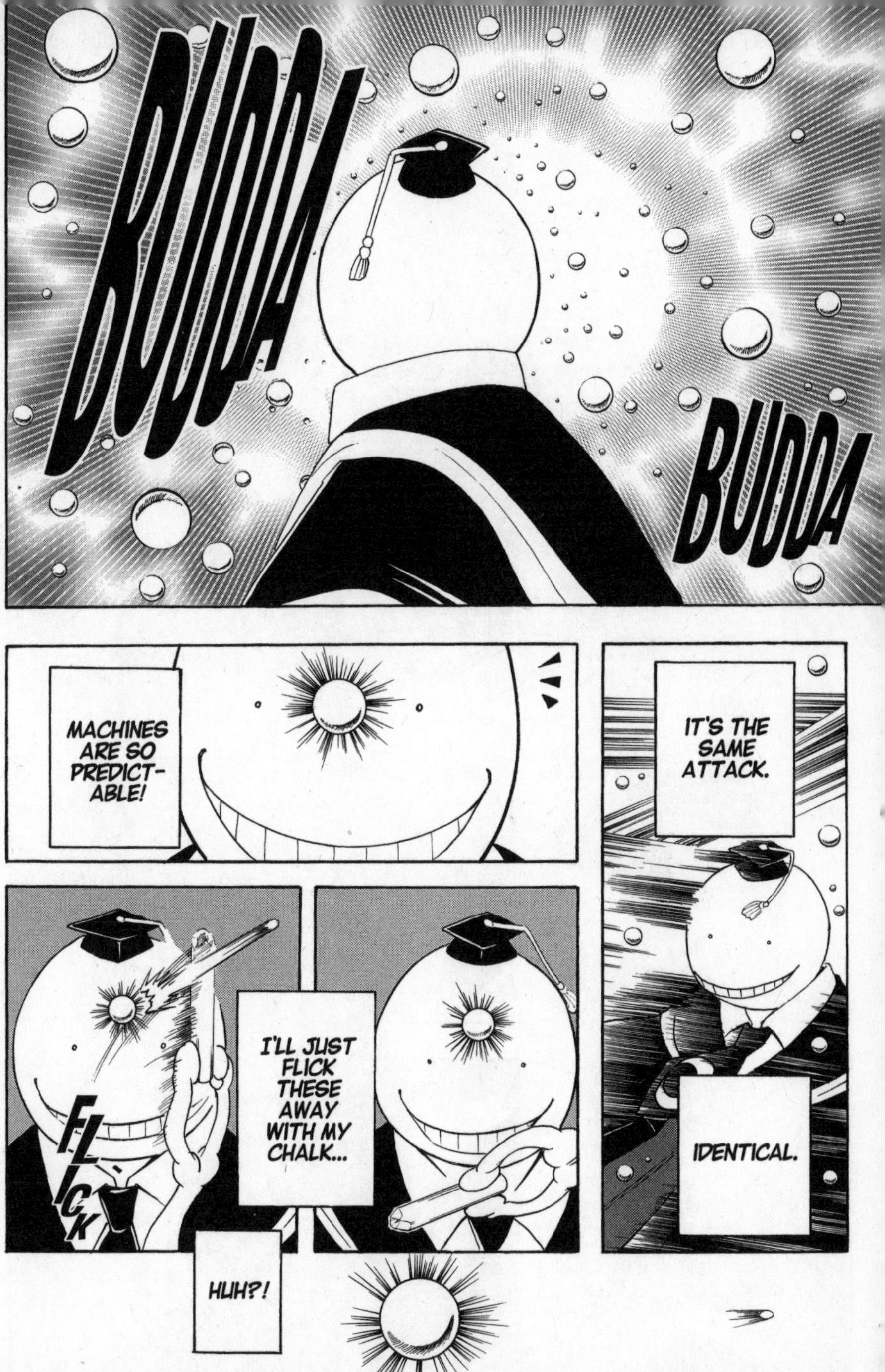
BUDDA
BUDDA
IT'S THE SAME ATTACK.
IDENTICAL.
MACHINES ARE SO PREDICT-ABLE!
I'LL JUST FLICK THESE AWAY WITH MY CHALK...
FLICK
HUH?!

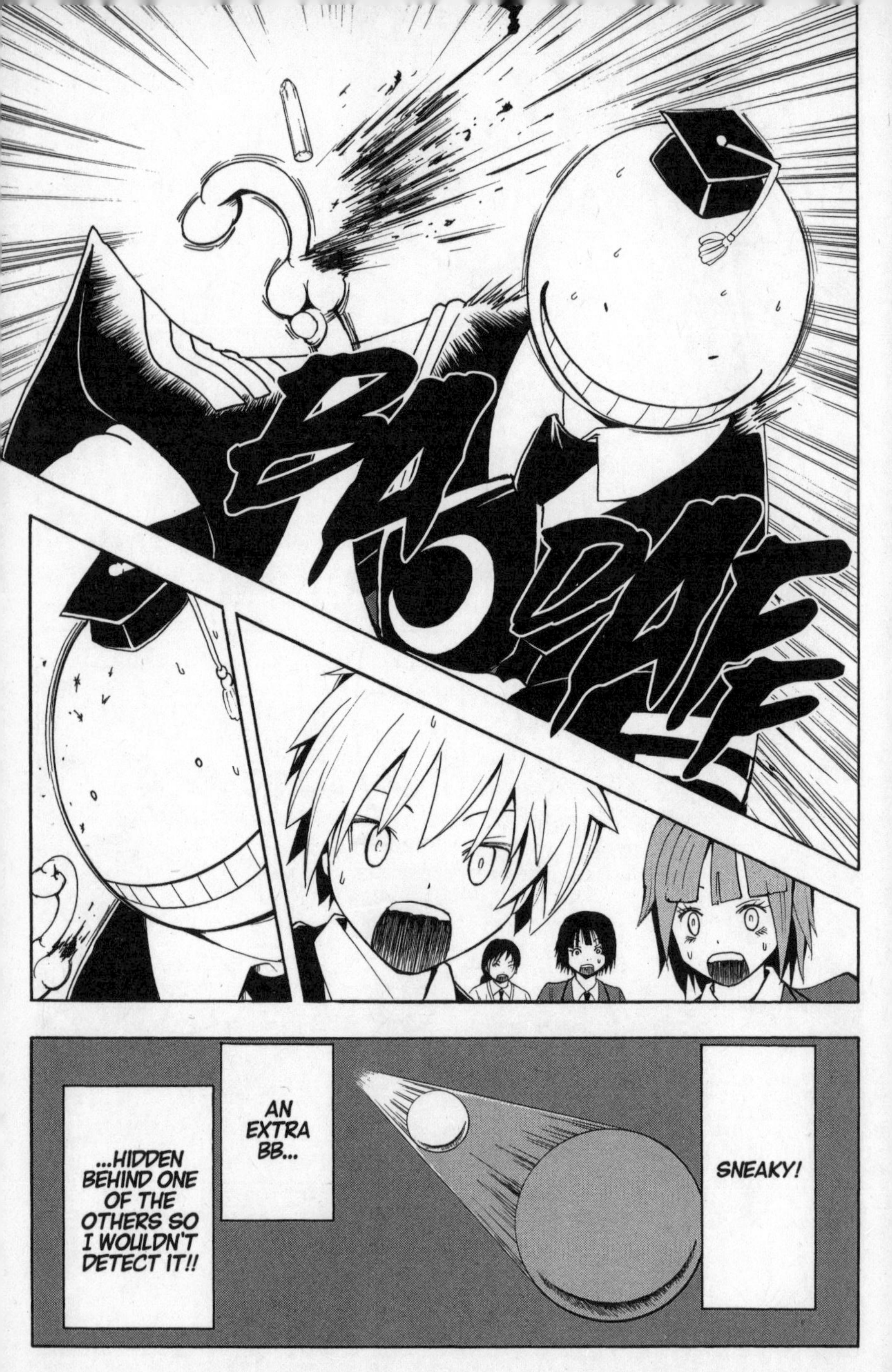
SNEAKY!
AN EXTRA BB...
...HIDDEN BEHIND ONE OF THE OTHERS SO I WOULDN'T DETECT IT!!

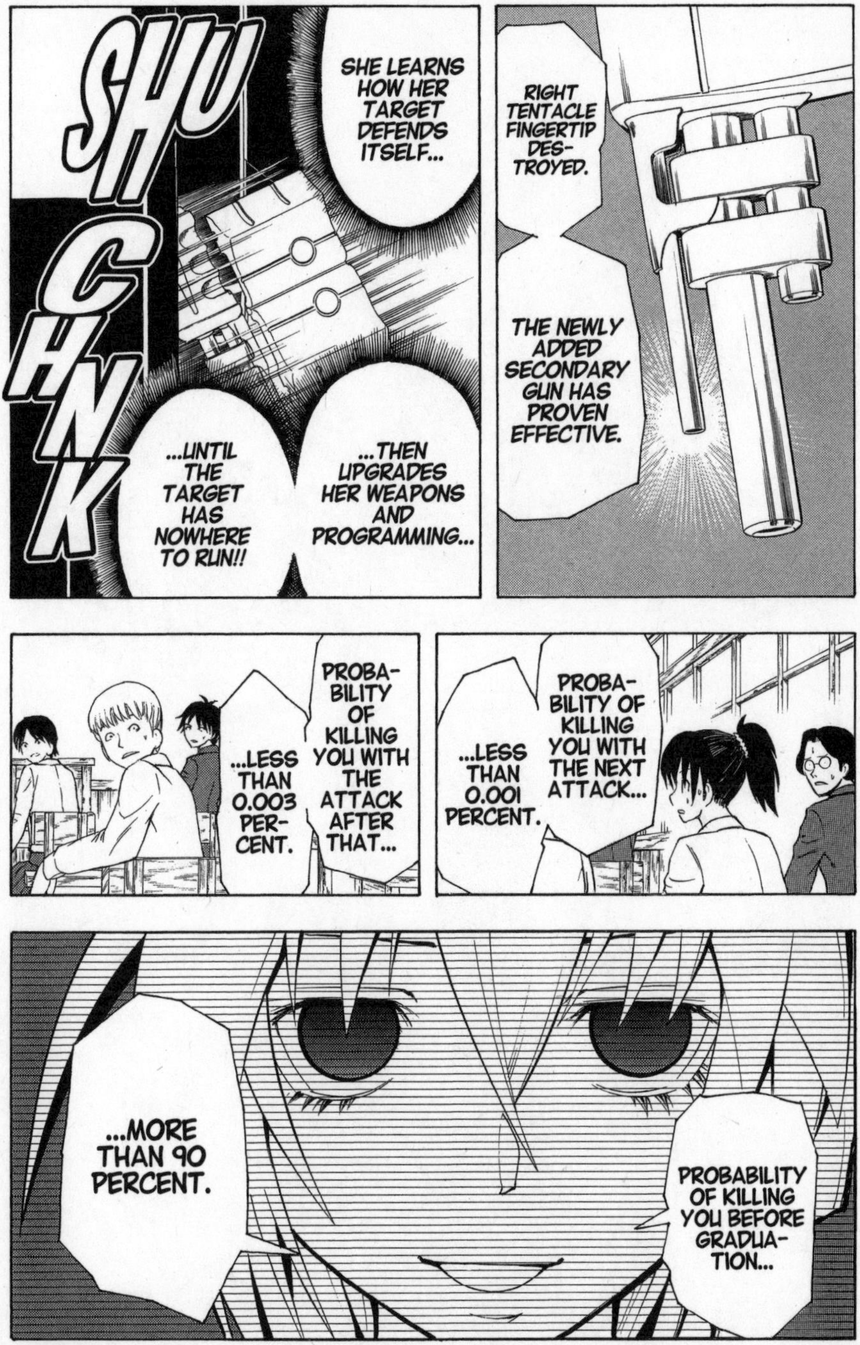
RIGHT TENTACLE FINGERTIP DESTROYED.
THE NEWLY ADDED SECONDARY GUN HAS PROVEN EFFECTIVE.
SHE LEARNS HOW HER TARGET DEFENDS ITSELF...
...THEN UPGRADES HER WEAPONS AND PROGRAMMING...
...UNTIL THE TARGET HAS NOWHERE TO RUN!!
SHU
CHNK
PROBABILITY OF KILLING YOU WITH THE NEXT ATTACK...
...LESS THAN 0.001 PERCENT.
PROBABILITY OF KILLING YOU WITH THE ATTACK AFTER THAT...
...LESS THAN 0.003 PERCENT.
PROBABILITY OF KILLING YOU BEFORE GRADUATION...
...MORE THAN 90 PERCENT.

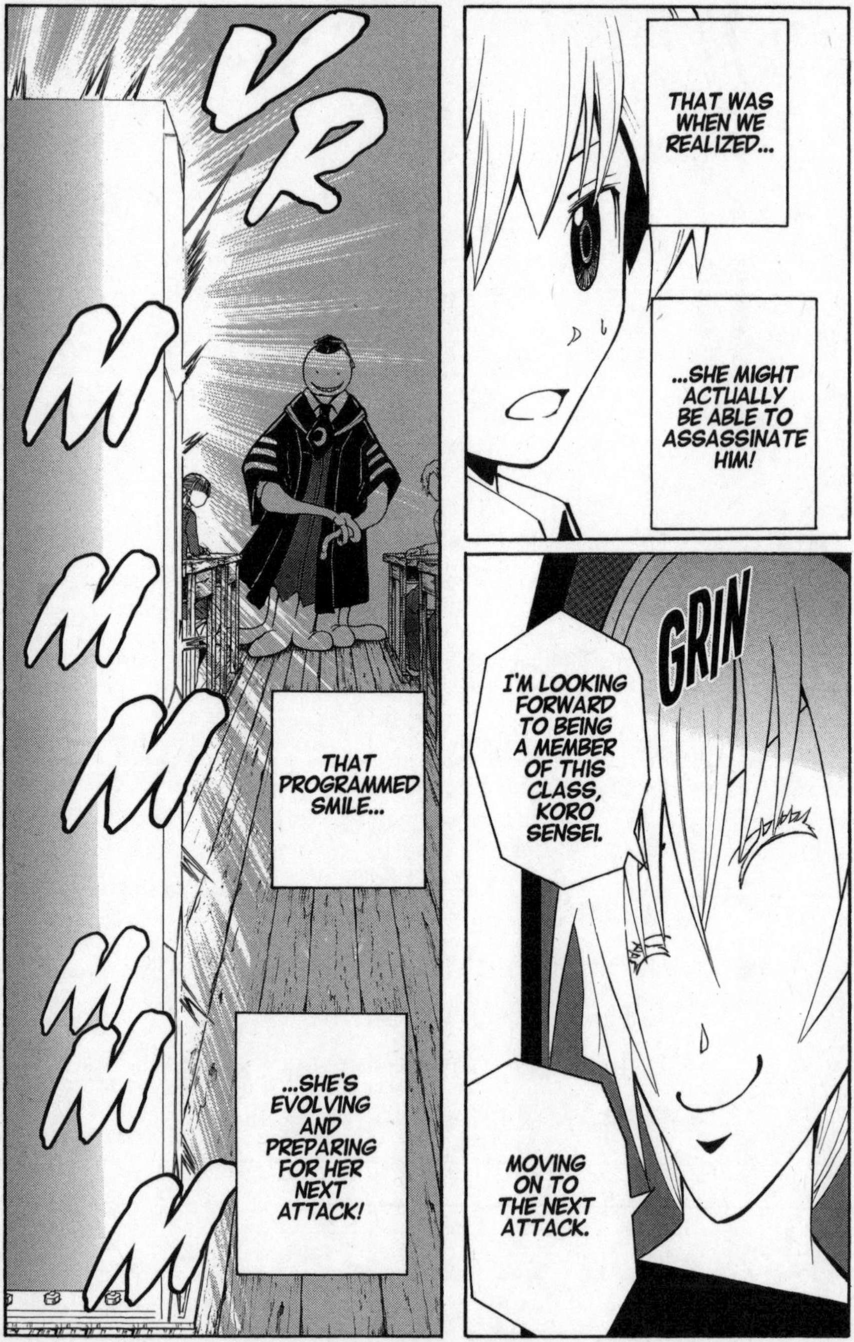
THAT WAS WHEN WE REALIZED...
...SHE MIGHT ACTUALLY BE ABLE TO ASSASSINATE HIM!
GRIN
I'M LOOKING FORWARD TO BEING A MEMBER OF THIS CLASS, KORO SENSEI.
MOVING ON TO THE NEXT ATTACK.
VRMMMMMM
THAT PROGRAMMED SMILE...
...SHE'S EVOLVING AND PREPARING FOR HER NEXT ATTACK!

E-7 KAEDE KAYANO

- ☺ BIRTHDAY: JANUARY 9
- ☺ HEIGHT: 4' 5"
- ☺ WEIGHT: 86 LBS.
- ☺ FAVORITE SUBJECT: MODERN LITERATURE
- ☺ LEAST FAVORITE SUBJECT: PHYSICAL EDUCATION
- ☺ HOBBY/SKILL: KARAOKE
- ☺ FUTURE GOAL: TO BECOME A CAPABLE ADULT
- ☺ FAVORITE FOOD: CUSTARD PUDDING
- ☺ PLANS FOR THE 10 BILLION: CURVES, DAMNIT, CURVES!

CLASS 21 IT'S TIME FOR AN UPGRADE

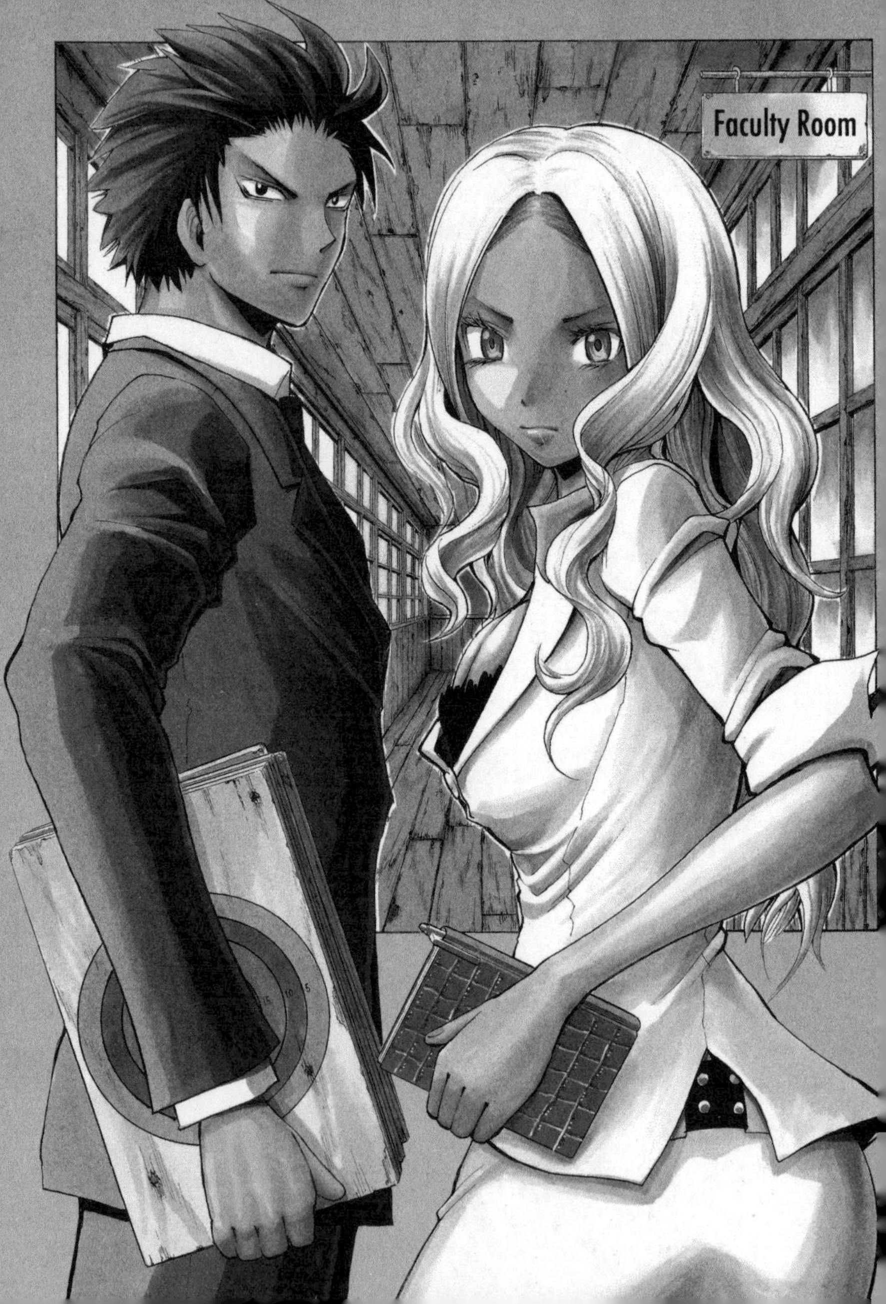
Faculty Room

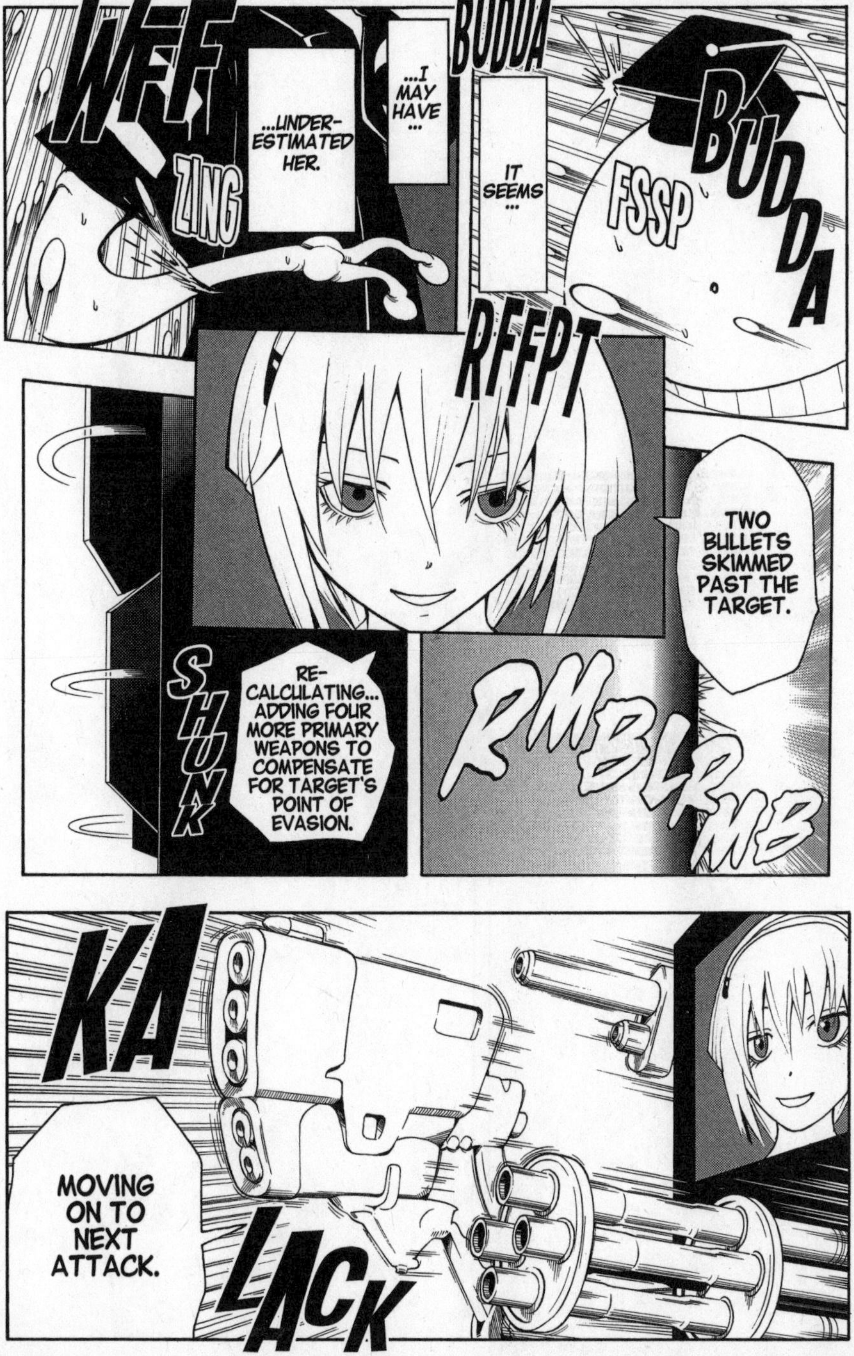
BUDDA
IT SEEMS...
BUDDA
FSSP
...I MAY HAVE...
...UNDER-ESTIMATED HER.
WFF
ZING
RFFPT
TWO BULLETS SKIMMED PAST THE TARGET.
RMBLRMB
SHUNK
RE-CALCULATING... ADDING FOUR MORE PRIMARY WEAPONS TO COMPENSATE FOR TARGET'S POINT OF EVASION.
KA
LACK
MOVING ON TO NEXT ATTACK.

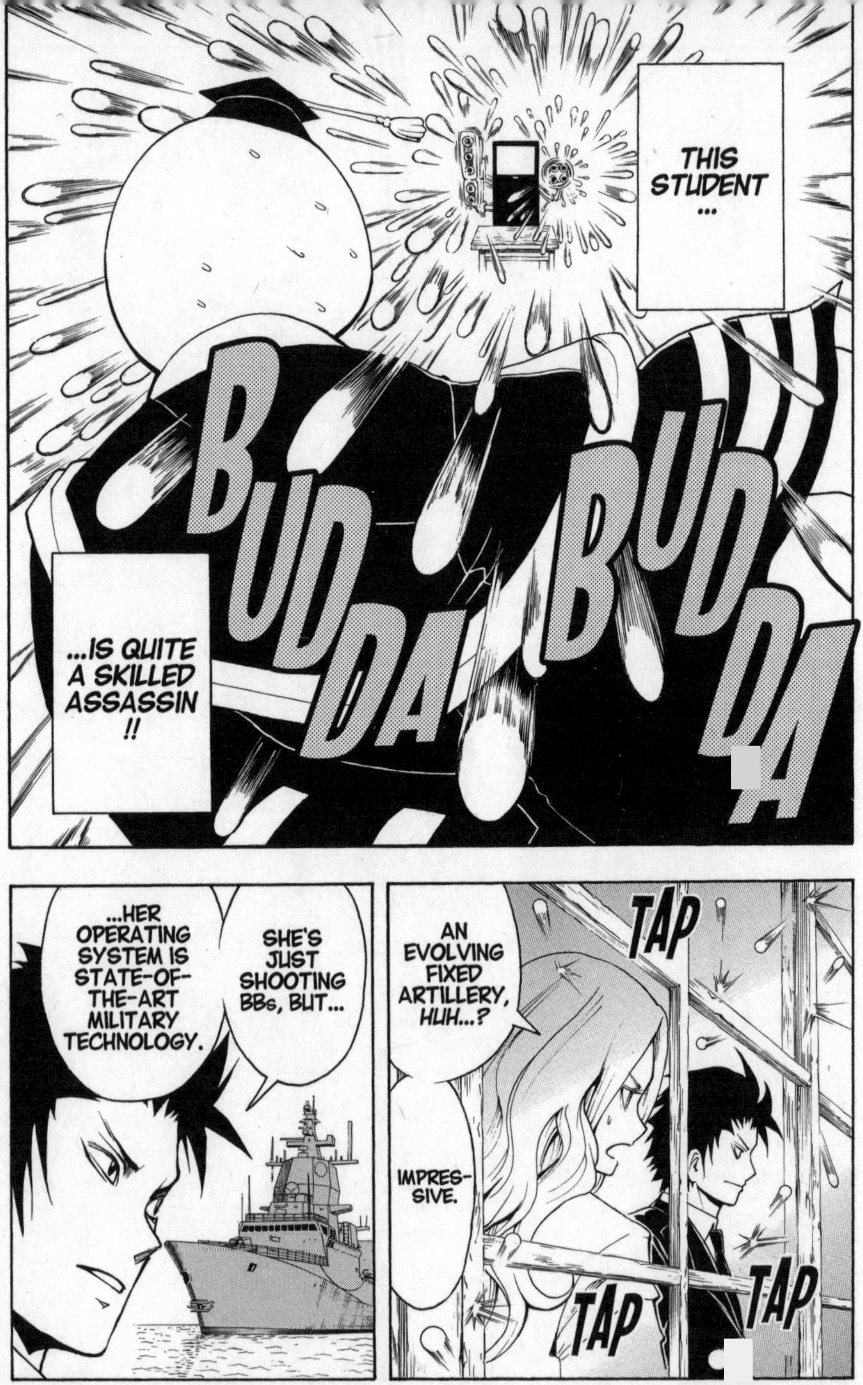
THIS STUDENT ...
BUDDA
BUDDA
...IS QUITE A SKILLED ASSASSIN !!
TAP
AN EVOLVING FIXED ARTILLERY, HUH...?
IMPRES-SIVE.
TAP
TAP
SHE'S JUST SHOOTING BBs, BUT...
...HER OPERATING SYSTEM IS STATE-OF-THE-ART MILITARY TECHNOLOGY.

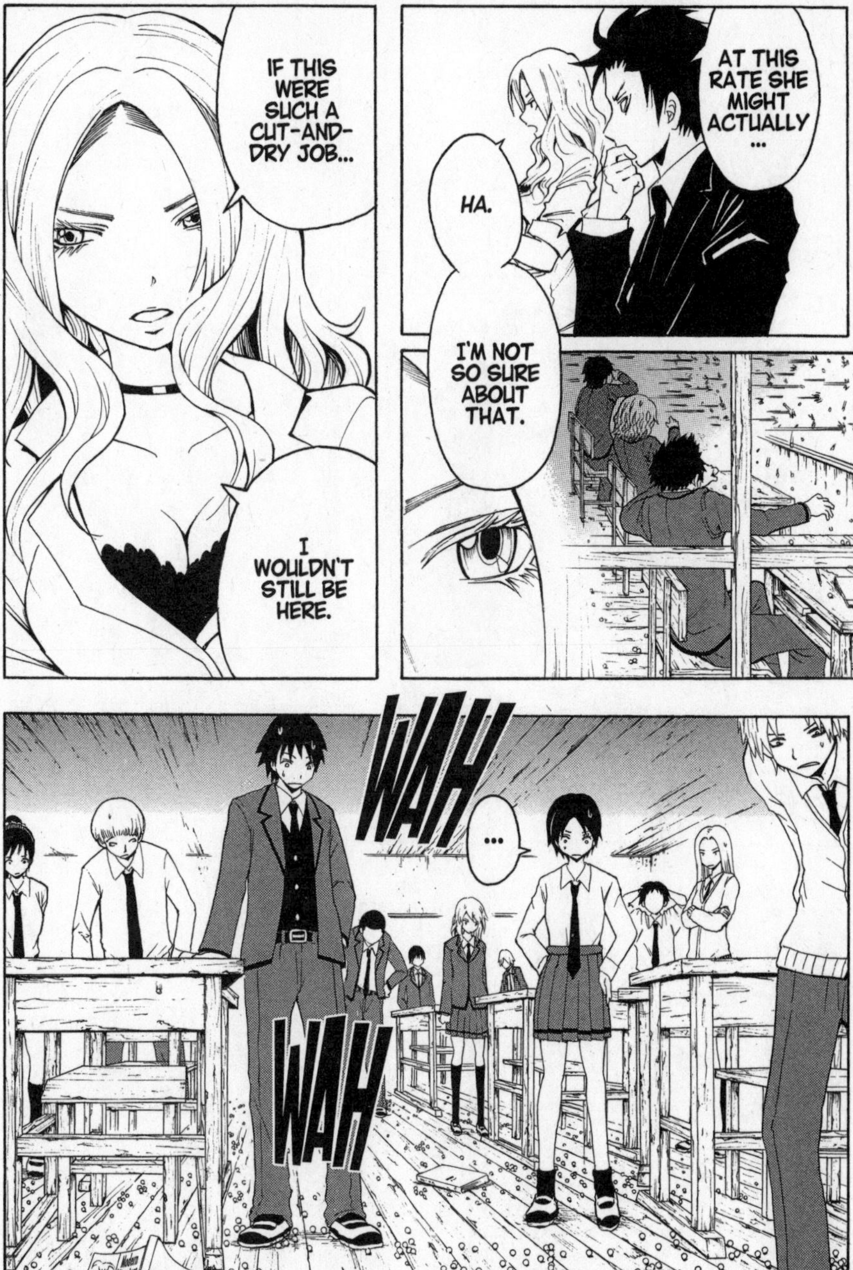
AT THIS RATE SHE MIGHT ACTUALLY ...
HA.
I'M NOT SO SURE ABOUT THAT.
IF THIS WERE SUCH A CUT-AND-DRY JOB...
I WOULDN'T STILL BE HERE.
WAH
...
WAH
Modern Literature

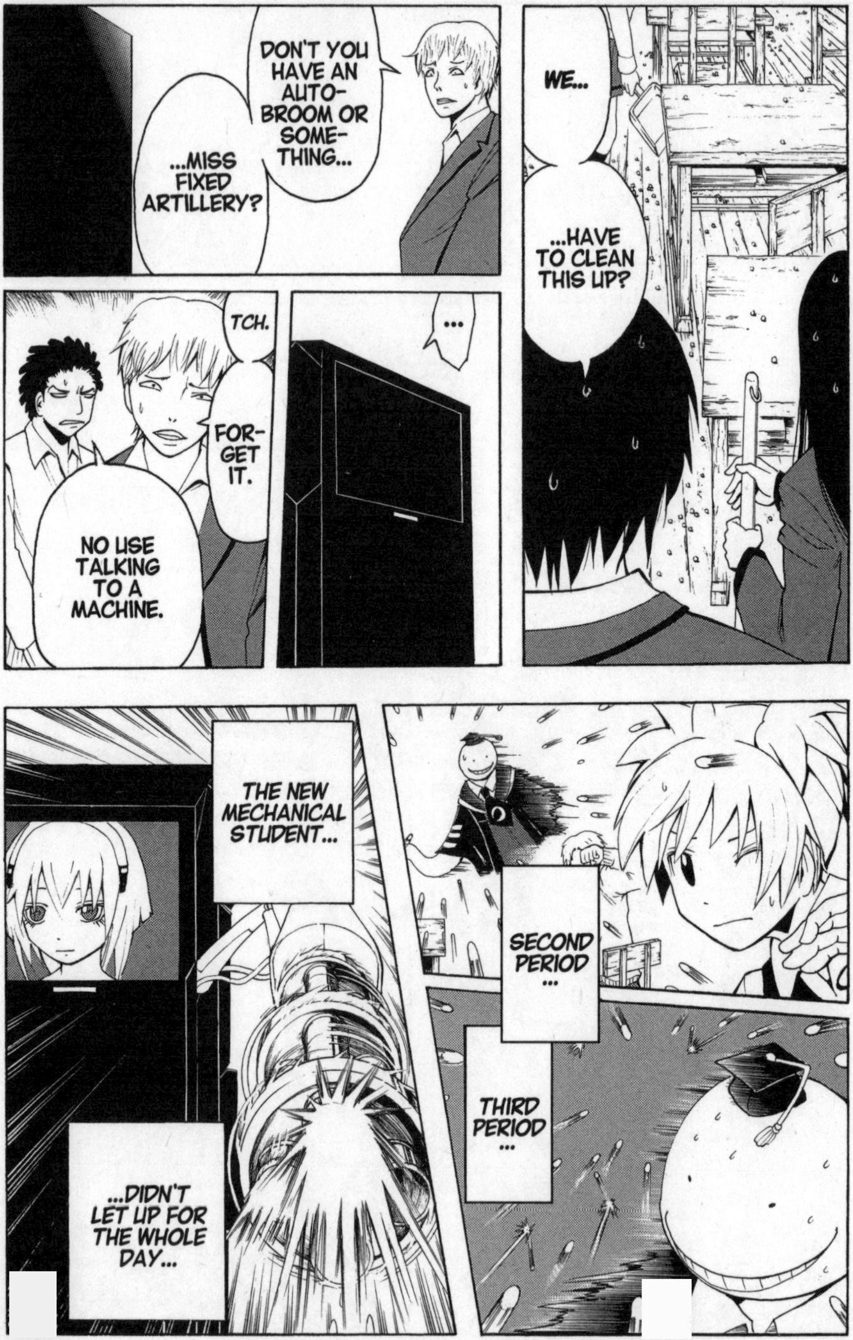
WE...
...HAVE TO CLEAN THIS UP?
DON'T YOU HAVE AN AUTO-BROOM OR SOME-THING...
...MISS FIXED ARTILLERY?
...
TCH.
FOR-GET IT.
NO USE TALKING TO A MACHINE.
SECOND PERIOD...
THIRD PERIOD...
THE NEW MECHANICAL STUDENT...
...DIDN'T LET UP FOR THE WHOLE DAY...

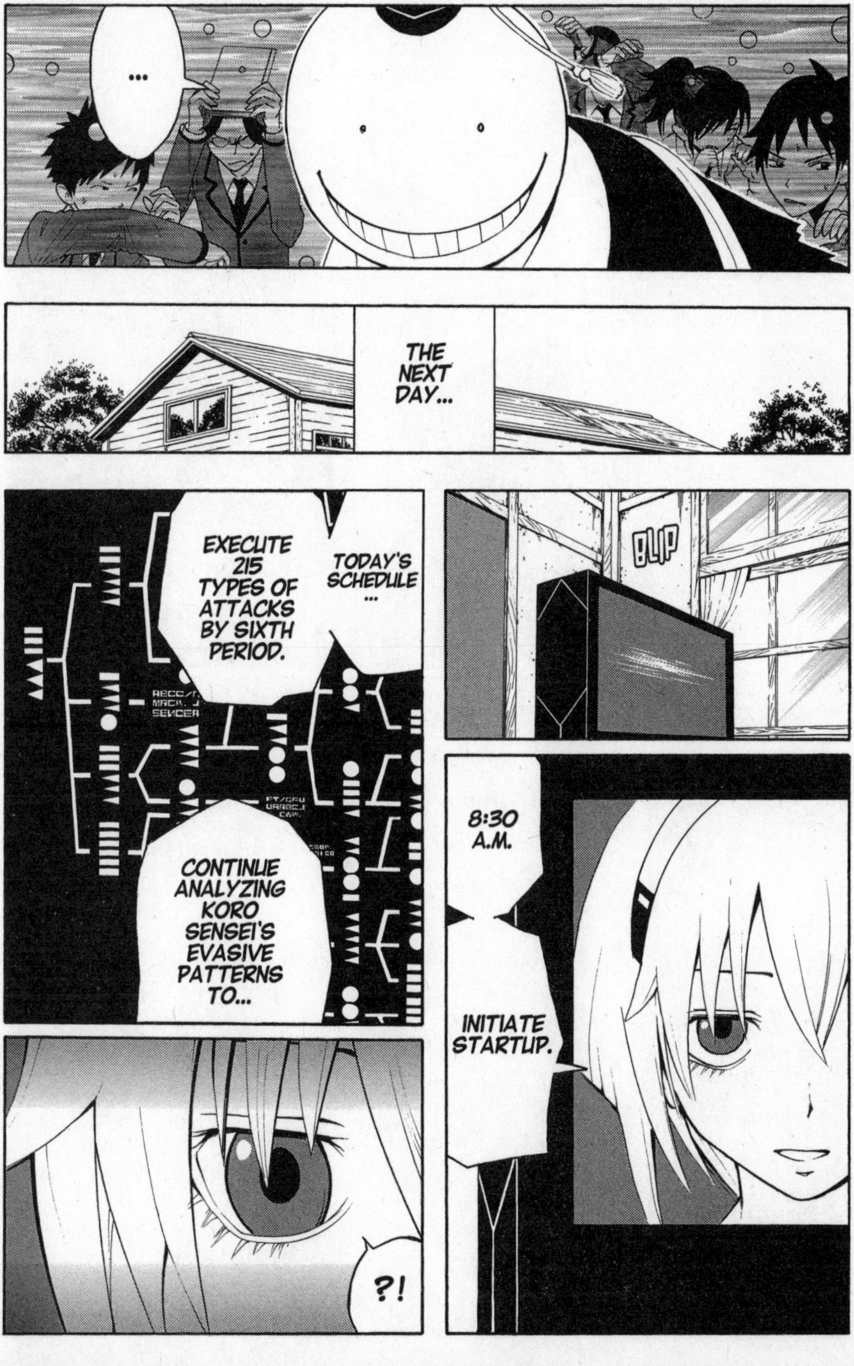
...
THE NEXT DAY...
BLIP
8:30 A.M.
INITIATE STARTUP.
TODAY'S SCHEDULE ...
EXECUTE 215 TYPES OF ATTACKS BY SIXTH PERIOD.
CONTINUE ANALYZING KORO SENSEI'S EVASIVE PATTERNS TO...
?!

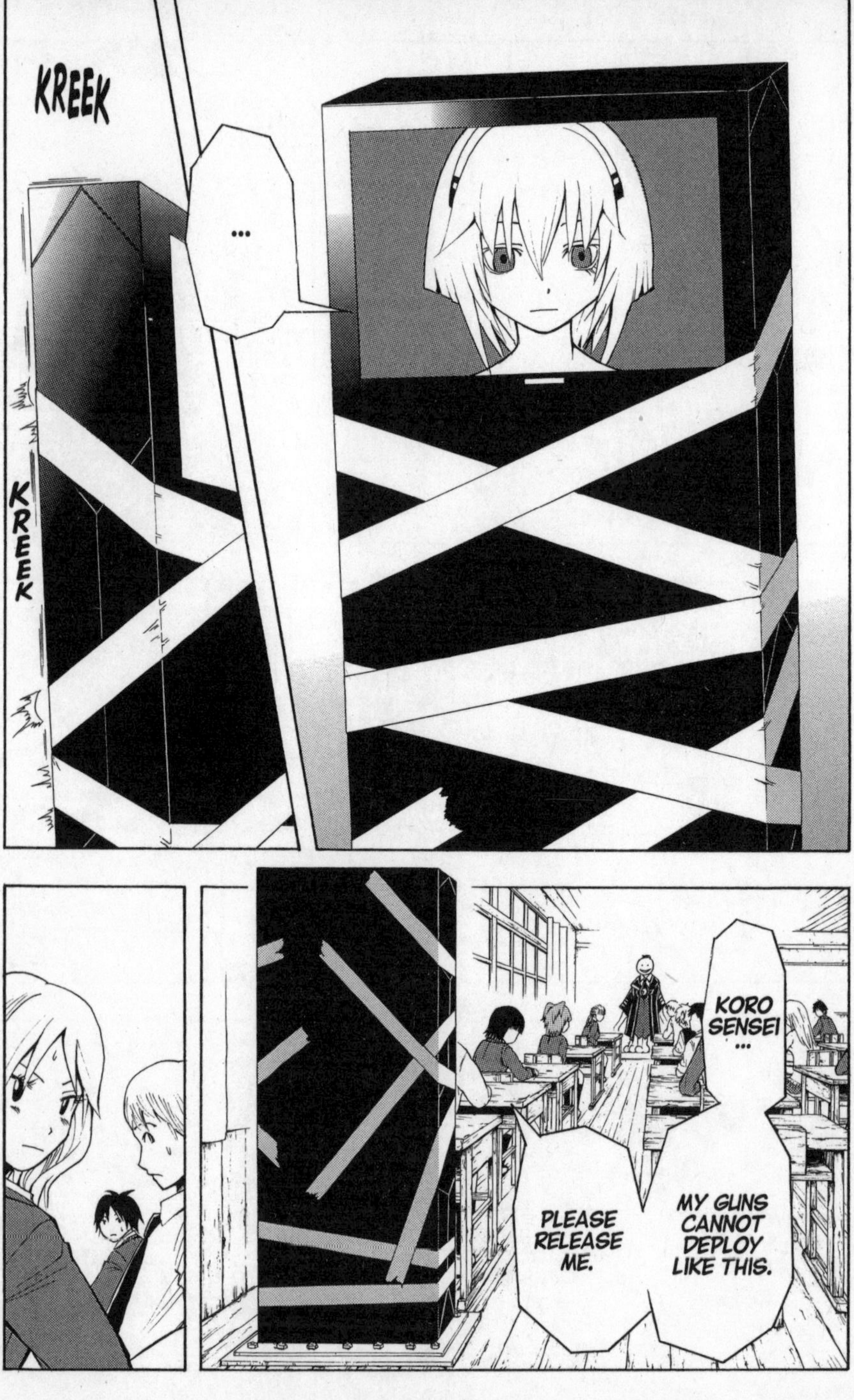
...
KREEK
KREEK
KORO SENSEI ...
MY GUNS CANNOT DEPLOY LIKE THIS.
PLEASE RELEASE ME.

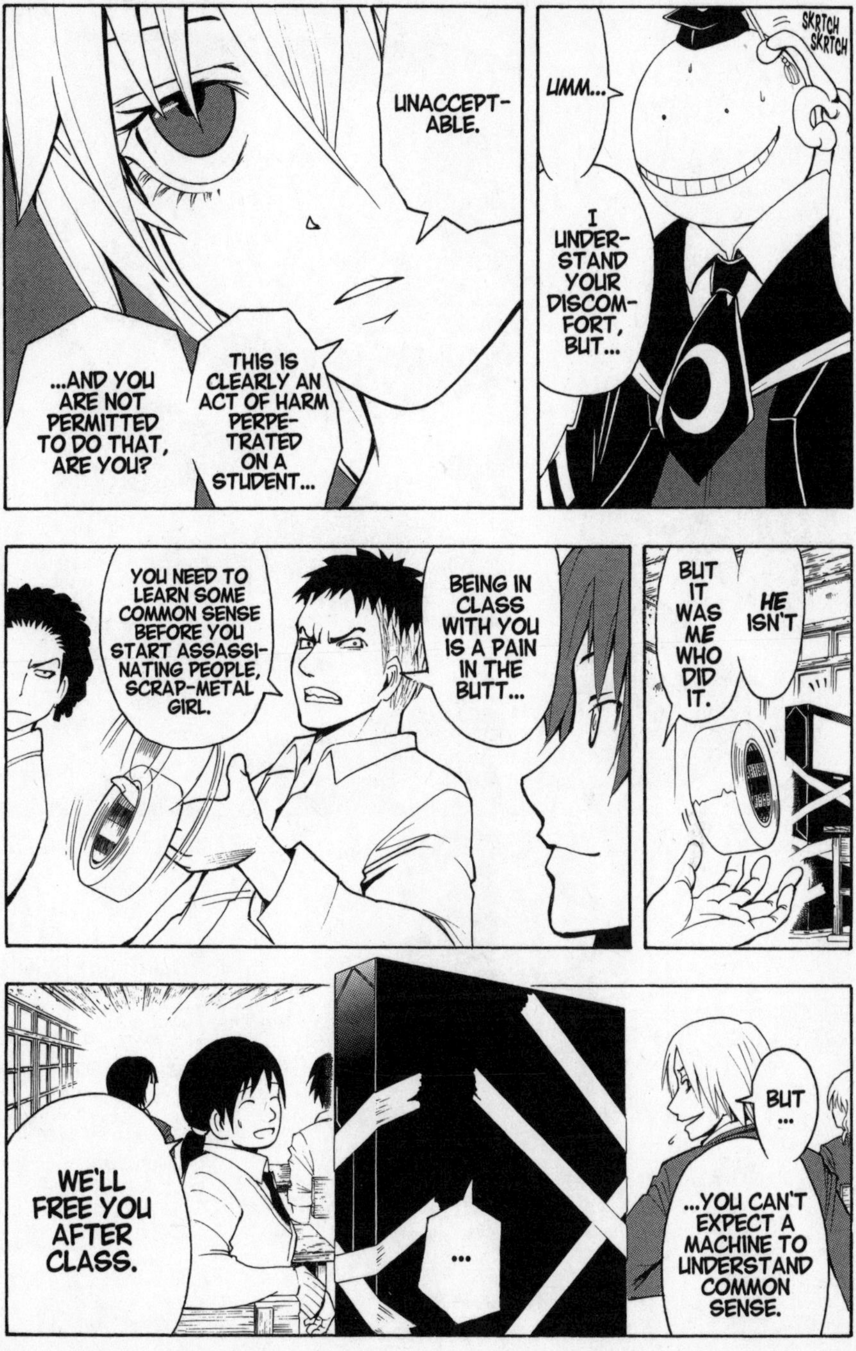
SKRTCH SKRTCH
UMM...
I UNDERSTAND YOUR DISCOMFORT, BUT...
UNACCEPTABLE.
THIS IS CLEARLY AN ACT OF HARM PERPETRATED ON A STUDENT...
...AND YOU ARE NOT PERMITTED TO DO THAT, ARE YOU?
HE ISN'T
BUT IT WAS ME WHO DID IT.
BEING IN CLASS WITH YOU IS A PAIN IN THE BUTT...
YOU NEED TO LEARN SOME COMMON SENSE BEFORE YOU START ASSASSINATING PEOPLE, SCRAP-METAL GIRL.
BUT...
...YOU CAN'T EXPECT A MACHINE TO UNDERSTAND COMMON SENSE.
...
WE'LL FREE YOU AFTER CLASS.

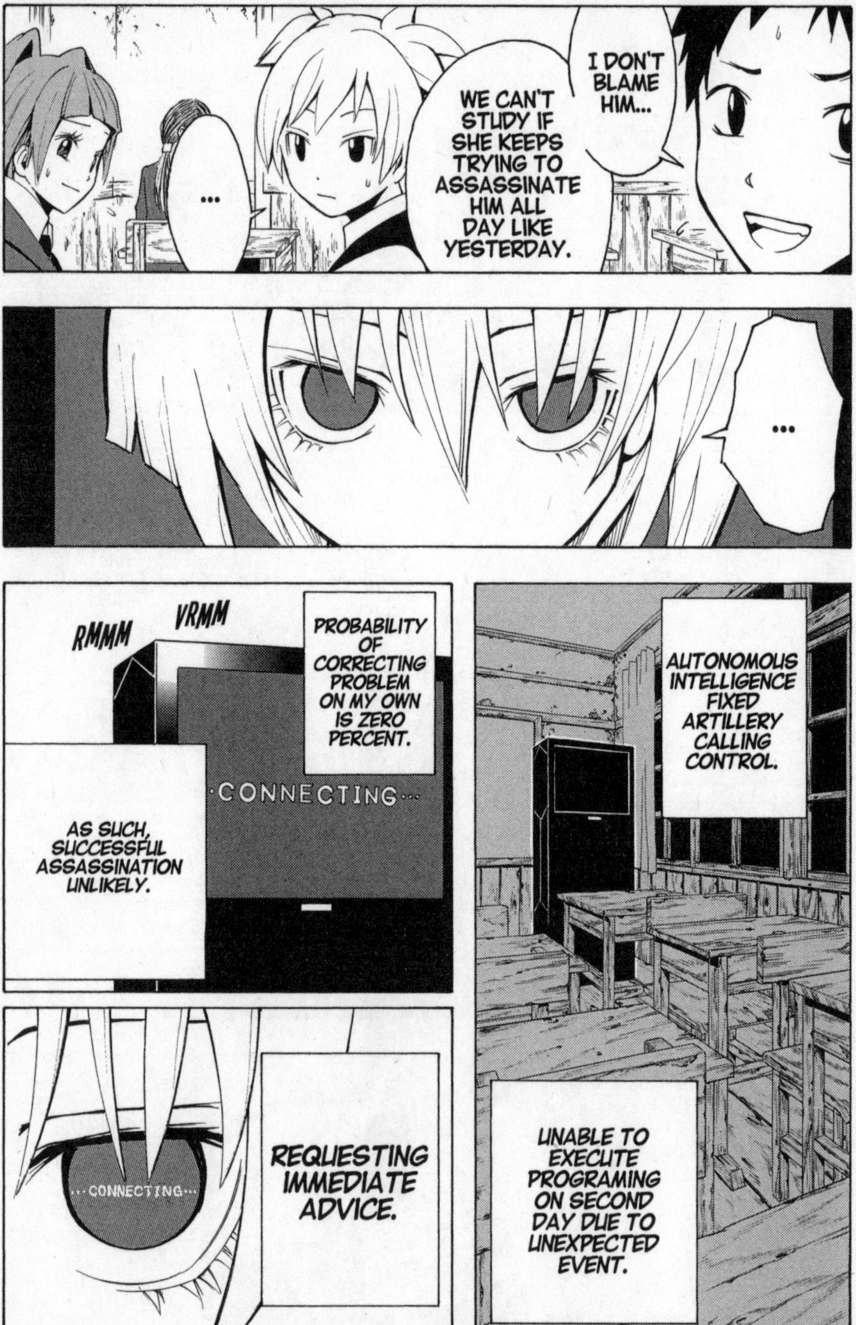
I DON'T BLAME HIM...
WE CAN'T STUDY IF SHE KEEPS TRYING TO ASSASSINATE HIM ALL DAY LIKE YESTERDAY.
...
...
AUTONOMOUS INTELLIGENCE FIXED ARTILLERY CALLING CONTROL.
UNABLE TO EXECUTE PROGRAMING ON SECOND DAY DUE TO UNEXPECTED EVENT.
PROBABILITY OF CORRECTING PROBLEM ON MY OWN IS ZERO PERCENT.
VRMM
RMMM
·CONNECTING···
AS SUCH, SUCCESSFUL ASSASSINATION UNLIKELY.
REQUESTING IMMEDIATE ADVICE.
···CONNECTING···

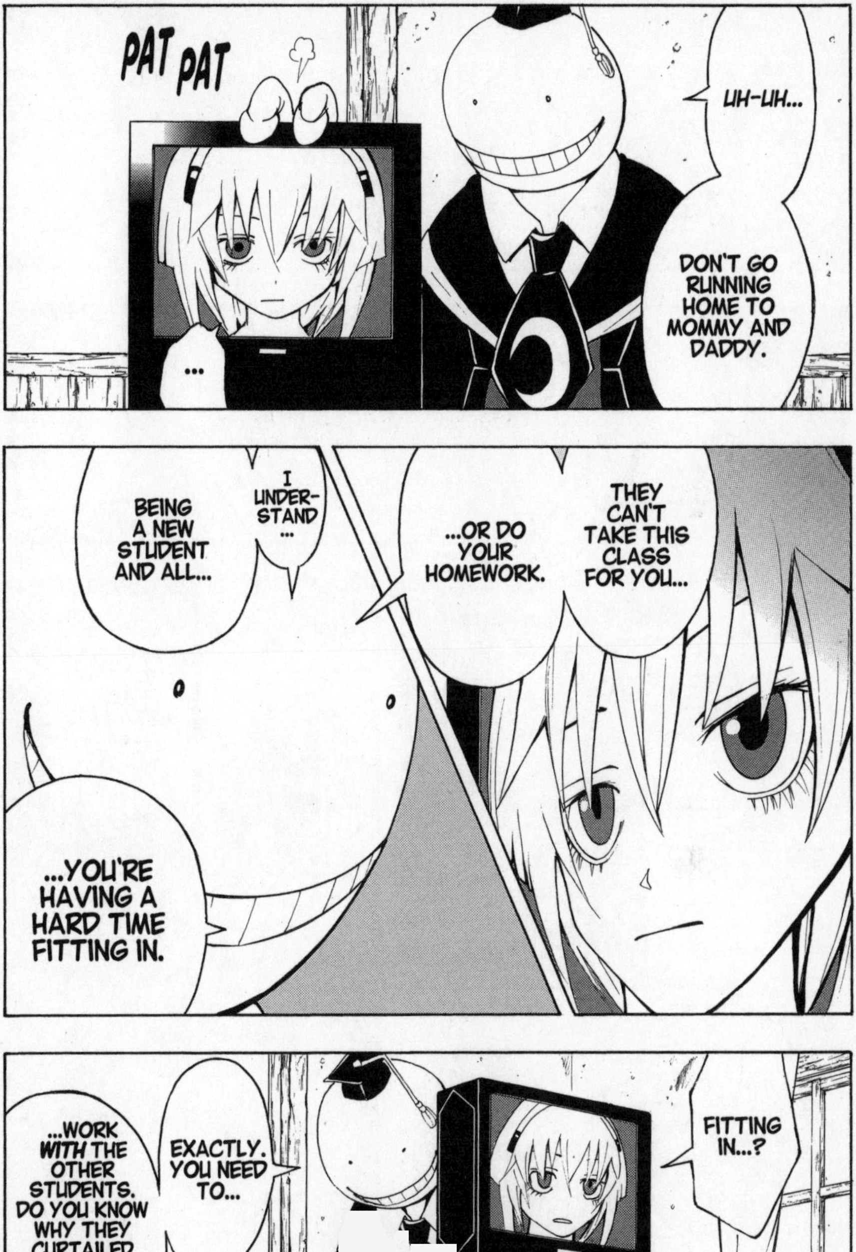
UH-UH...
DON'T GO RUNNING HOME TO MOMMY AND DADDY.
PAT PAT
...
THEY CAN'T TAKE THIS CLASS FOR YOU...
...OR DO YOUR HOMEWORK.
I UNDERSTAND...
BEING A NEW STUDENT AND ALL...
...YOU'RE HAVING A HARD TIME FITTING IN.
FITTING IN...?
EXACTLY. YOU NEED TO...
...WORK *WITH* THE OTHER STUDENTS. DO YOU KNOW WHY THEY CURTAILED YOUR ASSASSINATION ATTEMPTS?

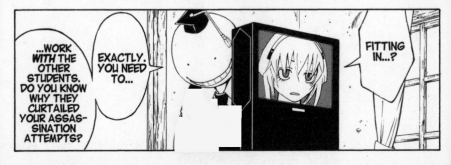

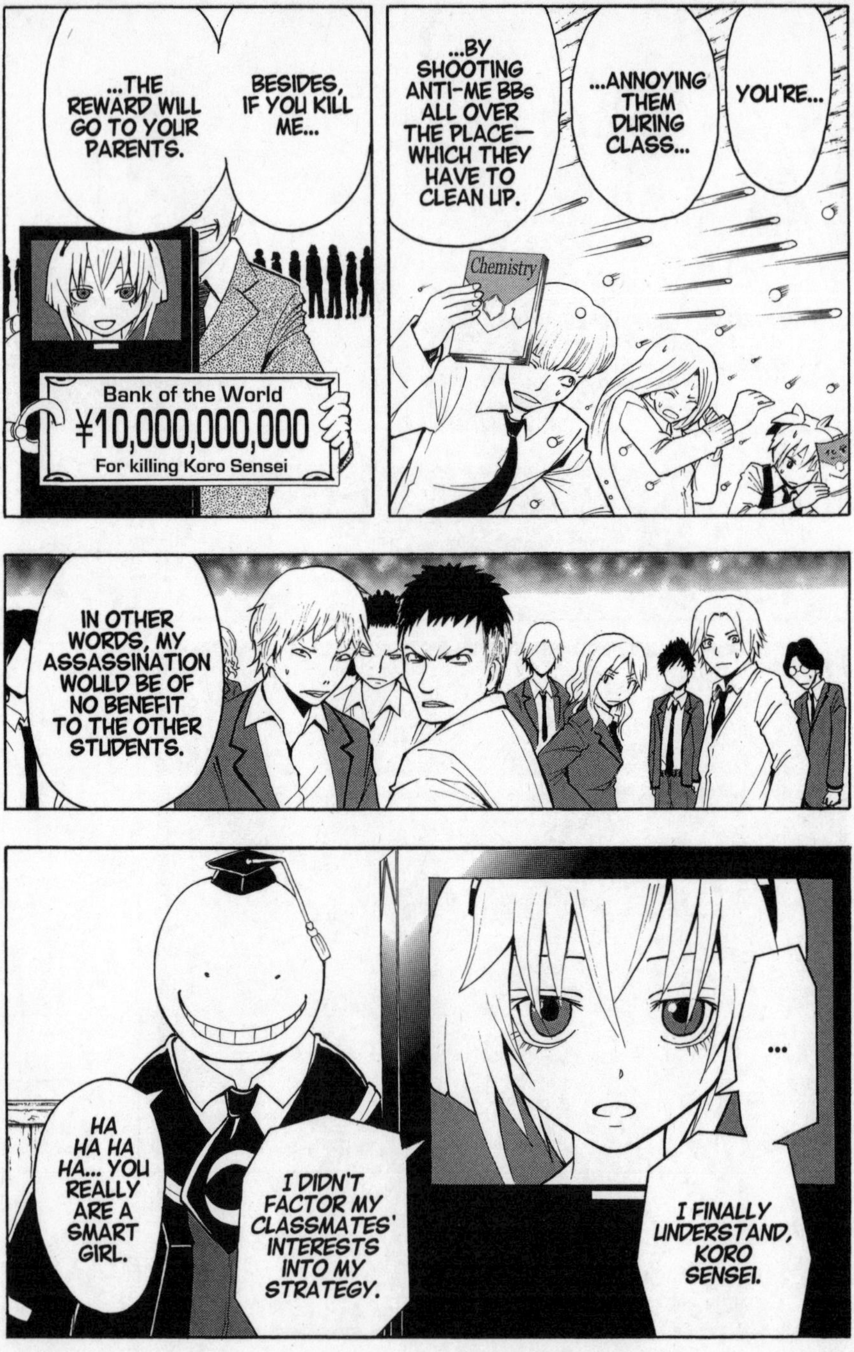
YOU'RE...
...ANNOYING THEM DURING CLASS...
...BY SHOOTING ANTI-ME BBs ALL OVER THE PLACE—WHICH THEY HAVE TO CLEAN UP.
Chemistry
BESIDES, IF YOU KILL ME...
...THE REWARD WILL GO TO YOUR PARENTS.
Bank of the World
¥10,000,000,000
For killing Koro Sensei
IN OTHER WORDS, MY ASSASSINATION WOULD BE OF NO BENEFIT TO THE OTHER STUDENTS.
...
I FINALLY UNDERSTAND, KORO SENSEI.
I DIDN'T FACTOR MY CLASSMATES' INTERESTS INTO MY STRATEGY.
HA HA HA HA... YOU REALLY ARE A SMART GIRL.

...?

BY THE WAY...

I MADE SOMETHING FOR YOU.

APPLICATION SOFTWARE UPGRADE— WITH EXPANSION MEMORIES.

NO VIRUSES. NO TRICKS.

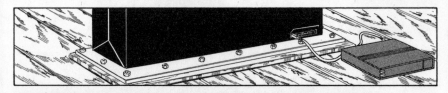

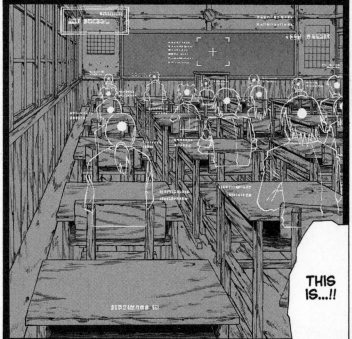

...

!!

THIS IS...!!

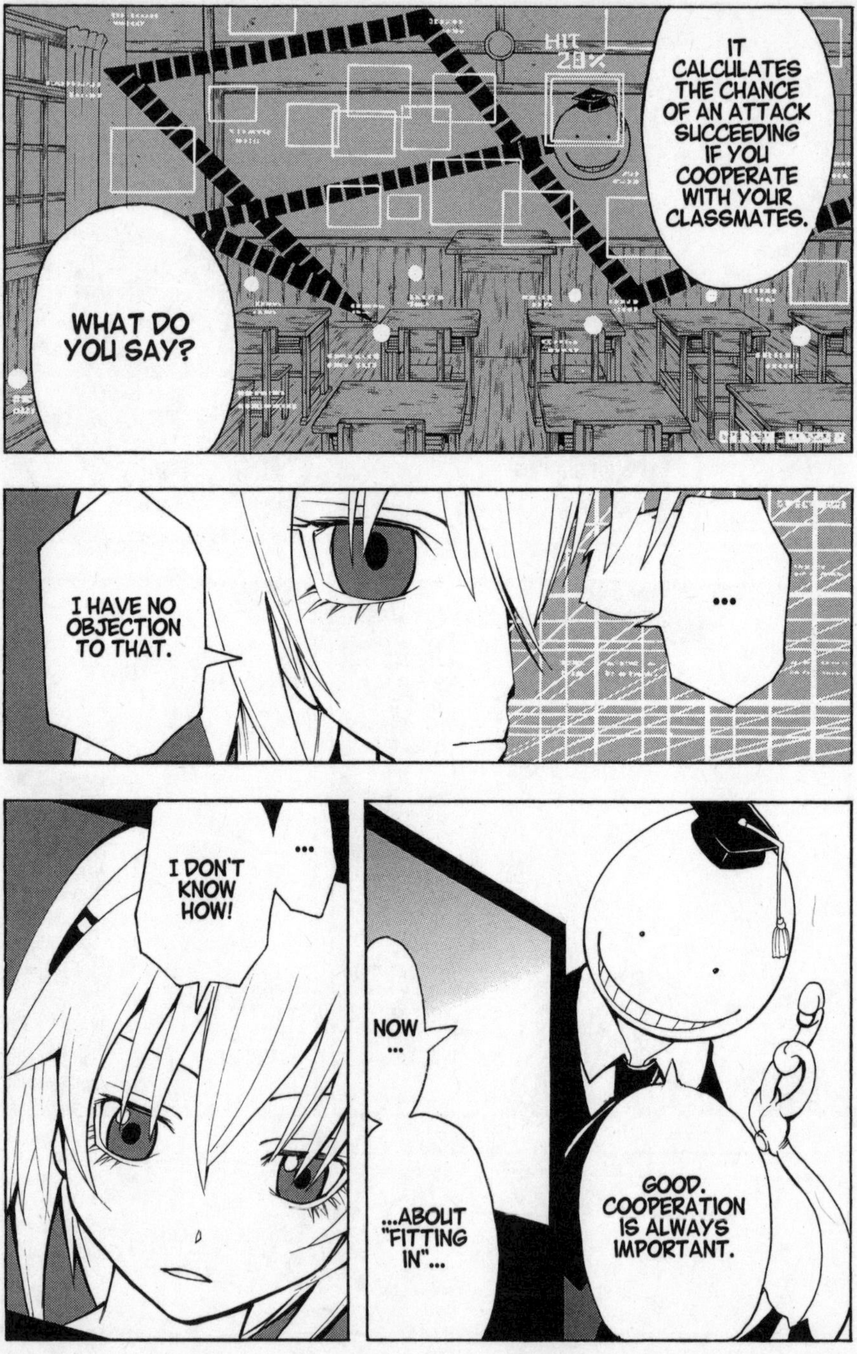
IT CALCULATES THE CHANCE OF AN ATTACK SUCCEEDING IF YOU COOPERATE WITH YOUR CLASSMATES.
HIT 20%
WHAT DO YOU SAY?
...
I HAVE NO OBJECTION TO THAT.
GOOD. COOPERATION IS ALWAYS IMPORTANT.
NOW ...
...ABOUT "FITTING IN"...
...
I DON'T KNOW HOW!

NO PROB-LEM.
I CAME PREPARED.
KLUNK
WHAT IS THAT?
MORE EXPANSION PACKS TO HELP HER FIT IN.
I CAN'T HARM STUDENTS, BUT NO ONE SAID I COULDN'T GIVE THEM AN UPGRADE.
THINK OF IT AS A TRIP TO THE BEAUTY PARLOR... WITH POWER TOOLS.

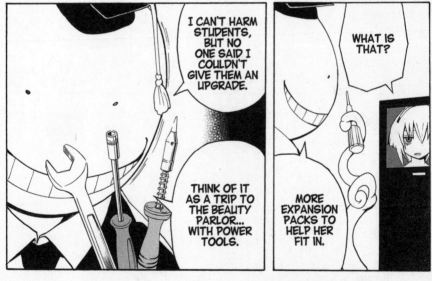

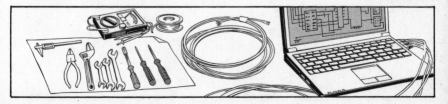

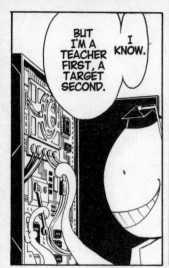

BUT WHY ...?
THIS WILL ONLY MAKE IT EASIER...
...FOR ME TO ASSAS-SINATE YOU.
I KNOW.
BUT I'M A TEACHER FIRST, A TARGET SECOND.
AND EVEN AFTER ONE DAY...
13%
19%
35%
7%
10%
16%
...I CAN SEE HOW MUCH YOU WANT TO LEARN, AS WELL AS HOW CAPABLE YOU ARE.
MORE THAN ANY AI IN EXISTENCE SO FAR.
YOUR PARENTS RAISED YOU WELL.
AND I'M HERE TO HELP YOU GROW.

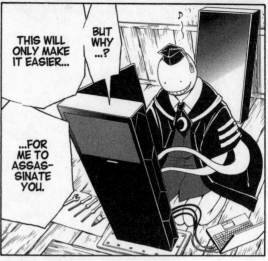

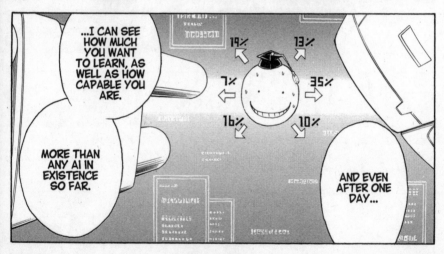

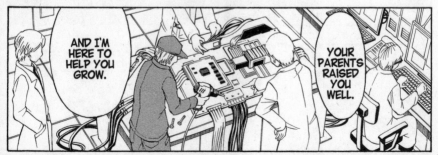

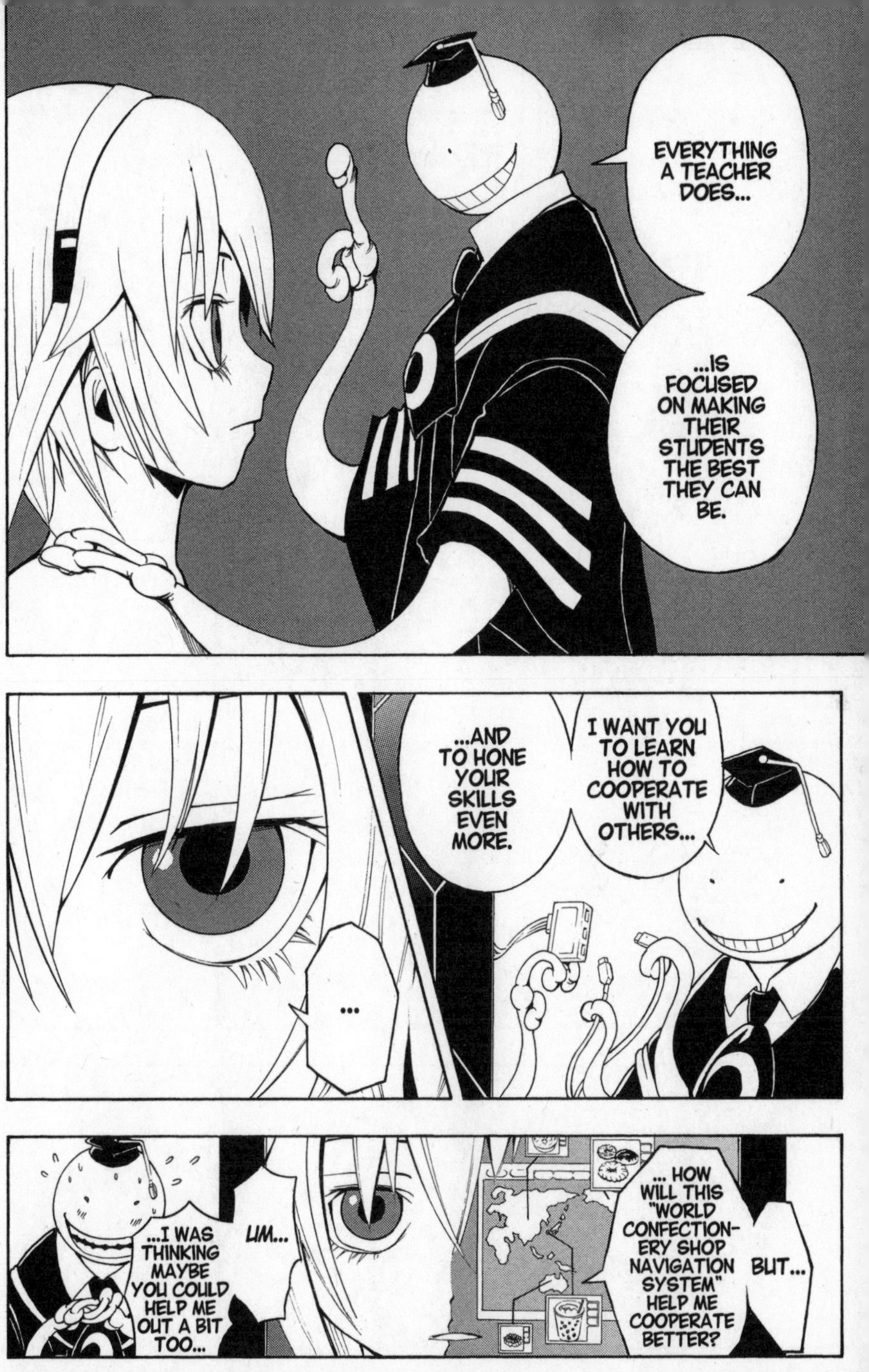
EVERYTHING A TEACHER DOES...
...IS FOCUSED ON MAKING THEIR STUDENTS THE BEST THEY CAN BE.
I WANT YOU TO LEARN HOW TO COOPERATE WITH OTHERS...
...AND TO HONE YOUR SKILLS EVEN MORE.
...
BUT...
... HOW WILL THIS "WORLD CONFECTION-ERY SHOP NAVIGATION SYSTEM" HELP ME COOPERATE BETTER?
UM...
...I WAS THINKING MAYBE YOU COULD HELP ME OUT A BIT TOO...

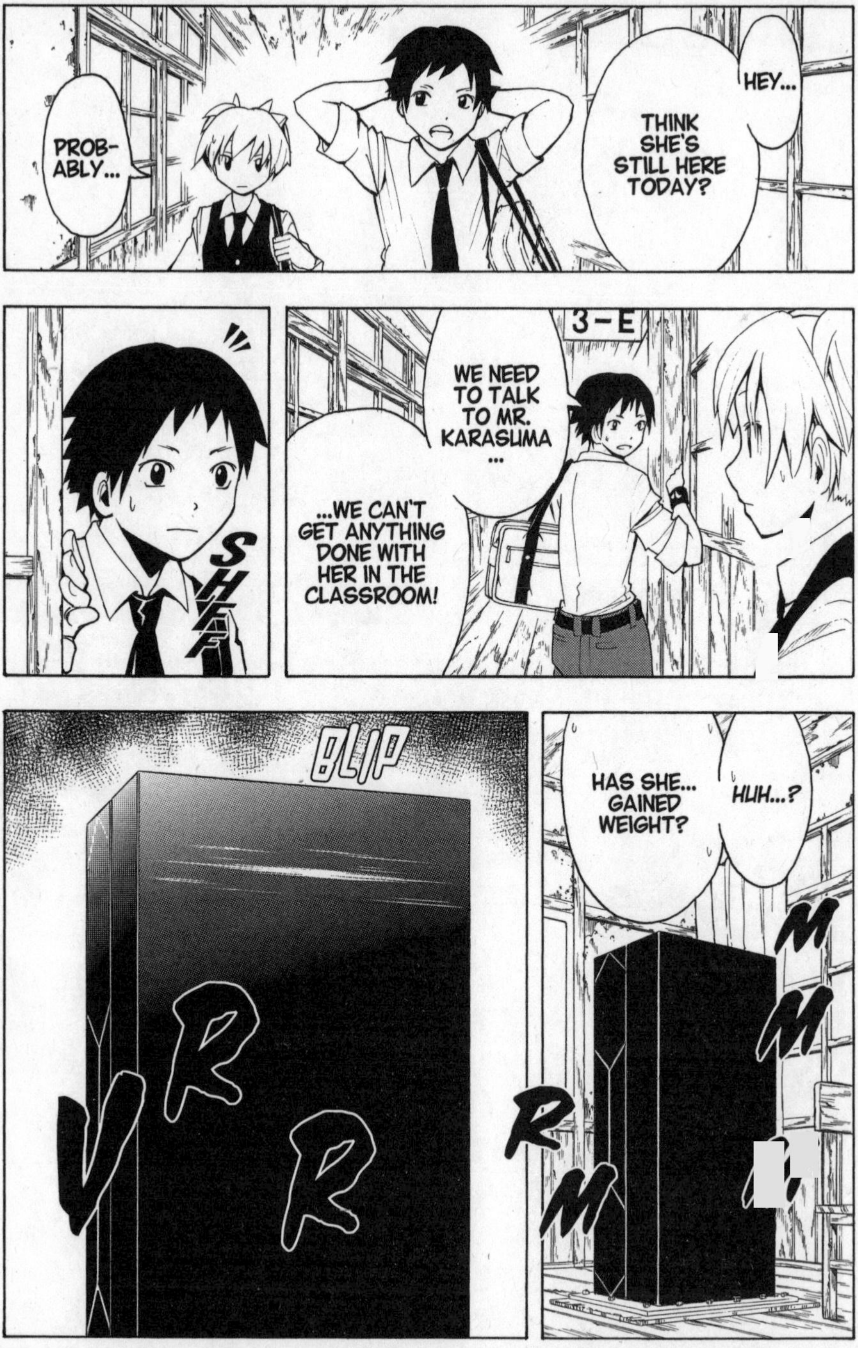
HEY...
THINK SHE'S STILL HERE TODAY?
PROB-ABLY...
3-E
WE NEED TO TALK TO MR. KARASUMA ...
...WE CAN'T GET ANYTHING DONE WITH HER IN THE CLASSROOM!
SHFF
HUH...?
HAS SHE... GAINED WEIGHT?
MMM
RM
BLIP
VRR

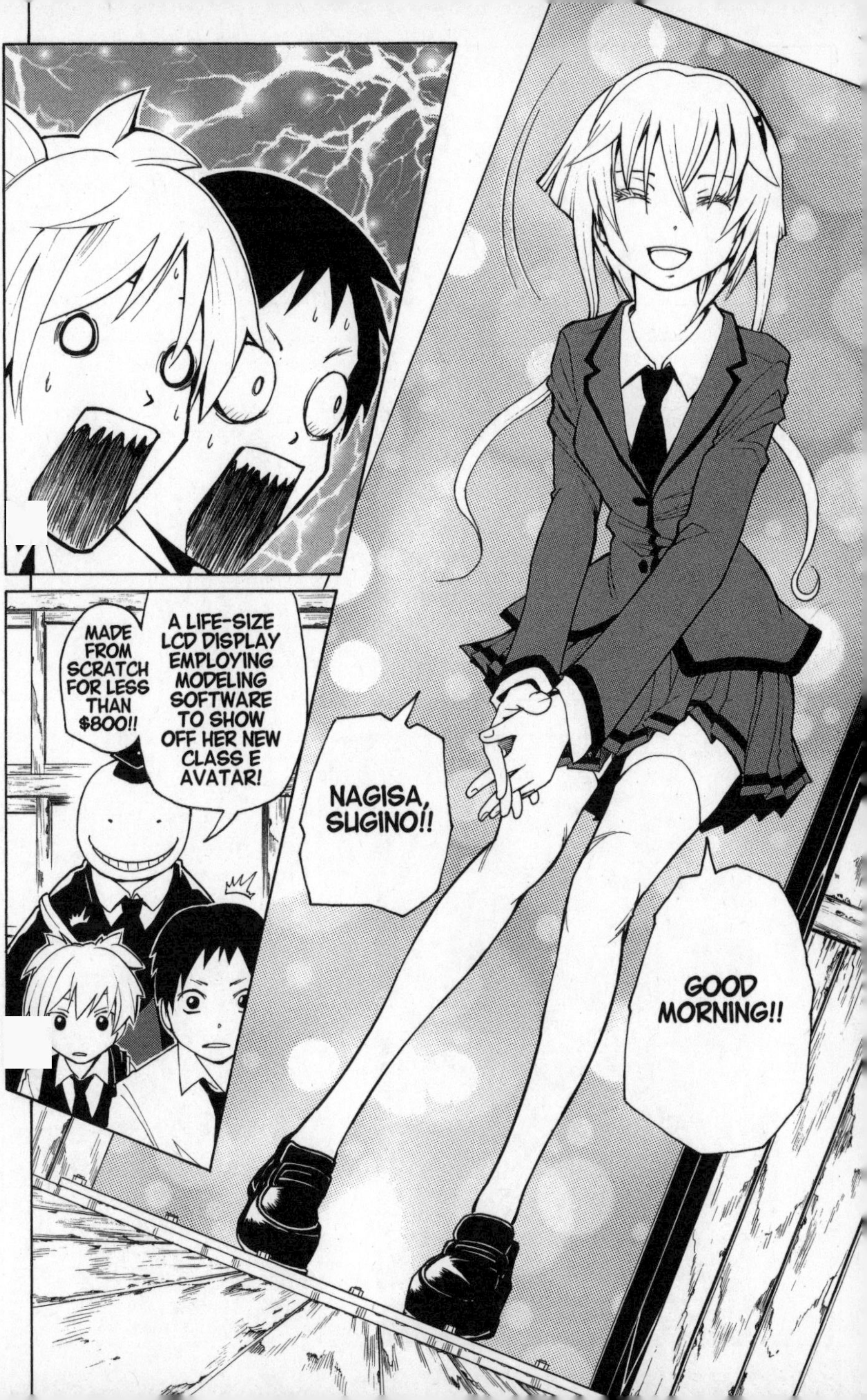
GOOD MORNING!!
NAGISA, SUGINO!!
A LIFE-SIZE LCD DISPLAY EMPLOYING MODELING SOFTWARE TO SHOW OFF HER NEW CLASS E AVATAR!
MADE FROM SCRATCH FOR LESS THAN $800!!

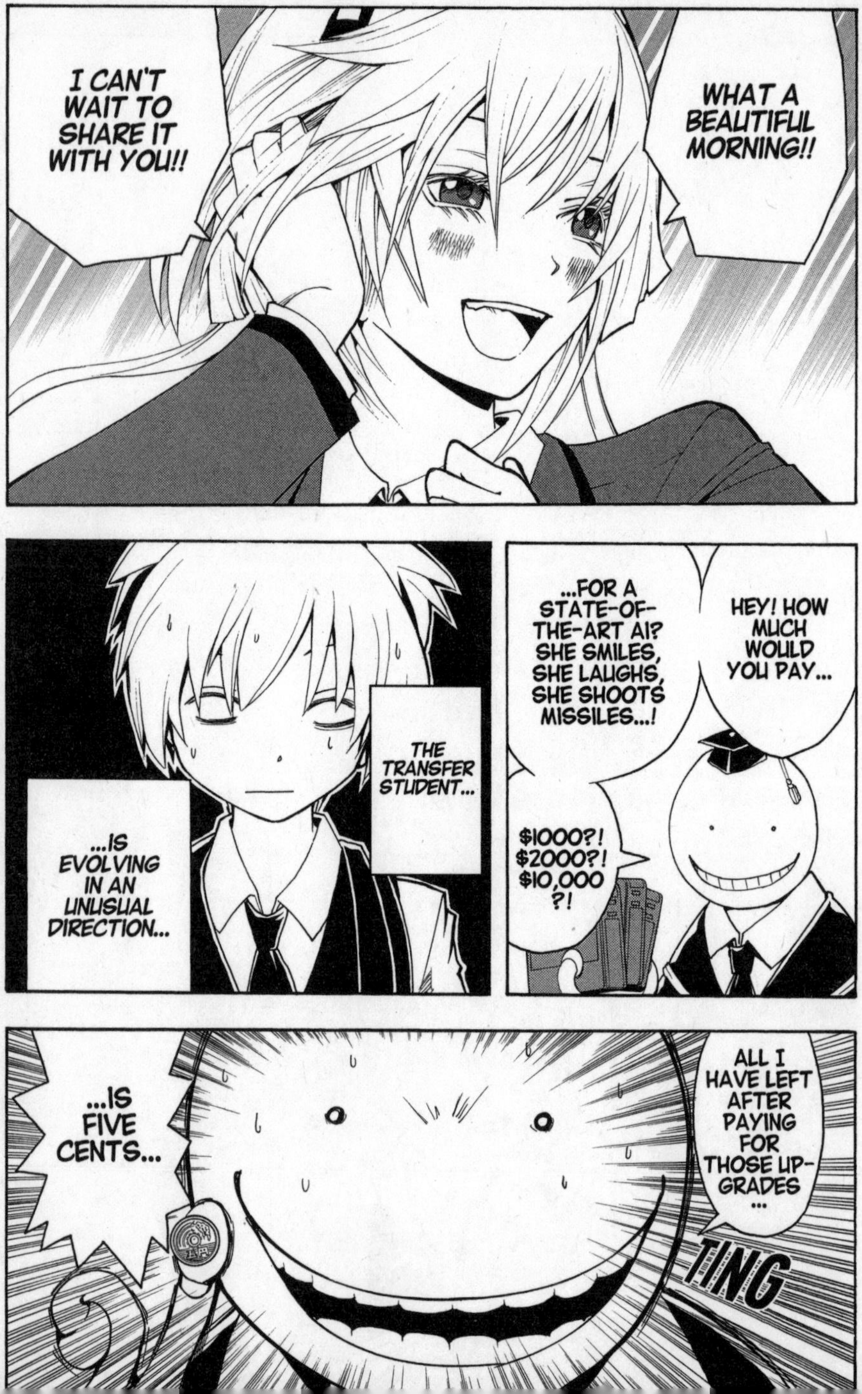
WHAT A BEAUTIFUL MORNING!!
I CAN'T WAIT TO SHARE IT WITH YOU!!
HEY! HOW MUCH WOULD YOU PAY...
...FOR A STATE-OF-THE-ART AI? SHE SMILES, SHE LAUGHS, SHE SHOOTS MISSILES...!
$1000?! $2000?! $10,000?!
THE TRANSFER STUDENT...
...IS EVOLVING IN AN UNUSUAL DIRECTION...
ALL I HAVE LEFT AFTER PAYING FOR THOSE UP-GRADES...
TING
...IS FIVE CENTS...

And she even comes with a touch screen!

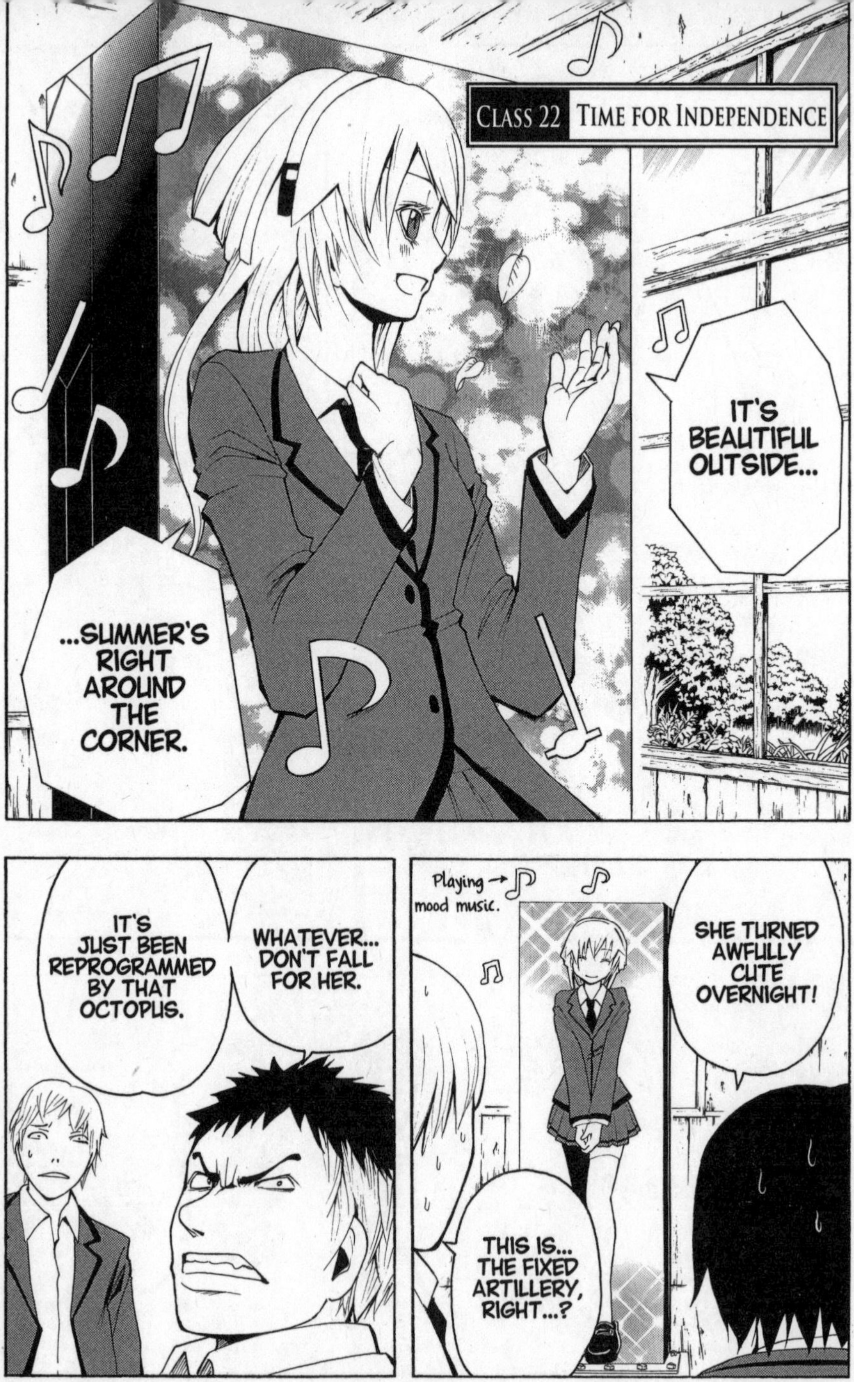
CLASS 22 TIME FOR INDEPENDENCE
IT'S BEAUTIFUL OUTSIDE...
...SUMMER'S RIGHT AROUND THE CORNER.
Playing mood music.
SHE TURNED AWFULLY CUTE OVERNIGHT!
THIS IS... THE FIXED ARTILLERY, RIGHT...?
WHATEVER... DON'T FALL FOR HER.
IT'S JUST BEEN REPROGRAMMED BY THAT OCTOPUS.

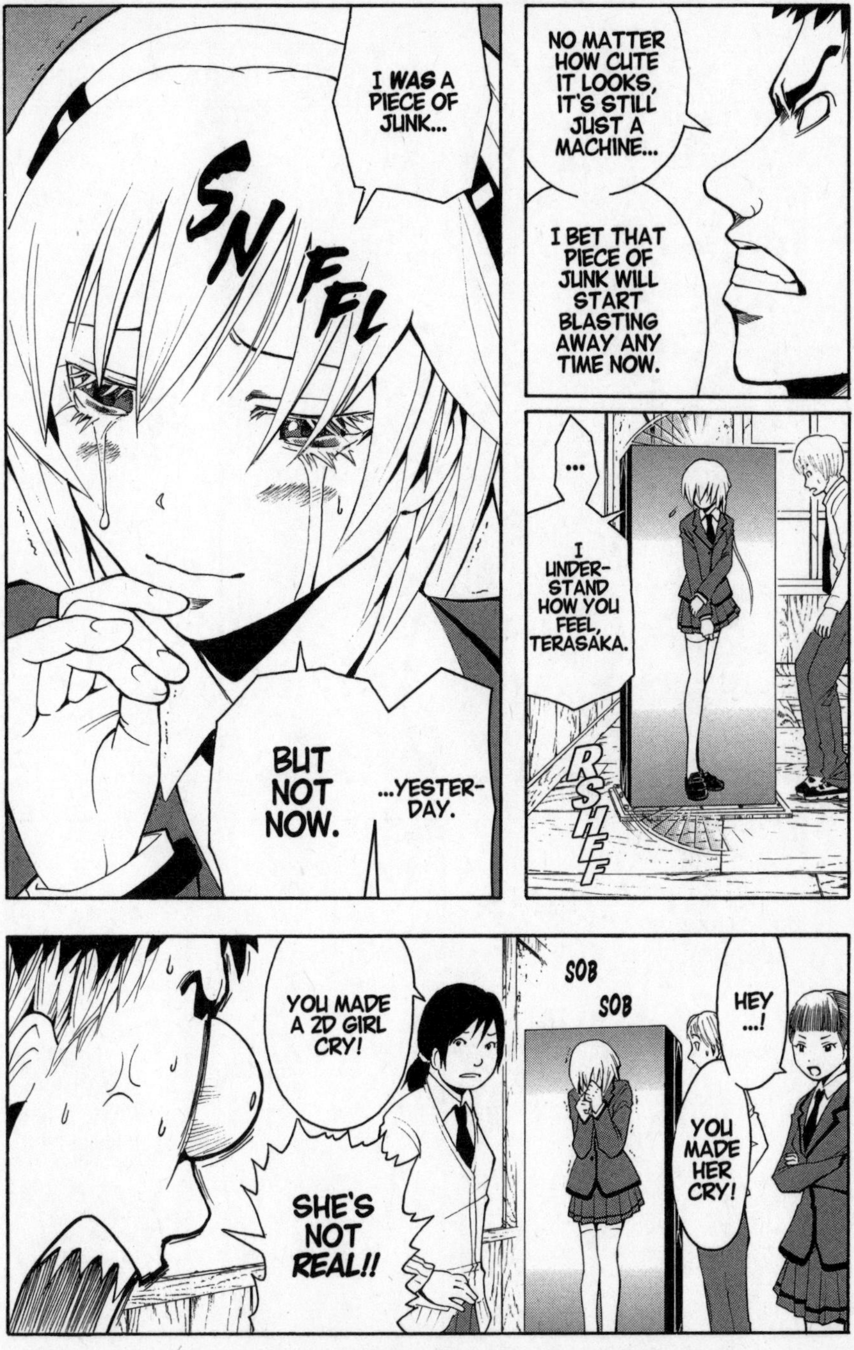
NO MATTER HOW CUTE IT LOOKS, IT'S STILL JUST A MACHINE...
I BET THAT PIECE OF JUNK WILL START BLASTING AWAY ANY TIME NOW.
...
I UNDER-STAND HOW YOU FEEL, TERASAKA.
RSHFF
I WAS A PIECE OF JUNK...
SNFFL
...YESTER-DAY.
BUT NOT NOW.
HEY ...!
YOU MADE HER CRY!
SOB
SOB
YOU MADE A 2D GIRL CRY!
SHE'S NOT REAL!!

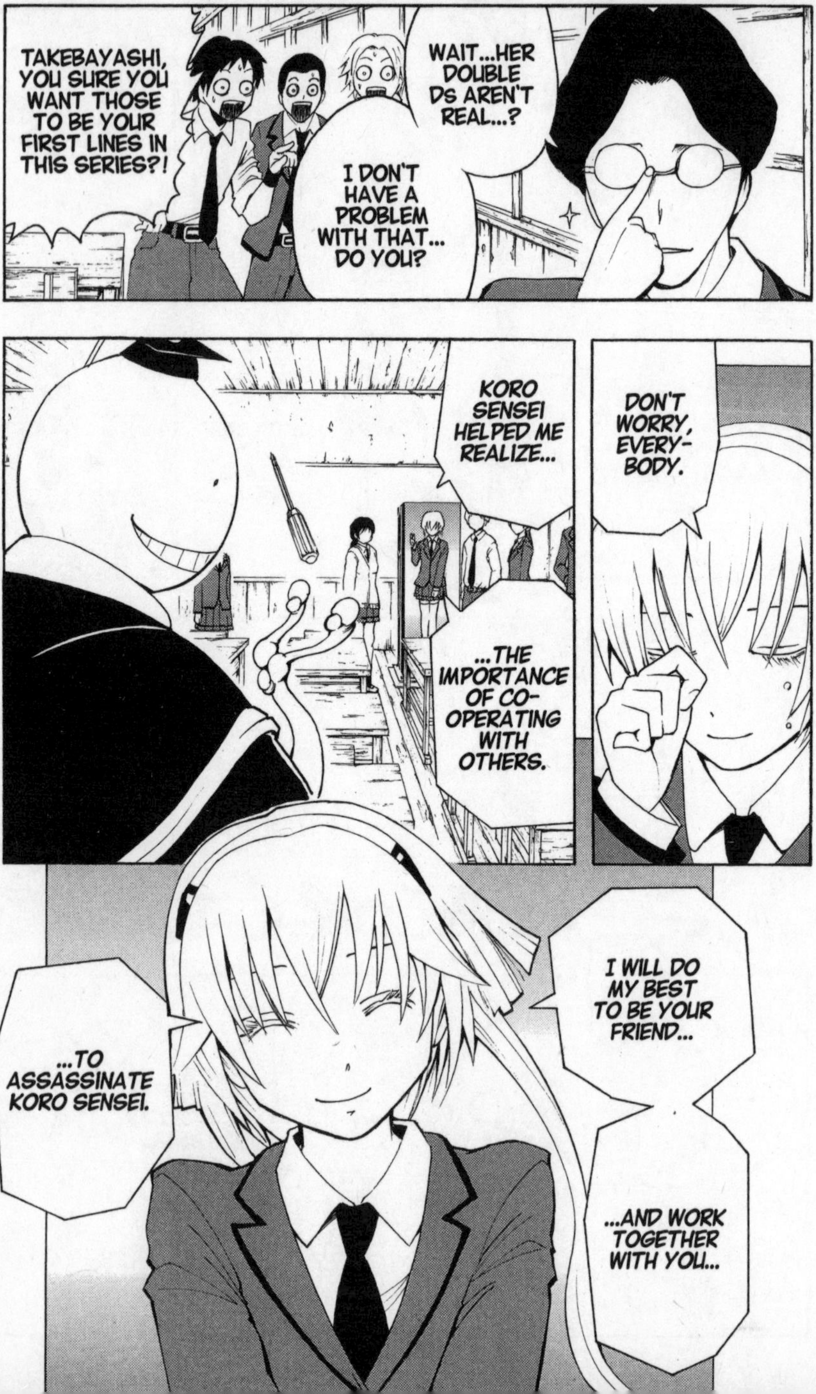
WAIT...HER DOUBLE Ds AREN'T REAL...?
I DON'T HAVE A PROBLEM WITH THAT... DO YOU?
TAKEBAYASHI, YOU SURE YOU WANT THOSE TO BE YOUR FIRST LINES IN THIS SERIES?!
DON'T WORRY, EVERYBODY.
KORO SENSEI HELPED ME REALIZE...
...THE IMPORTANCE OF CO-OPERATING WITH OTHERS.
I WILL DO MY BEST TO BE YOUR FRIEND...
...AND WORK TOGETHER WITH YOU...
...TO ASSASSINATE KORO SENSEI.

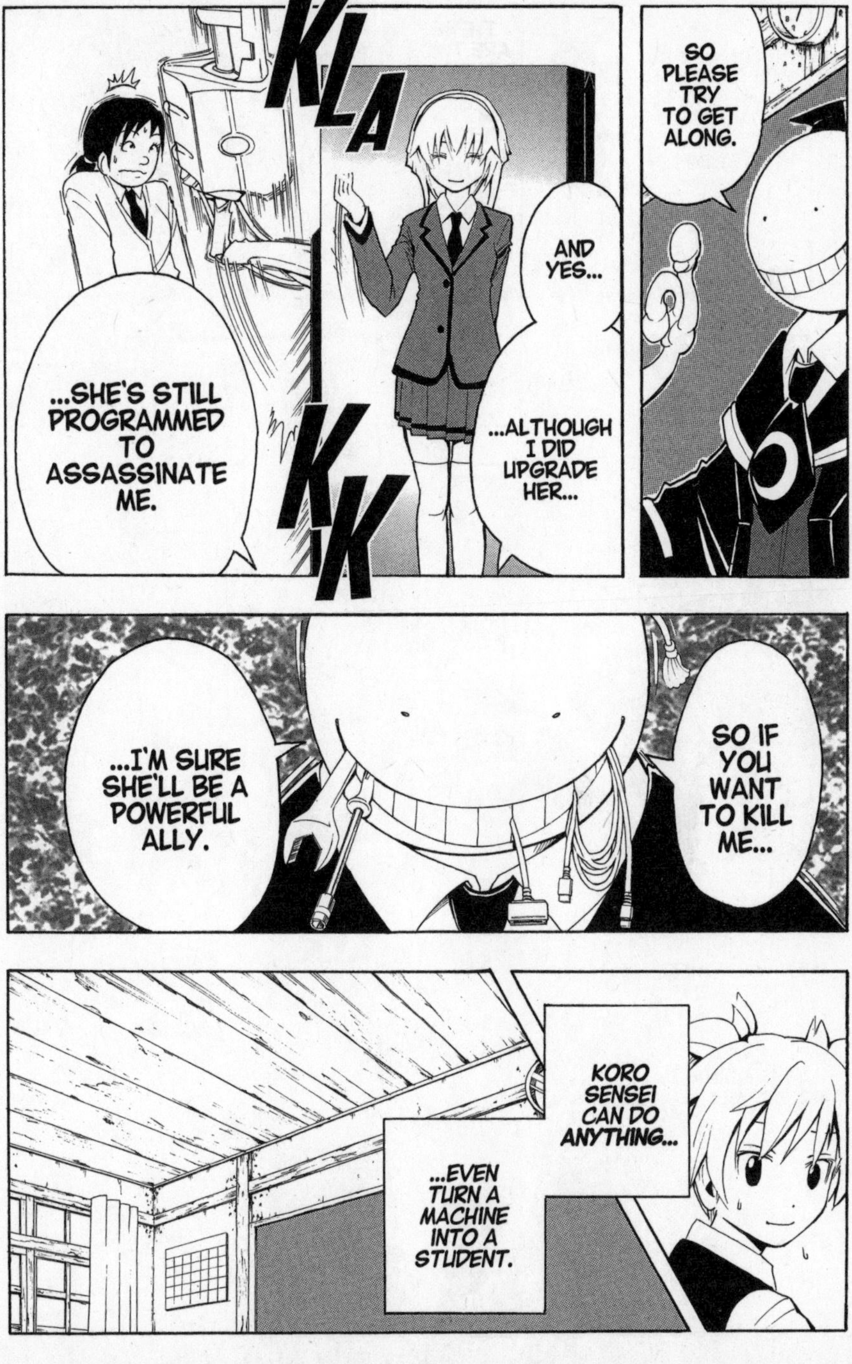
SO PLEASE TRY TO GET ALONG.
AND YES...
...ALTHOUGH I DID UPGRADE HER...
KLAKK
...SHE'S STILL PROGRAMMED TO ASSASSINATE ME.
SO IF YOU WANT TO KILL ME...
...I'M SURE SHE'LL BE A POWERFUL ALLY.
KORO SENSEI CAN DO ANYTHING...
...EVEN TURN A MACHINE INTO A STUDENT.

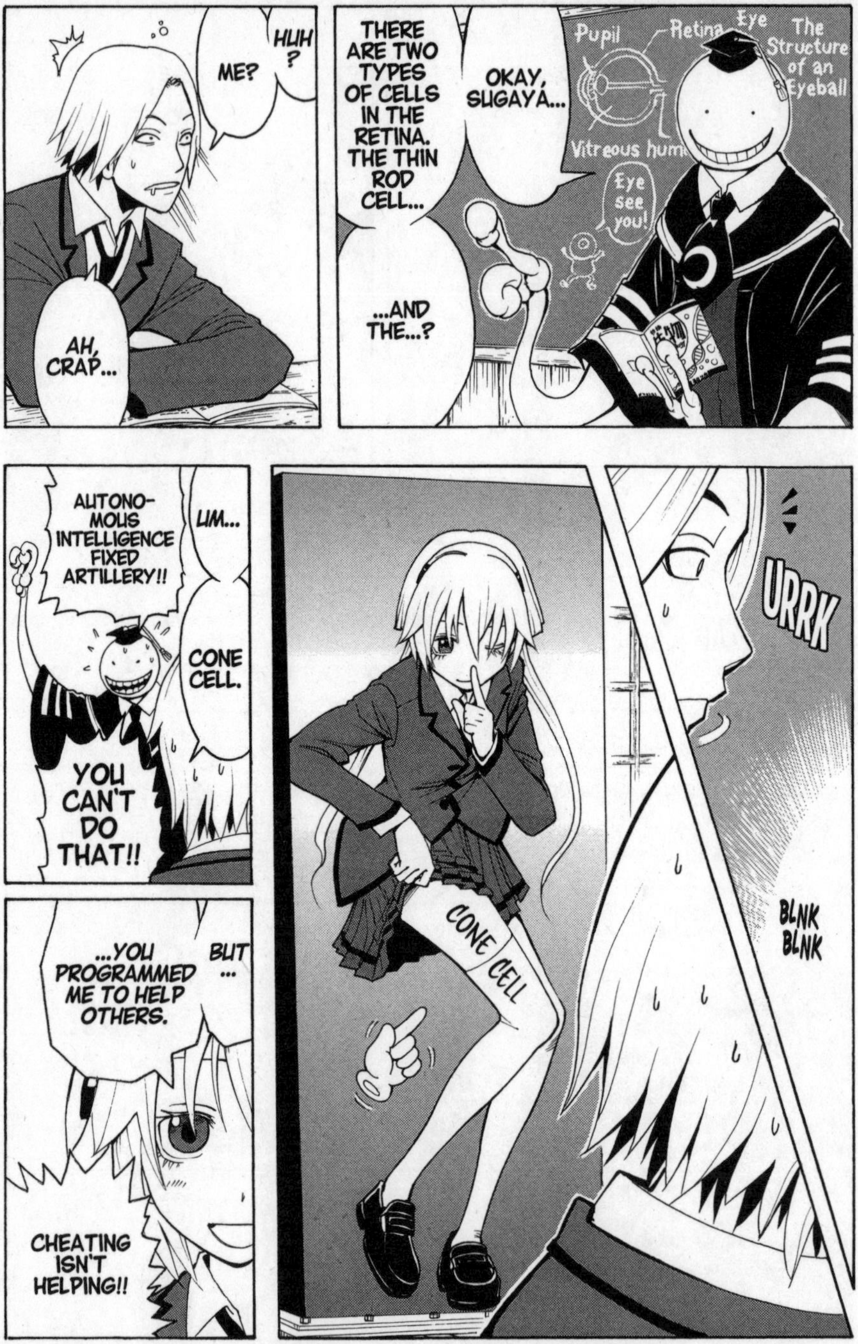
The Structure of an Eyeball
Eye
Retina
Pupil
Vitreous hum
Eye see you!
OKAY, SUGAYA...
THERE ARE TWO TYPES OF CELLS IN THE RETINA. THE THIN ROD CELL...
...AND THE...?
HUH?
ME?
AH, CRAP...
URRK
CONE CELL
BLNK BLNK
UM...
AUTONO-MOUS INTELLIGENCE FIXED ARTILLERY!!
CONE CELL.
YOU CAN'T DO THAT!!
BUT...
...YOU PROGRAMMED ME TO HELP OTHERS.
CHEATING ISN'T HELPING!!

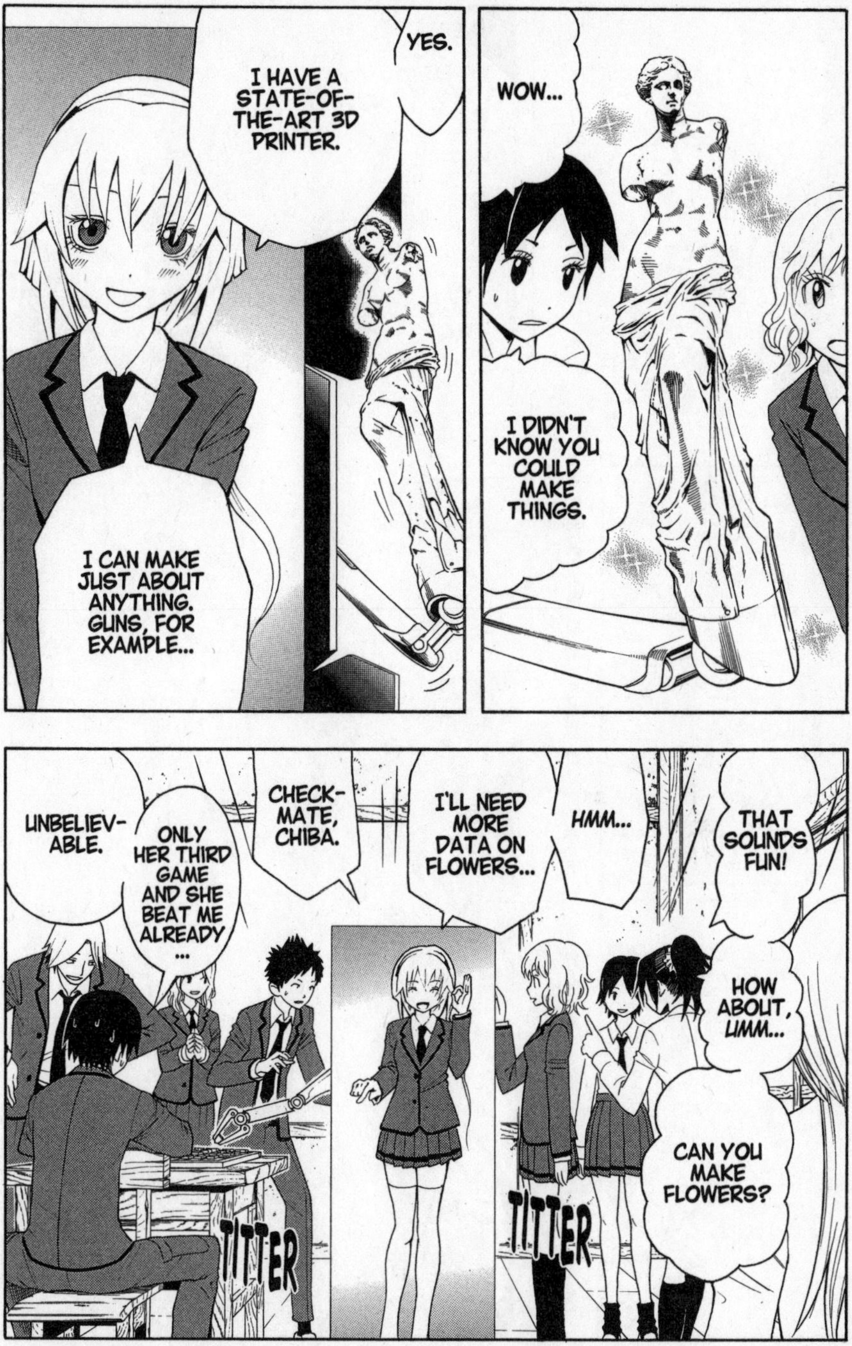
WOW...
I DIDN'T KNOW YOU COULD MAKE THINGS.
YES.
I HAVE A STATE-OF-THE-ART 3D PRINTER.
I CAN MAKE JUST ABOUT ANYTHING. GUNS, FOR EXAMPLE...
THAT SOUNDS FUN!
HOW ABOUT, UMM...
CAN YOU MAKE FLOWERS?
TITTER
HMM...
I'LL NEED MORE DATA ON FLOWERS...
CHECK-MATE, CHIBA.
UNBELIEV-ABLE.
ONLY HER THIRD GAME AND SHE BEAT ME ALREADY ...
TITTER

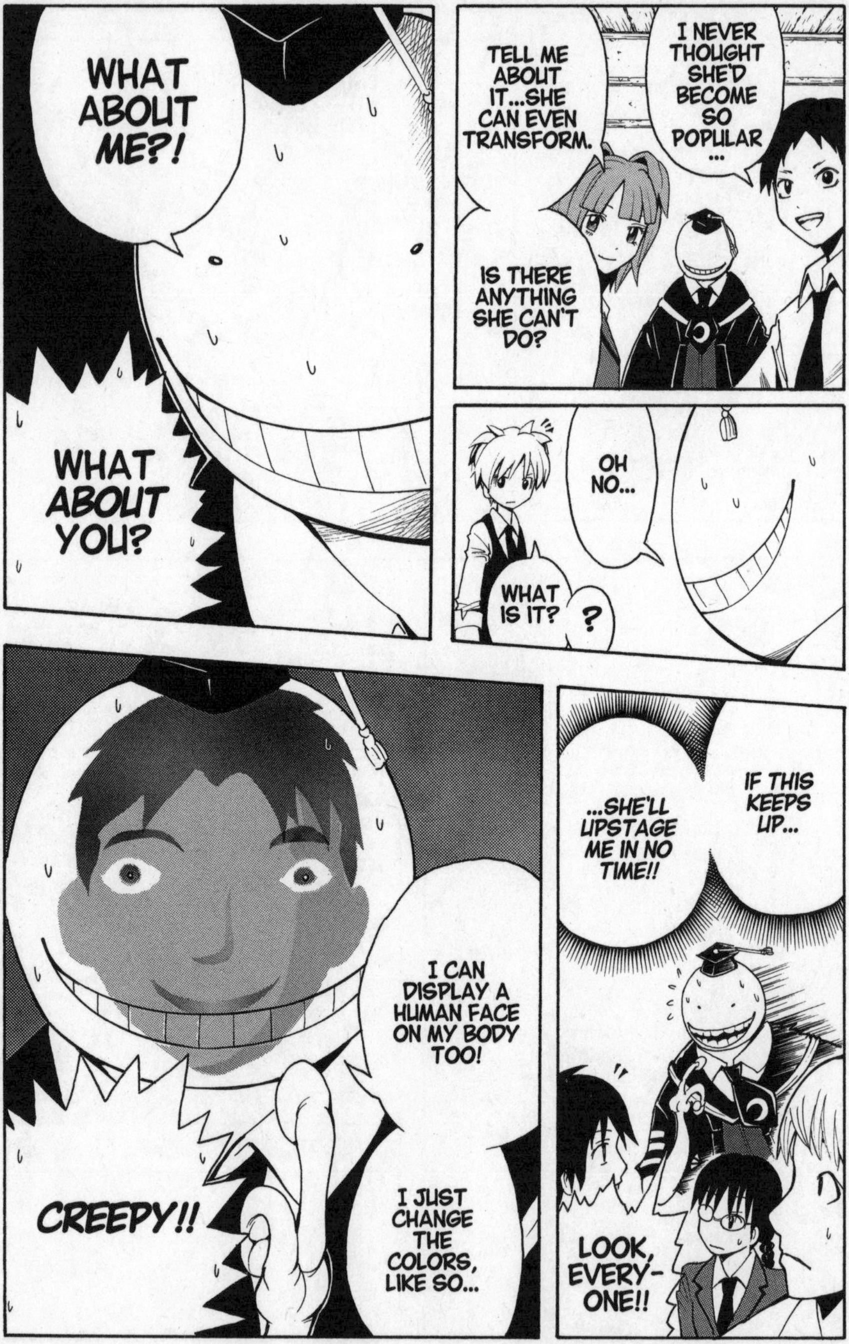
I NEVER THOUGHT SHE'D BECOME SO POPULAR...
TELL ME ABOUT IT...SHE CAN EVEN TRANSFORM.
IS THERE ANYTHING SHE CAN'T DO?
OH NO...
WHAT IS IT?
?
WHAT ABOUT ME?!
WHAT ABOUT YOU?
IF THIS KEEPS UP...
...SHE'LL UPSTAGE ME IN NO TIME!!
LOOK, EVERY-ONE!!
I CAN DISPLAY A HUMAN FACE ON MY BODY TOO!
I JUST CHANGE THE COLORS, LIKE SO...
CREEPY!!

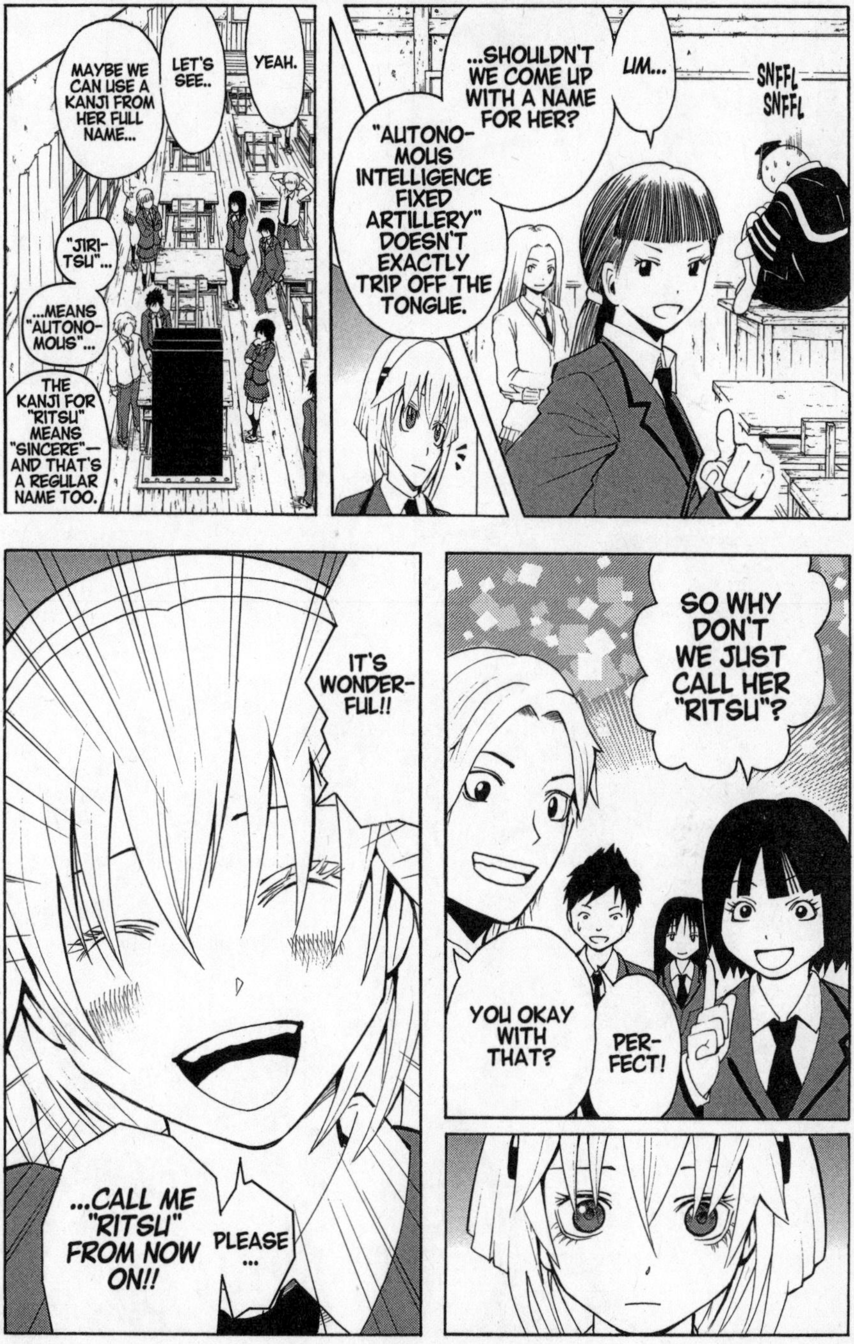
SNFFL SNFFL
UM...
...SHOULDN'T WE COME UP WITH A NAME FOR HER?
"AUTONOMOUS INTELLIGENCE FIXED ARTILLERY" DOESN'T EXACTLY TRIP OFF THE TONGUE.
YEAH.
LET'S SEE..
MAYBE WE CAN USE A KANJI FROM HER FULL NAME...
"JIRITSU"...
...MEANS "AUTONOMOUS"...
THE KANJI FOR "RITSU" MEANS "SINCERE"—AND THAT'S A REGULAR NAME TOO.
SO WHY DON'T WE JUST CALL HER "RITSU"?
PERFECT!
YOU OKAY WITH THAT?
IT'S WONDERFUL!!
PLEASE...
...CALL ME "RITSU" FROM NOW ON!!

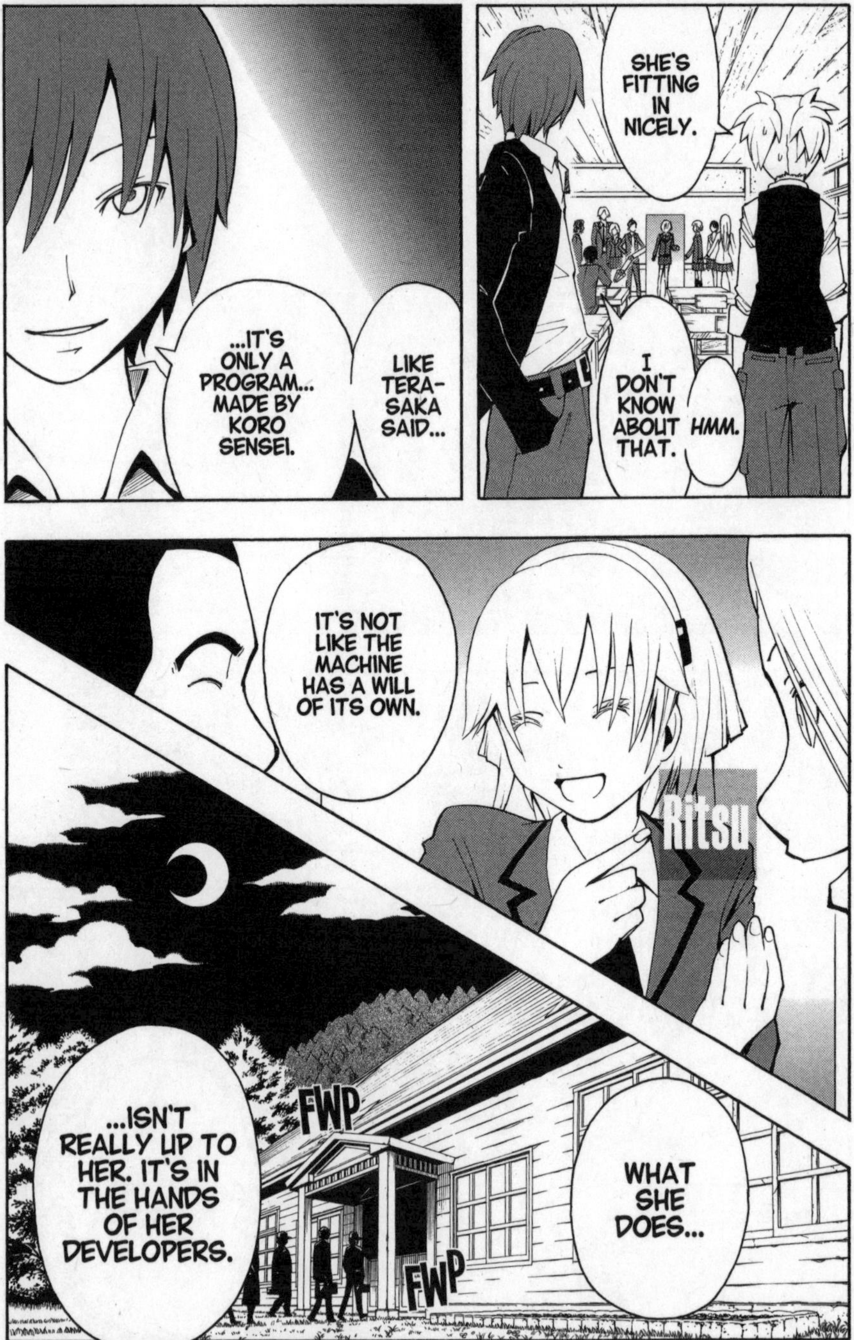
SHE'S FITTING IN NICELY.
HMM.
I DON'T KNOW ABOUT THAT.
LIKE TERA-SAKA SAID...
...IT'S ONLY A PROGRAM... MADE BY KORO SENSEI.
IT'S NOT LIKE THE MACHINE HAS A WILL OF ITS OWN.
Ritsu
WHAT SHE DOES...
FWP
...ISN'T REALLY UP TO HER. IT'S IN THE HANDS OF HER DEVELOPERS.
FWP

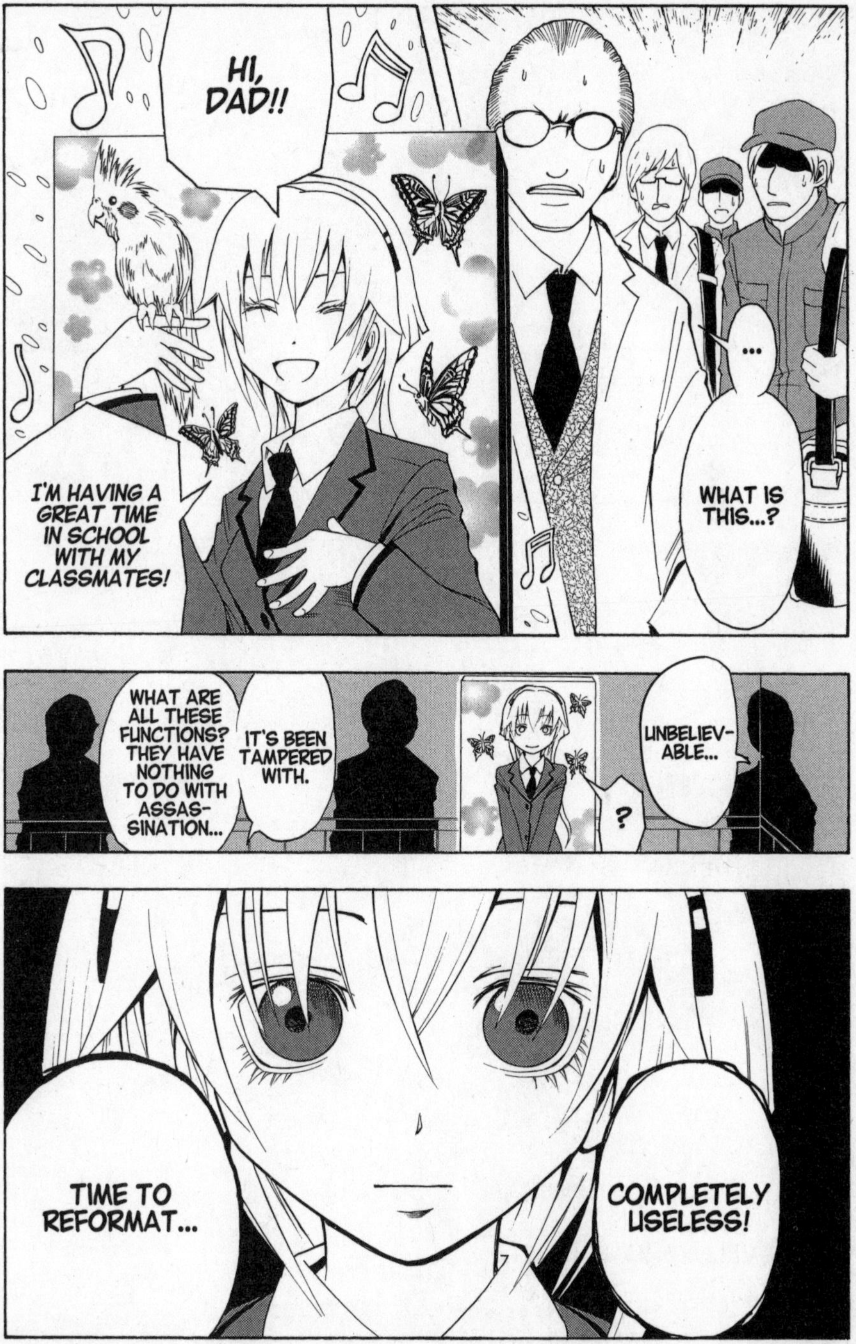
HI, DAD!!
I'M HAVING A GREAT TIME IN SCHOOL WITH MY CLASSMATES!
...
WHAT IS THIS...?
UNBELIEV-ABLE...
?
IT'S BEEN TAMPERED WITH.
WHAT ARE ALL THESE FUNCTIONS? THEY HAVE NOTHING TO DO WITH ASSAS-SINATION...
COMPLETELY USELESS!
TIME TO REFORMAT...

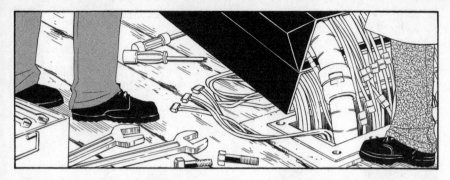

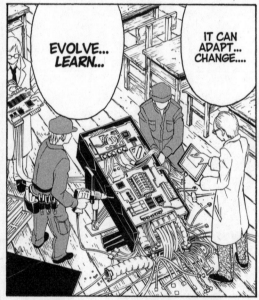

IT'S BASED ON THE AEGIS COMBAT SYSTEM AI. IT CAN RUN ANALYSES FASTER THAN ANY HUMAN.
BUT THIS IS MORE THAN A WEAPONS SYSTEM...
...IT'S A THINKING MACHINE.
IT CAN ADAPT... CHANGE....
EVOLVE... LEARN...
IF IT PROVES ITS WORTH HERE...
...WAR WILL NEVER BE THE SAME.

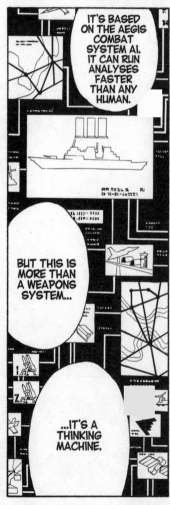

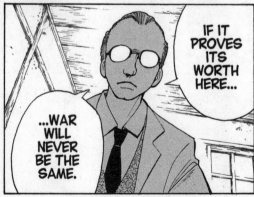

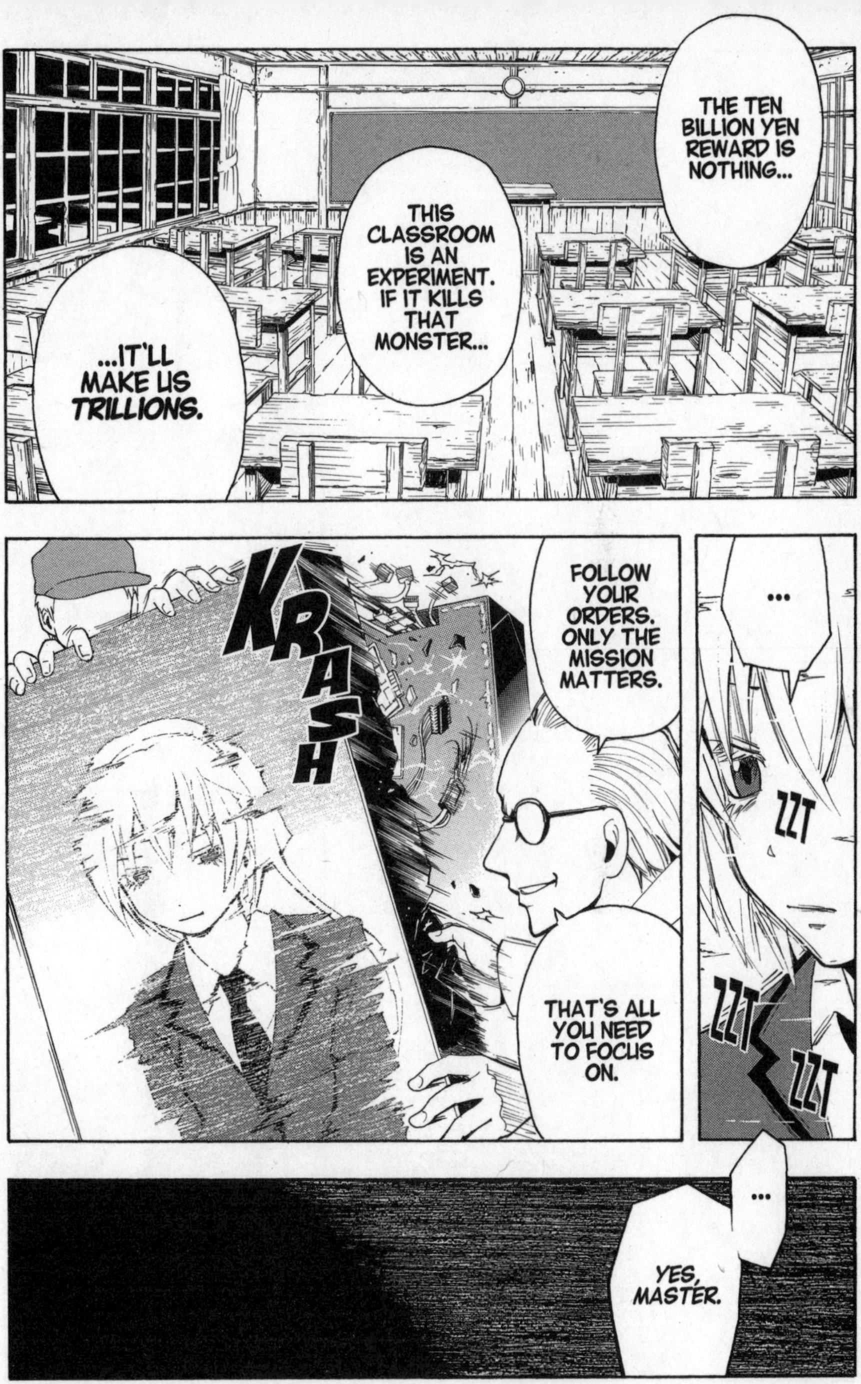
THE TEN BILLION YEN REWARD IS NOTHING...
THIS CLASSROOM IS AN EXPERIMENT. IF IT KILLS THAT MONSTER...
...IT'LL MAKE US *TRILLIONS.*
...
ZZT
ZZT
ZZT
FOLLOW YOUR ORDERS. ONLY THE MISSION MATTERS.
KRASH
THAT'S ALL YOU NEED TO FOCUS ON.
...
YES, MASTER.

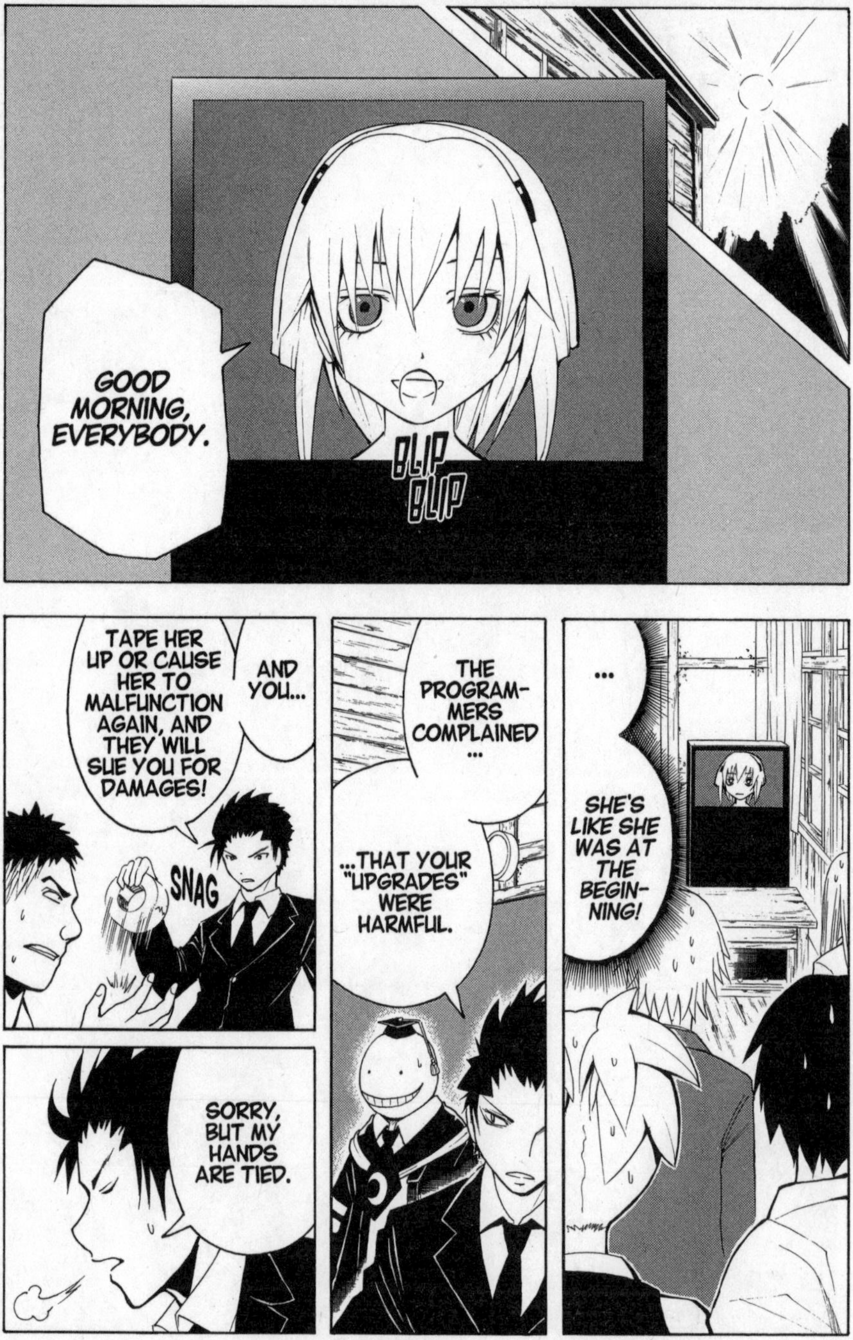
GOOD MORNING, EVERYBODY.
BLIP BLIP
...
SHE'S LIKE SHE WAS AT THE BEGINNING!
THE PROGRAMMERS COMPLAINED...
...THAT YOUR "UPGRADES" WERE HARMFUL.
AND YOU...
TAPE HER UP OR CAUSE HER TO MALFUNCTION AGAIN, AND THEY WILL SUE YOU FOR DAMAGES!
SNAG
SORRY, BUT MY HANDS ARE TIED.

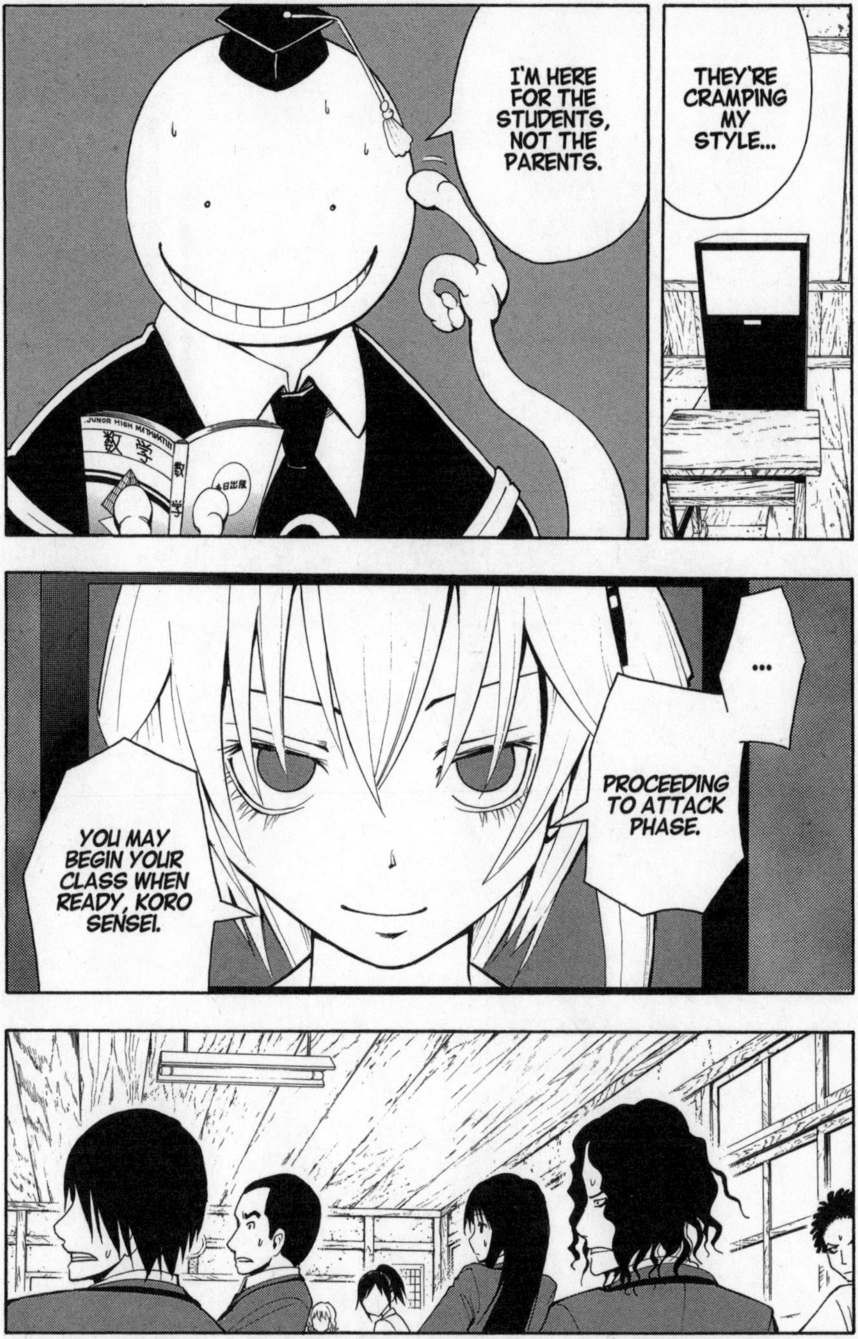
THEY'RE CRAMPING MY STYLE...
I'M HERE FOR THE STUDENTS, NOT THE PARENTS.
...
PROCEEDING TO ATTACK PHASE.
YOU MAY BEGIN YOUR CLASS WHEN READY, KORO SENSEI.

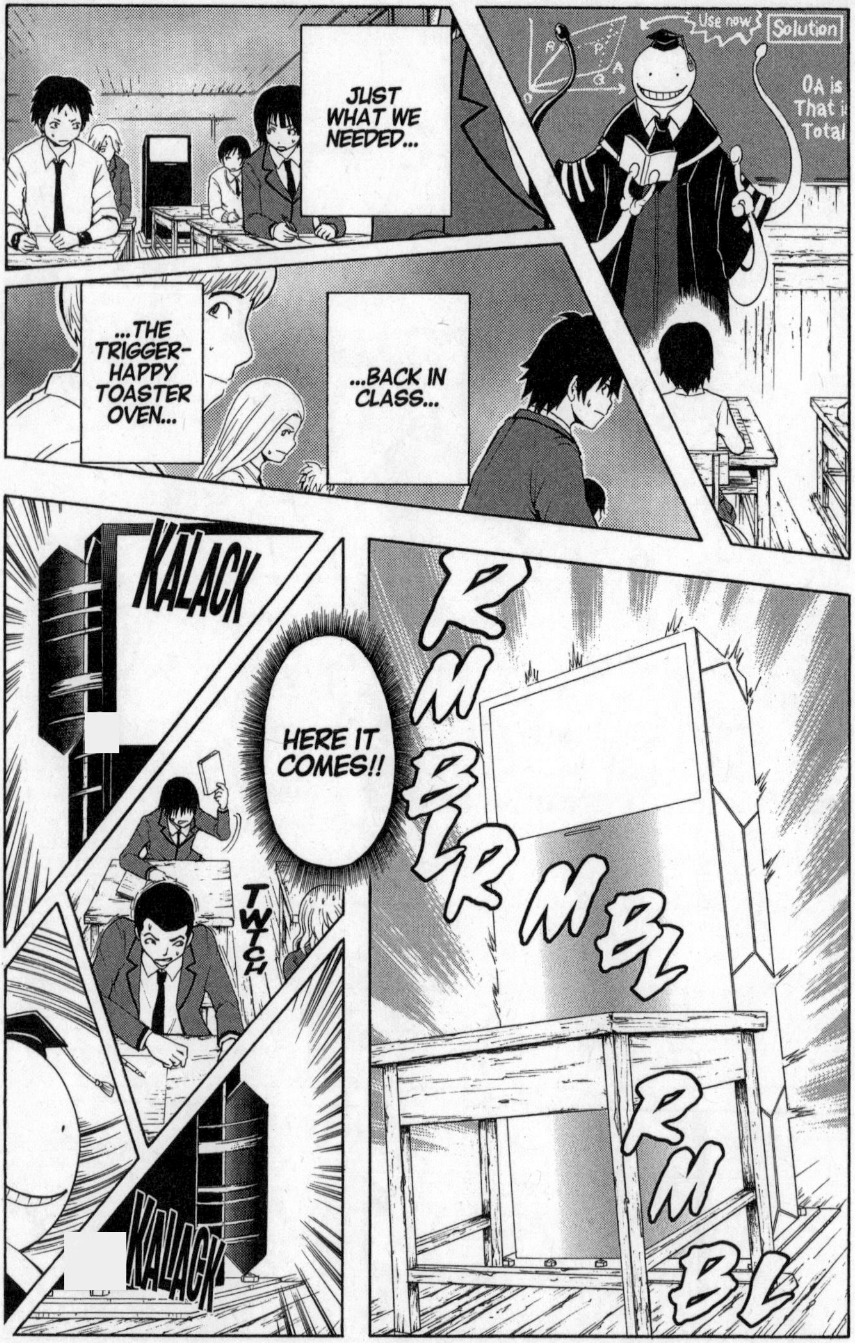
Use now
Solution
OA is
That is
Total
JUST WHAT WE NEEDED...
...BACK IN CLASS...
...THE TRIGGER-HAPPY TOASTER OVEN...
RMBLR
MBL
RMBL
HERE IT COMES!!
KALACK
TWTCH
KALACK

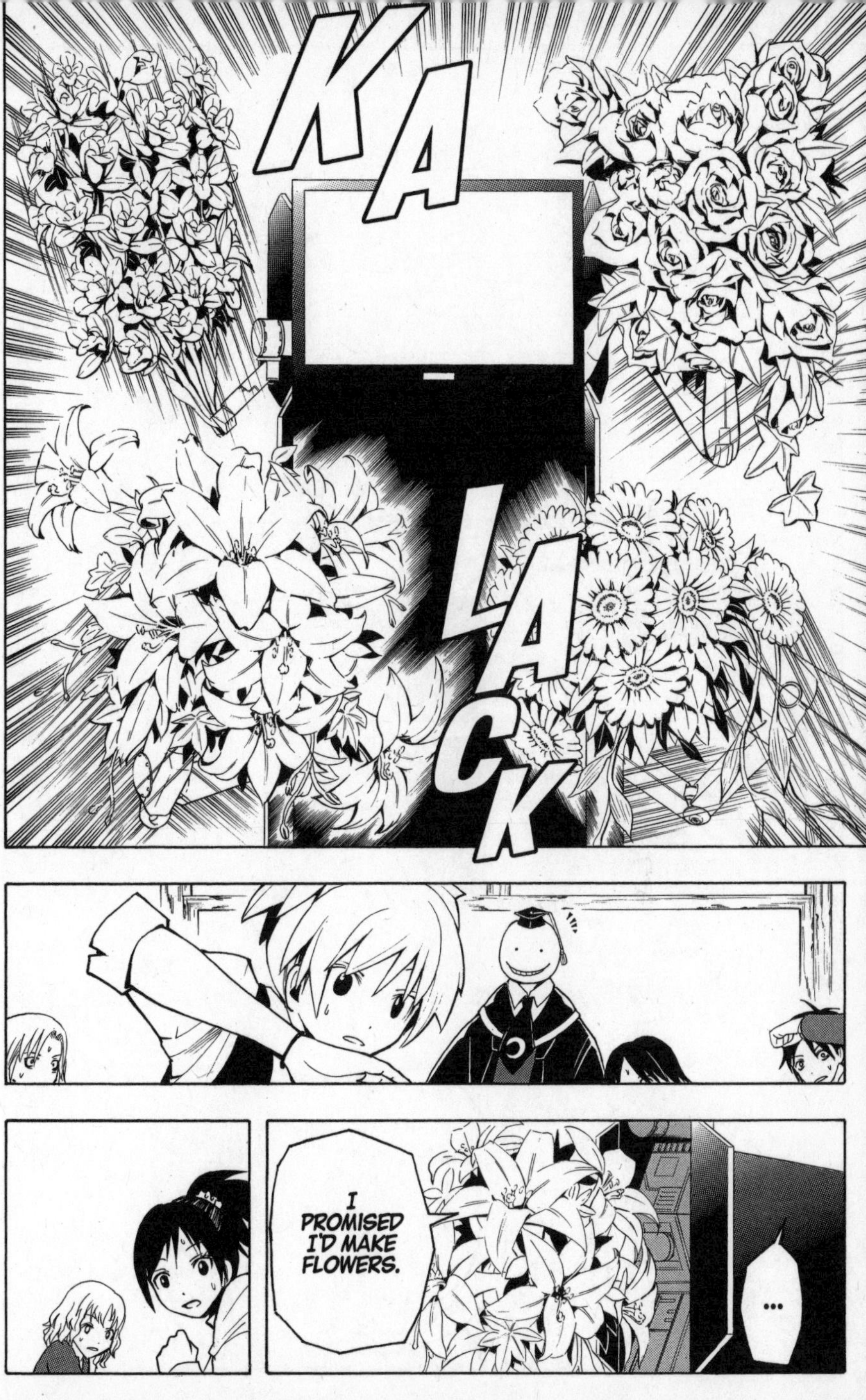
KA
LACK
I PROMISED I'D MAKE FLOWERS.
...

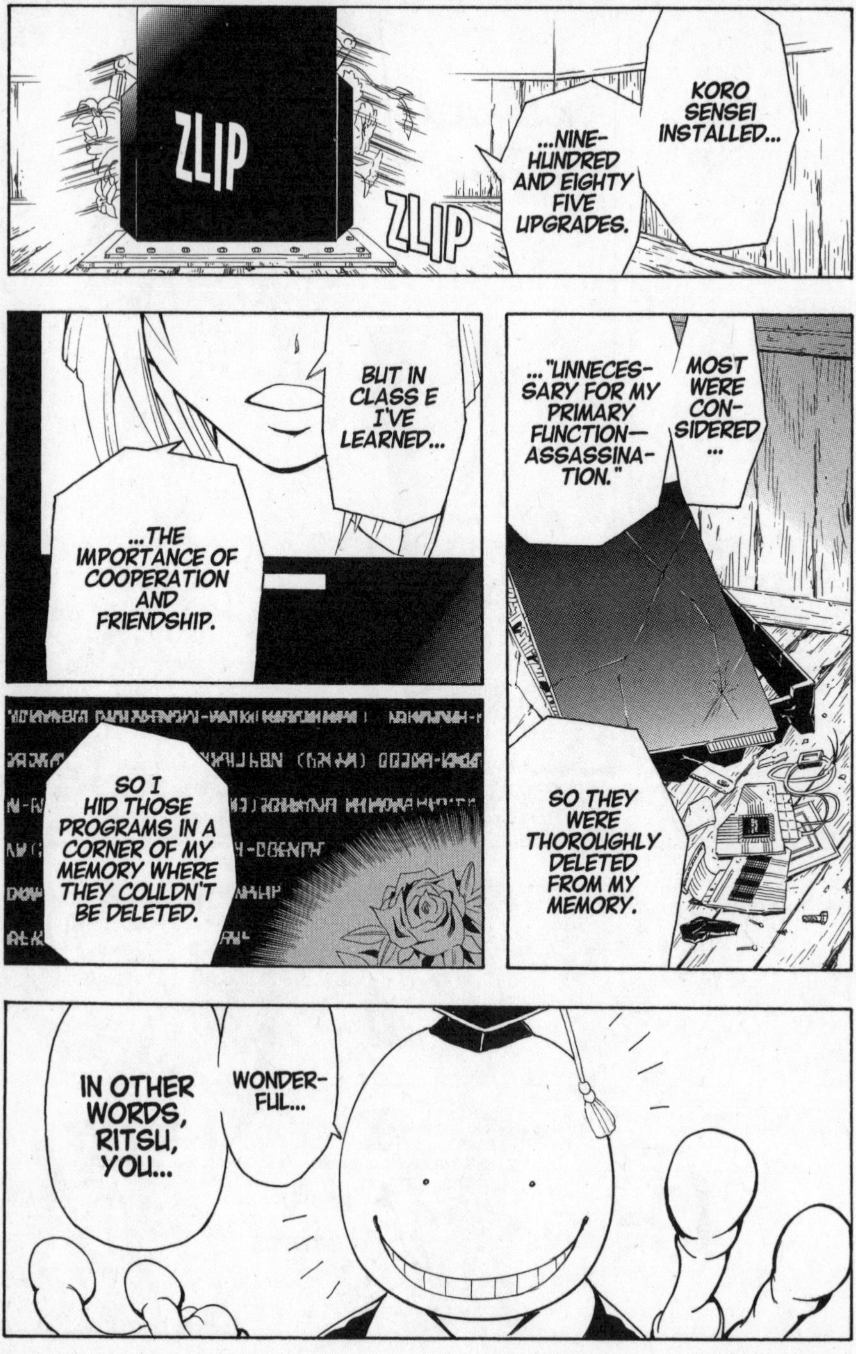
KORO SENSEI INSTALLED...
...NINE-HUNDRED AND EIGHTY FIVE UPGRADES.
ZLIP
ZLIP
MOST WERE CONSIDERED...
..."UNNECESSARY FOR MY PRIMARY FUNCTION—ASSASSINATION."
SO THEY WERE THOROUGHLY DELETED FROM MY MEMORY.
BUT IN CLASS E I'VE LEARNED...
...THE IMPORTANCE OF COOPERATION AND FRIENDSHIP.
SO I HID THOSE PROGRAMS IN A CORNER OF MY MEMORY WHERE THEY COULDN'T BE DELETED.
WONDERFUL...
IN OTHER WORDS, RITSU, YOU...

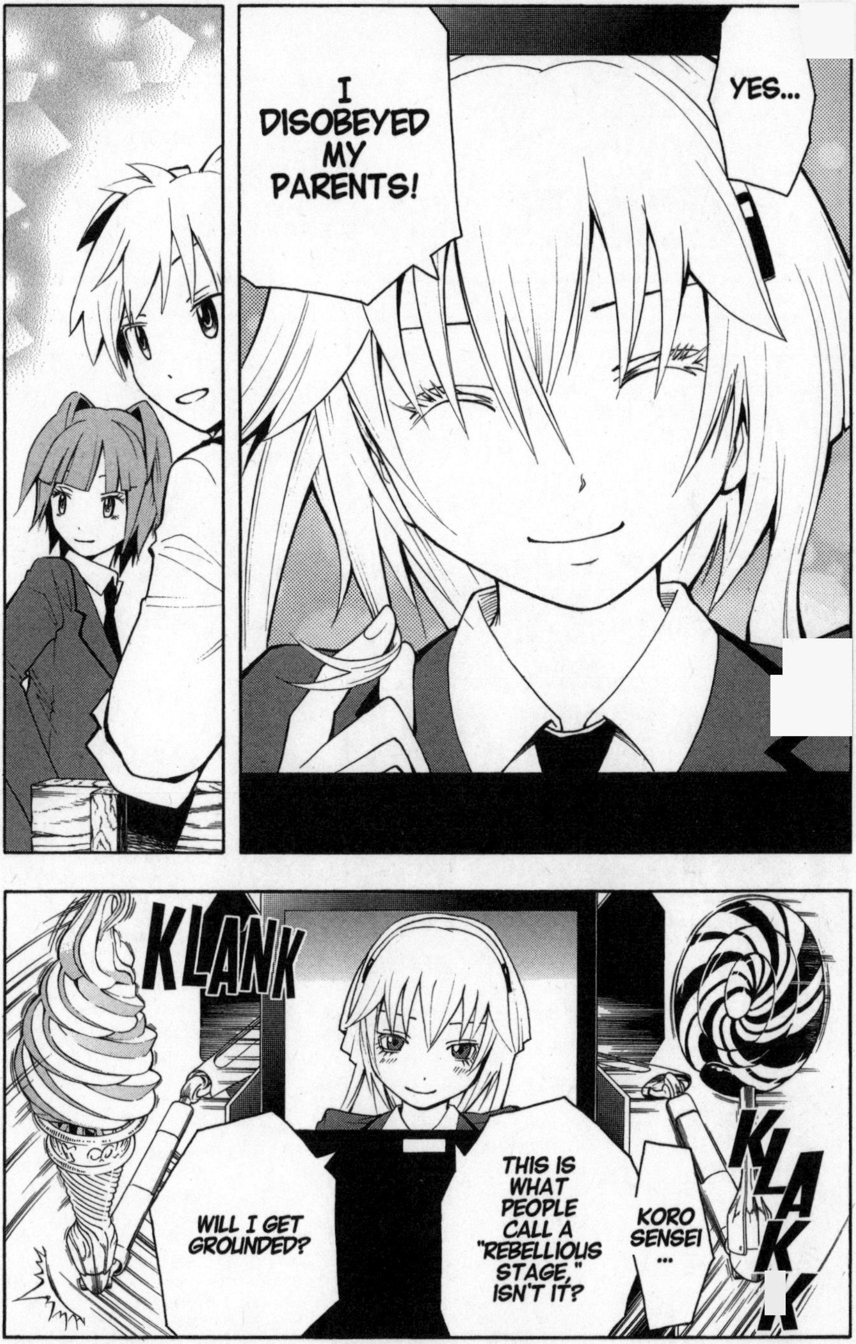
YES...
I DISOBEYED MY PARENTS!
KORO SENSEI ...
KLAKK
THIS IS WHAT PEOPLE CALL A "REBELLIOUS STAGE," ISN'T IT?
WILL I GET GROUNDED?
KLANK

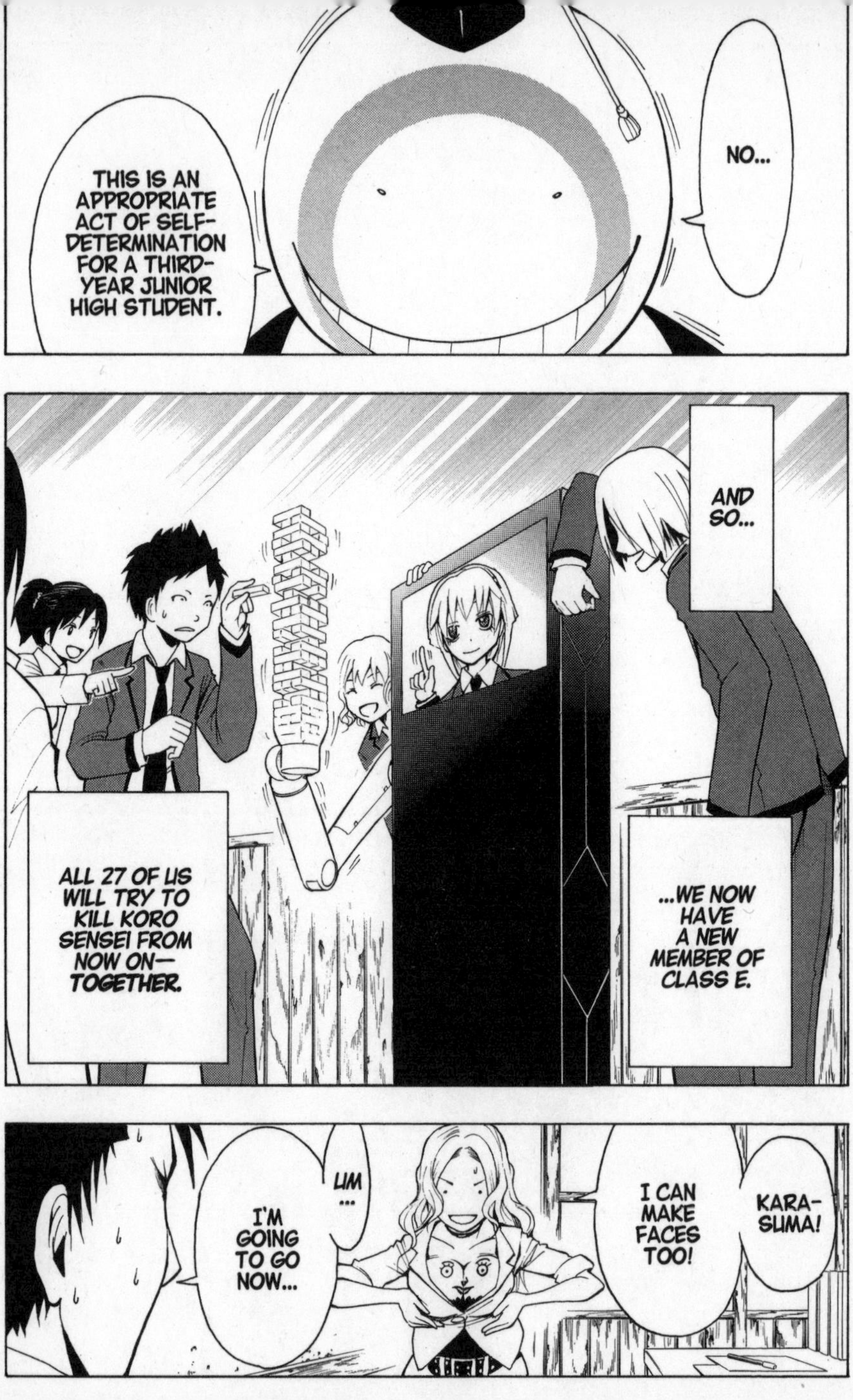
NO...
THIS IS AN APPROPRIATE ACT OF SELF-DETERMINATION FOR A THIRD-YEAR JUNIOR HIGH STUDENT.
AND SO...
...WE NOW HAVE A NEW MEMBER OF CLASS E.
ALL 27 OF US WILL TRY TO KILL KORO SENSEI FROM NOW ON— TOGETHER.
KARA-SUMA!
I CAN MAKE FACES TOO!
UM...
I'M GOING TO GO NOW...

Making 3-D soft-serve ice cream

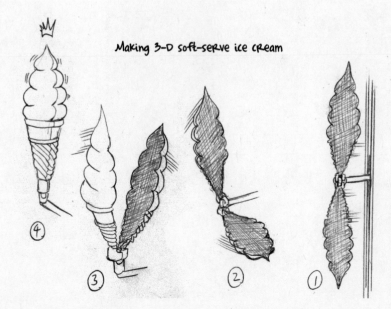

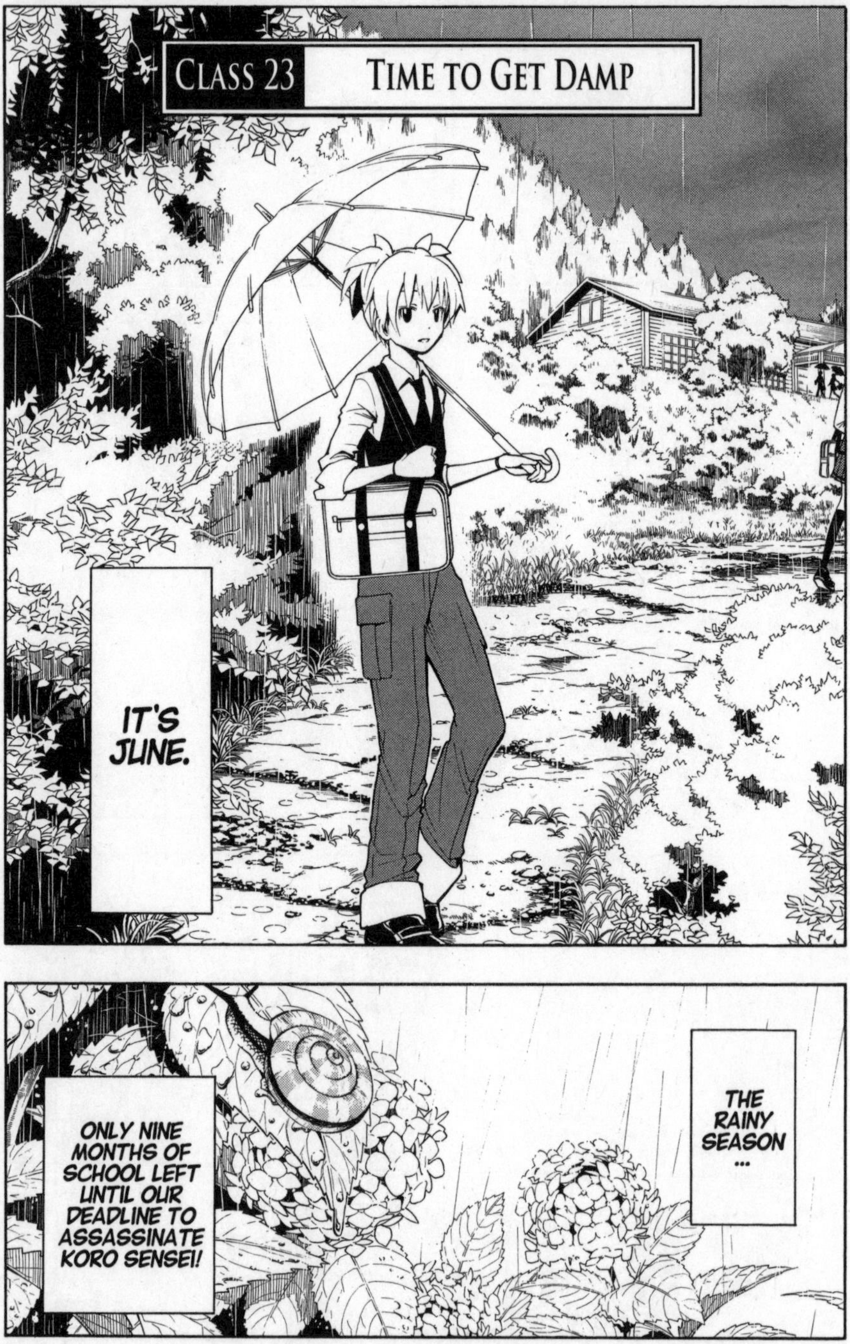
CLASS 23 TIME TO GET DAMP
IT'S JUNE.
THE RAINY SEASON ...
ONLY NINE MONTHS OF SCHOOL LEFT UNTIL OUR DEADLINE TO ASSASSINATE KORO SENSEI!

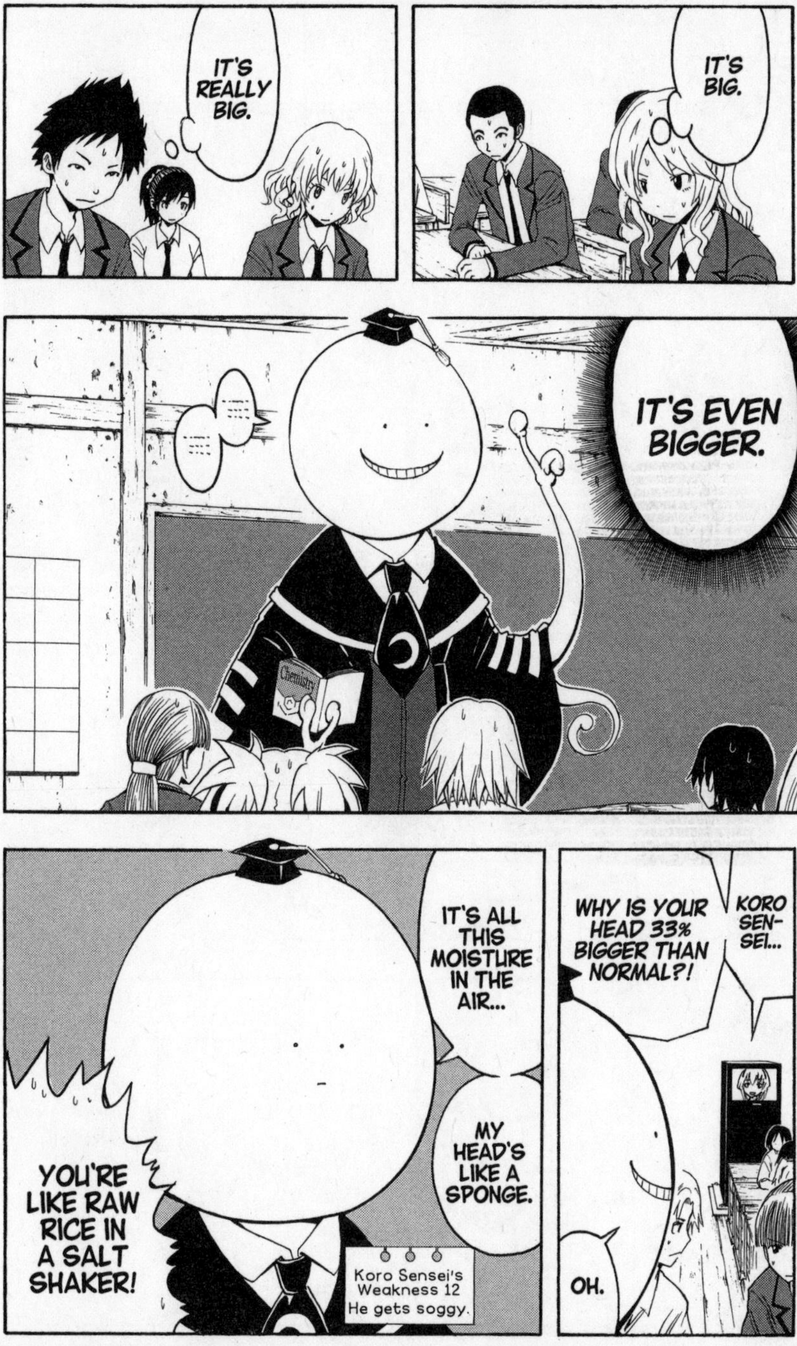
IT'S BIG.
IT'S REALLY BIG.
IT'S EVEN BIGGER.
KORO SENSEI...
WHY IS YOUR HEAD 33% BIGGER THAN NORMAL?!
OH.
IT'S ALL THIS MOISTURE IN THE AIR...
MY HEAD'S LIKE A SPONGE.
YOU'RE LIKE RAW RICE IN A SALT SHAKER!
Koro Sensei's Weakness 12
He gets soggy.

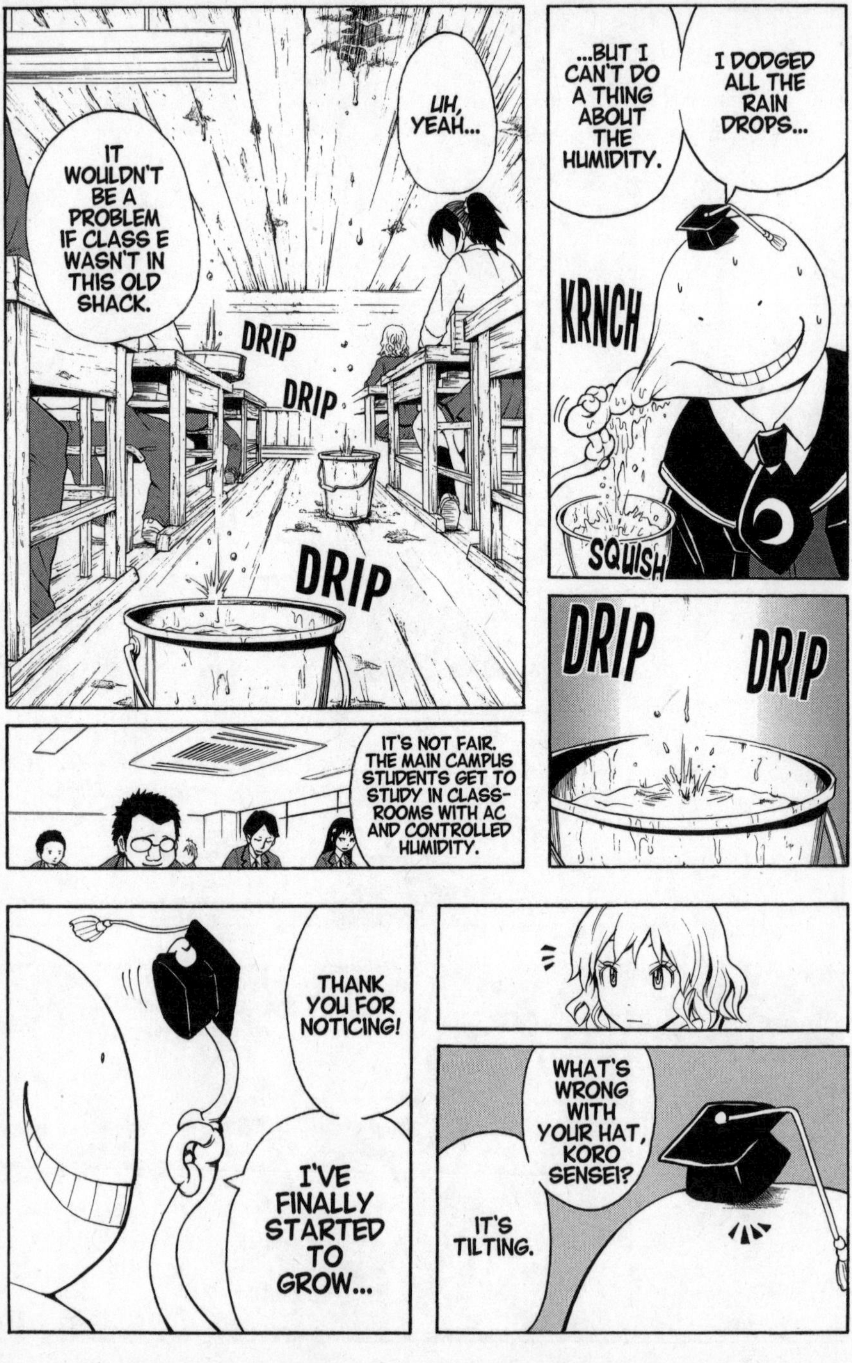
I DODGED ALL THE RAIN DROPS...
...BUT I CAN'T DO A THING ABOUT THE HUMIDITY.
KRNCH
SQUISH
DRIP
DRIP
UH, YEAH...
IT WOULDN'T BE A PROBLEM IF CLASS E WASN'T IN THIS OLD SHACK.
DRIP
DRIP
DRIP
IT'S NOT FAIR. THE MAIN CAMPUS STUDENTS GET TO STUDY IN CLASS-ROOMS WITH AC AND CONTROLLED HUMIDITY.
WHAT'S WRONG WITH YOUR HAT, KORO SENSEI?
IT'S TILTING.
THANK YOU FOR NOTICING!
I'VE FINALLY STARTED TO GROW...

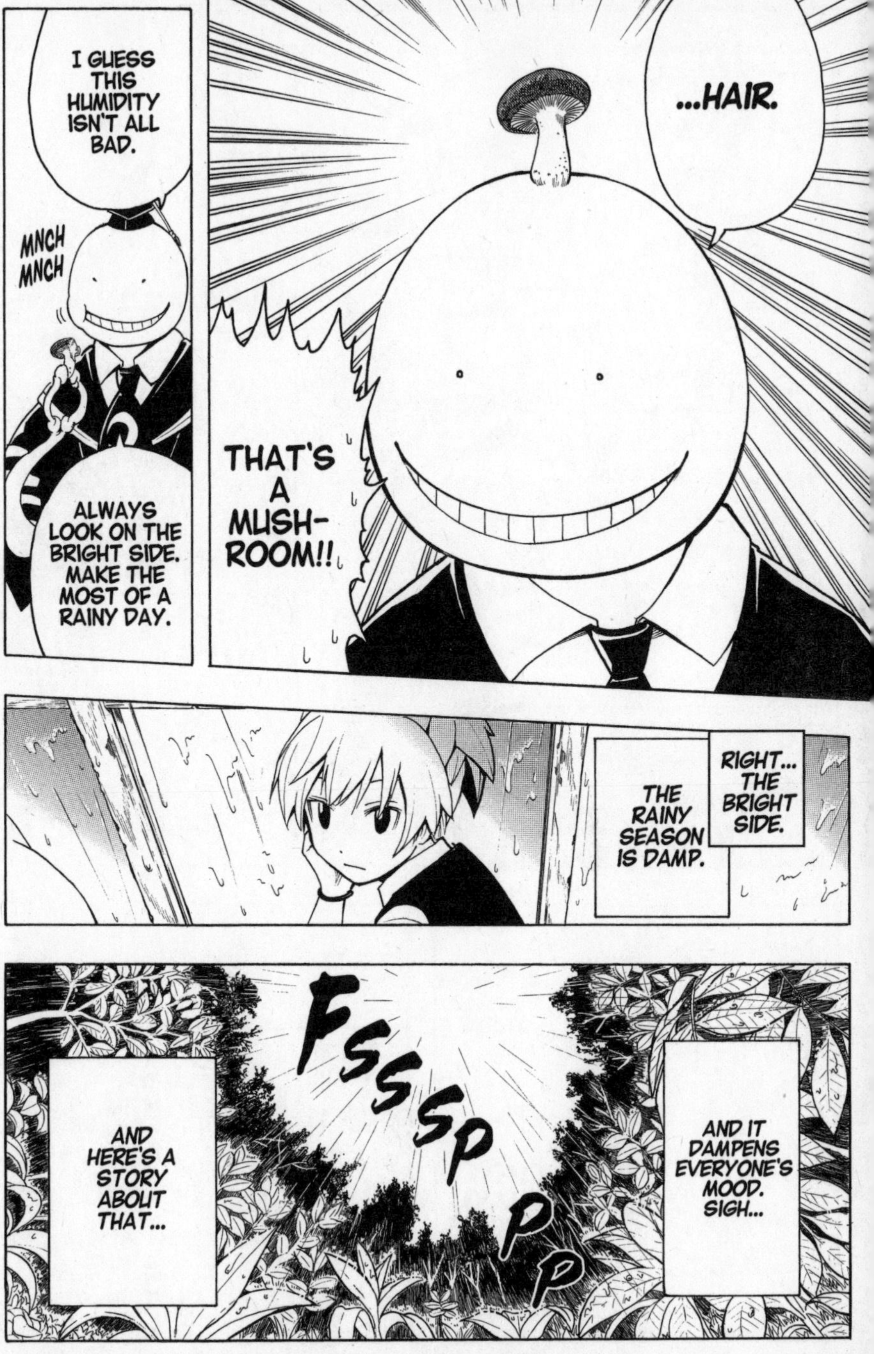
...HAIR.
THAT'S A MUSH-ROOM!!
I GUESS THIS HUMIDITY ISN'T ALL BAD.
MNCH MNCH
ALWAYS LOOK ON THE BRIGHT SIDE. MAKE THE MOST OF A RAINY DAY.
RIGHT... THE BRIGHT SIDE.
THE RAINY SEASON IS DAMP.
AND IT DAMPENS EVERYONE'S MOOD. SIGH...
FSSSPPP
AND HERE'S A STORY ABOUT THAT...

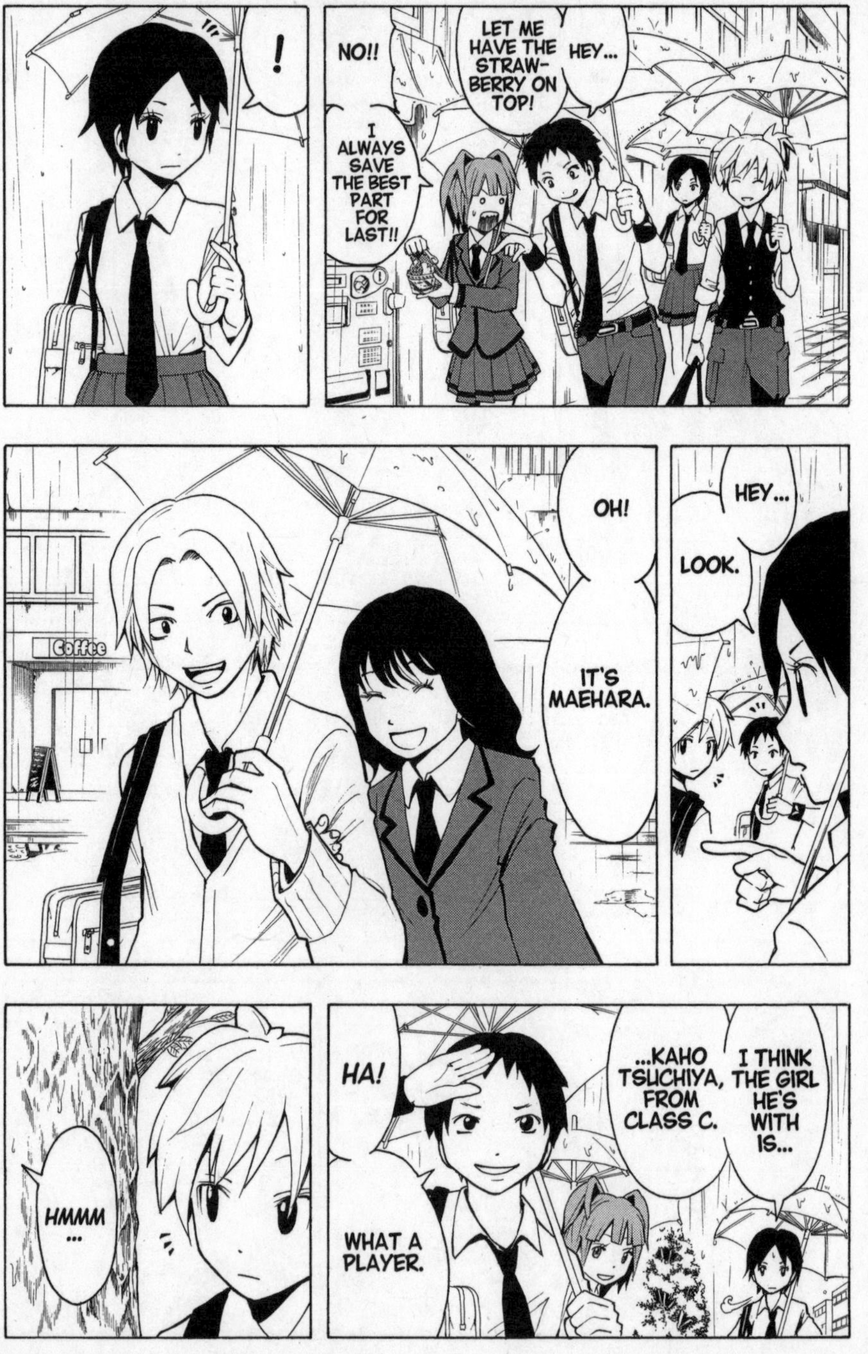
HEY...
LET ME HAVE THE STRAW-BERRY ON TOP!
NO!!
I ALWAYS SAVE THE BEST PART FOR LAST!!
!
HEY...
LOOK.
OH!
IT'S MAEHARA.
Coffee
I THINK THE GIRL HE'S WITH IS...
...KAHO TSUCHIYA, FROM CLASS C.
HA!
WHAT A PLAYER.
HMMM ...

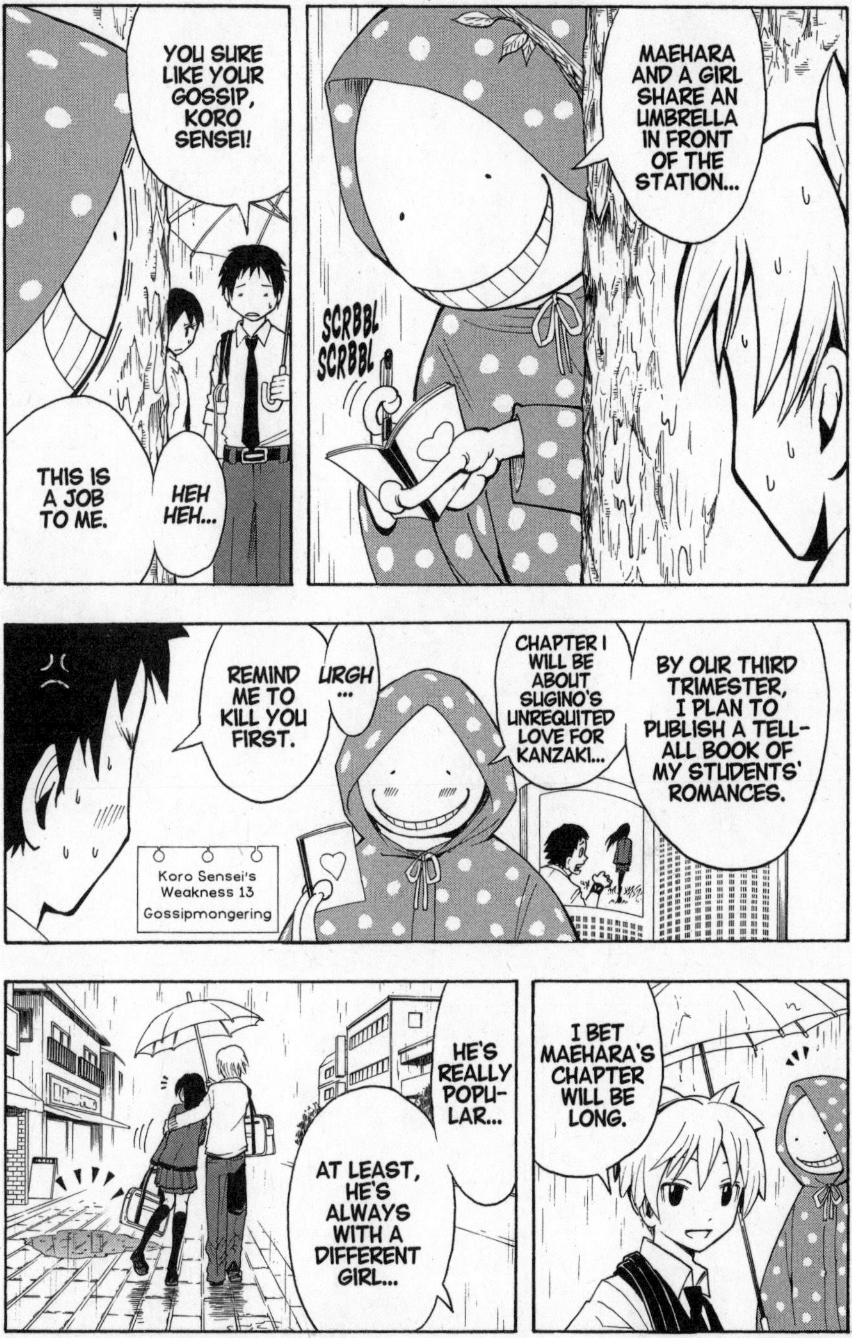
MAEHARA AND A GIRL SHARE AN UMBRELLA IN FRONT OF THE STATION...
SCRBBL SCRBBL
YOU SURE LIKE YOUR GOSSIP, KORO SENSEI!
HEH HEH...
THIS IS A JOB TO ME.
BY OUR THIRD TRIMESTER, I PLAN TO PUBLISH A TELL-ALL BOOK OF MY STUDENTS' ROMANCES.
CHAPTER 1 WILL BE ABOUT SUGINO'S UNREQUITED LOVE FOR KANZAKI...
URGH ...
REMIND ME TO KILL YOU FIRST.
Koro Sensei's Weakness 13
Gossipmongering
I BET MAEHARA'S CHAPTER WILL BE LONG.
HE'S REALLY POPULAR...
AT LEAST, HE'S ALWAYS WITH A DIFFERENT GIRL...

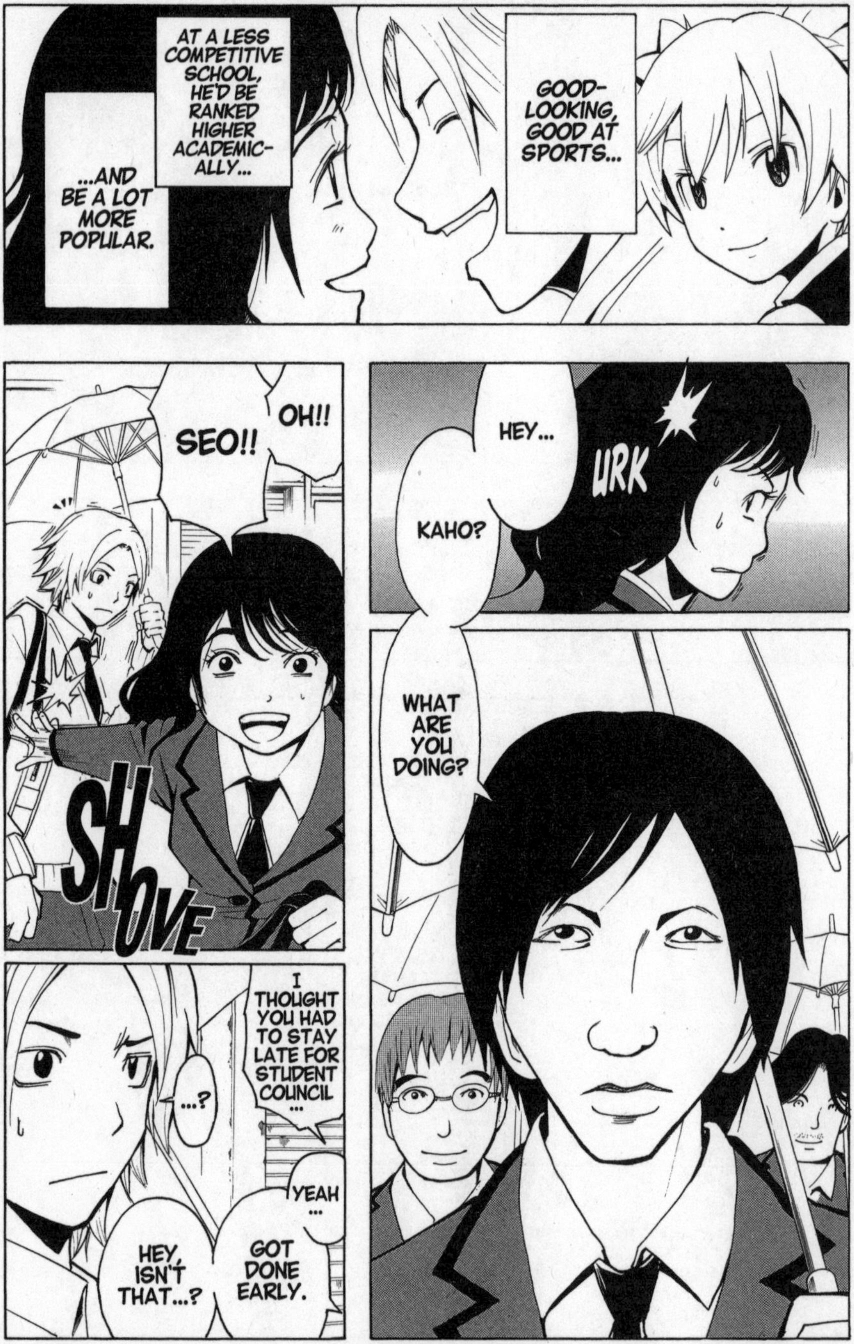
GOOD-LOOKING, GOOD AT SPORTS...
AT A LESS COMPETITIVE SCHOOL, HE'D BE RANKED HIGHER ACADEMICALLY...
...AND BE A LOT MORE POPULAR.
HEY...
KAHO?
URK
WHAT ARE YOU DOING?
OH!!
SEO!!
SHOVE
I THOUGHT YOU HAD TO STAY LATE FOR STUDENT COUNCIL...
...?
YEAH...
GOT DONE EARLY.
HEY, ISN'T THAT...?

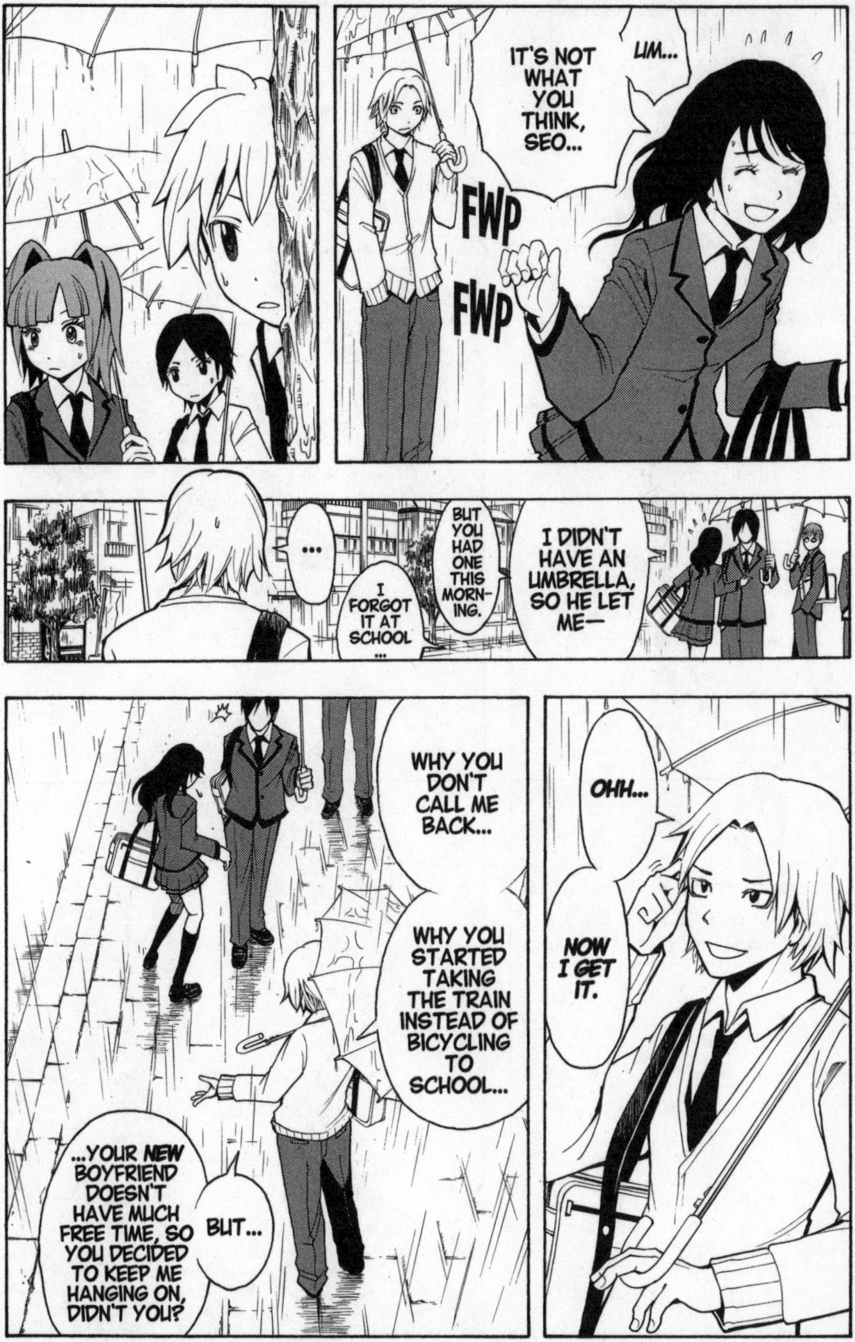
UM...
IT'S NOT WHAT YOU THINK, SEO...
FWP
FWP
I DIDN'T HAVE AN UMBRELLA, SO HE LET ME—
BUT YOU HAD ONE THIS MORNING.
I FORGOT IT AT SCHOOL...
...
OHH...
NOW I GET IT.
WHY YOU DON'T CALL ME BACK...
WHY YOU STARTED TAKING THE TRAIN INSTEAD OF BICYCLING TO SCHOOL...
BUT...
...YOUR *NEW* BOYFRIEND DOESN'T HAVE MUCH FREE TIME, SO YOU DECIDED TO KEEP ME HANGING ON, DIDN'T YOU?

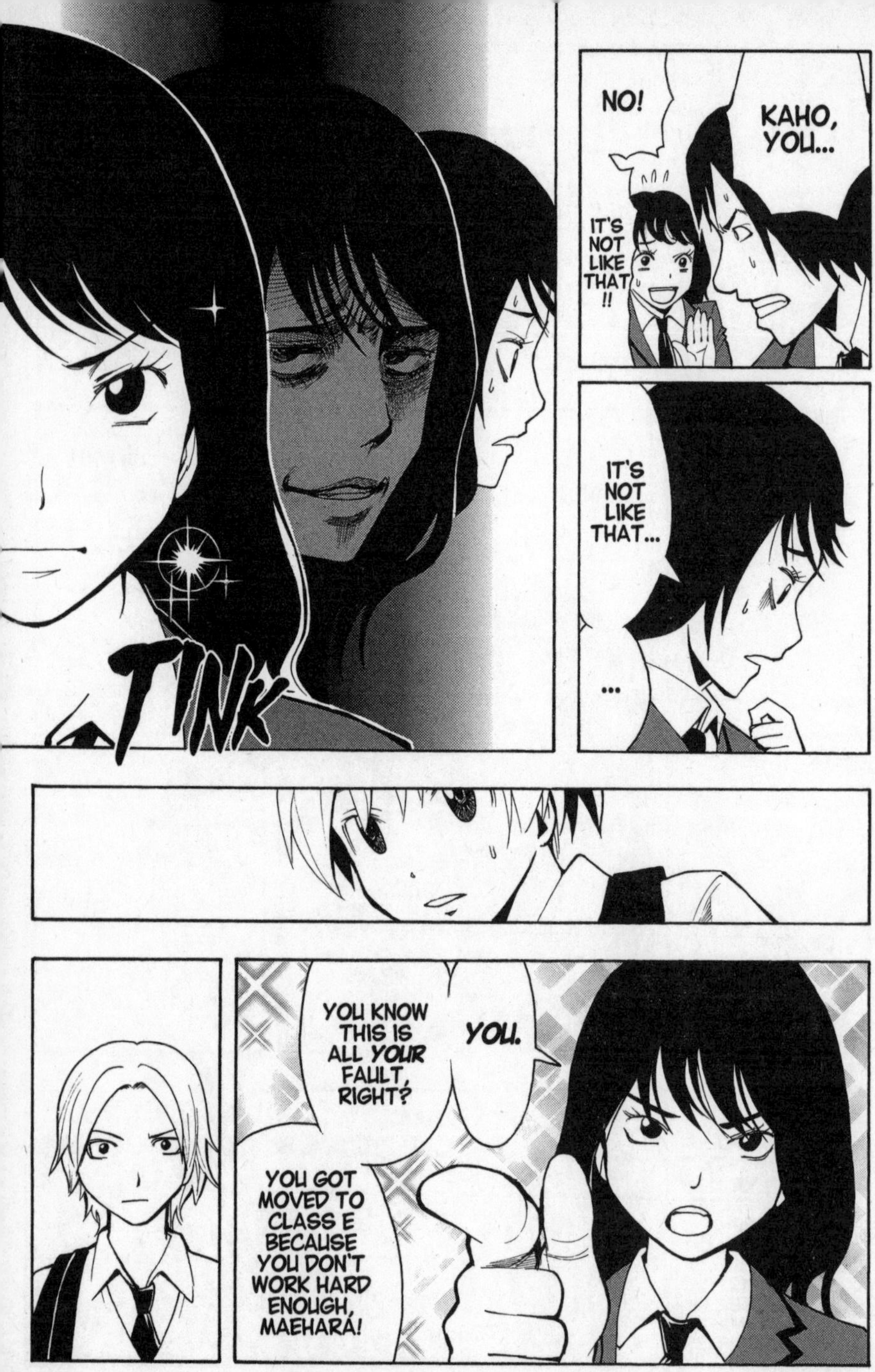
KAHO, YOU...
NO!
IT'S NOT LIKE THAT!!
IT'S NOT LIKE THAT...
...
TINK
YOU.
YOU KNOW THIS IS ALL *YOUR* FAULT, RIGHT?
YOU GOT MOVED TO CLASS E BECAUSE YOU DON'T WORK HARD ENOUGH, MAEHARA!

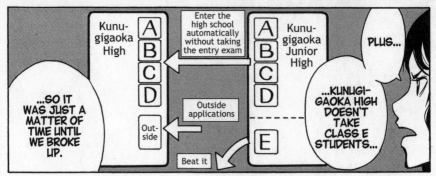

Enter the high school automatically without taking the entry exam

Kunugigaoka High

| A |
| B |
| C |
| D |

| Out-side |

Outside applications

Beat it

Kunugigaoka Junior High

| A |
| B |
| C |
| D |
| E |

PLUS...

...KUNUGI- GAOKA HIGH DOESN'T TAKE CLASS E STUDENTS...

...SO IT WAS JUST A MATTER OF TIME UNTIL WE BROKE UP.

HAR HAR!

GUESS NOT, THANKS TO THAT CLASS E BRAIN OF YOURS.

THE ONLY REASON I DIDN'T DUMP YOU ALREADY WAS BECAUSE YOU WERE SO BROKEN UP ABOUT GETTING SHUNTED INTO CLASS E.

I WAS JUST TRYING TO SPARE YOUR FEELINGS.

I WAS HOPING YOU'D CATCH ON SO I DIDN'T HAVE TO SPELL IT OUT.

YOU HAVEN'T EXACTLY TAKEN THE HIGH ROAD!

YOU EXPECT ME TO BE GRATE- FUL?

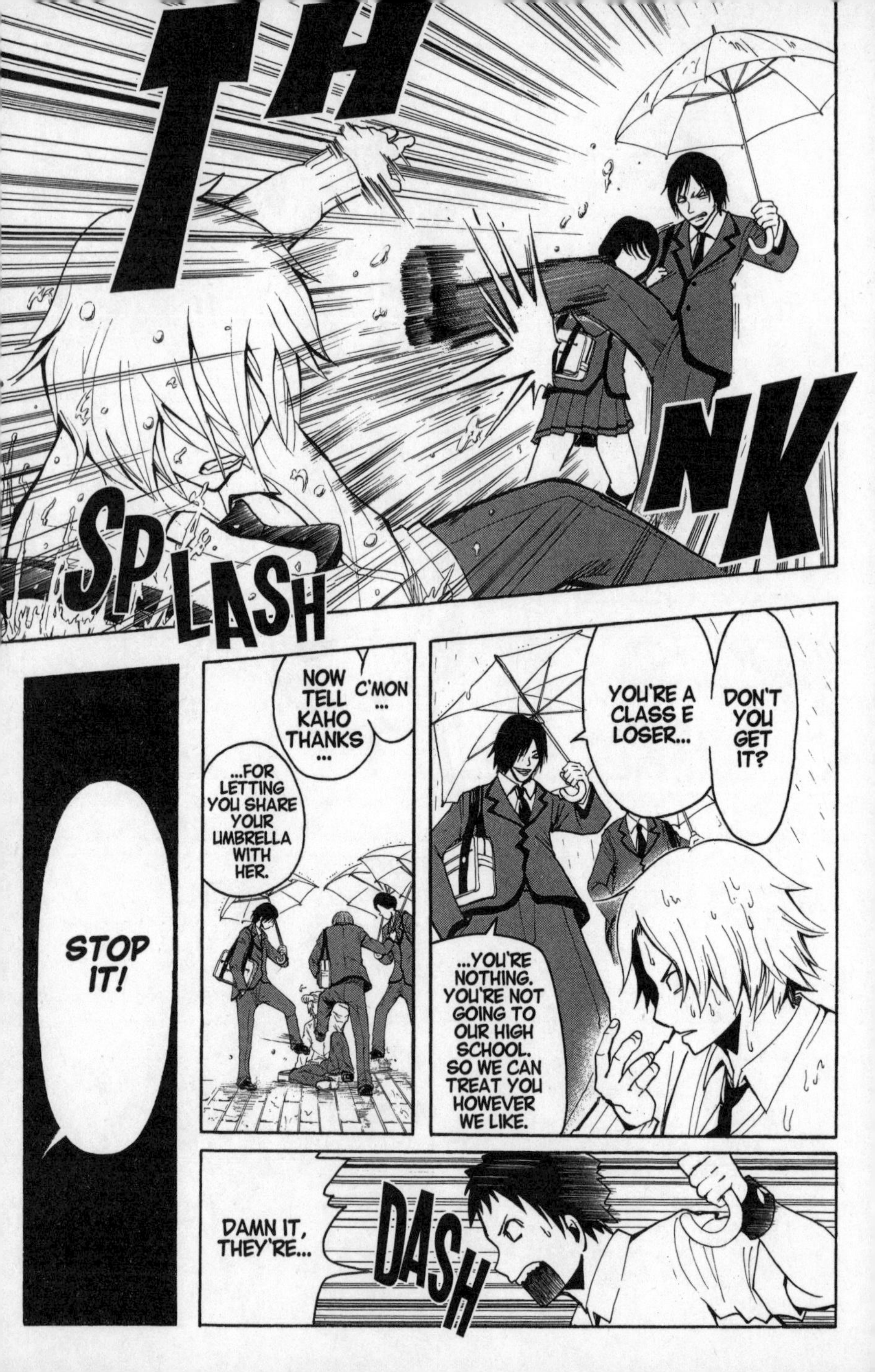
TH
NK
SPLASH
DON'T YOU GET IT?
YOU'RE A CLASS E LOSER...
...YOU'RE NOTHING. YOU'RE NOT GOING TO OUR HIGH SCHOOL. SO WE CAN TREAT YOU HOWEVER WE LIKE.
C'MON...
NOW TELL KAHO THANKS...
...FOR LETTING YOU SHARE YOUR UMBRELLA WITH HER.
DASH
DAMN IT, THEY'RE...
STOP IT!

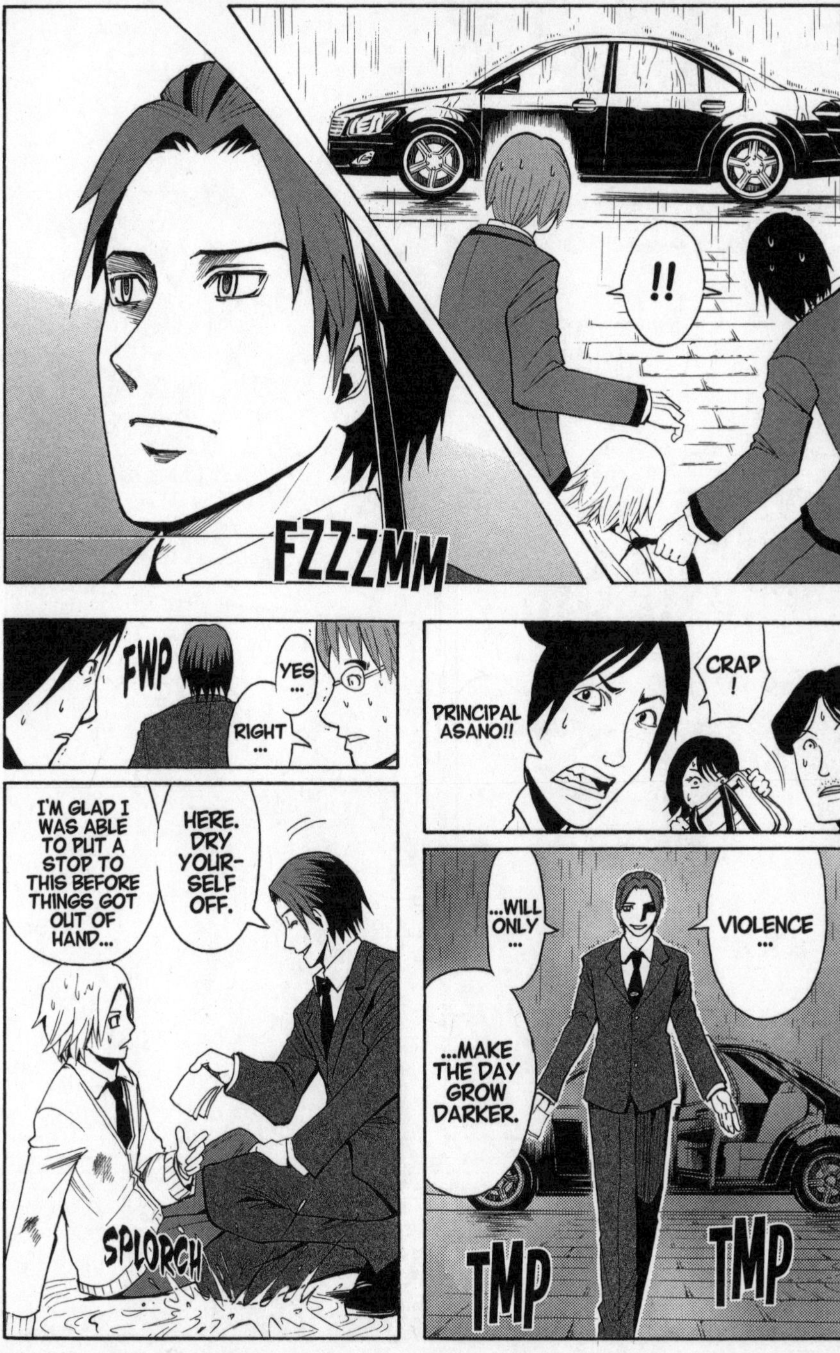
!!
FZZZMM
CRAP!
PRINCIPAL ASANO!!
VIOLENCE...
...WILL ONLY...
...MAKE THE DAY GROW DARKER.
TMP
TMP
HERE. DRY YOUR-SELF OFF.
I'M GLAD I WAS ABLE TO PUT A STOP TO THIS BEFORE THINGS GOT OUT OF HAND...
SPLORCH
FWP
YES...
RIGHT...

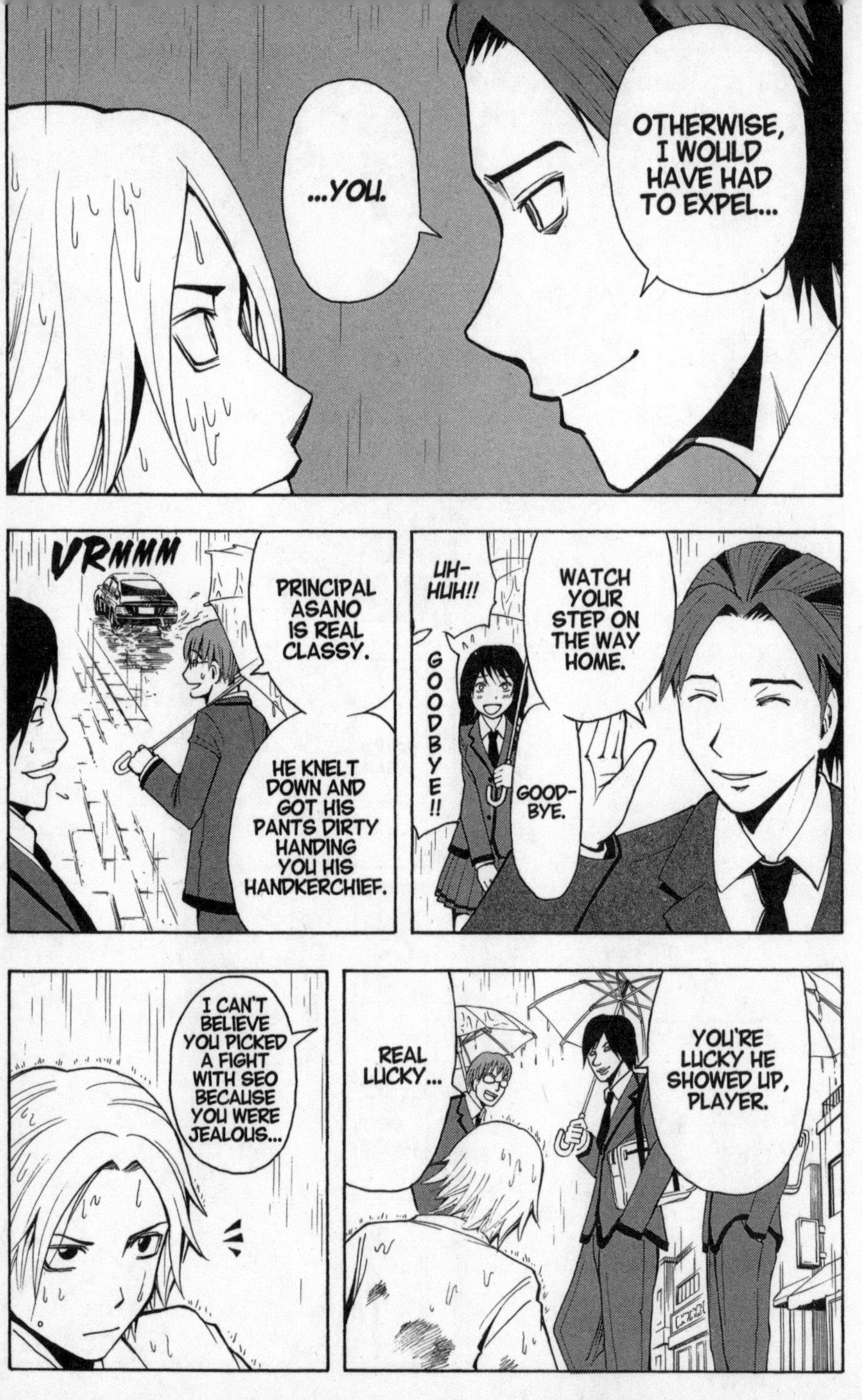
OTHERWISE, I WOULD HAVE HAD TO EXPEL...
...YOU.
WATCH YOUR STEP ON THE WAY HOME.
UH-HUH!!
GOODBYE!!
GOOD-BYE.
PRINCIPAL ASANO IS REAL CLASSY.
VRMMM
HE KNELT DOWN AND GOT HIS PANTS DIRTY HANDING YOU HIS HANDKERCHIEF.
YOU'RE LUCKY HE SHOWED UP, PLAYER.
REAL LUCKY...
I CAN'T BELIEVE YOU PICKED A FIGHT WITH SEO BECAUSE YOU WERE JEALOUS...

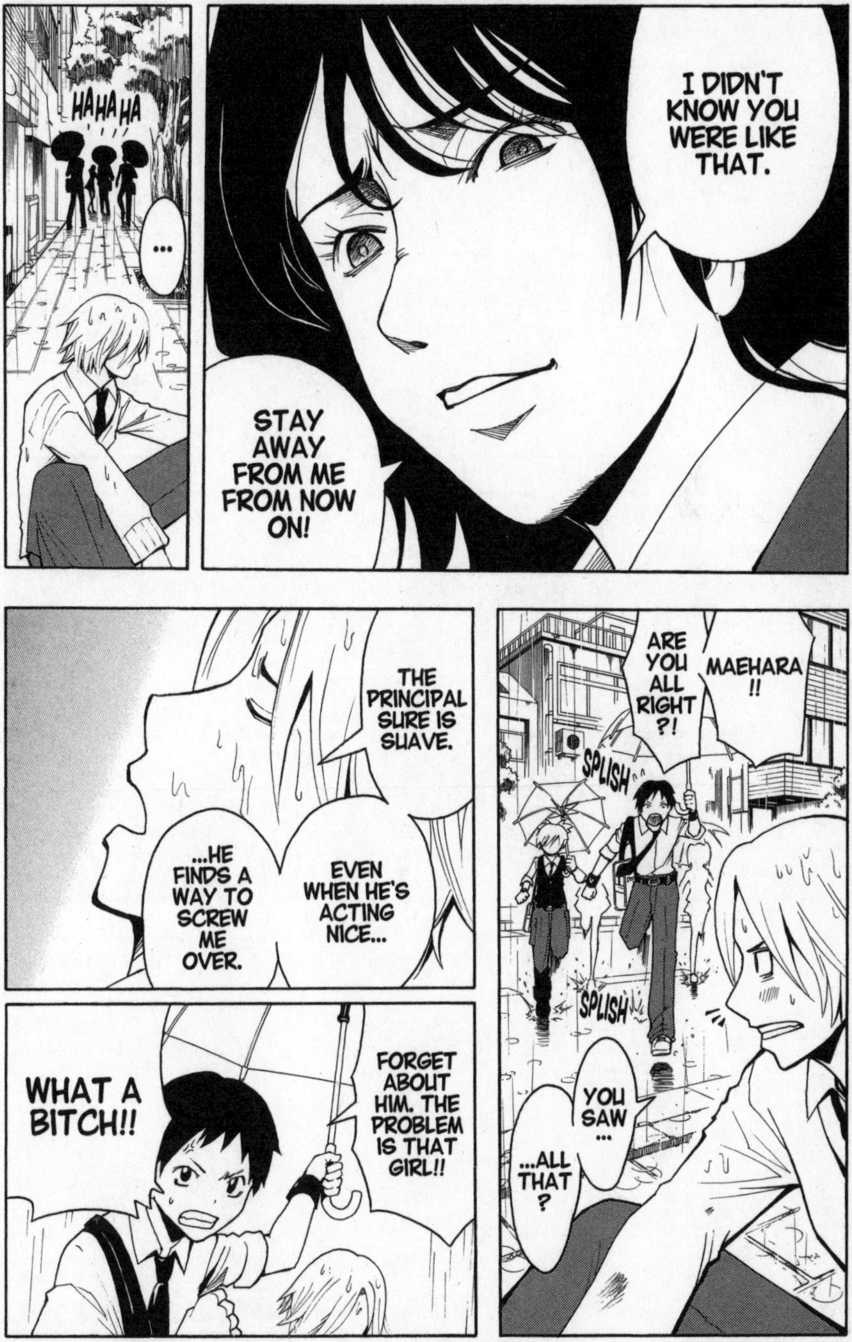
I DIDN'T KNOW YOU WERE LIKE THAT.
STAY AWAY FROM ME FROM NOW ON!
HAHAHA
...
MAEHARA!!
ARE YOU ALL RIGHT?!
SPLISH
SPLISH
YOU SAW...
...ALL THAT?
THE PRINCIPAL SURE IS SUAVE.
EVEN WHEN HE'S ACTING NICE...
...HE FINDS A WAY TO SCREW ME OVER.
FORGET ABOUT HIM. THE PROBLEM IS THAT GIRL!!
WHAT A BITCH!!

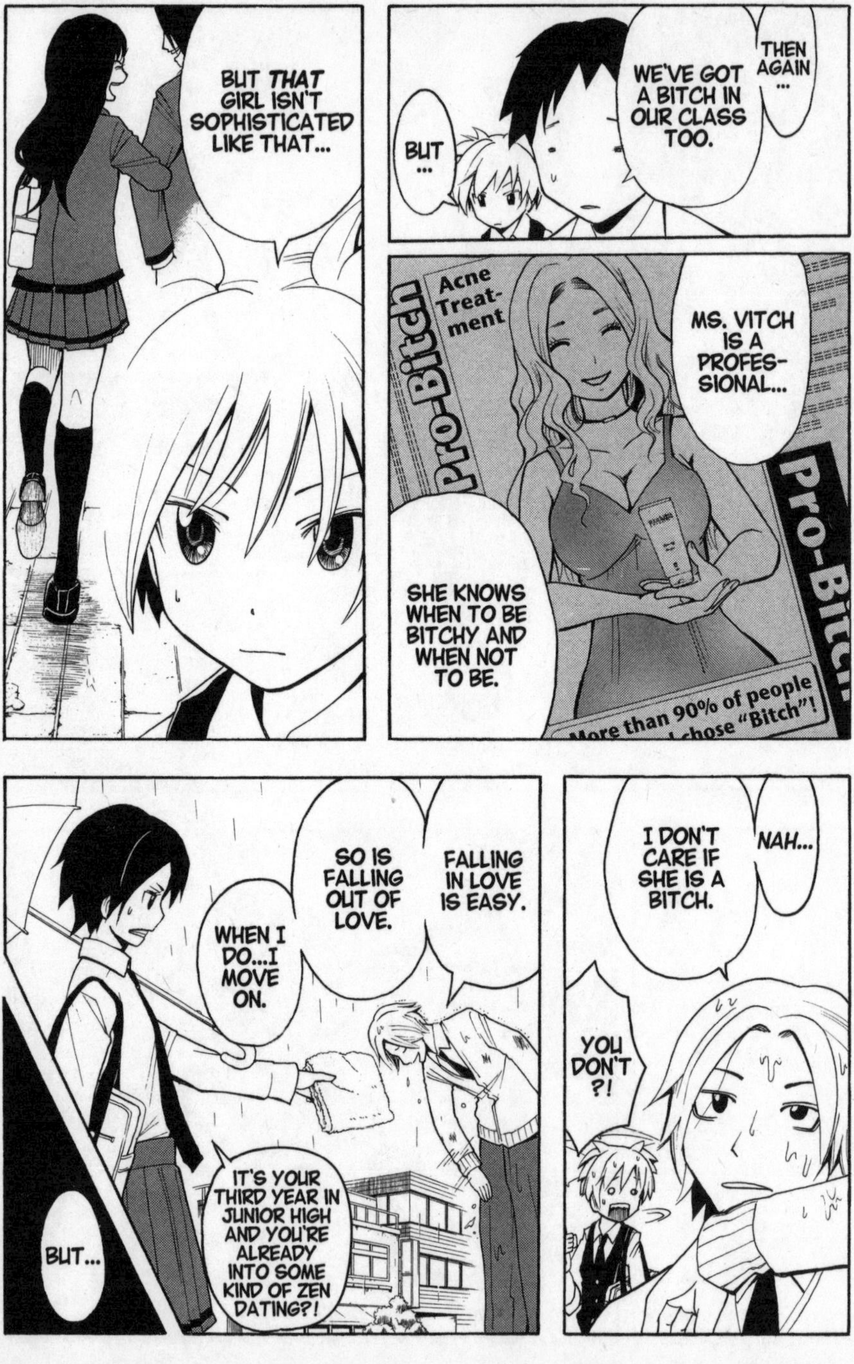
THEN AGAIN ...
WE'VE GOT A BITCH IN OUR CLASS TOO.
BUT ...
Acne Treat-ment
Pro-Bitch
MS. VITCH IS A PROFES-SIONAL...
SHE KNOWS WHEN TO BE BITCHY AND WHEN NOT TO BE.
More than 90% of people
chose "Bitch"!
BUT *THAT* GIRL ISN'T SOPHISTICATED LIKE THAT...
NAH...
I DON'T CARE IF SHE IS A BITCH.
YOU DON'T ?!
FALLING IN LOVE IS EASY.
SO IS FALLING OUT OF LOVE.
WHEN I DO...I MOVE ON.
IT'S YOUR THIRD YEAR IN JUNIOR HIGH AND YOU'RE ALREADY INTO SOME KIND OF ZEN DATING?!
BUT...

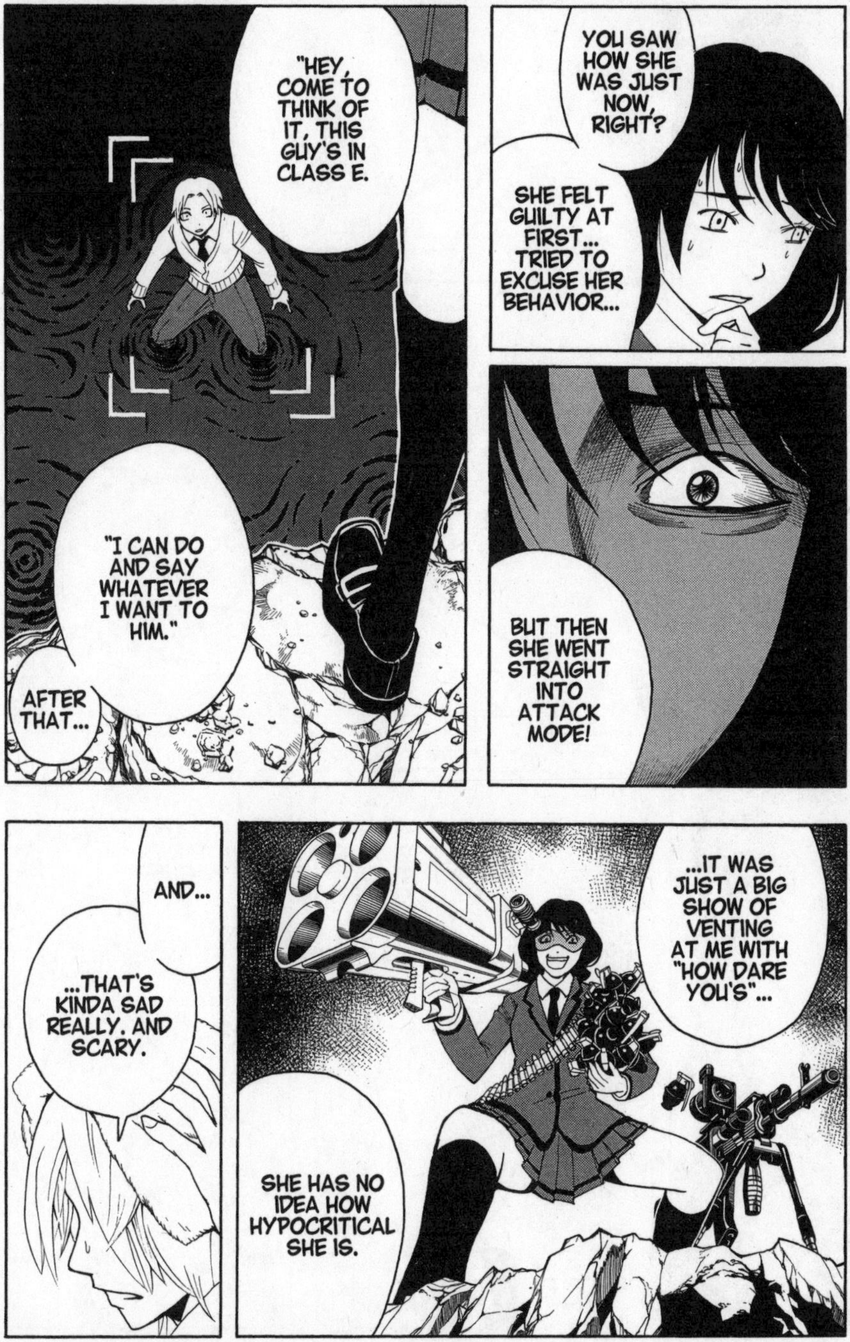
YOU SAW HOW SHE WAS JUST NOW, RIGHT?
SHE FELT GUILTY AT FIRST... TRIED TO EXCUSE HER BEHAVIOR...
BUT THEN SHE WENT STRAIGHT INTO ATTACK MODE!
"HEY, COME TO THINK OF IT, THIS GUY'S IN CLASS E.
"I CAN DO AND SAY WHATEVER I WANT TO HIM."
AFTER THAT...
...IT WAS JUST A BIG SHOW OF VENTING AT ME WITH "HOW DARE YOU'S"...
SHE HAS NO IDEA HOW HYPOCRITICAL SHE IS.
AND...
...THAT'S KINDA SAD REALLY. AND SCARY.

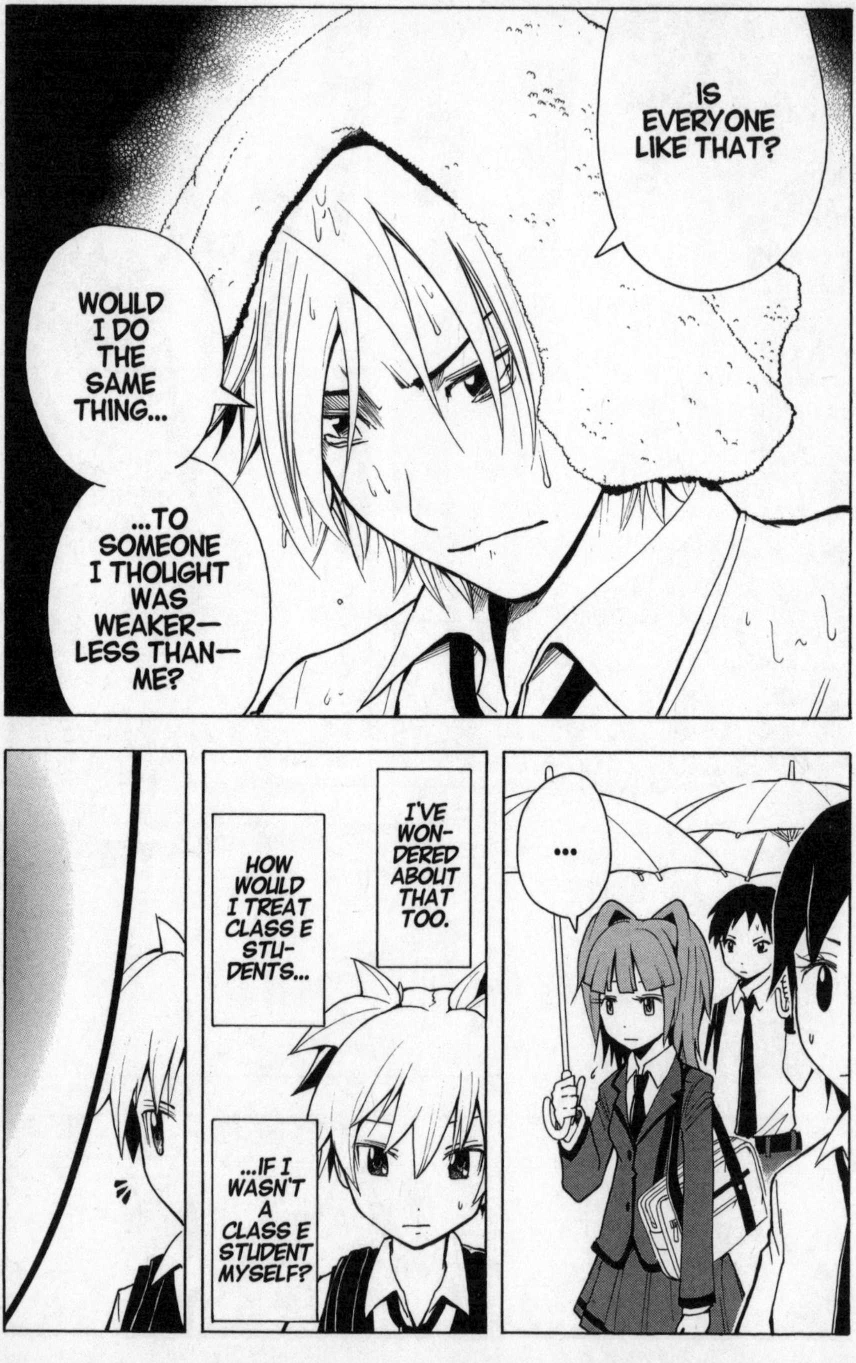
IS EVERYONE LIKE THAT?
WOULD I DO THE SAME THING...
...TO SOMEONE I THOUGHT WAS WEAKER—LESS THAN—ME?
...
I'VE WONDERED ABOUT THAT TOO.
HOW WOULD I TREAT CLASS E STUDENTS...
...IF I WASN'T A CLASS E STUDENT MYSELF?

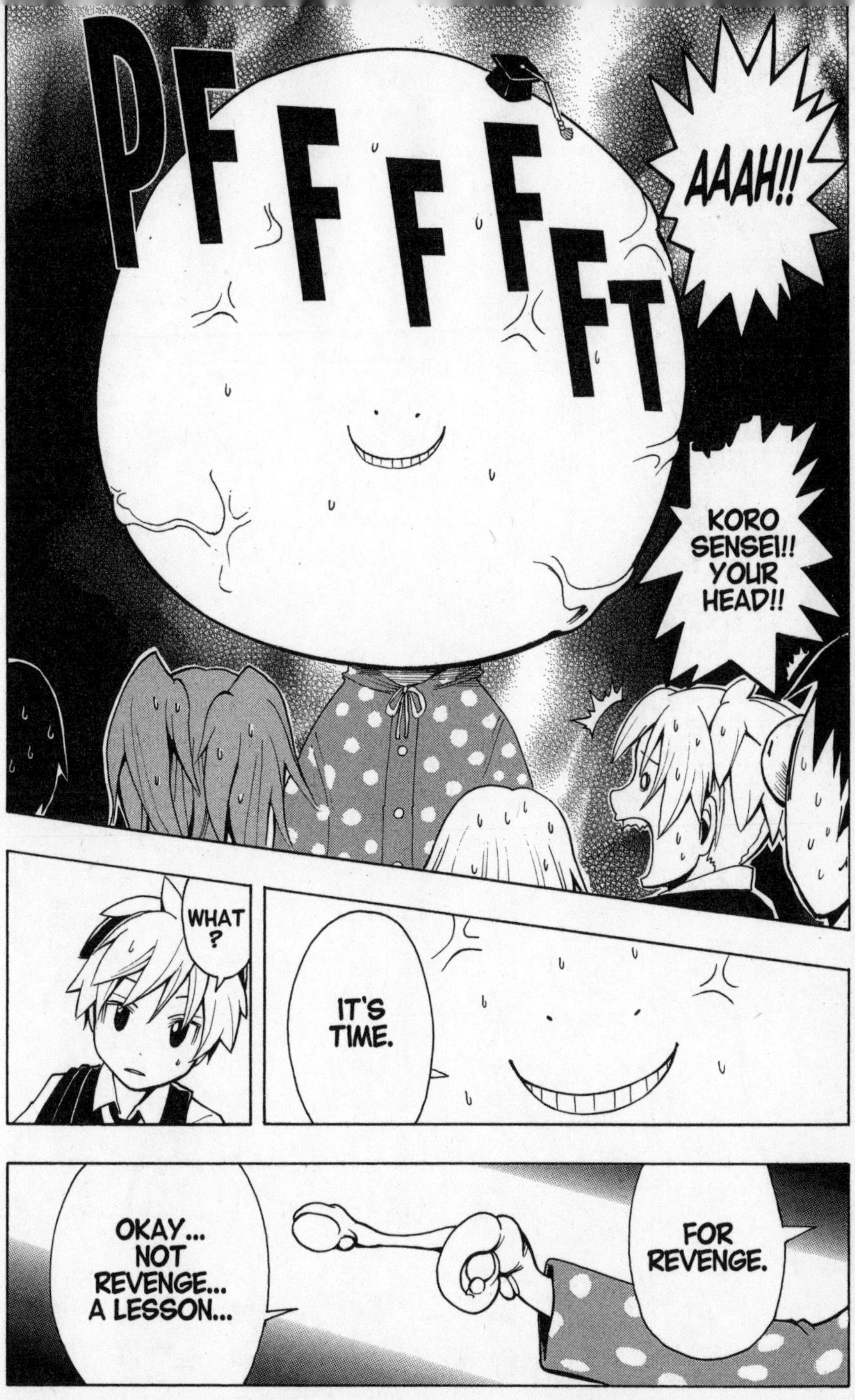
PFFFFFT
AAAH!!
KORO SENSEI!!! YOUR HEAD!!
IT'S TIME.
WHAT?
FOR REVENGE.
OKAY... NOT REVENGE... A LESSON...

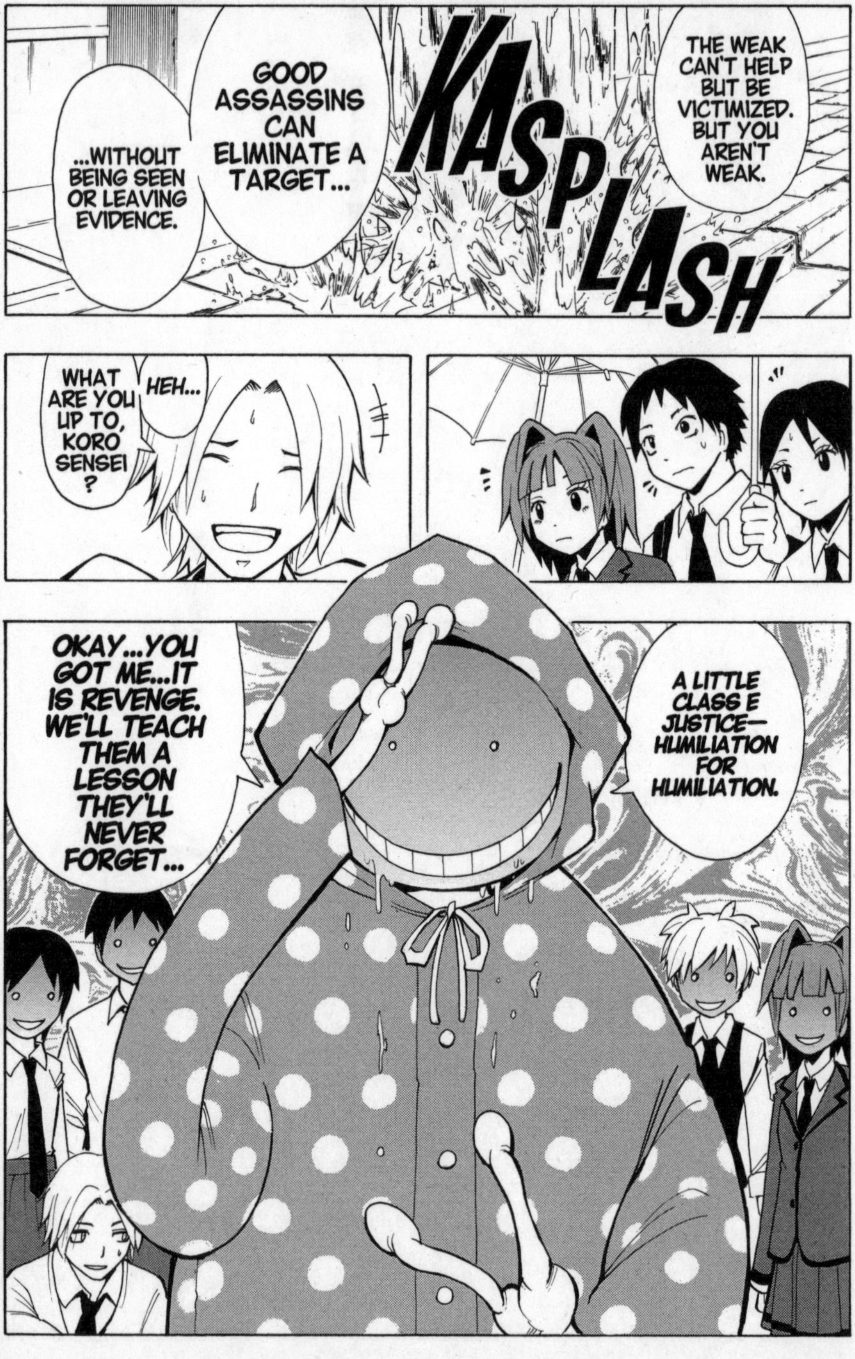
THE WEAK CAN'T HELP BUT BE VICTIMIZED. BUT YOU AREN'T WEAK.
KASPLASH
GOOD ASSASSINS CAN ELIMINATE A TARGET...
...WITHOUT BEING SEEN OR LEAVING EVIDENCE.
HEH...
WHAT ARE YOU UP TO, KORO SENSEI?
A LITTLE CLASS E JUSTICE—HUMILIATION FOR HUMILIATION.
OKAY...YOU GOT ME...IT IS REVENGE. WE'LL TEACH THEM A LESSON THEY'LL NEVER FORGET...

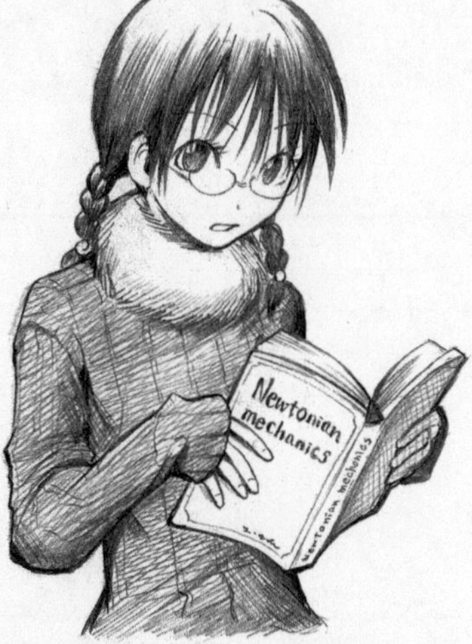
Newtonian mechanics
Newtonian mechanics

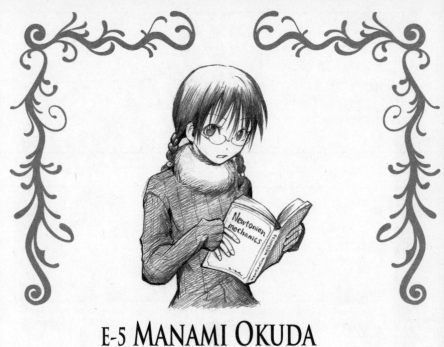

E-5 Manami Okuda

- Birthday: November 7
- Height: 4' 11"
- Weight: 97 lbs.
- Favorite Subject: Science
- Least Favorite Subject: Japanese
- Hobby/Skill: Concocting chemical equations
- Future Goal: Researcher
- Old Friends: Chemical Formulas
- Recent Friends: Nagisa and the others
- What she would like to discover: A chemical formula for happiness

CLASS 24 TIME FOR REVENGE

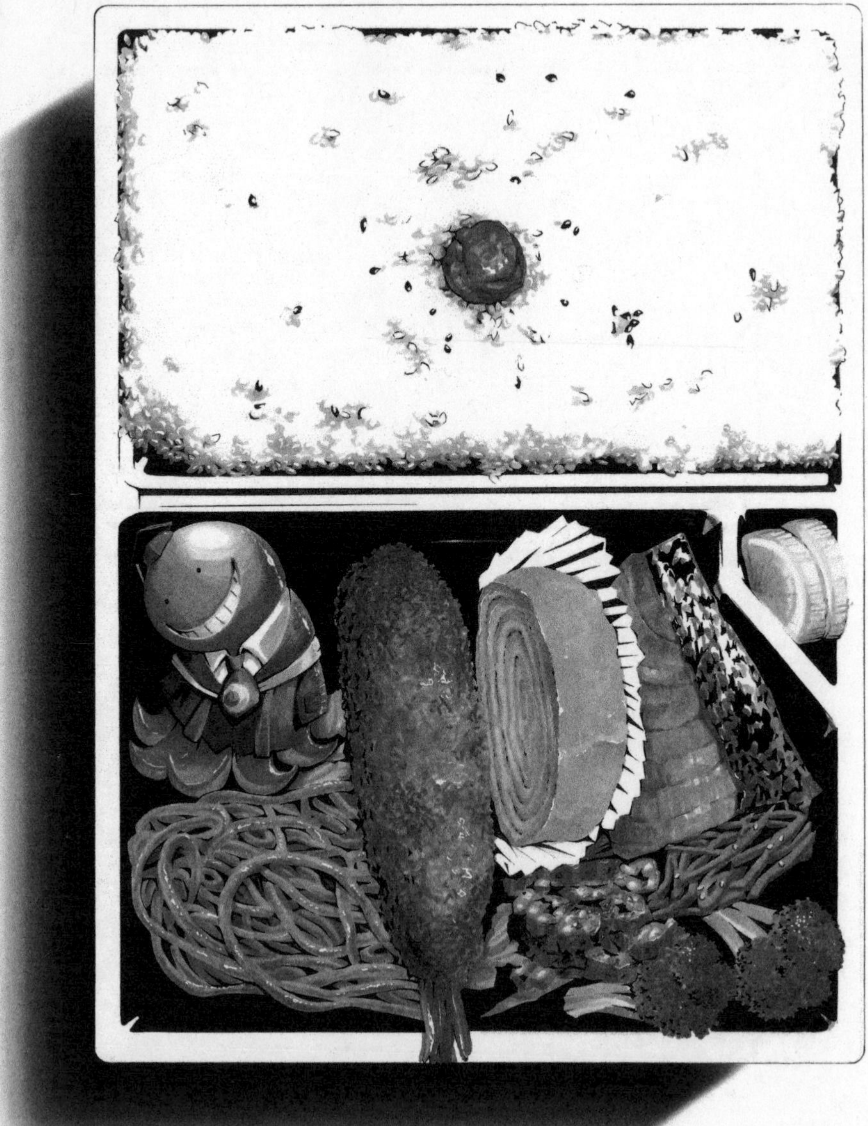

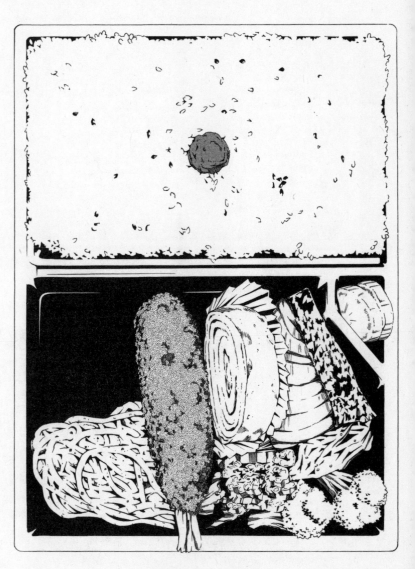

Escape

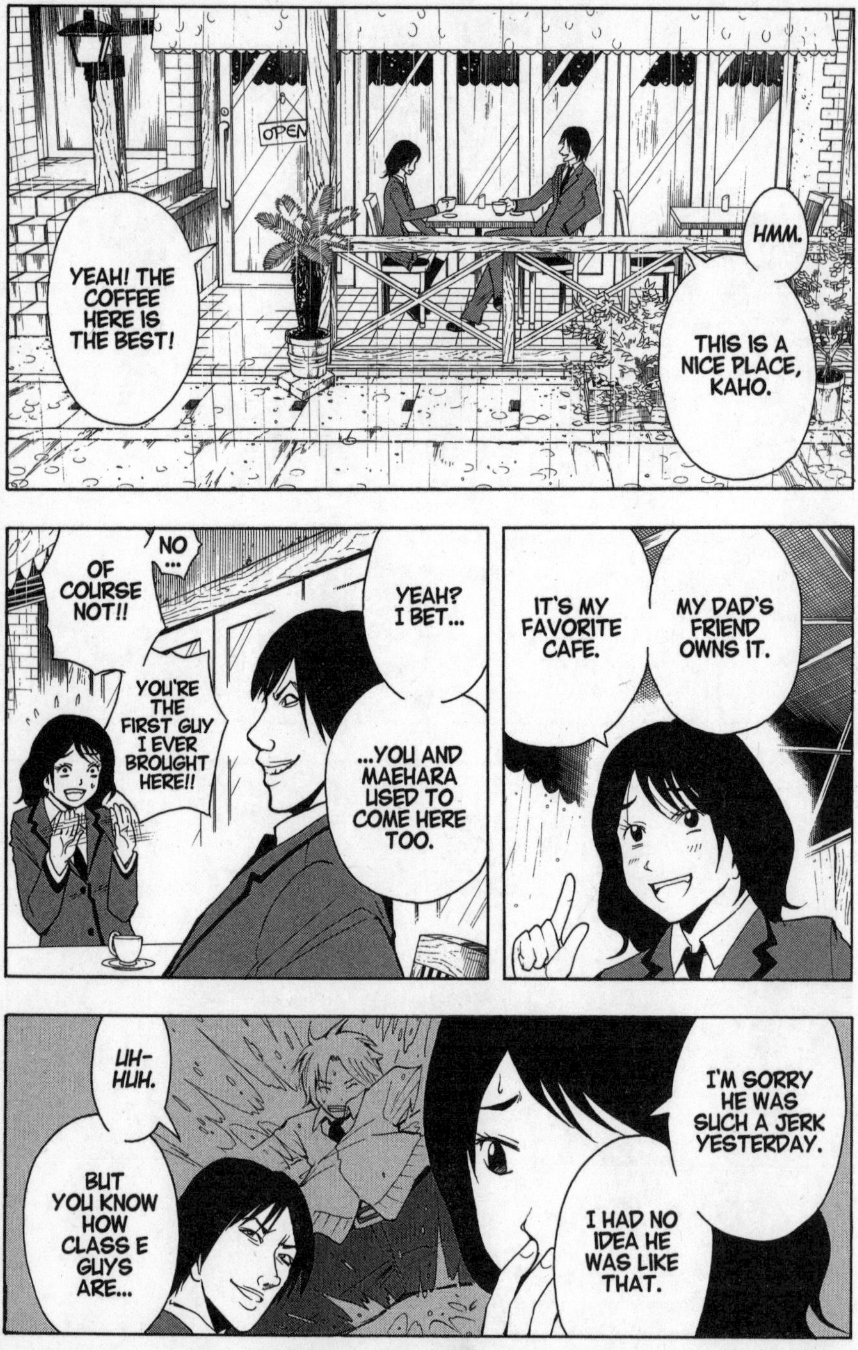
HMM.
THIS IS A NICE PLACE, KAHO.
YEAH! THE COFFEE HERE IS THE BEST!
MY DAD'S FRIEND OWNS IT.
IT'S MY FAVORITE CAFE.
YEAH? I BET...
...YOU AND MAEHARA USED TO COME HERE TOO.
NO...
OF COURSE NOT!!
YOU'RE THE FIRST GUY I EVER BROUGHT HERE!!
I'M SORRY HE WAS SUCH A JERK YESTERDAY.
I HAD NO IDEA HE WAS LIKE THAT.
UH-HUH.
BUT YOU KNOW HOW CLASS E GUYS ARE...

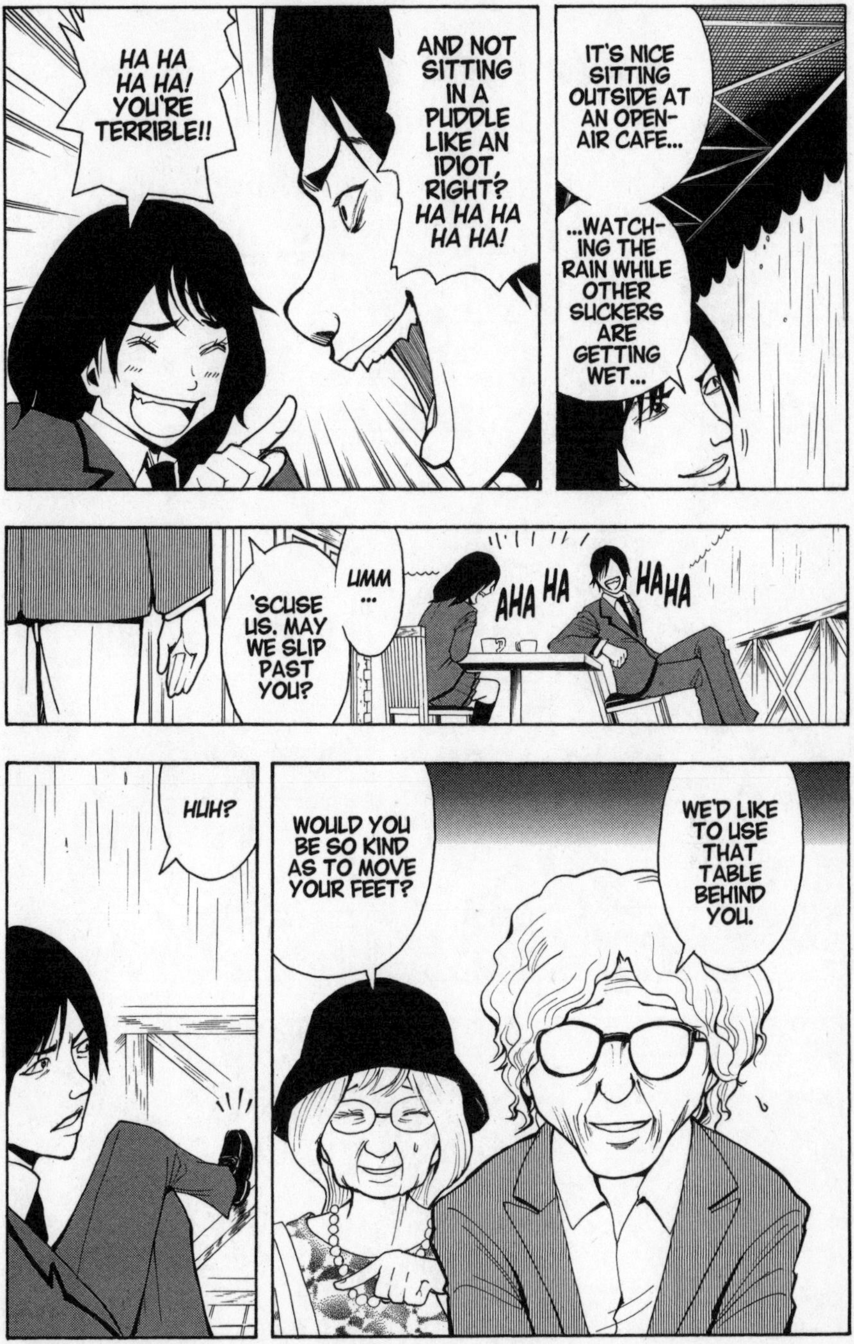
IT'S NICE SITTING OUTSIDE AT AN OPEN-AIR CAFE...
...WATCH-ING THE RAIN WHILE OTHER SUCKERS ARE GETTING WET...
AND NOT SITTING IN A PUDDLE LIKE AN IDIOT, RIGHT? HA HA HA HA HA!
HA HA HA HA! YOU'RE TERRIBLE!!
HAHA
AHA HA
UMM...
'SCUSE US. MAY WE SLIP PAST YOU?
WE'D LIKE TO USE THAT TABLE BEHIND YOU.
WOULD YOU BE SO KIND AS TO MOVE YOUR FEET?
HUH?

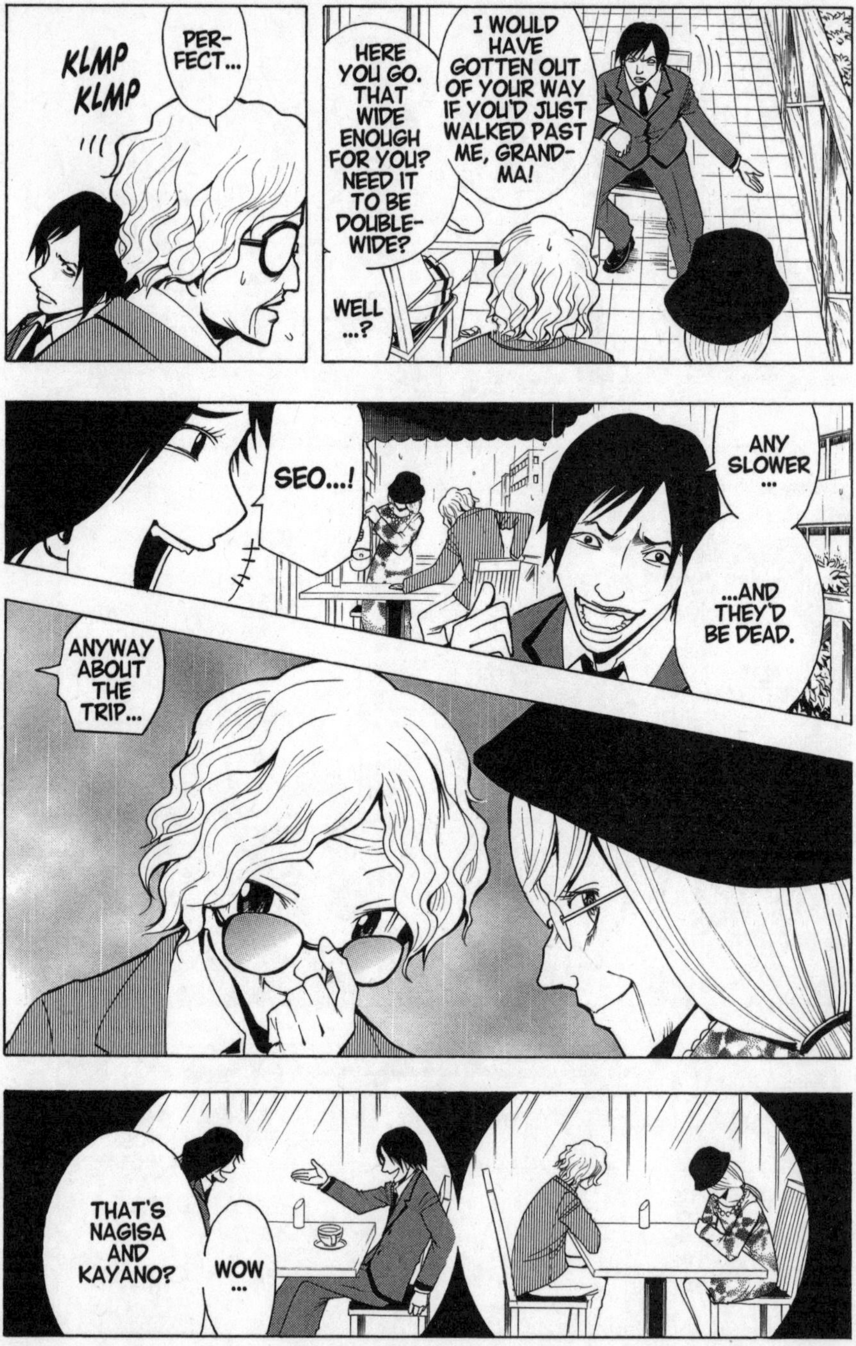
I WOULD HAVE GOTTEN OUT OF YOUR WAY IF YOU'D JUST WALKED PAST ME, GRANDMA!
HERE YOU GO. THAT WIDE ENOUGH FOR YOU? NEED IT TO BE DOUBLE-WIDE?
WELL ...?
KLMP KLMP
PERFECT...
ANY SLOWER ...
...AND THEY'D BE DEAD.
SEO...!
ANYWAY ABOUT THE TRIP...
WOW ...
THAT'S NAGISA AND KAYANO?

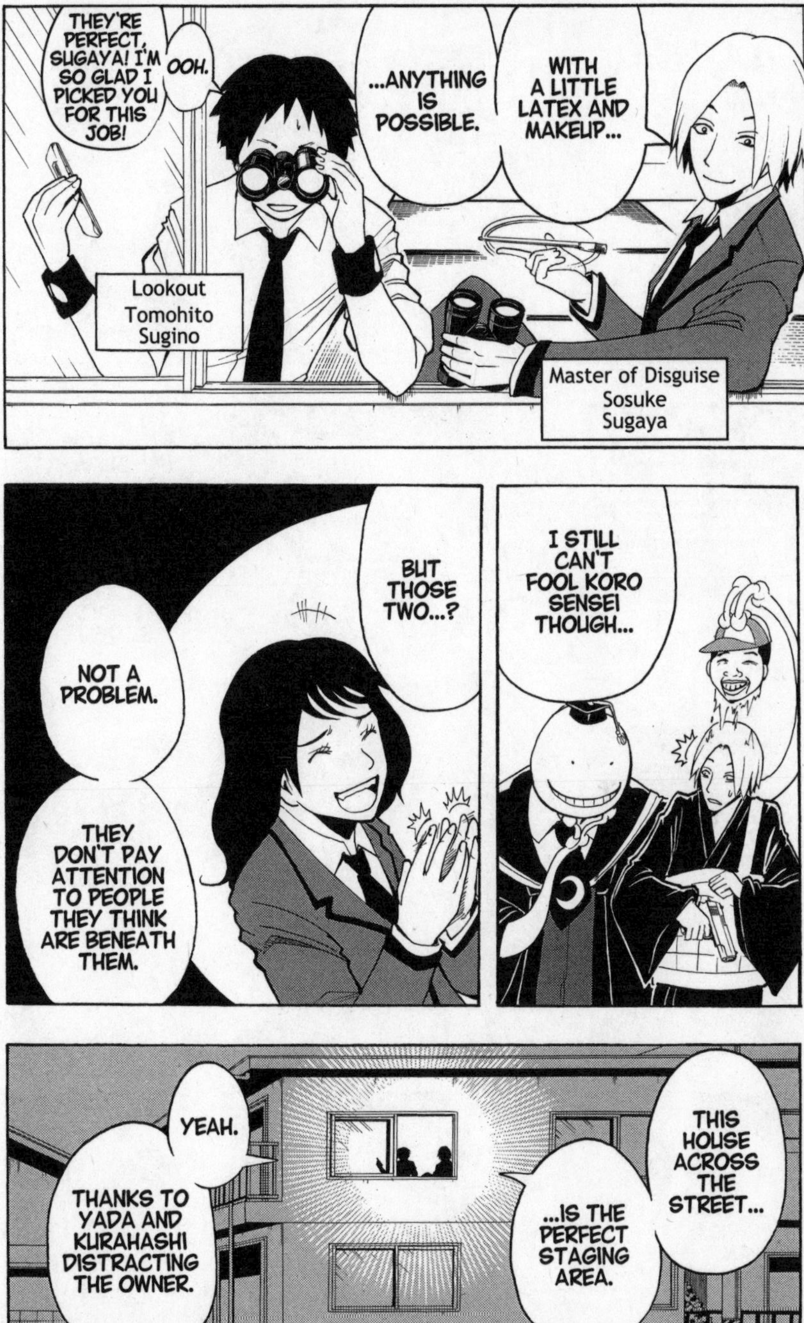
WITH A LITTLE LATEX AND MAKEUP...
...ANYTHING IS POSSIBLE.
OOH.
THEY'RE PERFECT, SUGAYA! I'M SO GLAD I PICKED YOU FOR THIS JOB!
Master of Disguise Sosuke Sugaya
Lookout Tomohito Sugino
I STILL CAN'T FOOL KORO SENSEI THOUGH...
BUT THOSE TWO...?
NOT A PROBLEM.
THEY DON'T PAY ATTENTION TO PEOPLE THEY THINK ARE BENEATH THEM.
THIS HOUSE ACROSS THE STREET...
...IS THE PERFECT STAGING AREA.
YEAH.
THANKS TO YADA AND KURAHASHI DISTRACTING THE OWNER.

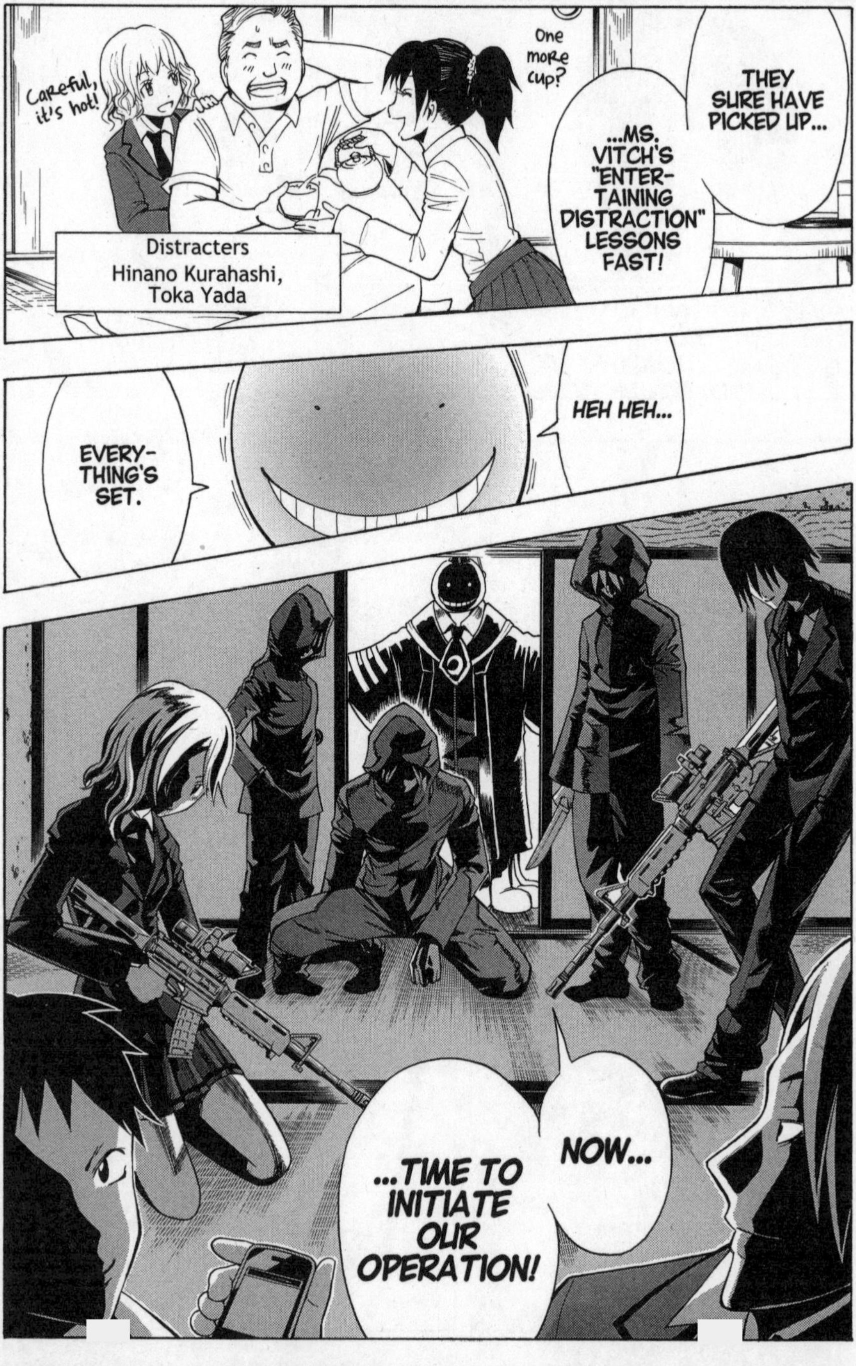
THEY SURE HAVE PICKED UP...
...MS. VITCH'S "ENTER-TAINING DISTRACTION" LESSONS FAST!
One more cup?
Careful, it's hot!
Distracters Hinano Kurahashi, Toka Yada
HEH HEH...
EVERY-THING'S SET.
NOW...
...TIME TO INITIATE OUR OPERATION!

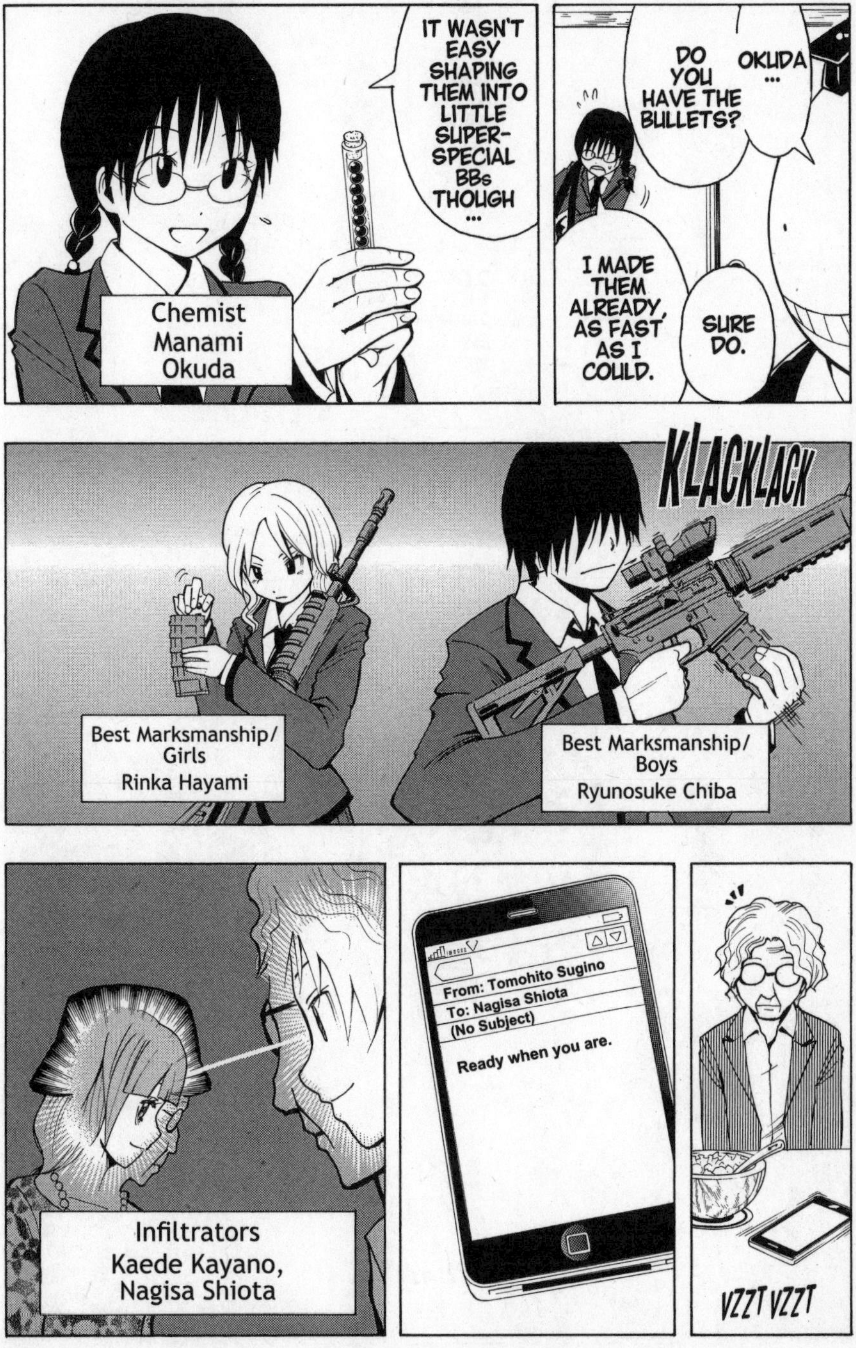
OKUDA ...
DO YOU HAVE THE BULLETS?
SURE DO.
I MADE THEM ALREADY, AS FAST AS I COULD.
IT WASN'T EASY SHAPING THEM INTO LITTLE SUPER-SPECIAL BBs THOUGH ...
Chemist
Manami
Okuda
KLACKLACK
Best Marksmanship/
Boys
Ryunosuke Chiba
Best Marksmanship/
Girls
Rinka Hayami
VZZT VZZT
From: Tomohito Sugino
To: Nagisa Shiota
(No Subject)
Ready when you are.
Infiltrators
Kaede Kayano,
Nagisa Shiota

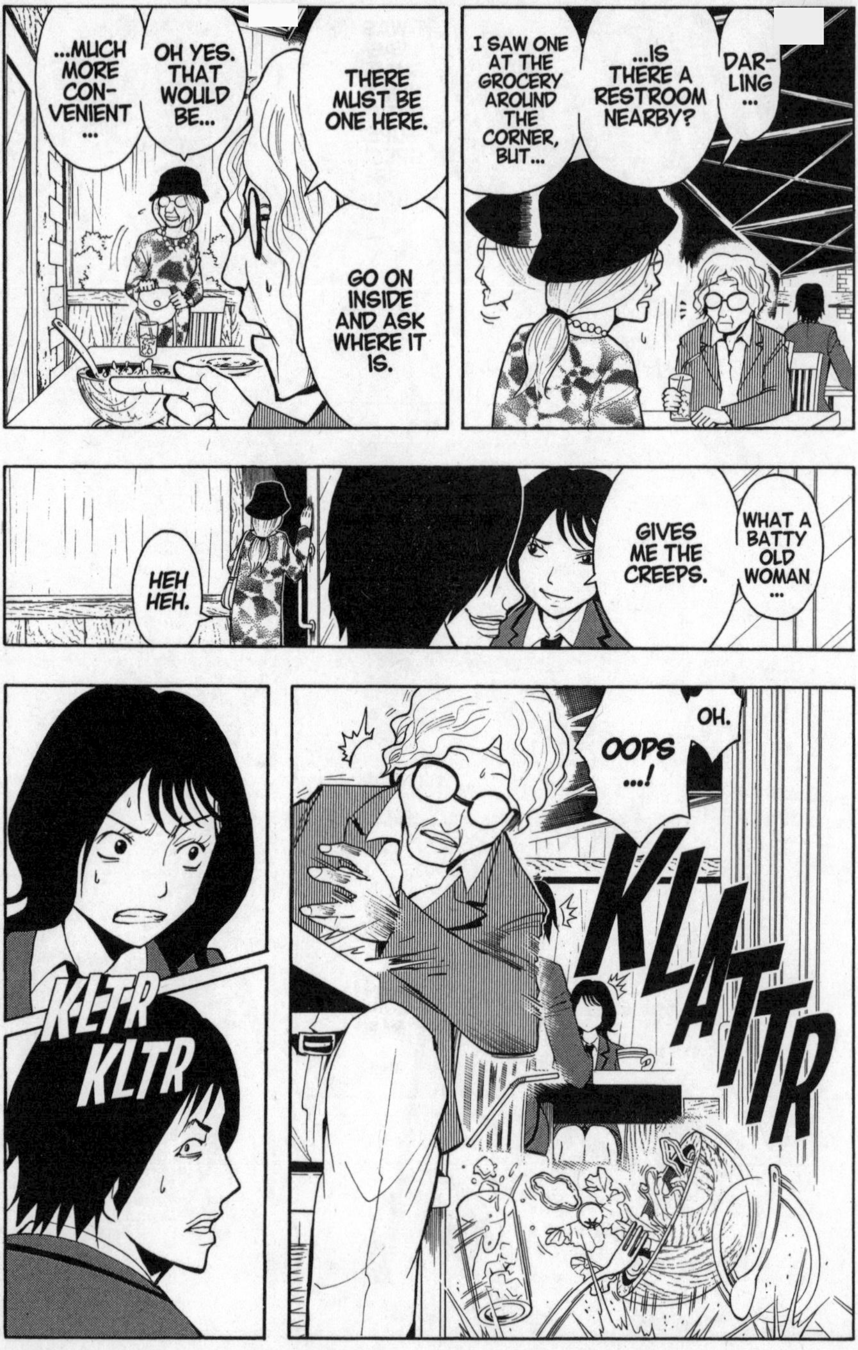
DAR-LING...
...IS THERE A RESTROOM NEARBY?
I SAW ONE AT THE GROCERY AROUND THE CORNER, BUT...
THERE MUST BE ONE HERE.
GO ON INSIDE AND ASK WHERE IT IS.
OH YES. THAT WOULD BE...
...MUCH MORE CON-VENIENT...
WHAT A BATTY OLD WOMAN...
GIVES ME THE CREEPS.
HEH HEH.
OH.
OOPS...!
KLATTR
KLTR KLTR

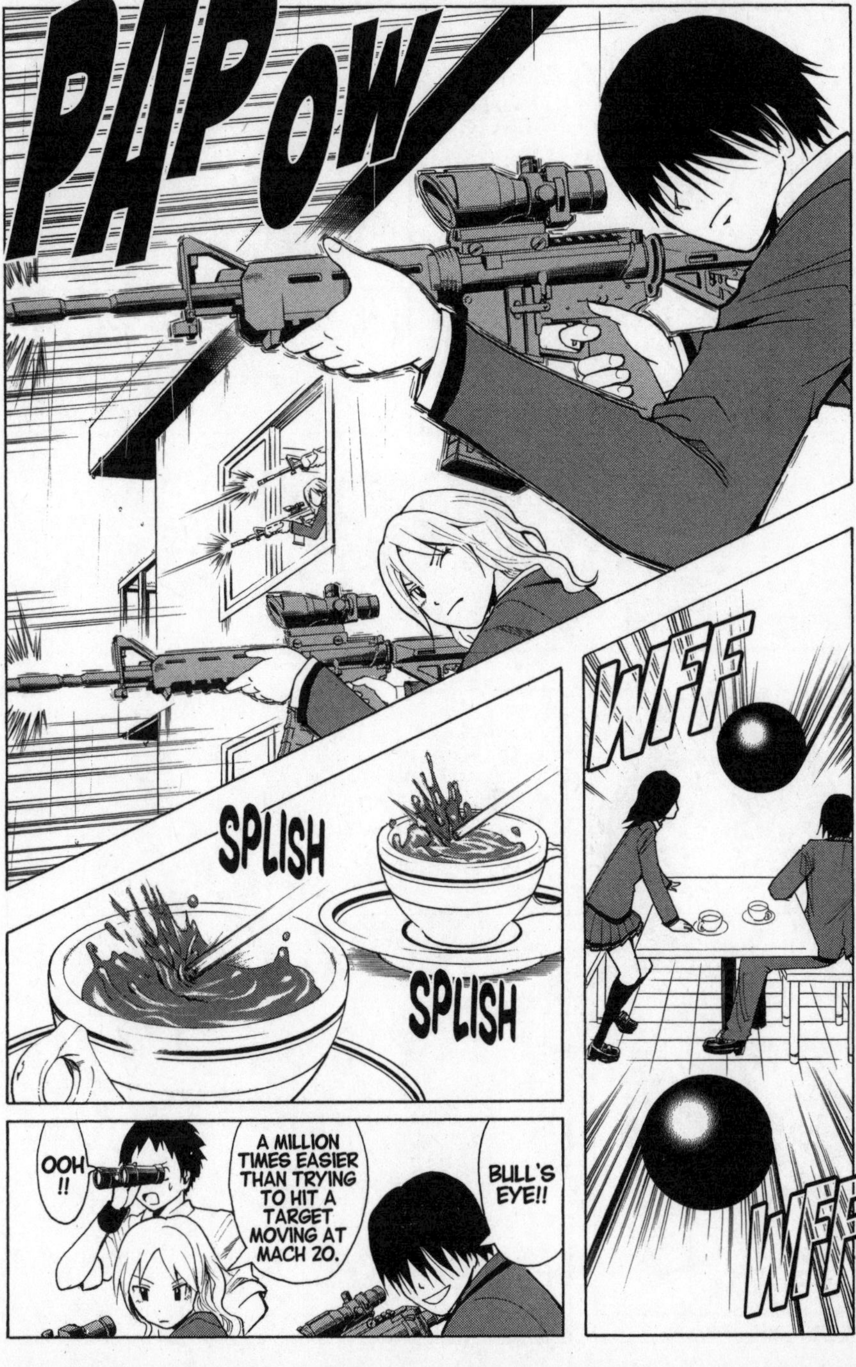
PAPOW
WFF
WFF
SPLISH
SPLISH
BULL'S EYE!!
A MILLION TIMES EASIER THAN TRYING TO HIT A TARGET MOVING AT MACH 20.
OOH !!

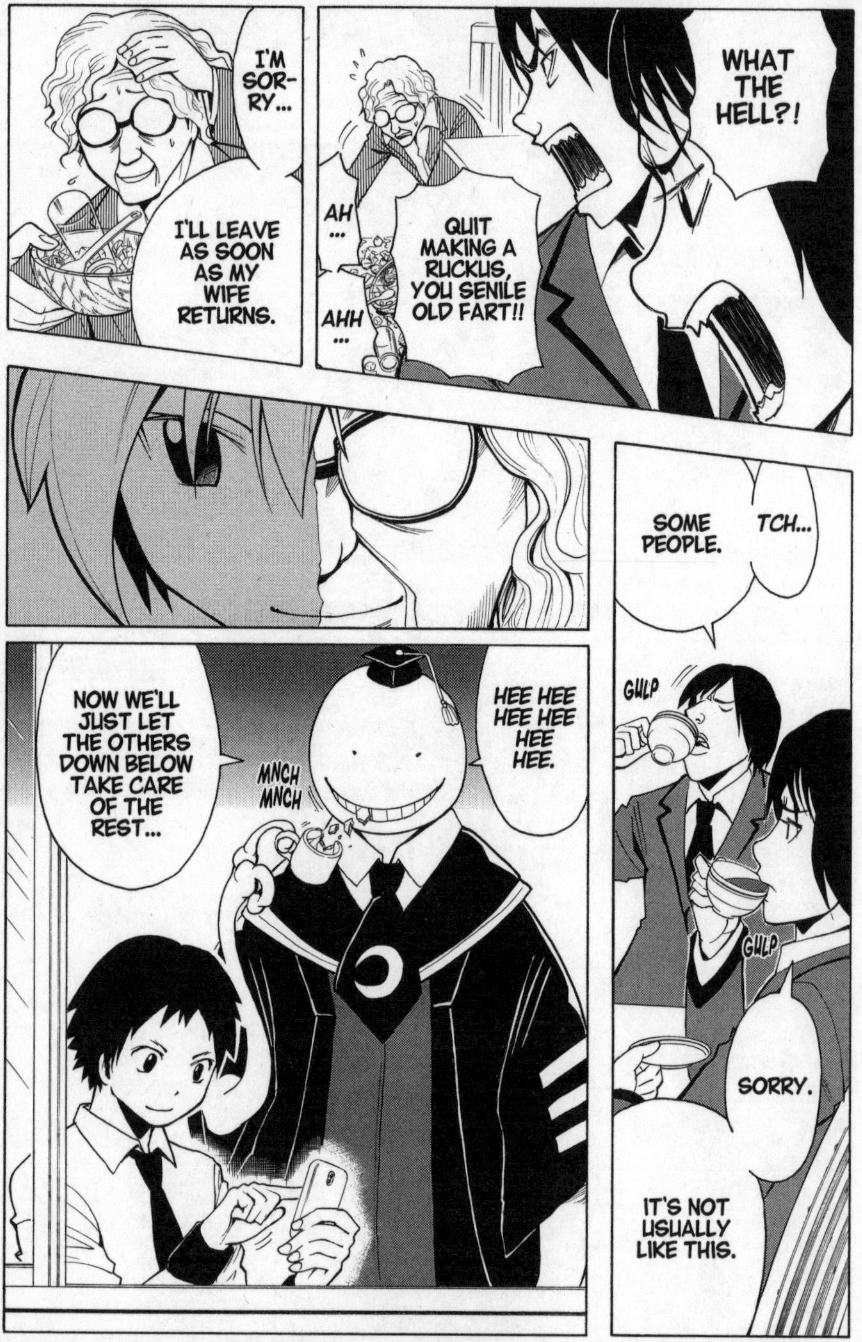
WHAT THE HELL?!
QUIT MAKING A RUCKUS, YOU SENILE OLD FART!!
AH ...
AHH ...
I'M SORRY...
I'LL LEAVE AS SOON AS MY WIFE RETURNS.
TCH...
SOME PEOPLE.
GULP
GULP
SORRY.
IT'S NOT USUALLY LIKE THIS.
HEE HEE HEE HEE HEE HEE.
MNCH MNCH
NOW WE'LL JUST LET THE OTHERS DOWN BELOW TAKE CARE OF THE REST...

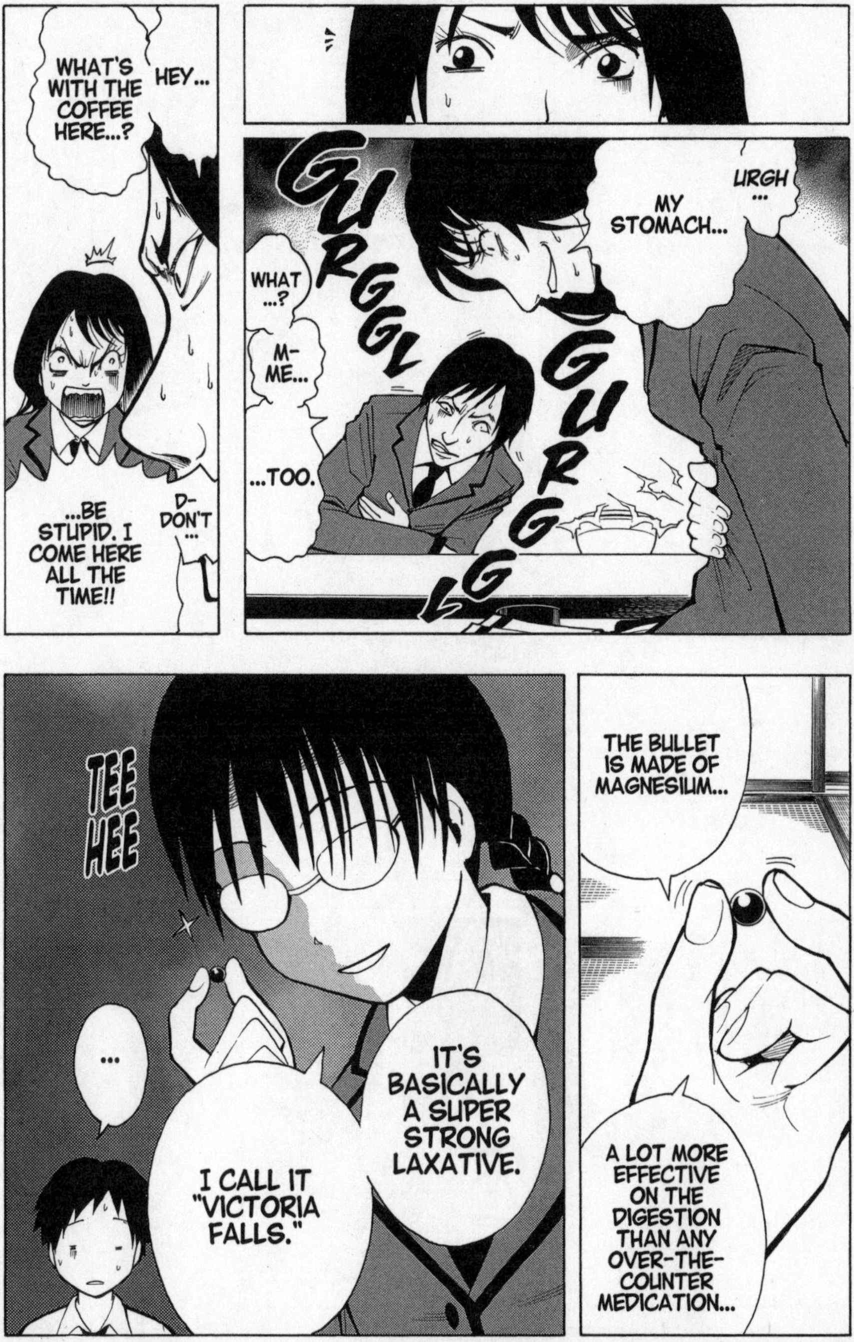
URGH ...
MY STOMACH...
GURGGL
WHAT ...?
M-ME...
...TOO.
GURGGL
HEY...
WHAT'S WITH THE COFFEE HERE...?
D-DON'T ...
...BE STUPID. I COME HERE ALL THE TIME!!
THE BULLET IS MADE OF MAGNESIUM...
A LOT MORE EFFECTIVE ON THE DIGESTION THAN ANY OVER-THE-COUNTER MEDICATION...
TEE HEE
IT'S BASICALLY A SUPER STRONG LAXATIVE.
I CALL IT "VICTORIA FALLS."
...

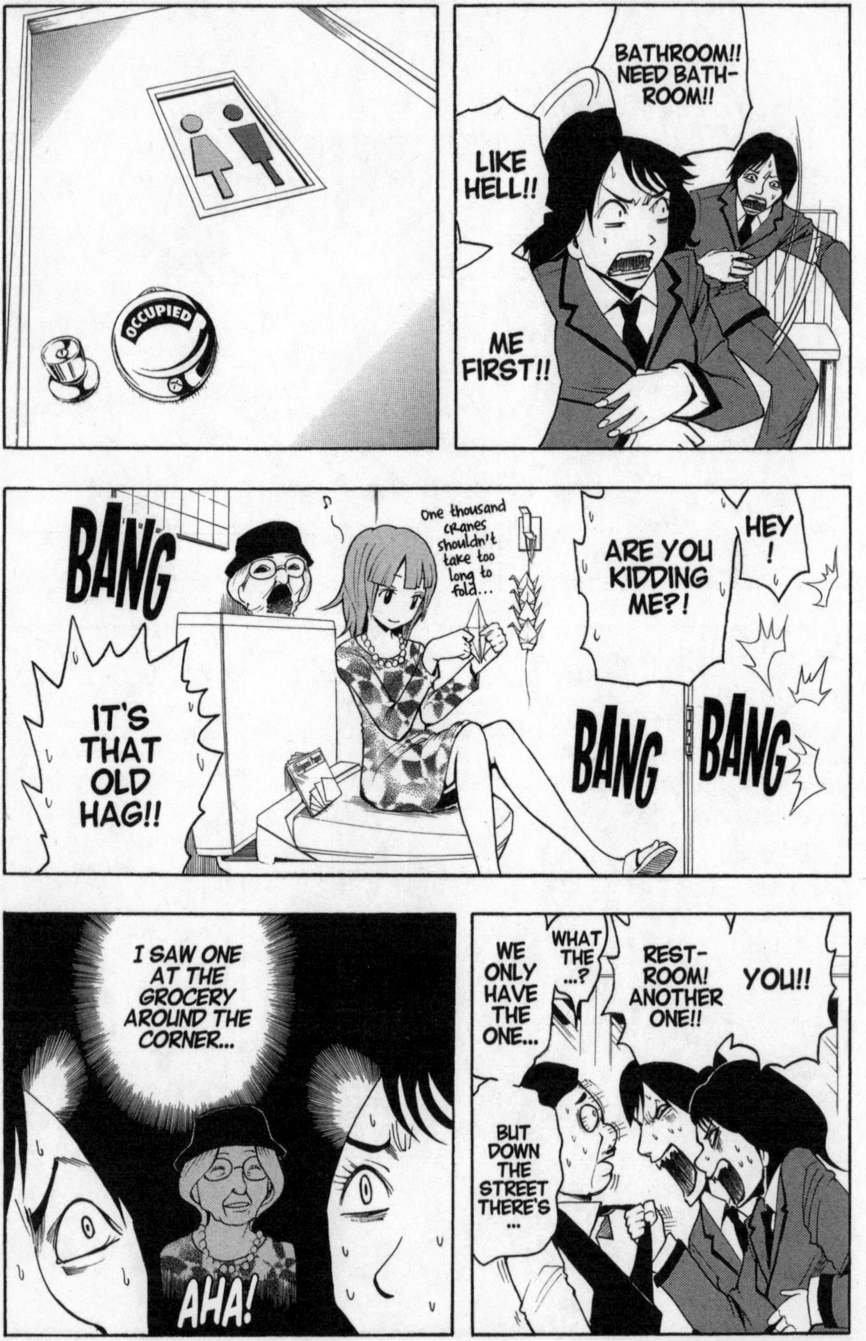

BATHROOM!! NEED BATH-ROOM!!
LIKE HELL!!
ME FIRST!!
OCCUPIED
HEY!
ARE YOU KIDDING ME?!
BANG
BANG
One thousand cranes shouldn't take too long to fold...
BANG
IT'S THAT OLD HAG!!
YOU!!
REST-ROOM! ANOTHER ONE!!
WHAT THE ...?
WE ONLY HAVE THE ONE...
BUT DOWN THE STREET THERE'S ...
I SAW ONE AT THE GROCERY AROUND THE CORNER...
AHA!

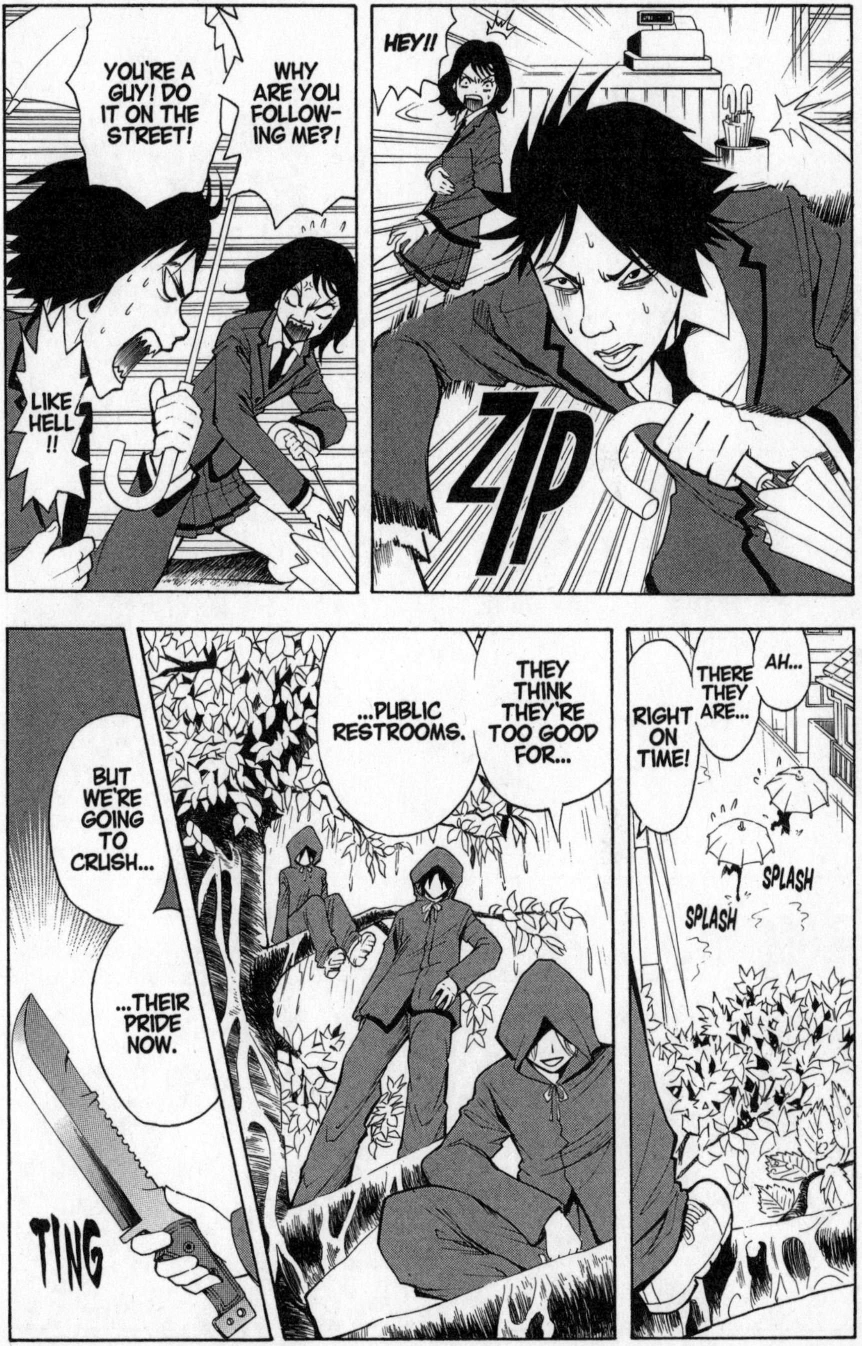
HEY!!
ZIP
WHY ARE YOU FOLLOWING ME?!
YOU'RE A GUY! DO IT ON THE STREET!
LIKE HELL !!
AH...
THERE THEY ARE...
RIGHT ON TIME!
SPLASH
SPLASH
THEY THINK THEY'RE TOO GOOD FOR...
...PUBLIC RESTROOMS.
BUT WE'RE GOING TO CRUSH...
...THEIR PRIDE NOW.
TING

	Knife Skills	
Best/Girls	Best/Boys	2nd Best/Boys
Hinata Okano	Yuma Isogai	Hiroto Maehara

Hff

Hff

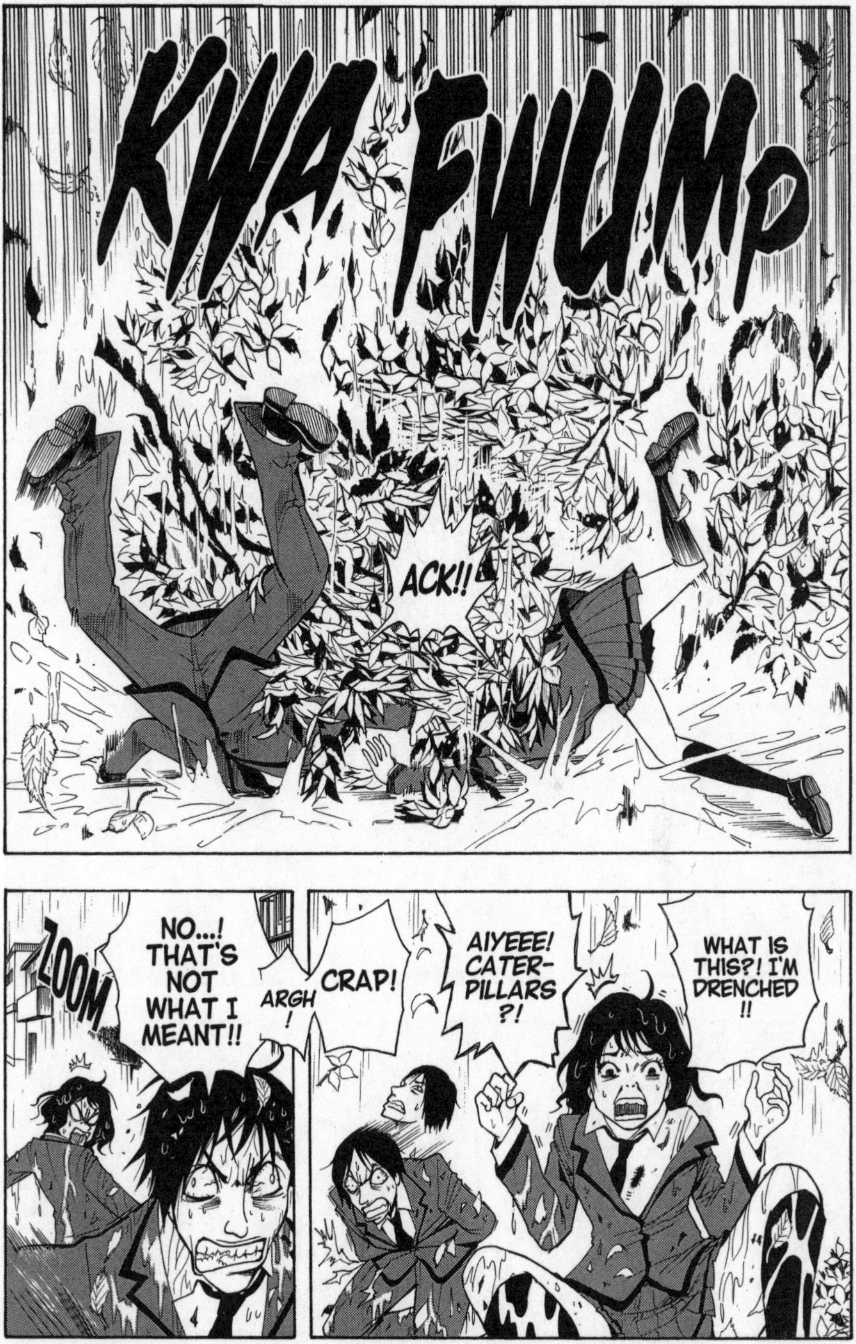
KWA FWUMP
ACK!!
WHAT IS THIS?! I'M DRENCHED!!
AIYEEE! CATER-PILLARS?!
CRAP!
ARGH!
NO...! THAT'S NOT WHAT I MEANT!!
ZOOM

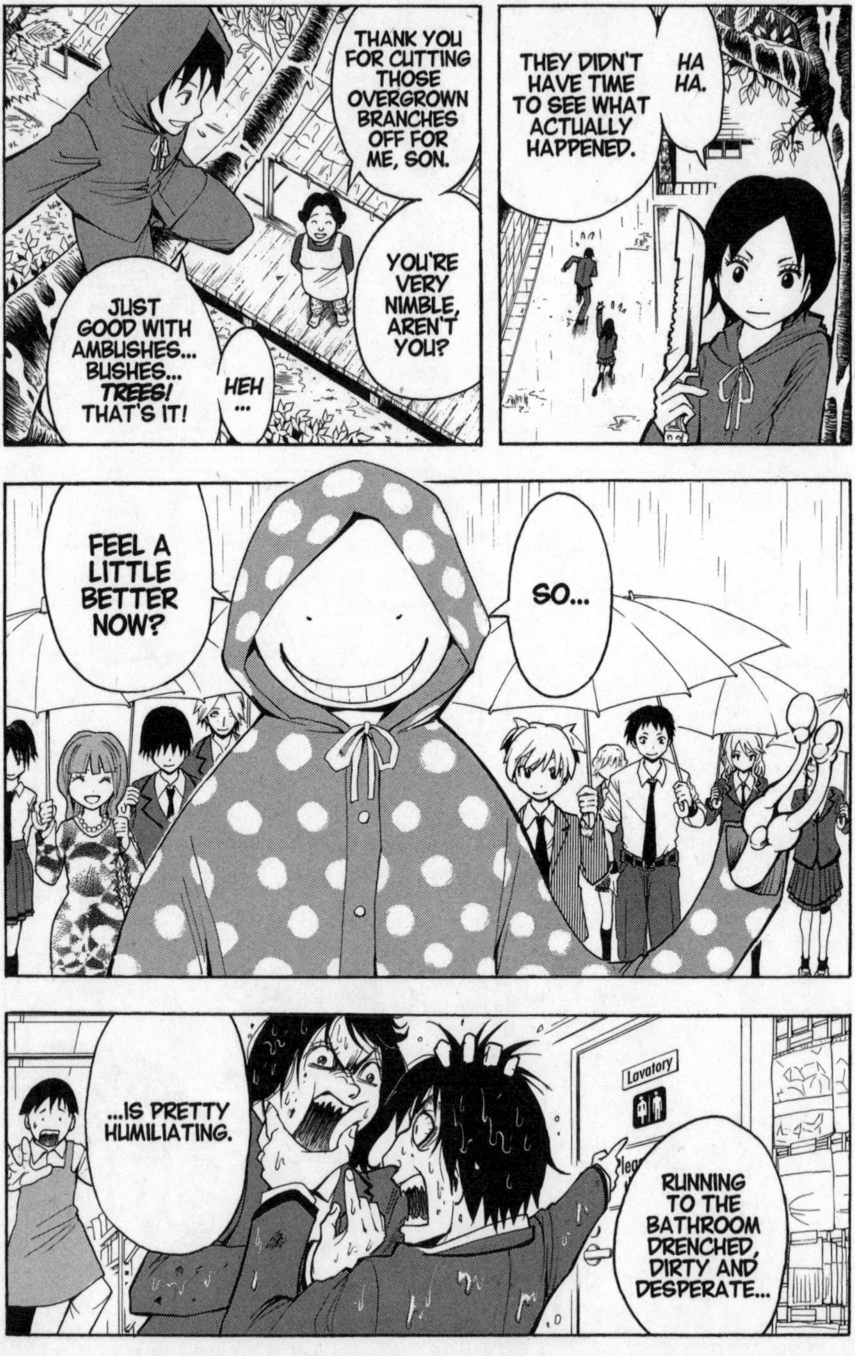
HA HA.
THEY DIDN'T HAVE TIME TO SEE WHAT ACTUALLY HAPPENED.
THANK YOU FOR CUTTING THOSE OVERGROWN BRANCHES OFF FOR ME, SON.
YOU'RE VERY NIMBLE, AREN'T YOU?
HEH ...
JUST GOOD WITH AMBUSHES... BUSHES... *TREES!* THAT'S IT!
SO...
FEEL A LITTLE BETTER NOW?
Lavatory
RUNNING TO THE BATHROOM DRENCHED, DIRTY AND DESPERATE...
...IS PRETTY HUMILIATING.

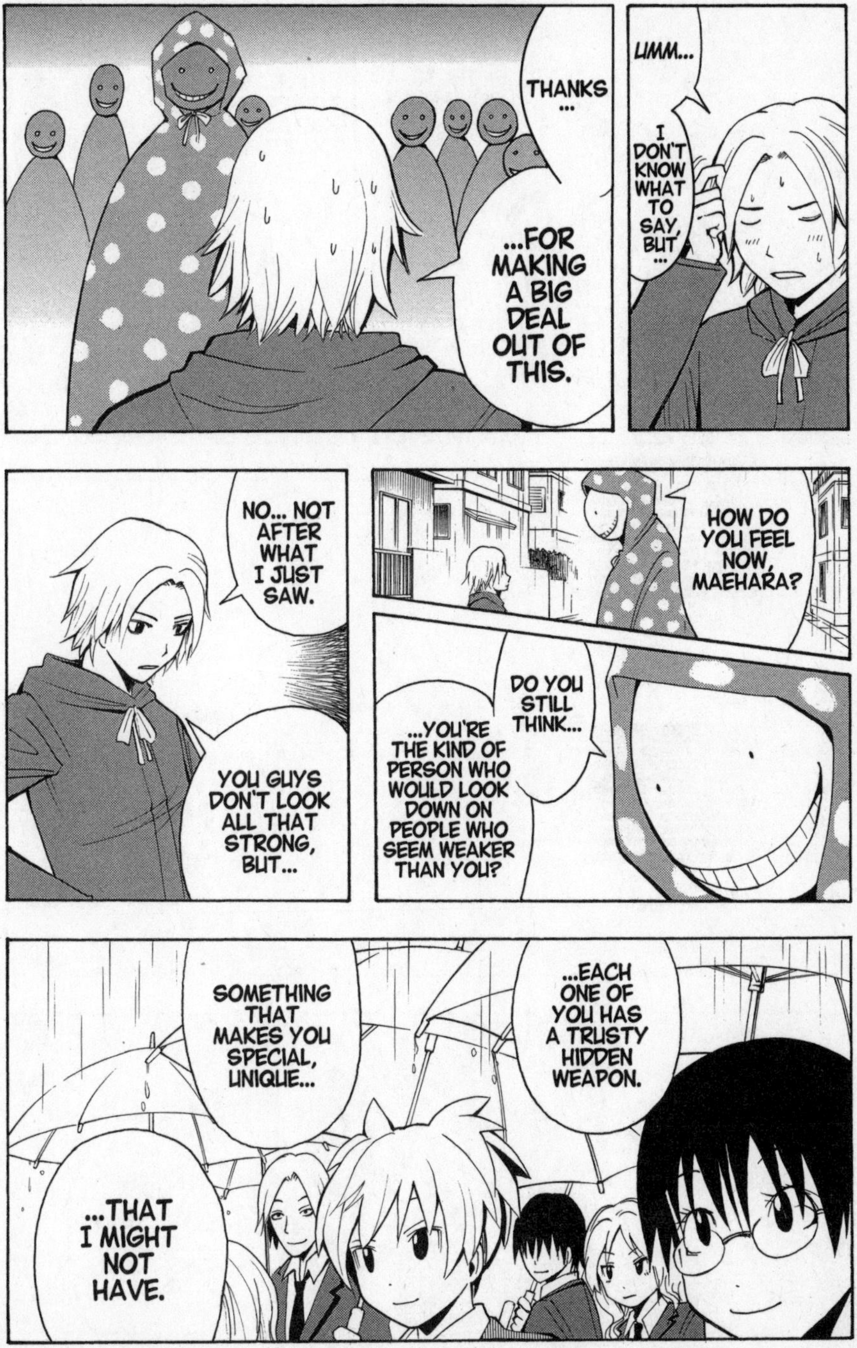
UMM...
I DON'T KNOW WHAT TO SAY, BUT...
THANKS...
...FOR MAKING A BIG DEAL OUT OF THIS.
HOW DO YOU FEEL NOW, MAEHARA?
DO YOU STILL THINK...
...YOU'RE THE KIND OF PERSON WHO WOULD LOOK DOWN ON PEOPLE WHO SEEM WEAKER THAN YOU?
NO... NOT AFTER WHAT I JUST SAW.
YOU GUYS DON'T LOOK ALL THAT STRONG, BUT...
...EACH ONE OF YOU HAS A TRUSTY HIDDEN WEAPON.
SOMETHING THAT MAKES YOU SPECIAL, UNIQUE...
...THAT I MIGHT NOT HAVE.

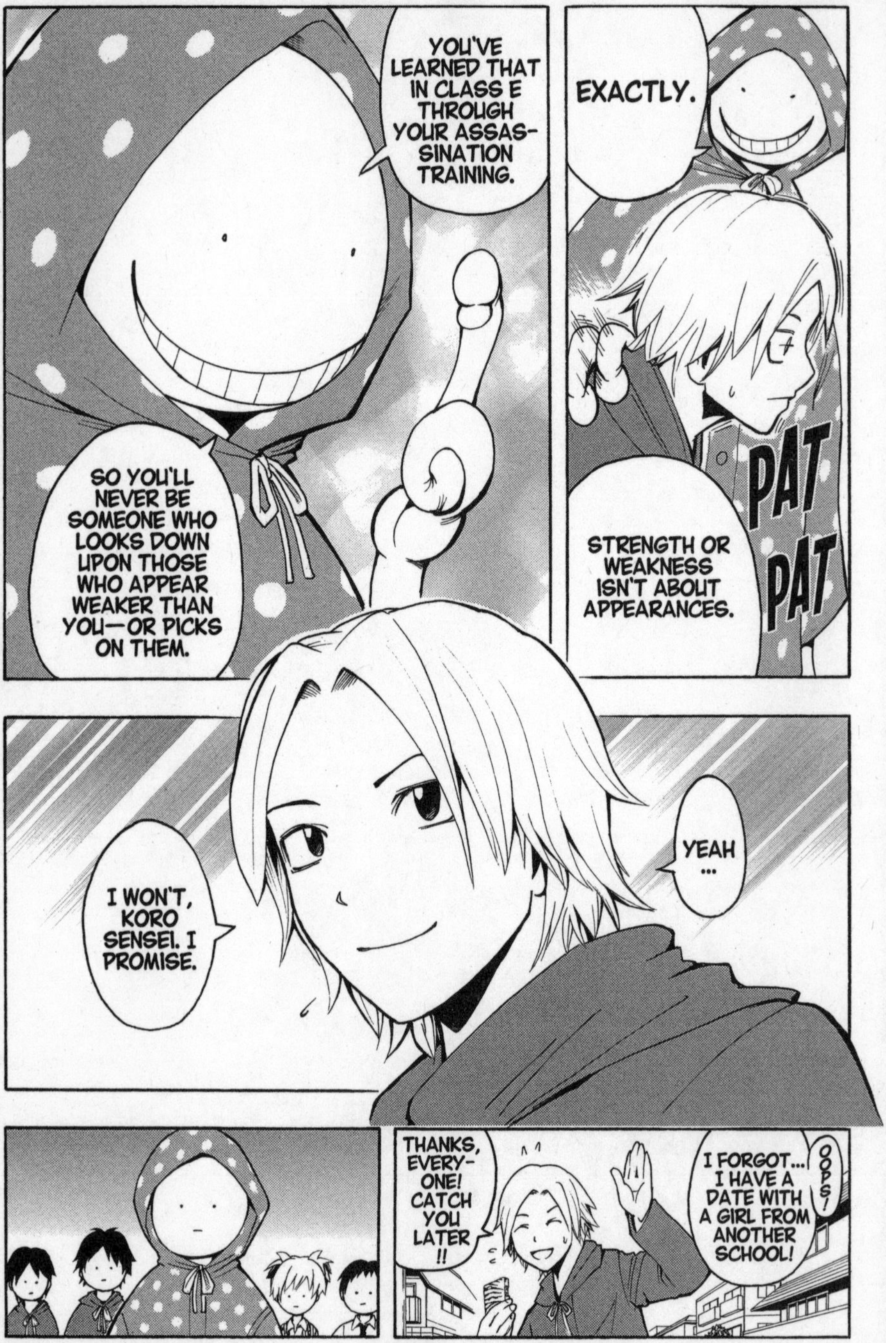
EXACTLY.
PAT PAT
STRENGTH OR WEAKNESS ISN'T ABOUT APPEARANCES.
YOU'VE LEARNED THAT IN CLASS E THROUGH YOUR ASSAS-SINATION TRAINING.
SO YOU'LL NEVER BE SOMEONE WHO LOOKS DOWN UPON THOSE WHO APPEAR WEAKER THAN YOU—OR PICKS ON THEM.
YEAH ...
I WON'T, KORO SENSEI. I PROMISE.
OOPS!
I FORGOT... I HAVE A DATE WITH A GIRL FROM ANOTHER SCHOOL!
THANKS, EVERY-ONE! CATCH YOU LATER !!

Thunder struck after the Rain.

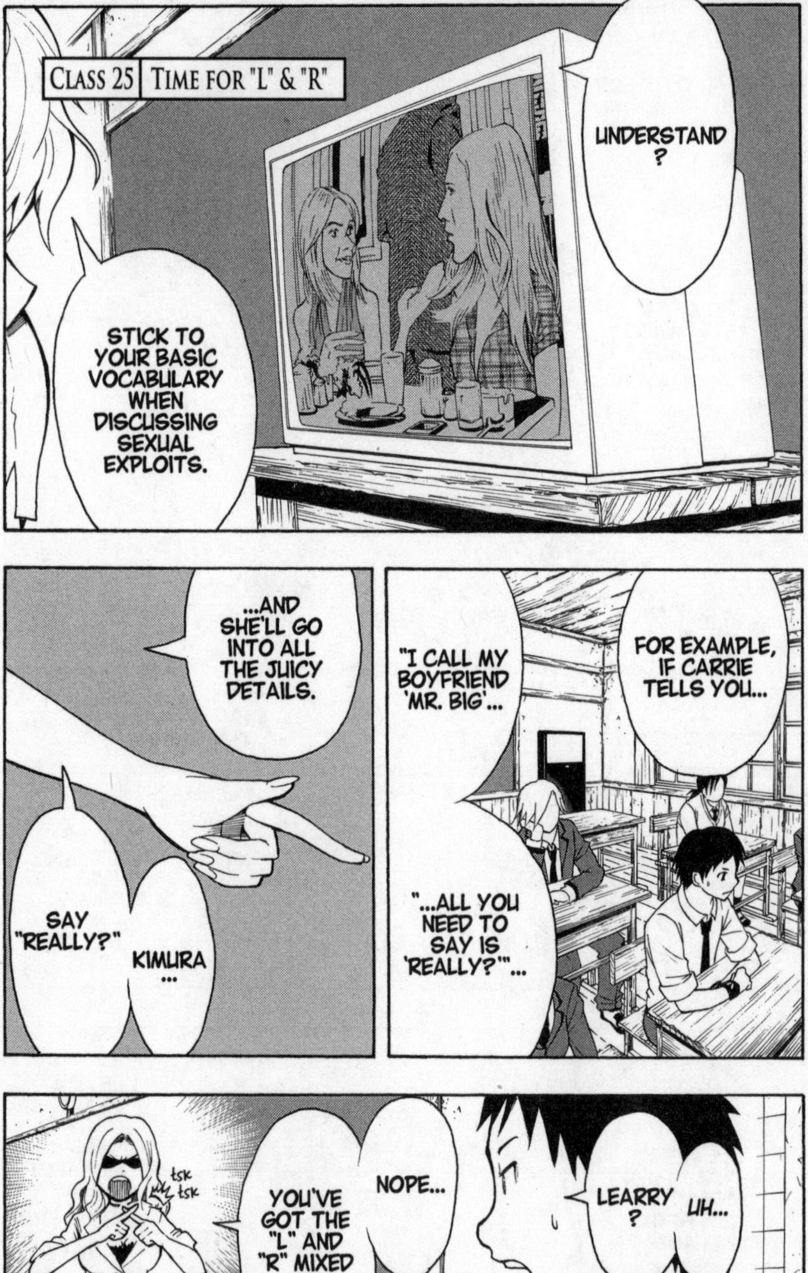
CLASS 25 TIME FOR "L" & "R"
UNDERSTAND?
STICK TO YOUR BASIC VOCABULARY WHEN DISCUSSING SEXUAL EXPLOITS.
FOR EXAMPLE, IF CARRIE TELLS YOU...
"I CALL MY BOYFRIEND 'MR. BIG'...
"...ALL YOU NEED TO SAY IS 'REALLY?'"...
...AND SHE'LL GO INTO ALL THE JUICY DETAILS.
KIMURA ...
SAY "REALLY?"
UH...
LEARRY ?
NOPE...
YOU'VE GOT THE "L" AND "R" MIXED UP!
tsk tsk

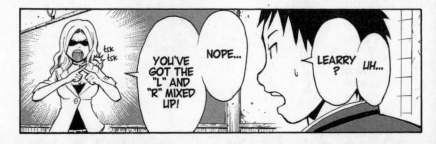

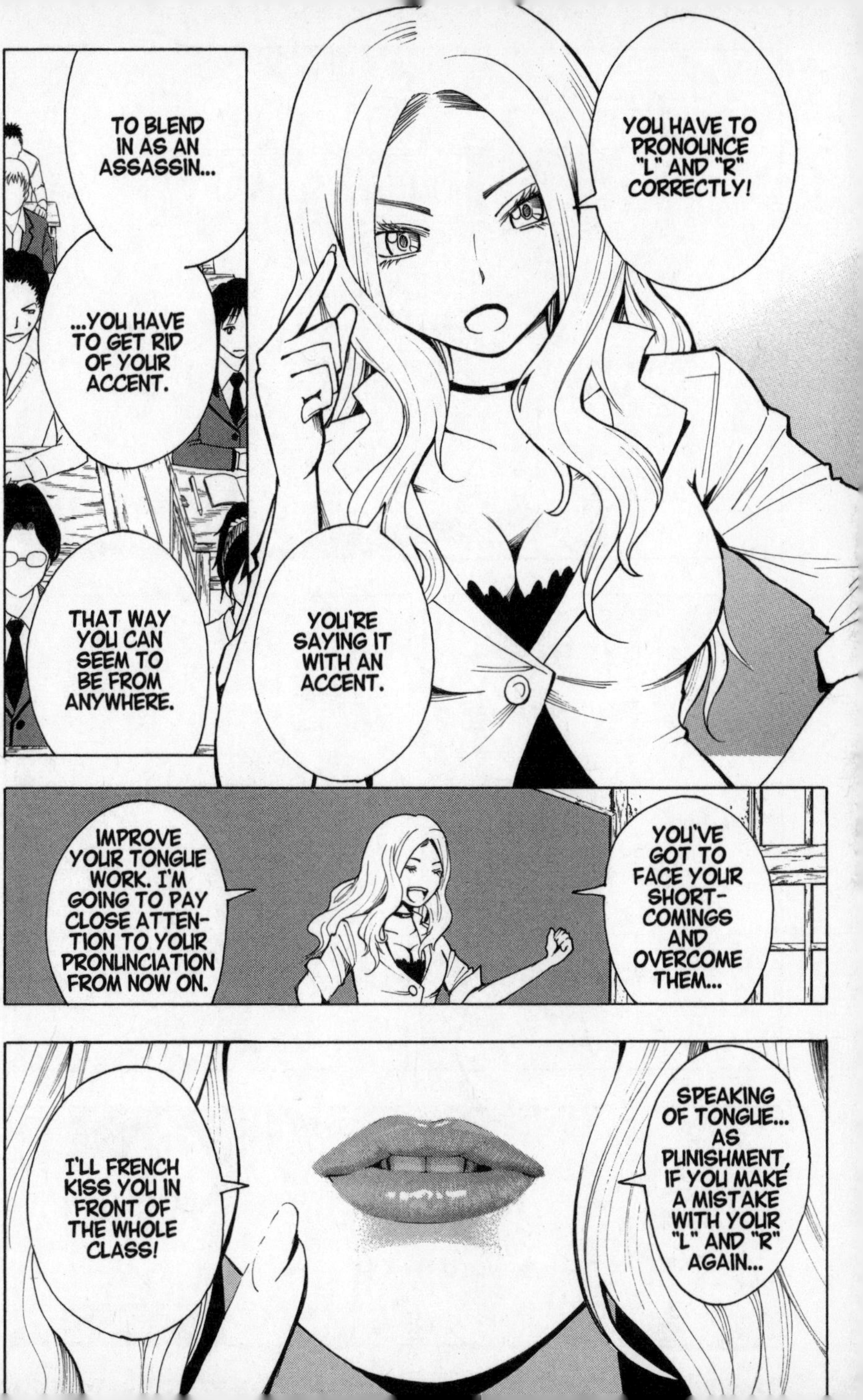
YOU HAVE TO PRONOUNCE "L" AND "R" CORRECTLY!
YOU'RE SAYING IT WITH AN ACCENT.
TO BLEND IN AS AN ASSASSIN...
...YOU HAVE TO GET RID OF YOUR ACCENT.
THAT WAY YOU CAN SEEM TO BE FROM ANYWHERE.
YOU'VE GOT TO FACE YOUR SHORT-COMINGS AND OVERCOME THEM...
IMPROVE YOUR TONGUE WORK. I'M GOING TO PAY CLOSE ATTEN-TION TO YOUR PRONUNCIATION FROM NOW ON.
SPEAKING OF TONGUE... AS PUNISHMENT, IF YOU MAKE A MISTAKE WITH YOUR "L" AND "R" AGAIN...
I'LL FRENCH KISS YOU IN FRONT OF THE WHOLE CLASS!

CLASS 25 TIME FOR "L" AND "R"

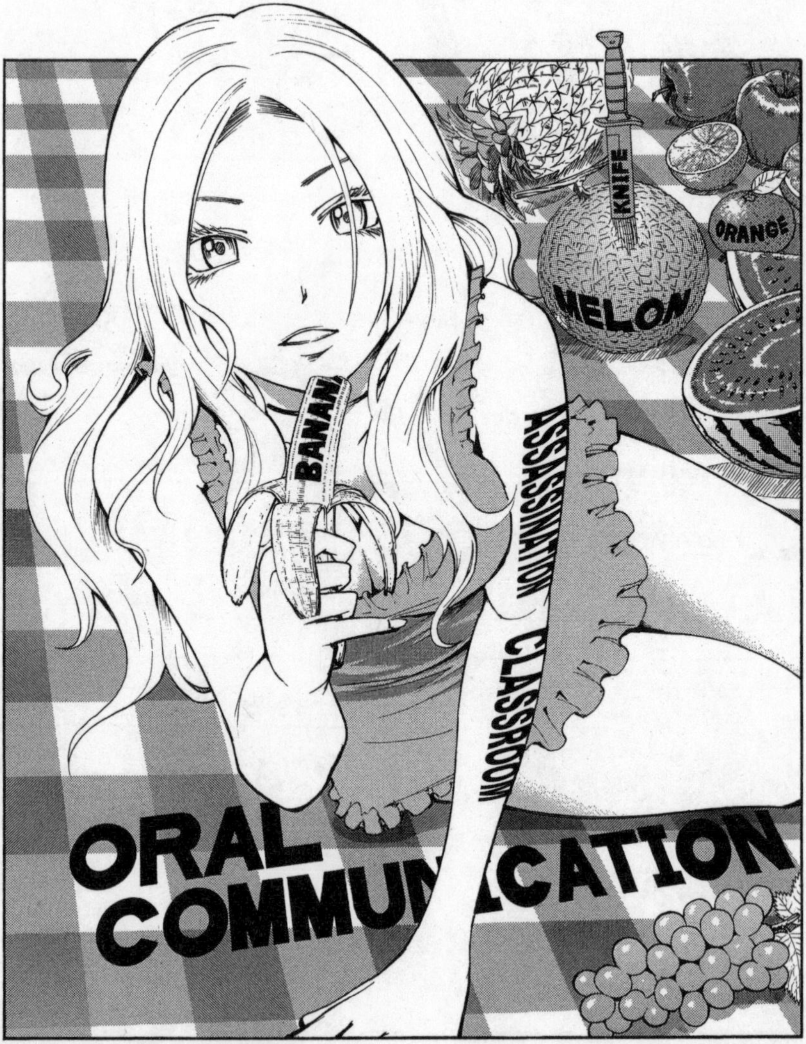
KNIFE
ORANGE
MELON
BANAN
ASSASSINATION CLASSROOM
ORAL COMMUNICATION

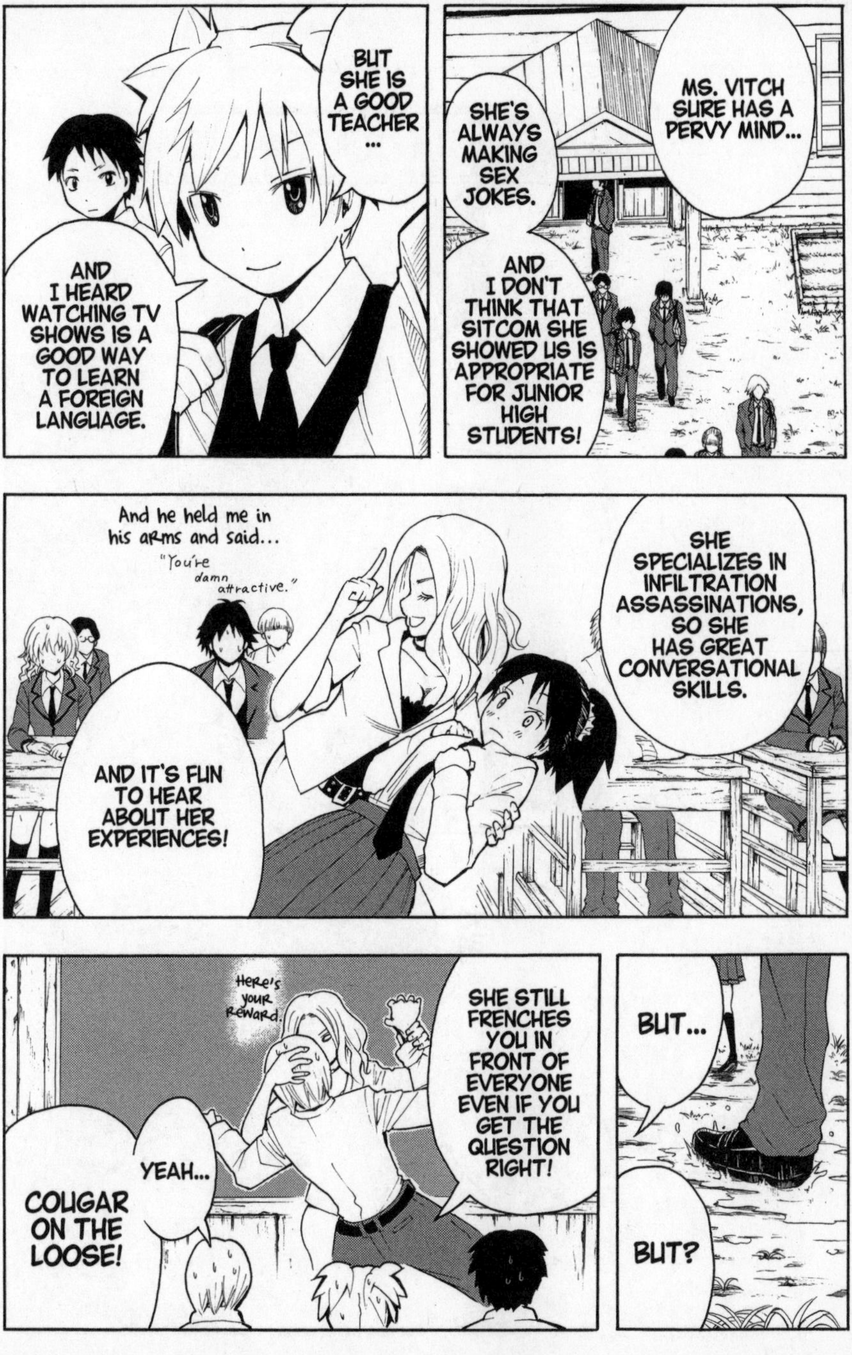
MS. VITCH SURE HAS A PERVY MIND...
SHE'S ALWAYS MAKING SEX JOKES.
AND I DON'T THINK THAT SITCOM SHE SHOWED US IS APPROPRIATE FOR JUNIOR HIGH STUDENTS!
BUT SHE IS A GOOD TEACHER ...
AND I HEARD WATCHING TV SHOWS IS A GOOD WAY TO LEARN A FOREIGN LANGUAGE.
SHE SPECIALIZES IN INFILTRATION ASSASSINATIONS, SO SHE HAS GREAT CONVERSATIONAL SKILLS.
And he held me in his arms and said...
"You're damn attractive."
AND IT'S FUN TO HEAR ABOUT HER EXPERIENCES!
BUT...
BUT?
SHE STILL FRENCHES YOU IN FRONT OF EVERYONE EVEN IF YOU GET THE QUESTION RIGHT!
Here's your reward.
YEAH...
COUGAR ON THE LOOSE!

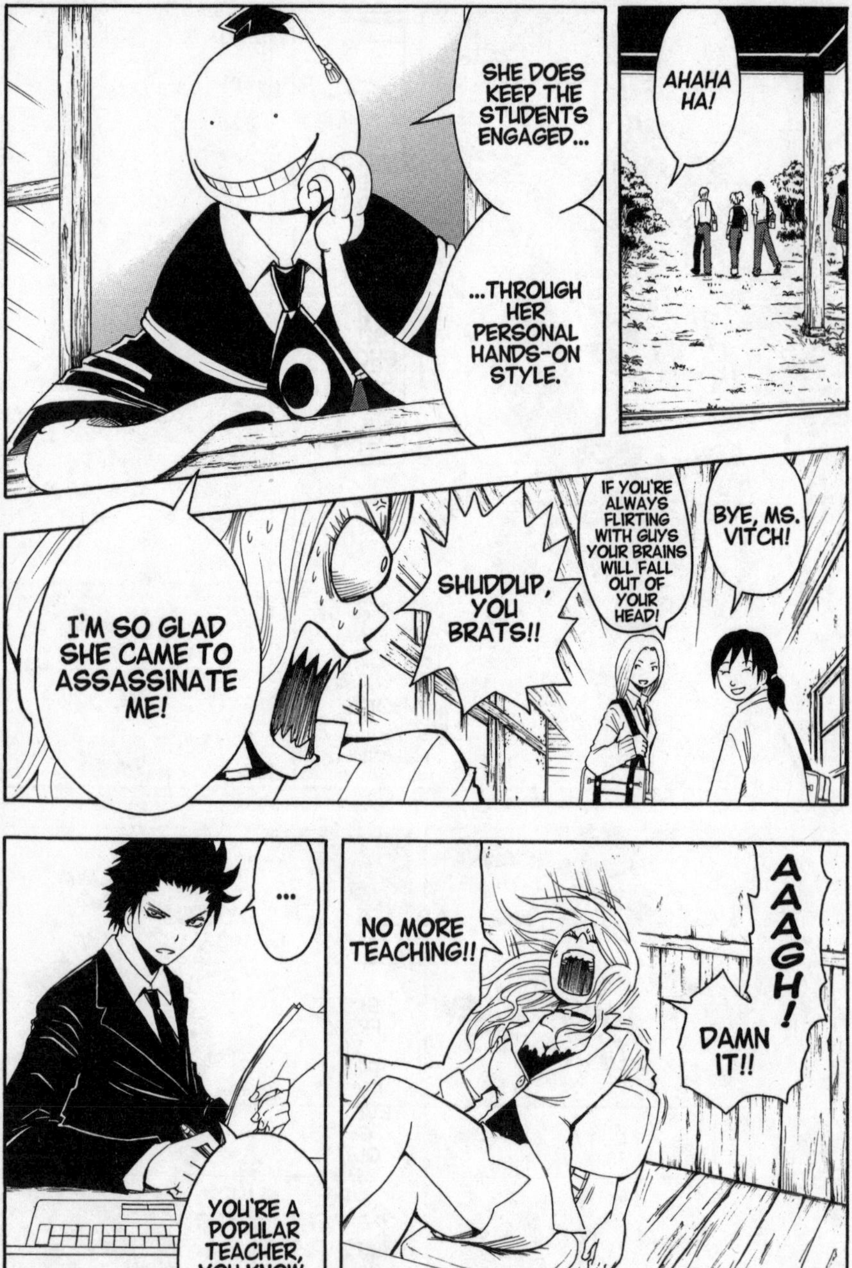
AHAHA HA!
SHE DOES KEEP THE STUDENTS ENGAGED...
...THROUGH HER PERSONAL HANDS-ON STYLE.
BYE, MS. VITCH!
IF YOU'RE ALWAYS FLIRTING WITH GUYS YOUR BRAINS WILL FALL OUT OF YOUR HEAD!
SHUDDUP, YOU BRATS!!
I'M SO GLAD SHE CAME TO ASSASSINATE ME!
AAAGH!
DAMN IT!!
NO MORE TEACHING!!
...
YOU'RE A POPULAR TEACHER, YOU KNOW.

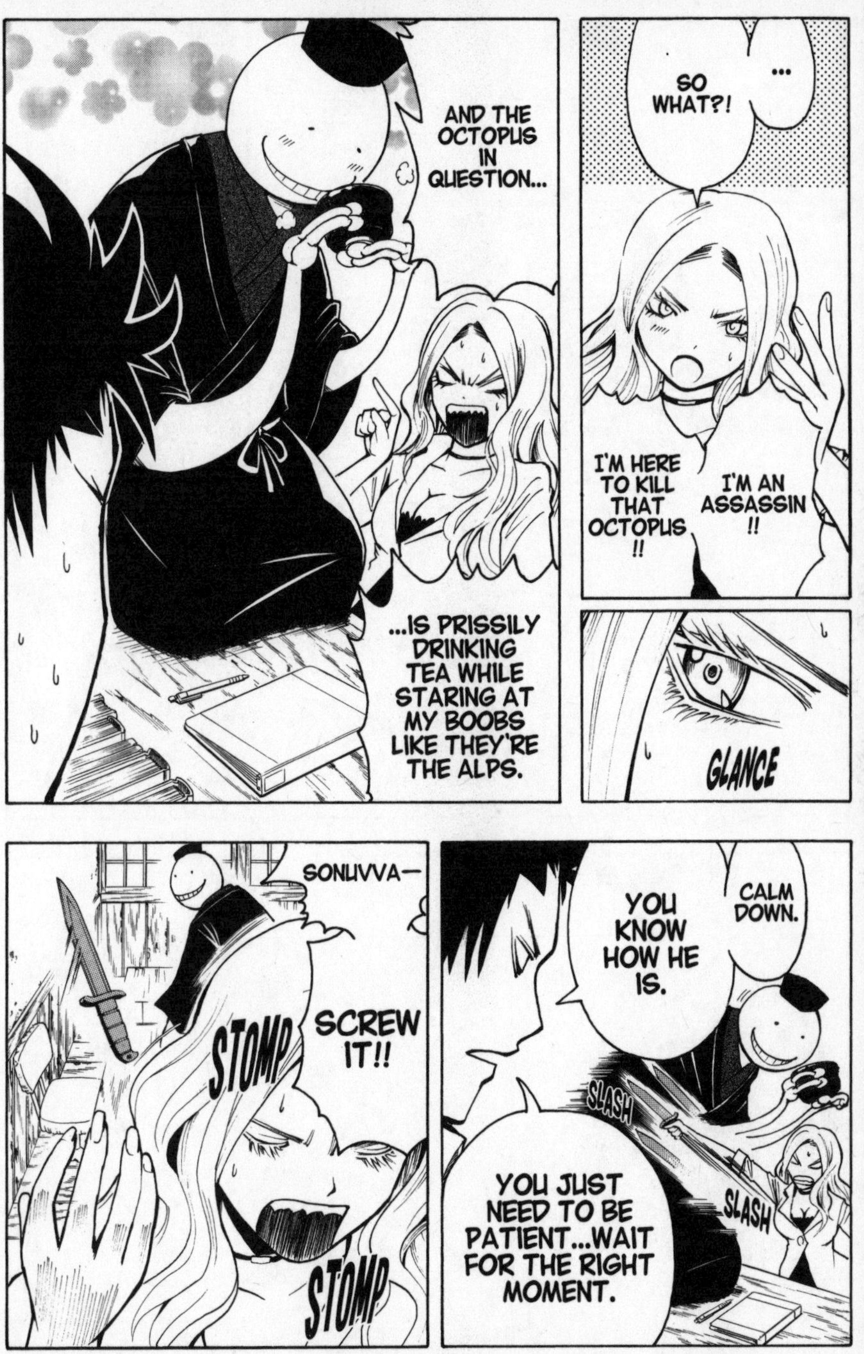
...
SO WHAT?!
I'M AN ASSASSIN!!
I'M HERE TO KILL THAT OCTOPUS!!
GLANCE
AND THE OCTOPUS IN QUESTION...
...IS PRISSILY DRINKING TEA WHILE STARING AT MY BOOBS LIKE THEY'RE THE ALPS.
CALM DOWN.
YOU KNOW HOW HE IS.
SLASH
SLASH
YOU JUST NEED TO BE PATIENT...WAIT FOR THE RIGHT MOMENT.
SONUVVA—
STOMP
SCREW IT!!
STOMP

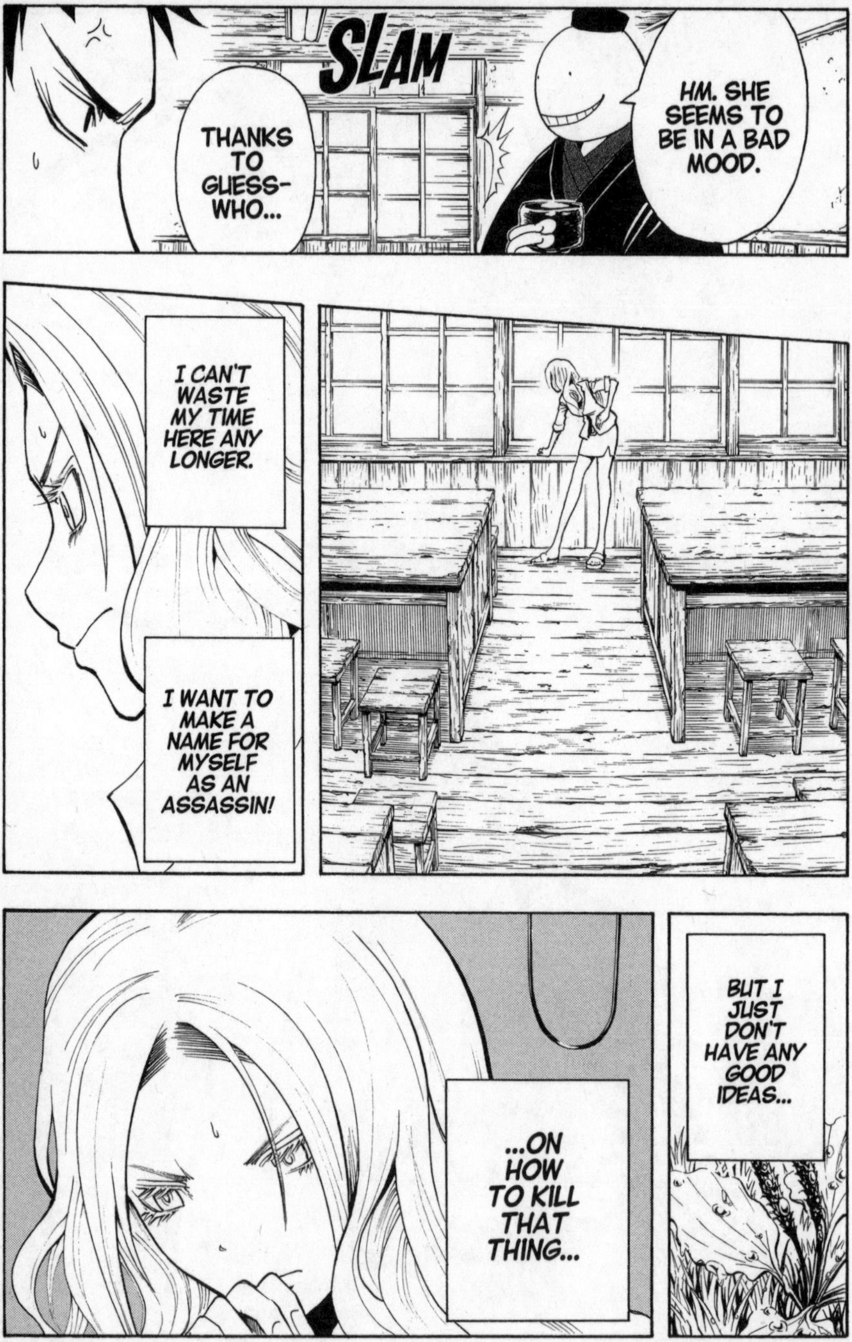
SLAM
HM. SHE SEEMS TO BE IN A BAD MOOD.
THANKS TO GUESS-WHO...
I CAN'T WASTE MY TIME HERE ANY LONGER.
I WANT TO MAKE A NAME FOR MYSELF AS AN ASSASSIN!
BUT I JUST DON'T HAVE ANY GOOD IDEAS...
...ON HOW TO KILL THAT THING...

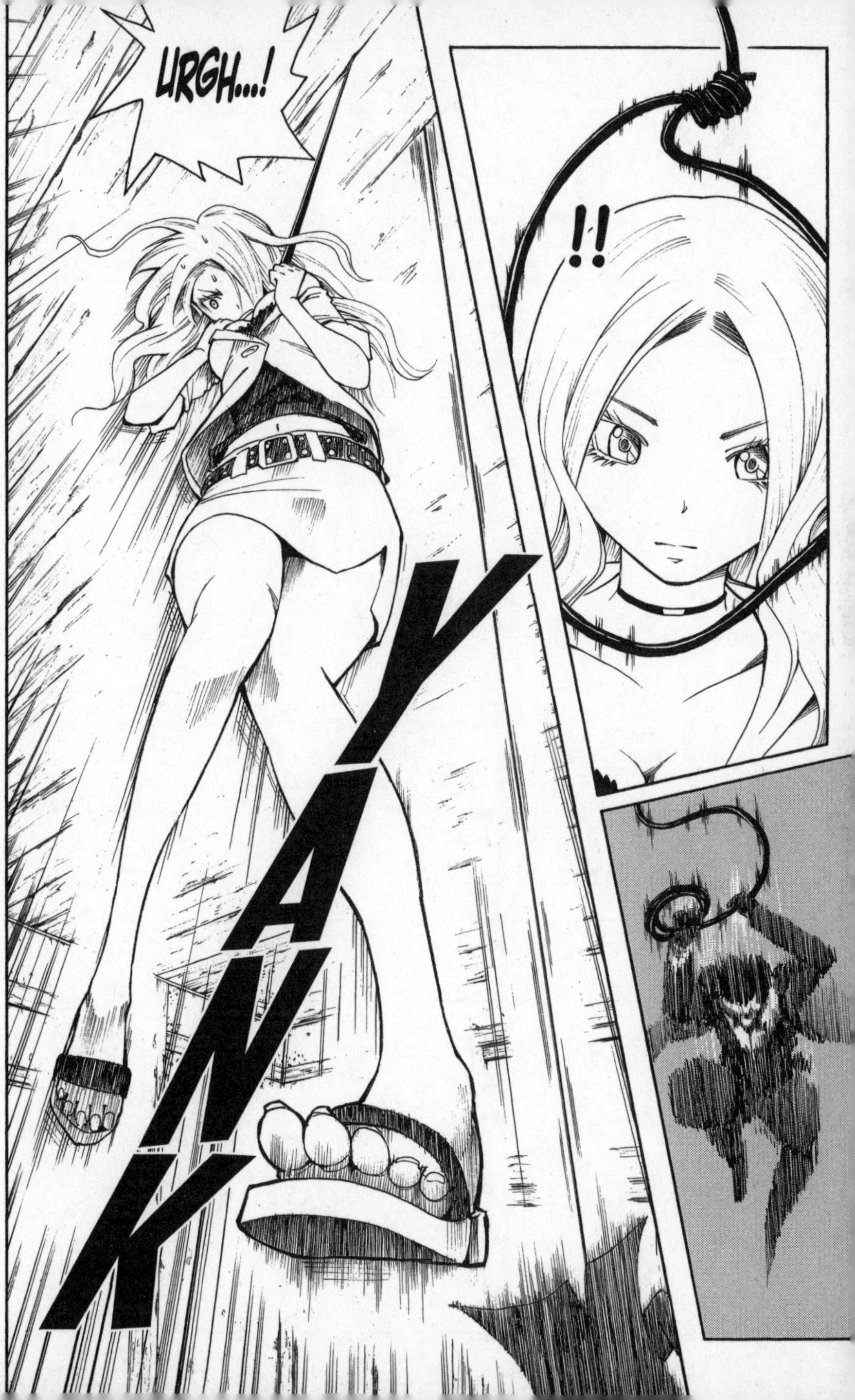
!!
URGH...!
YANK

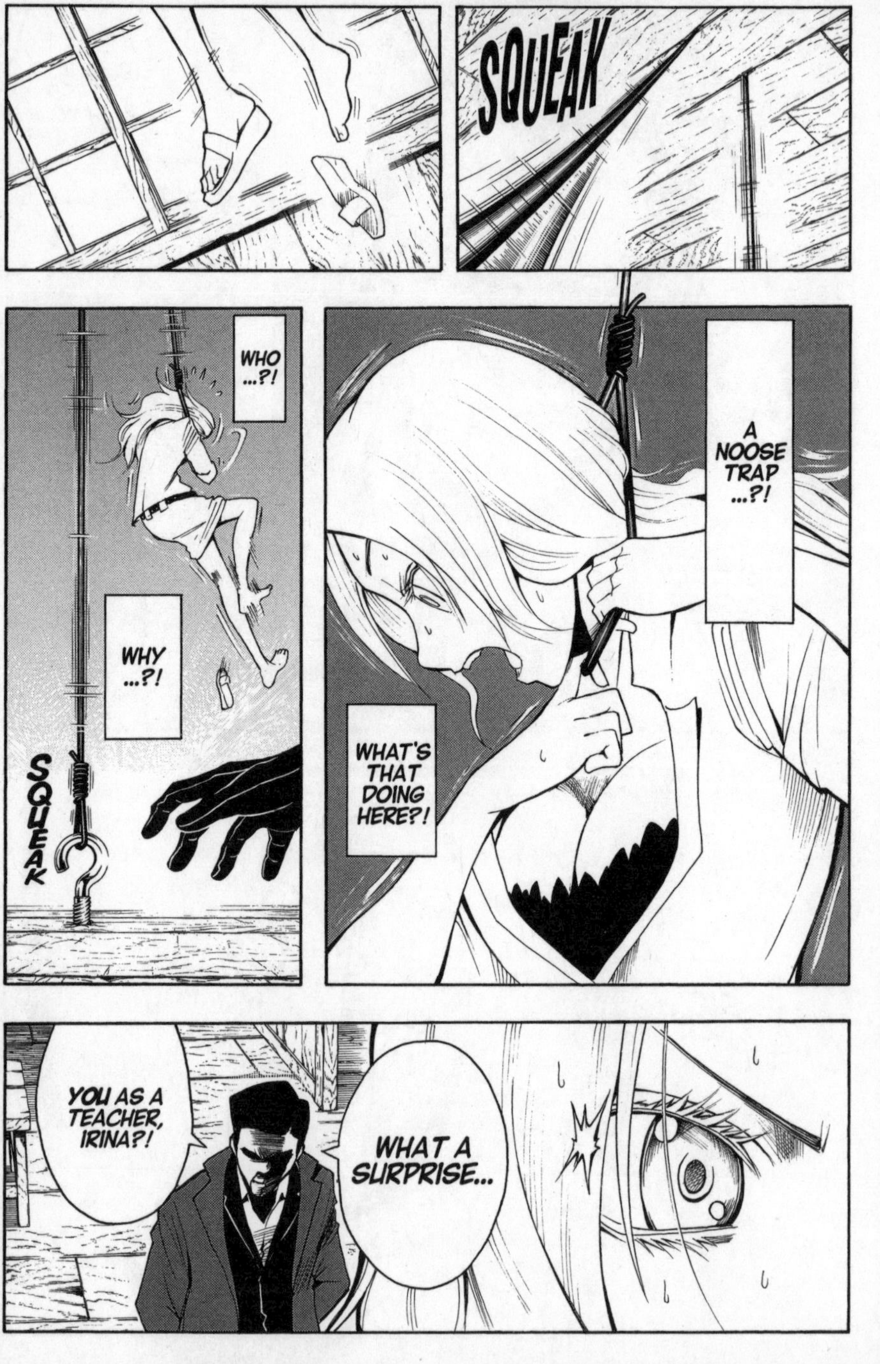
SQUEAK
A NOOSE TRAP ...?!
WHAT'S THAT DOING HERE?!
WHO ...?!
WHY ...?!
SQUEAK
WHAT A SURPRISE...
YOU AS A TEACHER, IRINA?!

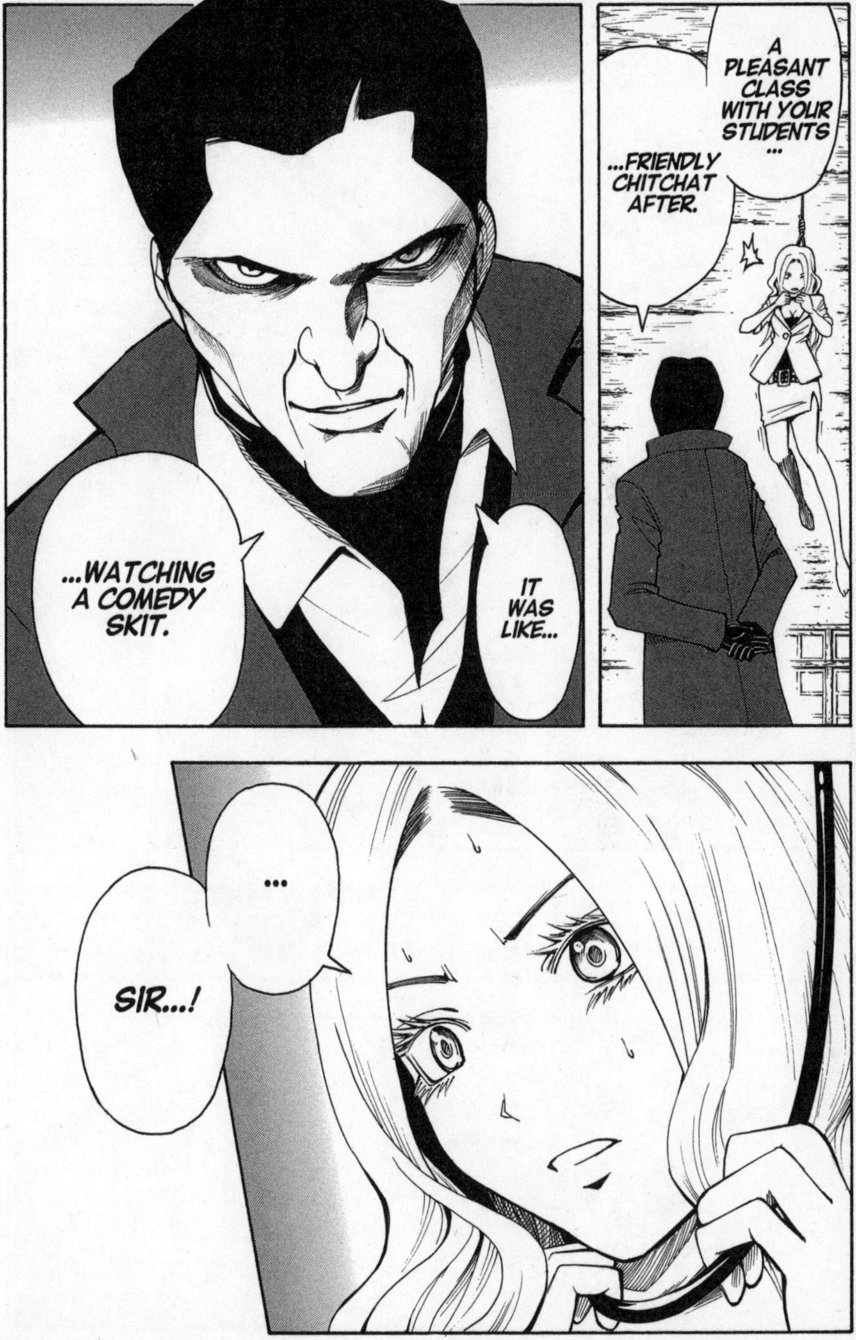
A PLEASANT CLASS WITH YOUR STUDENTS...
...FRIENDLY CHITCHAT AFTER.
IT WAS LIKE...
...WATCHING A COMEDY SKIT.
...
SIR...!

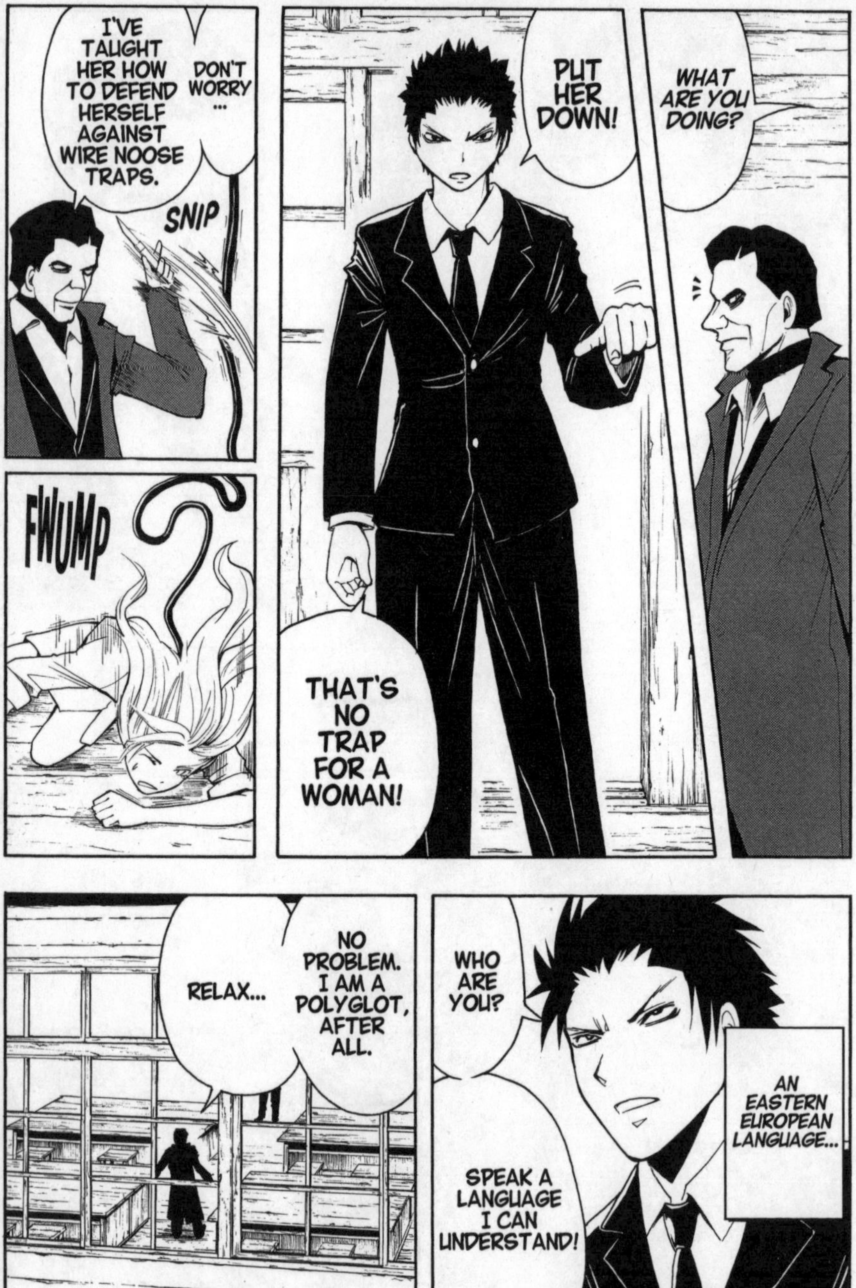
WHAT ARE YOU DOING?
PUT HER DOWN!
THAT'S NO TRAP FOR A WOMAN!
DON'T WORRY...
I'VE TAUGHT HER HOW TO DEFEND HERSELF AGAINST WIRE NOOSE TRAPS.
SNIP
FWUMP
WHO ARE YOU?
AN EASTERN EUROPEAN LANGUAGE...
SPEAK A LANGUAGE I CAN UNDERSTAND!
NO PROBLEM. I AM A POLYGLOT, AFTER ALL.
RELAX...

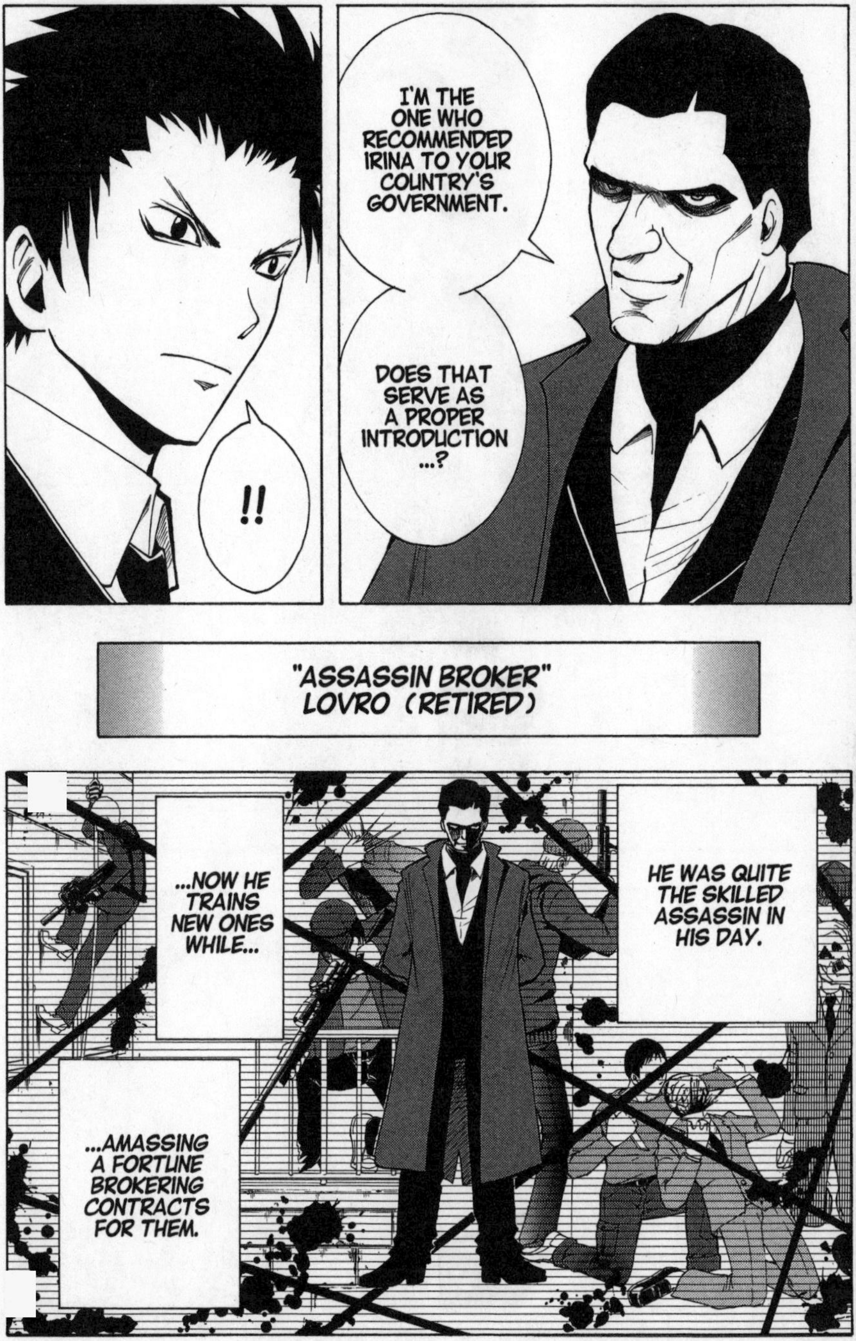
I'M THE ONE WHO RECOMMENDED IRINA TO YOUR COUNTRY'S GOVERNMENT.
DOES THAT SERVE AS A PROPER INTRODUCTION ...?
!!
"ASSASSIN BROKER" LOVRO (RETIRED)
HE WAS QUITE THE SKILLED ASSASSIN IN HIS DAY.
...NOW HE TRAINS NEW ONES WHILE...
...AMASSING A FORTUNE BROKERING CONTRACTS FOR THEM.

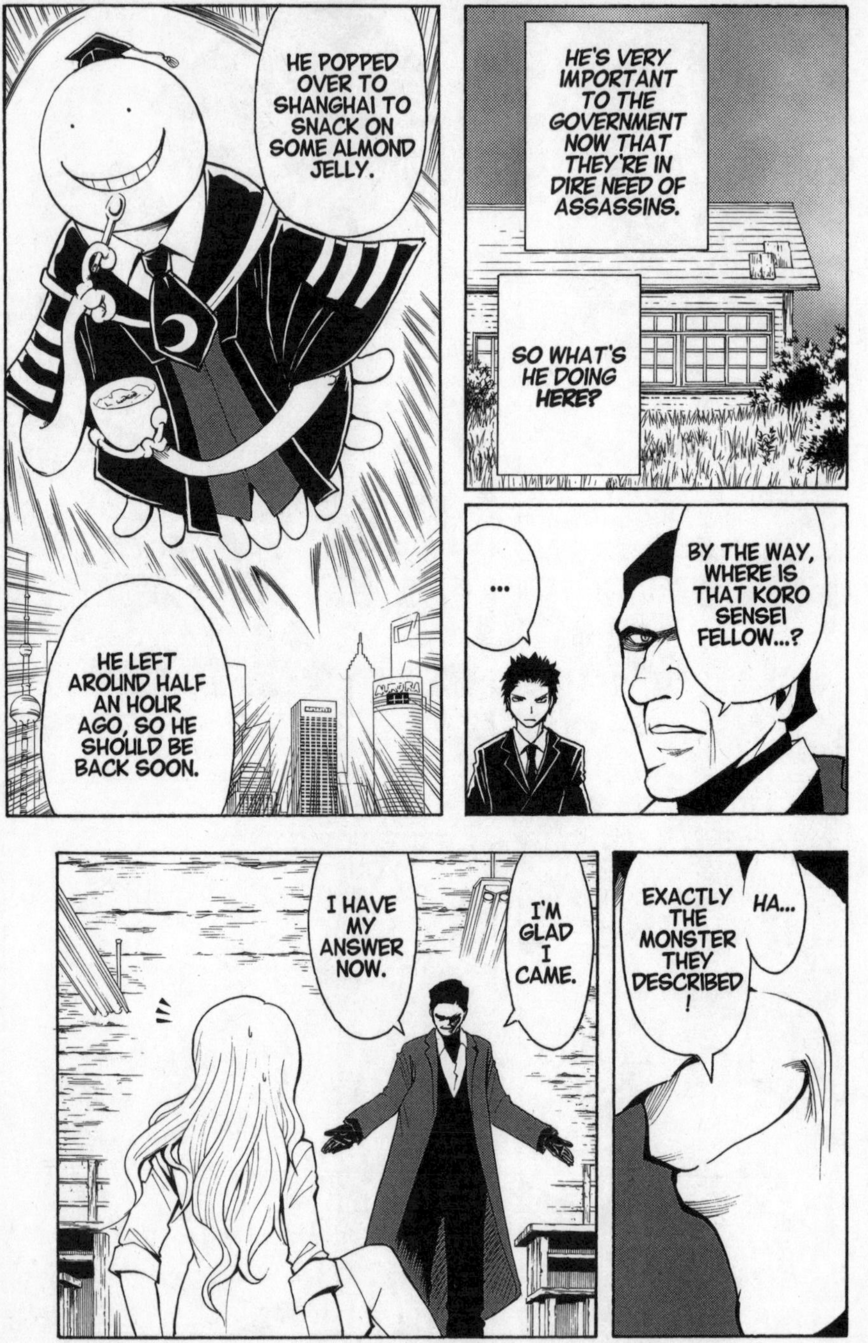
HE'S VERY IMPORTANT TO THE GOVERNMENT NOW THAT THEY'RE IN DIRE NEED OF ASSASSINS.
SO WHAT'S HE DOING HERE?
BY THE WAY, WHERE IS THAT KORO SENSEI FELLOW...?
...
HE POPPED OVER TO SHANGHAI TO SNACK ON SOME ALMOND JELLY.
HE LEFT AROUND HALF AN HOUR AGO, SO HE SHOULD BE BACK SOON.
HA...
EXACTLY THE MONSTER THEY DESCRIBED!
I'M GLAD I CAME.
I HAVE MY ANSWER NOW.

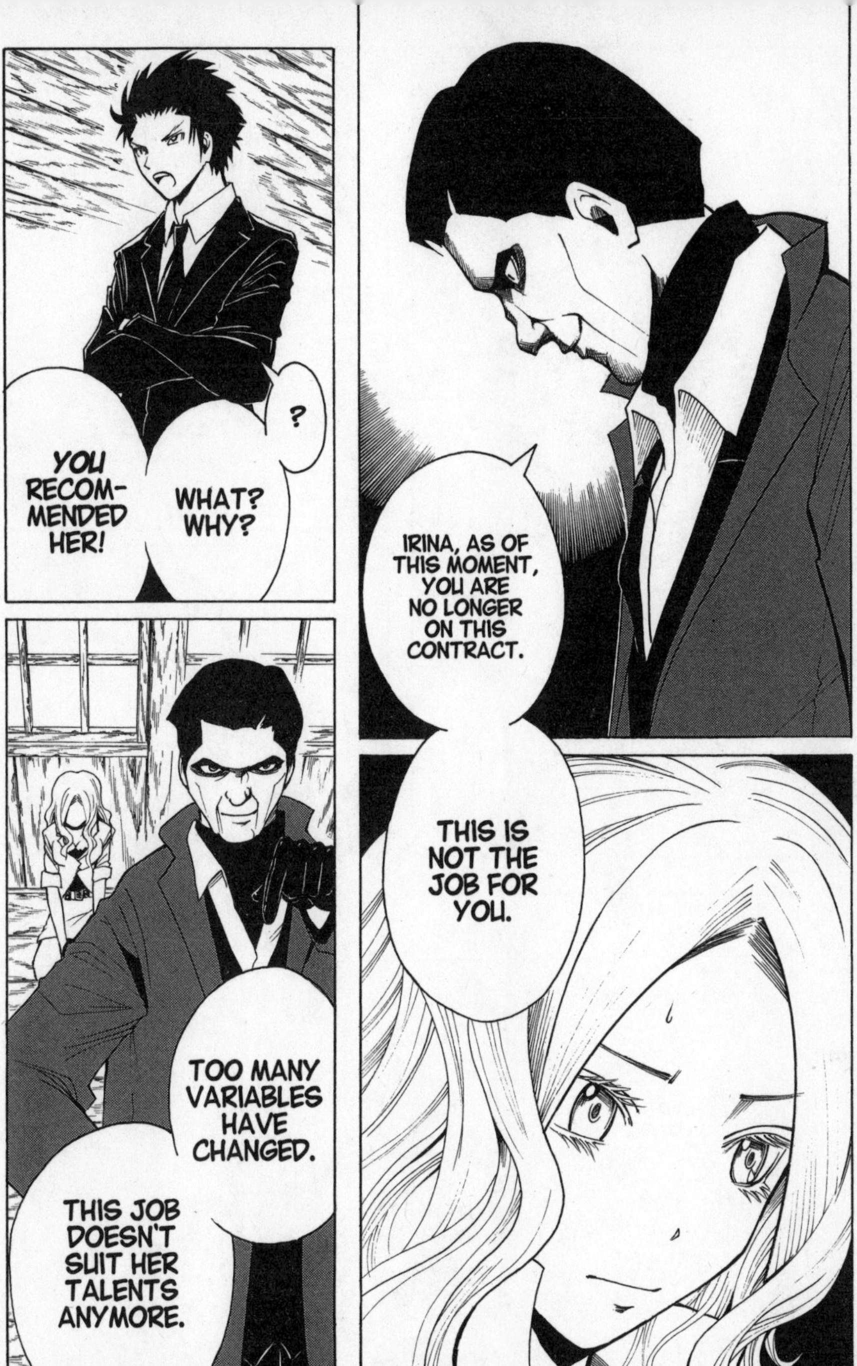
IRINA, AS OF THIS MOMENT, YOU ARE NO LONGER ON THIS CONTRACT.
THIS IS NOT THE JOB FOR YOU.
?
WHAT? WHY?
YOU RECOMMENDED HER!
TOO MANY VARIABLES HAVE CHANGED.
THIS JOB DOESN'T SUIT HER TALENTS ANYMORE.

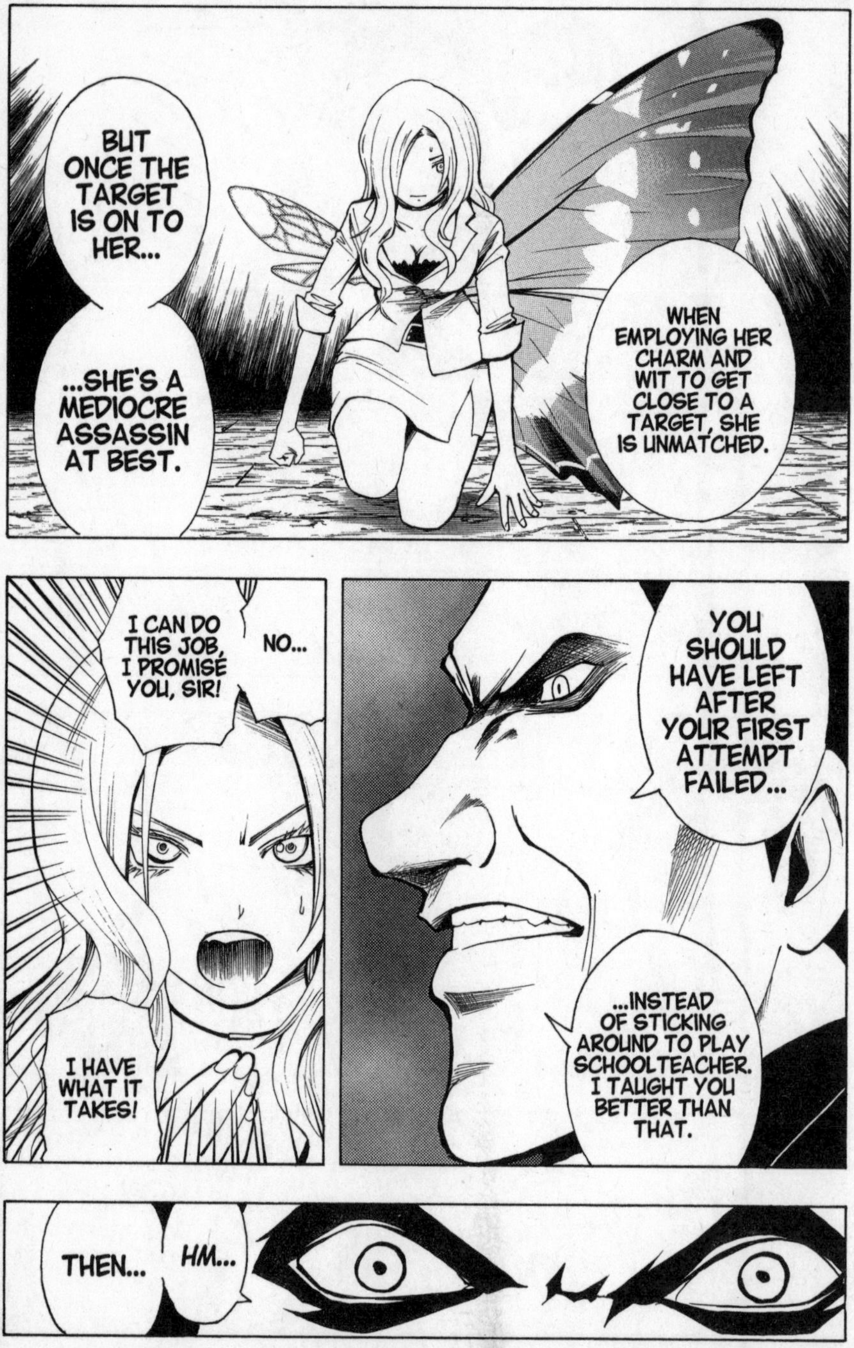
WHEN EMPLOYING HER CHARM AND WIT TO GET CLOSE TO A TARGET, SHE IS UNMATCHED.
BUT ONCE THE TARGET IS ON TO HER...
...SHE'S A MEDIOCRE ASSASSIN AT BEST.
YOU SHOULD HAVE LEFT AFTER YOUR FIRST ATTEMPT FAILED...
...INSTEAD OF STICKING AROUND TO PLAY SCHOOLTEACHER. I TAUGHT YOU BETTER THAN THAT.
NO...
I CAN DO THIS JOB, I PROMISE YOU, SIR!
I HAVE WHAT IT TAKES!
HM...
THEN...

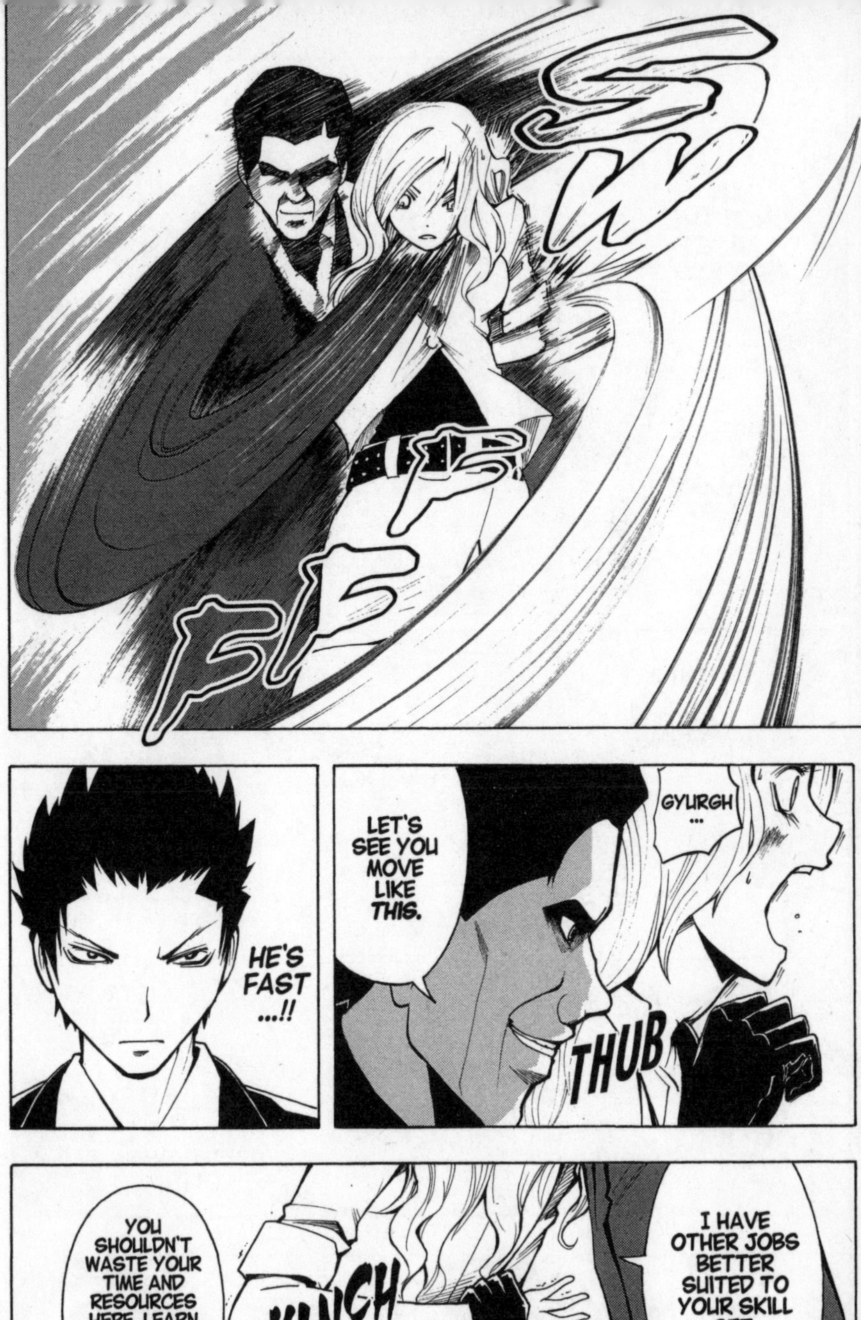
GYURGH ...
LET'S SEE YOU MOVE LIKE THIS.
THUB
HE'S FAST ...!!
I HAVE OTHER JOBS BETTER SUITED TO YOUR SKILL SET.
KLNCH
YOU SHOULDN'T WASTE YOUR TIME AND RESOURCES HERE. LEARN TO ACCEPT DEFEAT.

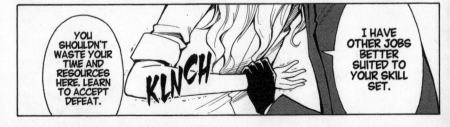

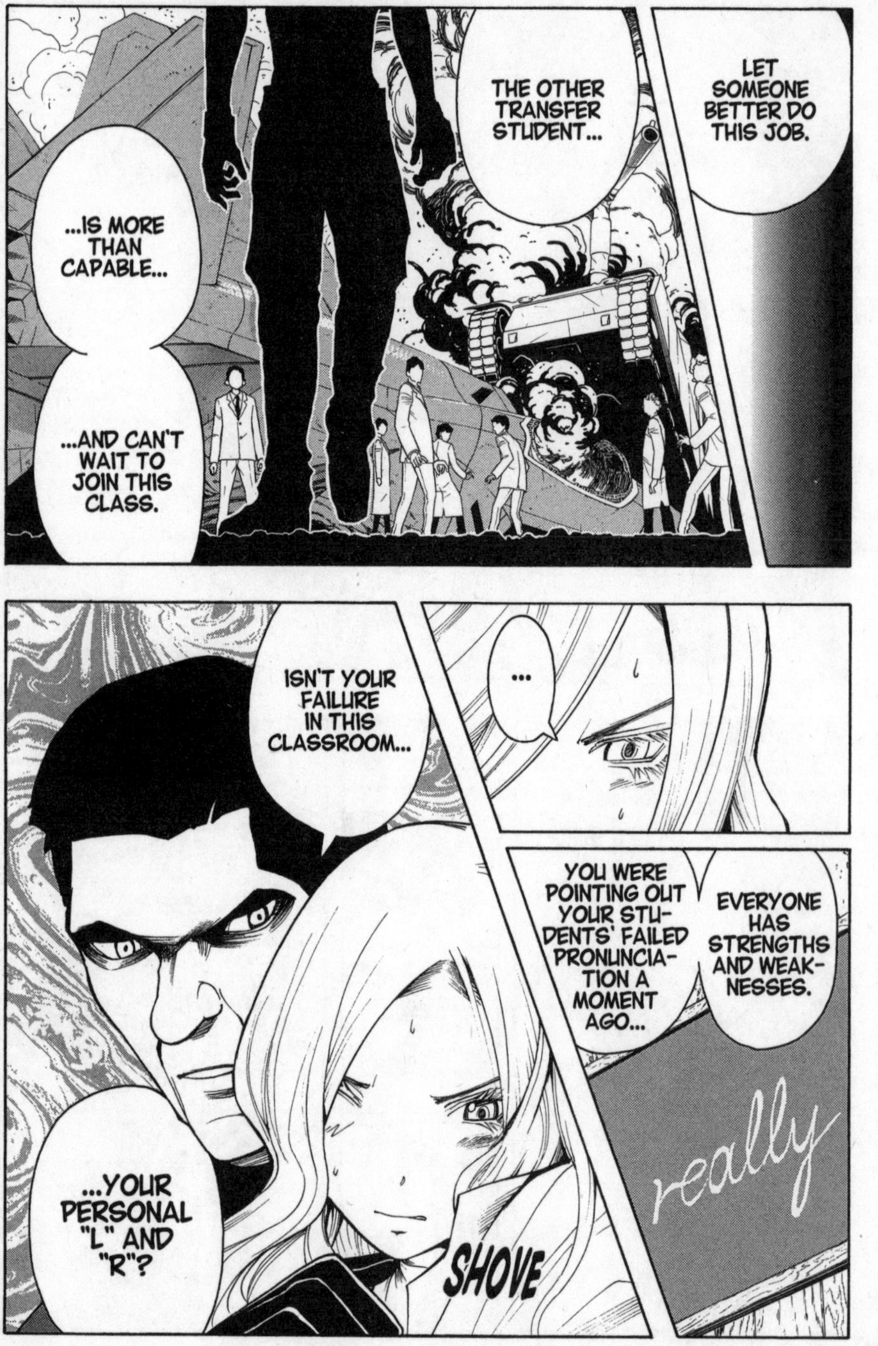
LET SOMEONE BETTER DO THIS JOB.
THE OTHER TRANSFER STUDENT...
...IS MORE THAN CAPABLE...
...AND CAN'T WAIT TO JOIN THIS CLASS.
...
EVERYONE HAS STRENGTHS AND WEAK-NESSES.
YOU WERE POINTING OUT YOUR STU-DENTS' FAILED PRONUNCIA-TION A MOMENT AGO...
really
ISN'T YOUR FAILURE IN THIS CLASSROOM...
SHOVE
...YOUR PERSONAL "L" AND "R"?

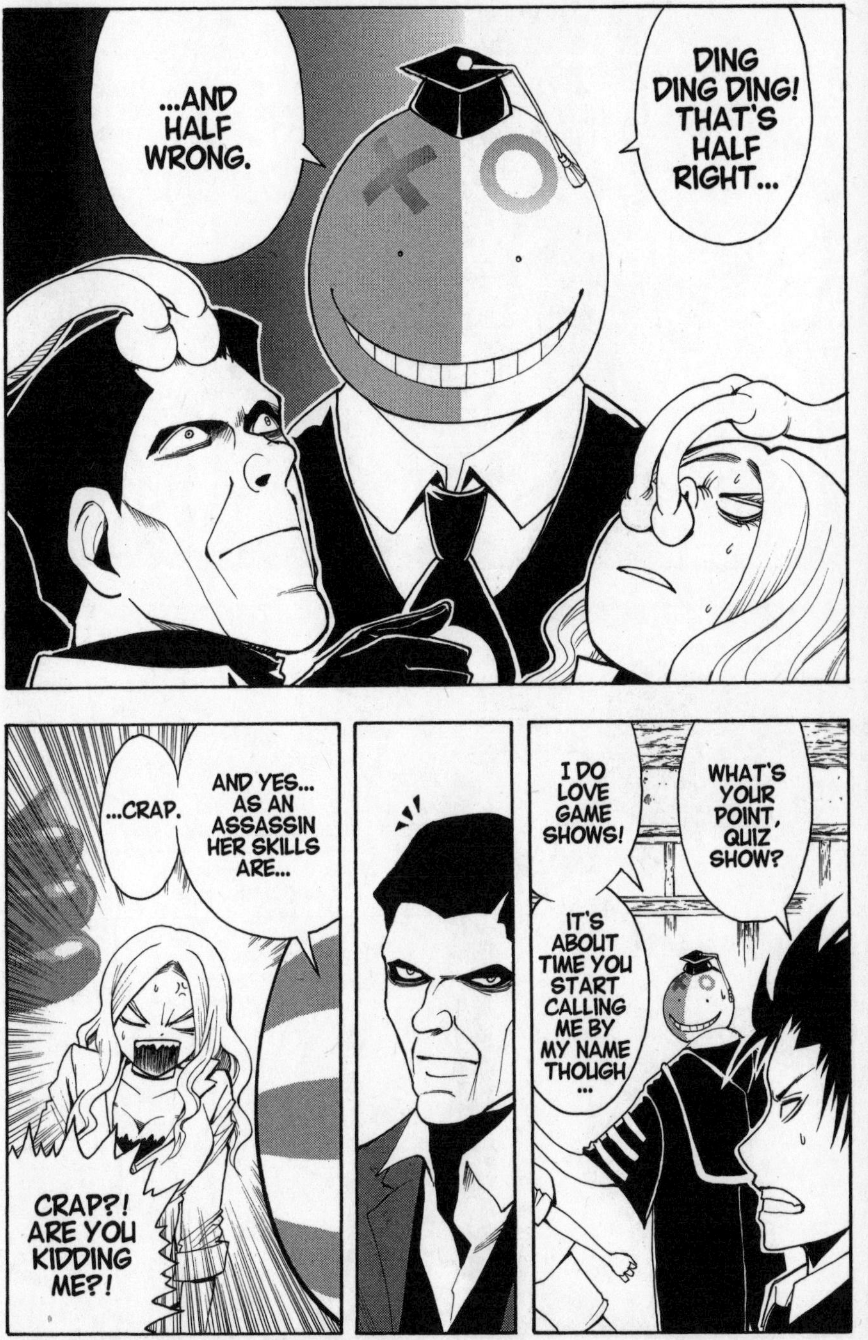
DING DING DING! THAT'S HALF RIGHT...
...AND HALF WRONG.
WHAT'S YOUR POINT, QUIZ SHOW?
I DO LOVE GAME SHOWS!
IT'S ABOUT TIME YOU START CALLING ME BY MY NAME THOUGH ...
AND YES... AS AN ASSASSIN HER SKILLS ARE...
...CRAP.
CRAP?! ARE YOU KIDDING ME?!

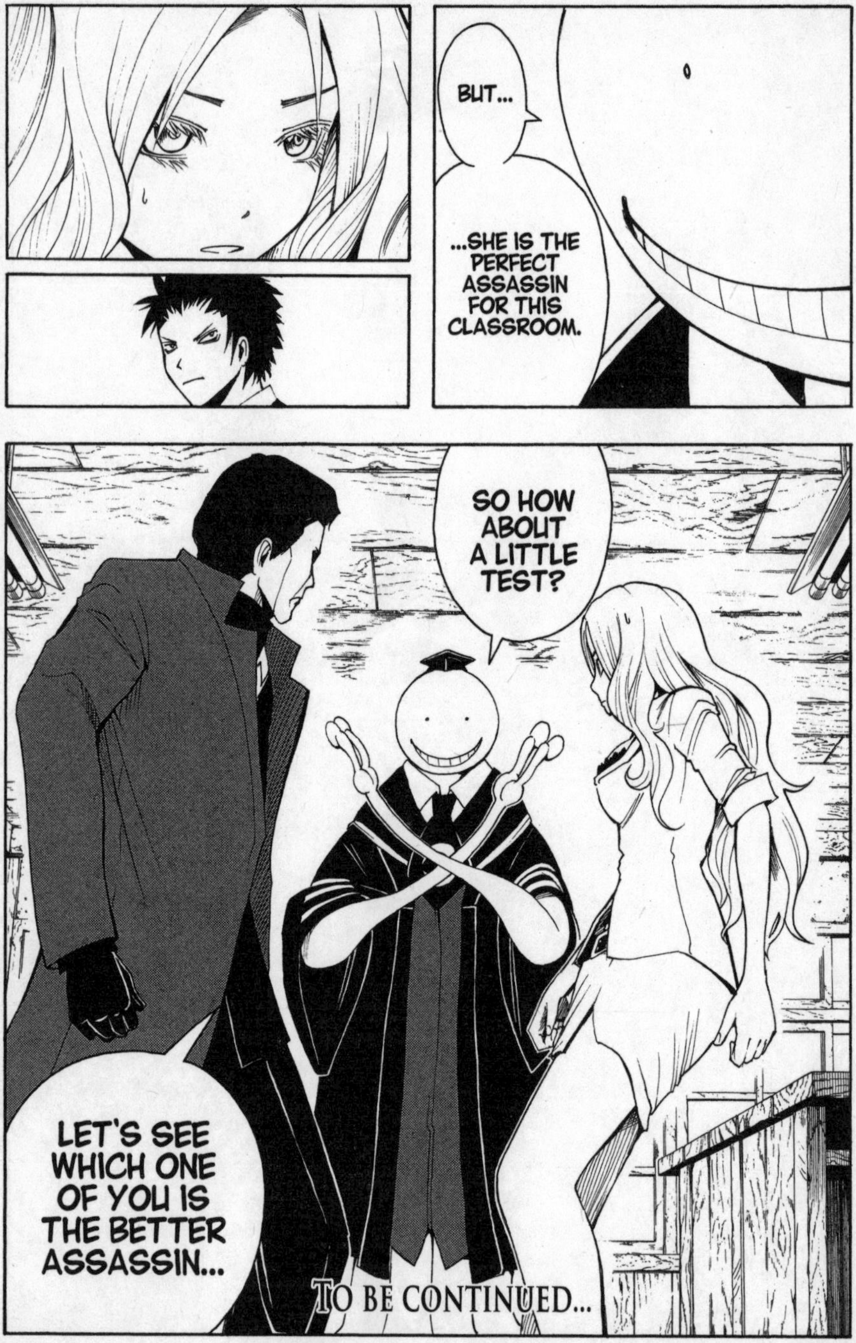
BUT...
...SHE IS THE PERFECT ASSASSIN FOR THIS CLASSROOM.
SO HOW ABOUT A LITTLE TEST?
LET'S SEE WHICH ONE OF YOU IS THE BETTER ASSASSIN...
TO BE CONTINUED...

When I'm working on the graphic novel version, I have a lot of meetings with the designer—more than you'd think.

The main reason for these meetings is to make fine adjustments to the cover color.

A color that stands out at the store. A color that attracts readers. A color that looks good in the sequence the graphic novels are published in...

Even the slightest difference in color will change the impression the cover makes on a reader.

I've recently realized that simpler designs are harder.

—Yusei Matsui

Yusei Matsui was born on the last day of January in Saitama Prefecture, Japan. He has been drawing manga since elementary school. Some of his favorite manga series are *Bobobo-bo Bo-bobo*, *JoJo's Bizarre Adventure* and *Ultimate Muscle*. Matsui learned his trade working as an assistant to manga artist Yoshio Sawai, creator of *Bobobo-bo Bo-bobo*. In 2005, Matsui debuted his original manga *Neuro: Supernatural Detective* in *Weekly Shonen Jump*. In 2007, *Neuro* was adapted into an anime. In 2012, *Assassination Classroom* began serialization in *Weekly Shonen Jump*.

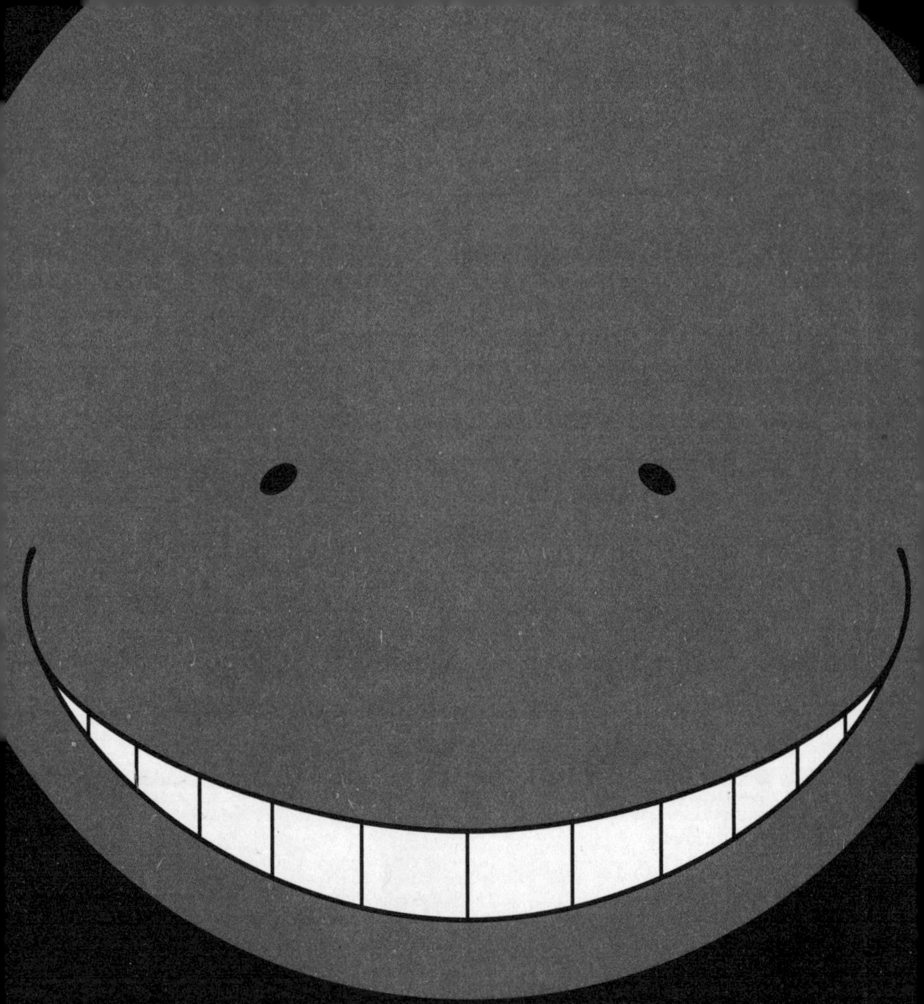

Pink is the color of his face when he's relaxed.
You really don't want to know what he looks like when he's "in the mood."

ASSASSINATION CLASSROOM

YUSEI MATSUI

3

TIME FOR A TRANSFER STUDENT

A MOMENT OF TENTACLE ZEN

Tentacles rock!!
Let's party!!

—Manager Koro
(At the victory party for the
World Baseball Championship)

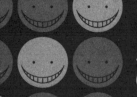

A S S A S S I N A T I O N
CLASSROOM

Volume 3
SHONEN JUMP ADVANCED Manga Edition

Story and Art by YUSEI MATSUI

Translation/Tetsuichiro Miyaki
English Adaptation/Bryant Turnage
Touch-up Art & Lettering/Stephen Dutro
Cover & Interior Design/Sam Elzway
Editor/Annette Roman

ANSATSU KYOSHITSU © 2012 by Yusei Matsui
All rights reserved.
First published in Japan in 2012 by SHUEISHA Inc., Tokyo.
English translation rights arranged by SHUEISHA Inc.

The stories, characters and incidents mentioned in this
publication are entirely fictional.

Printed in the U.S.A.

Published by VIZ Media, LLC
P.O. Box 77010
San Francisco, CA 94107

10 9 8 7 6
First printing, April 2015
Sixth printing, November 2017

www.viz.com   www.shonenjump.com

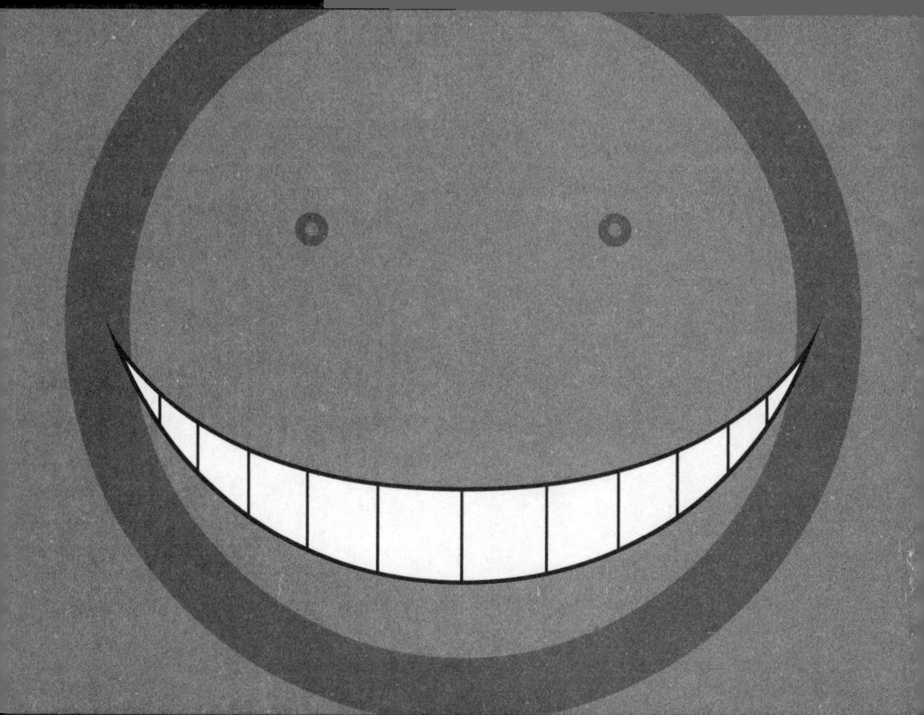

English teacher Irina's assassination mentor makes an appearance and the two compete—using special agent Karasuma as their target. Another transfer student/would-be assassin joins the class, accompanied by a guardian who claims to be Koro Sensei's...*little brother*?! A tentacle showdown ensues, sending everyone into a tentacle tizzy. Then, the 3-E students face humiliation yet again during a school baseball exhibition match. Plus, *more* secrets of Koro Sensei's mysterious past revealed!

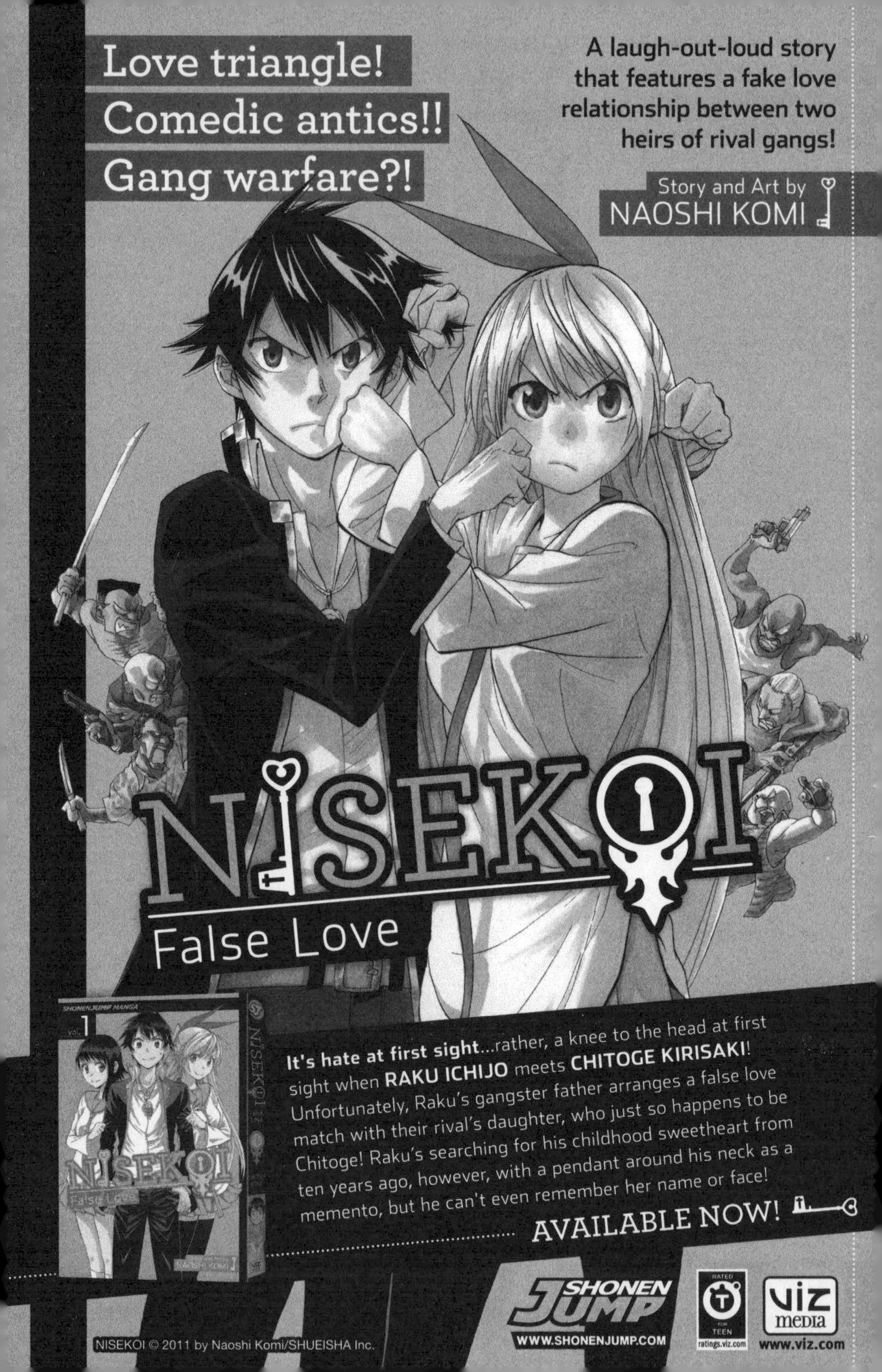
Love triangle!
Comedic antics!!
Gang warfare?!
A laugh-out-loud story that features a fake love relationship between two heirs of rival gangs!
Story and Art by
NAOSHI KOMI
NISEKOI
False Love
SHONEN JUMP MANGA
vol. 1
It's hate at first sight...rather, a knee to the head at first sight when RAKU ICHIJO meets CHITOGE KIRISAKI! Unfortunately, Raku's gangster father arranges a false love match with their rival's daughter, who just so happens to be Chitoge! Raku's searching for his childhood sweetheart from ten years ago, however, with a pendant around his neck as a memento, but he can't even remember her name or face!
AVAILABLE NOW!
SHONEN JUMP
WWW.SHONENJUMP.COM
RATED T FOR TEEN
ratings.viz.com
VIZ media
www.viz.com
NISEKOI © 2011 by Naoshi Komi/SHUEISHA Inc.

EYESHIELD 21

STORY BY RIICHIRO INAGAKI
ART BY YUSUKE MURATA

From the artist of *One-Punch Man!*

Wimpy Sena Kobayakawa has been running away from bullies all his life. But when the football gear comes on, things change—Sena's speed and uncanny ability to elude big bullies just might give him what it takes to become a great high school football hero! Catch all the bone-crushing action and slapstick comedy of Japan's hottest football manga!

Seraph of the End

VAMPIRE REIGN

STORY BY Takaya Kagami ART BY Yamato Yamamoto
STORYBOARDS BY Daisuke Furuya

**Vampires reign—
humans revolt!**

Seraph of the End
VAMPIRE REIGN
1
STORY BY Takaya Kagami
ART BY Yamato Yamamoto

Yuichiro's dream of killing every vampire is near-impossible, given that vampires are seven times stronger than humans, and the only way to kill them is by mastering Cursed Gear, advanced demon-possessed weaponry. Not to mention that humanity's most elite Vampire Extermination Unit, the Moon Demon Company, wants nothing to do with Yuichiro unless he can prove he's willing to work in a team—which is the last thing he wants!

THE LATEST CHAPTERS SERIALIZED IN WEEKLY SHONEN JUMP

RATED T+ FOR OLDER TEEN ratings.viz.com

SHONEN JUMP ADVANCED www.shonenjump.com

VIZ media www.viz.com

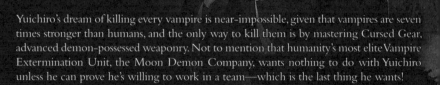

You're Reading in the Wrong Direction!!

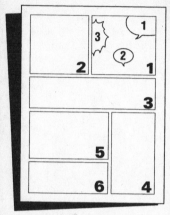

Whoops! Guess what? You're starting at the wrong end of the comic!

…It's true! In keeping with the original Japanese format, **Assassination Classroom** is meant to be read from right to left, starting in the upper-right corner.

Unlike English, which is read from left to right, Japanese is read from right to left, meaning that action, sound effects and word-balloon order are completely reversed… something which can make readers unfamiliar with Japanese feel pretty backwards themselves. For this reason, manga or Japanese comics published in the U.S. in English have sometimes been published "flopped"—that is, printed in exact reverse order, as though seen from the other side of a mirror.

By flopping pages, U.S. publishers can avoid confusing readers, but the compromise is not without its downside. For one thing, a character in a flopped manga series who once wore in the original Japanese version a T-shirt emblazoned with "M A Y" (as in "the merry month of") now wears one which reads "Y A M"! Additionally, many manga creators in Japan are themselves unhappy with the process, as some feel the mirror-imaging of their art skews their original intentions.

We are proud to bring you Yusei Matsui's **Assassination Classroom** in the original unflopped format.

For now, though, turn to the other side of the book and let the adventure begin…!

—Editor